Advanced Manufacturing

Advanced Manufacturing

The New American Innovation Policies

William B. Bonvillian and Peter L. Singer

The MIT Press
Cambridge, Massachusetts
London, England

This book was set in Stone Serif by Westchester Publishing Services. Printed and bound in the United States of America.

Library of Congress Cataloging-in-Publication Data

Names: Bonvillian, William, author. | Singer, Peter L., author.
Title: Advanced manufacturing : the new American innovation policies /
    William B. Bonvillian and Peter L. Singer.
Description: Cambridge, MA : MIT Press, [2017] | Includes bibliographical
    references and index.
Identifiers: LCCN 2017014250 | ISBN 9780262037037 (hardcover : alk. paper)
Subjects: LCSH: Manufacturing industries—Government policy—United States. |
    Manufacturing industries—Technological innovations—United States. |
    Industrial policy—United States.
Classification: LCC HD9726 .B656 2017 | DDC 338/.0640973—dc23
    LC record available at https://lccn.loc.gov/2017014250

10 9 8 7 6 5 4 3 2 1

Contents

Acknowledgments

The authors have many to thank for advice and assistance in the preparation of this book. Phillip Singerman, Jason Miller, Johanna Wolfson, Megan Brewster, Adele Ratcliff, Stephen Luckowski, and Susan Singer, who worked in the executive branch to develop advanced manufacturing policies, read various parts of the draft and provided very helpful insights. From the manufacturing institutes, Craig Blue of IACMI, Yoel Fink of AFFOA, and Emily DeRocco of LIFT, in particular, provided information and details that helped us describe what is developing within the institutes.

Our colleagues at the Massachusetts Institute of Technology (MIT) who are working on advanced manufacturing also provided ideas that helped shape this work, and they have our sincere thanks. These included Suzanne Berger, Martin Schmidt, Krystyn VanVliet, Elizabeth Reynolds, David Autor, Sanjay Sarma, Brian Anthony, Tom Kochan, David Mindell, John Hart and Philip Lippel, as well as Israel Soibelman of MIT's Lincoln Lab. MIT's presidents Rafael Reif and Susan Hockfield worked hard on these manufacturing issues as co-chairs of the industry-university Advanced Manufacturing Partnership (AMP), and it was a special pleasure to serve with them on these projects and learn from them. From the MIT Washington Office, interns and fellows Joseff Kolman, Nathalie Bockelt, Katherine Nazemi, and Ben Chazen performed highly useful research on "innovation orchard" models for MIT cited here, and Eliza Eddison, Maggie Lloyd, Katherine Hewitt, Daniel Kuhner, Yiliu Zhang, and Aneesh Anand undertook examinations of federal programs and manufacturing studies for MIT manufacturing efforts also helpful for this work. All are posted as "policy resources" on the MIT Washington Office website.

Many who staffed the Advanced Manufacturing Partnership, from agencies, industry, and universities, deserve a special thanks for helping to create a new generation of manufacturing policies and for providing advice during the period during which these programs were formed. Those who contributed particular insights from the executive branch, in addition to those already named, included J. J. Raynor, Thomas Kalil, David Hart, and Sridhar Kota at the National Economic Council and Office of Science and Technology Policy; Pat Gallagher, Susan Helper, Gregory Tassey, and Michael Molnar from the Commerce Department; David Danielson and Mark Johnson from the Energy Department; Steven McKnight and Bruce Kramer from the National Science Foundation; Brett Lambert and Neil Orringer from the Defense Department's Manufacturing and Industrial Base office; and Mick Maher from the Defense Advanced Research Projects Agency (DARPA). From the industry side of AMP, Carrie Houtman, Theresa Kotanchek, Ravi Shankar, and Mark Jones of Dow, along with Joseph Ensor of Northrop Grumman and Rebecca Taylor of the National Center for Manufacturing Sciences, deserve our particular thanks, along with other colleagues who worked on the AMP reports. From the university side of AMP, Robert Knotts and Tom Kurfess of Georgia Tech were of particular assistance. From the U.S. Senate, we thank Chris Slevin, who worked on the Revitalize American Manufacturing and Innovation (RAMI) Act, for his review of the legislative issues. Information Technology and Innovation Foundation's (ITIF) Rob Atkinson, Stephen Ezell and their colleagues deserve special thanks for their extensive work over the years on manufacturing, work that is reflected here.

At MIT Press, we thank Emily Taber, our editor, and Amy Brand, the Press's director, for their very helpful work, advice, and continuing support for this project, as well as Laura Keeler for her assistance with manuscript and figure preparation, and Erin Hasley for the cover design. The authors also thank reviewers Mike Trebing, senior economic analyst at the Philadelphia Federal Reserve Bank, and Adams Nager, economic policy analyst at the Information Technology and Innovation Foundation (ITIF), who made detailed, thoughtful, and careful reviews of this work. They made a number of very helpful suggestions that we have worked to incorporate.

It must be emphasized, however, that the views expressed in this work are solely the responsibility of the authors.

The authors also thank Albert N. Link, editor of *Annals of Science and Technology Policy*, for publishing in that journal material on manufacturing policy, institutes, and start-ups that appears here. They also thank Kevin Finneran, editor of *Issues in Science Technology Policy*, Phillip E. Auerswald, editor of the journal *Innovations*, Alistair Nolan, senior policy analyst for science and technology at the Organization for Economic Cooperation and Development (OECD), and editor of its report on advanced manufacturing, "The Next Production Revolution," and Rob Atkinson, president of ITIF, for initially publishing articles with our ideas on manufacturing that are drawn on here. This work is specifically acknowledged in notes to the text.

Finally, the authors thank their families for their support in so many ways during the preparation of this work.

1 Introduction: Social Disruption, Legacy Barriers, and Innovation Challenges in U.S. Manufacturing

In the first decade of the twenty-first century, the manufacturing sector in the United States experienced significant disruption. The Great Recession of 2007–2009 accelerated the changes, but they were structural, not simply caused by the economic crisis. There was trouble with jobs, capital investment, output, productivity, and trade.

To briefly summarize the story set out in chapter 3, the number of manufacturing jobs in the United States declined by 5.8 million between 2000 and 2010. Manufacturing employment had been relatively stable between 1965 and 2000 at around 17 million, then fell to under 12 million by 2010, returning to only 12.3 million in 2016. Fixed capital investment in manufacturing in the United States declined by 1.8% over the course of the decade, the first recorded decade of decline since data collection began in 1947. This was not the result of a decline in a few sectors but rather was pervasive: there was a decline, sometimes sharp, in 13 of 19 industrial sectors and another three were stagnant. Manufacturing output grew only 0.5% between 2000 and 2007 and then fell by 10.3% in the Great Recession period from 2007 to 2009. It is slowly growing again, but real output only surpassed pre-recession levels halfway through 2016. Manufacturing productivity reflects stagnating output; it grew 4.1% per year on average between 1989 and 2000 but then fell to 1.7% between 2007 and 2014. Therefore, contrary to what many believe, productivity gains have not been the cause of the manufacturing employment declines. The sector has been hollowing out.

These disruptions are mirrored in the patterns of trade in manufactured goods. The trade deficit in manufactured goods was a remarkable $800 billion in 2015. Importantly, of that, there was a $92 billion trade deficit in advanced technology goods. The trade deficit in U.S. manufacturing will not be offset by the U.S. trade surplus in services—services are only a quarter of the level of trade in goods.

This economic disruption has resulted in growing social disruption.[1] While most Americans once assumed we were becoming one big middle class, instead, a working class that has been facing declining incomes is now in clear, angry view. For example, the full-year employment rate of men with a high school diploma but no college degree went from 76% in 1990 to 68% in 2013.[2] The share of these men who did not work at all went from 11% in 1990 to 18% in 2013. Importantly, the *median income of men without a high school diploma fell by 20%* between 1990 and 2013; for men *with high school diplomas or some college, median income fell by 13%*.[3] The decline of American manufacturing between 2000 and 2010 hit this group particularly hard. Overall, real household income, measured both at the median (the middle) and the mean (the average), declined between 1999 and 2014.[4] Importantly, there is a growing gap between median household income—the statistical center of the middle class—and average, which includes the higher gains going to the upper middle and upper classes.[5] This spells middle class decline.

It also spells growing income inequality. As labor economist Richard Freeman put it, "Inequality is now at Third World levels."[6] It can be traced in significant part to the stagnation in college graduation rates since the mid-1970s: workforce skill requirements kept growing but education output failed to keep up.[7] Those with the education captured a wage premium, but those without it faced the opposite. The one-third decline in manufacturing jobs between 2000 and 2010, which generally offered better pay, exacerbated that inequality split.

The massive trade imbalance in manufacturing hit many industrial communities hard. Economists David Autor, David Dorn, and Gordon Hanson, in an article titled "The China Shock," examined trade effects in seven hundred urban areas.[8] Those areas that faced direct impacts from Chinese imports faced an average annual income loss per adult of $549 between 1990 and 2007. This was offset by federal adjustment assistance of only $58 per capita. As Nobel Prize–winning economist Michael Spence has found, "Globalization hurts some subgroups. . . . The result is growing disparities in income and employment."[9]

Given these new realities, an effort across industry, federal and state governments, and universities materialized in the wake of the Great Recession. This effort sought to bring strong innovation back to U.S. manufacturing. Known under the broad brand of "advanced manufacturing," it is the story of this book.

Before we can tell it, though, we need to grapple with a central reality about the great difficulty of this task. Manufacturing is not a rising frontier sector of the economy, such as information technology, that absorbs inno-vations like a magnet. It is a complex, established, legacy sector. Innovation in legacy sectors faces a multitude of barriers that multiply the innova-tion challenge. That is why this task is far from easy and why this story is complicated.

The Legacy Sector Challenge for Manufacturing

The rise of information technology and biotechnology and the new eco-nomic sectors they have created has tended to blind us to the problem of our complex, established, innovation-resistant, legacy economic sectors.[10] This blind spot has helped lead us into a neglected problem: we are limiting our growth and therefore job creation. The focus of the field of innovation policy has for decades been on the problem of the "Valley of Death"—the gap between research and late-stage development that creates barriers to frontier innovation. Researchers have failed to focus on a challenge in plain view: how to bring innovation to legacy sectors. We have been after "the next big thing"—the next technology frontier—and have neglected opportunities in existing economic sectors. This frontier focus ignores these legacy sectors, where the new technology ideas are blocked by deeply entrenched paradigms.

These legacy sectors make up the majority of the U.S. economy. Accord-ing to recent Bureau of Economic Analysis data,[11] legacy sectors (such as utilities, civil construction, building, agriculture, transport, education, health delivery, mining, finance, government, education, and manufactur-ing, among others) make up over two-thirds of U.S. gross domestic product (GDP). Add in significant parts of sectors such as retail and business ser-vices, and the total rises significantly higher. In contrast, the information sector value added accounts for only 4.8% of U.S. GDP.[12] This total still includes areas such as copper wire telephones and hardback books. Legacy sectors are monster-size, and we have been ignoring the monster in our room. In innovation, the United States tends to move on, not look back at its legacy.

As a result, we rely on creating new technology frontiers to boost our growth rate. The IT revolution did exactly that in the 1990s, creating a remarkable run of increased productivity gains and corresponding growth. But, by limiting innovation to the frontier, we are curtailing our growth rate. The growth economists tell us that technological and related innova-tion is the dominant causative factor in economic growth. If we tend to limit innovation to frontier sectors, and wall it off—particularly disruptive innovation—from legacy sectors, we limit our growth. At a time when there is an outcry about quality job creation and income inequality, this is a serious problem.

Some of the nation's greatest needs for innovation now lie in legacy economic sectors that resist innovation that could alter their established technology routines and business models. Prime examples include fossil fuel energy, the electric grid, the health care delivery system, highway-intensive transport, and input-intensive agriculture.[13] Perhaps at the top of the list is the manufacturing sector, because of its long-standing role as a job multiplier and its steep decline since 2000. All of these sectors, and especially manufacturing, are areas in which innovation can broaden our growth base beyond frontier-based growth. It is not bad to promote frontier technology—the economic gains of the IT revolution in the 1990s show how powerful new innovation waves can be. The problem is that we do not have a broader base for our innovation applications; we typically fail to extend our innovation capability into our existing sectors.

Legacy sectors tend to protect themselves from disruption by maintaining a technological, economic, political, and social paradigm. That is, they lock in on their existing technologies, driving them toward efficiencies and lower costs that hinder competing new entrants. They lock in on economic and business models that protect their own returns and systems and limit entry by competitors. They build systems of political support that lock in policies and subsidies that protect their own technologies and systems. And they build social systems that assure their supplies of workers and public support. These obstacles must be addressed if new disruptive innovations are to enter legacy sectors. The technologies behind legacy sectors often work well, and these sectors will adopt incremental improvements to keep meeting the sector's established requirements. A sector will also adopt new innovations if they further the existing economic model behind the legacy sector. For example, fracking technology fits the legacy fossil fuel sector well. But legacy sectors are not organized to accommodate disruptive new advances that counter elements of the legacy system.

The established legacy sectors share a series of common features, as previous work has described.[14] The descriptions in the next two paragraphs are densely packed but need to be briefly set out at the outset as an important context for considering manufacturing innovation. These legacy sector characteristics can include the following: *perverse subsidies and price structures* that favor incumbents and can also ignore externalities such as sustainability and health; an *established institutional architecture* that imposes regulatory hurdles or other policy disincentives in order to favor existing technology; established, powerful *vested interests* that protect their sectors, politically and otherwise, and resist the introduction of technologies; an *innovation financing system* that will not support the longer-term, higher-risk technologies typically required for legacy sectors; *public habits and expectations* that offer popular support to policies and government expenditures to existing technology; a *knowledge and human resources structure*—educational curricula, training, career paths, and professional standards in medical, legal, and technical fields—oriented toward the needs of existing technology; and *limited research and development* in both public and private spheres that limits availability of innovative technologies ready for implementation.

The dominance of existing technologies is further reinforced by a series of market imperfections that affect the introduction of new technology. These can include *network economies* (the large scale of the legacy sector's technology network allows only entry at scale), *lumpiness* (major investment is required to introduce the new technology), *split incentives* (the incentives for introducing a new technology cannot be appropriated by its developer), *collective action* (the economic actors in a sector are small scale and undercapitalized, limiting their ability to absorb new technology), and *governmental institutional and regulatory structure* (a pattern of government regulation, activity, or incentives that supports existing technologies).

Legacy sectors do not share all of these characteristics, but they all share some of them. Manufacturing is a legacy sector that shares many of them. Sometimes some or even many of the actors within a legacy sector are interested in embracing change, but they still face the many characteristics in the legacy sector that resist change. This is also the case with manufacturing.

How do these characteristics apply to U.S. manufacturing? There are many examples, but some key ones follow. The sector faces *perverse pricing* effects because a high-value dollar often tends to overprice U.S. manufactured goods relative to those of foreign competitors, who may also undervalue their currencies. The U.S. manufacturing sector faces an established *innovation financing system* that limits the availability of support for innovation for small and midsize firms and for start-ups that must manufacture. There are *vested interests* in manufacturing; for example, multinationals that limit their U.S. production investments because of pressure to expand and produce abroad to stay in foreign markets. These actors can be reluctant to take the risk of innovating in advanced production processes in the United States because they already have lower-cost production facilities abroad or because of a finance system that focuses on international return models and has abandoned the local banking that historically served small manufacturers. There are *public habits and expectations* that affect manufacturing; for example, the unwillingness of mainstream economic policy, in the past accepted by the public and politicians, to focus policies on the manufacturing sector, or of the public to encourage the next generation to take manufacturing jobs, as will be discussed in subsequent chapters. There is a *knowledge and human resources structure* that supports a highly decentralized labor market and is not organized to produce the highly skilled workforce future manufacturing will require. There is *limited research and development* (R&D) in U.S. manufacturing on the federal side because government-supported R&D has never focused on production. Also, most small and midsize manufacturers, the majority of U.S. manufacturing, simply cannot afford the added cost of R&D, given heavy global competition. The list of reasons goes on.

There are market imperfections in U.S. manufacturing as well. There are *network economy* problems because complex manufacturing supply chains are hard to penetrate or to reorganize, or if they have been lost to foreign competition, to ever reconstitute. There are *lumpiness* problems because small and midsize producers will find it hard to afford the major investments that may be required to introduce new advanced manufacturing technologies. There are *split incentives* because the incentives for introducing new manufacturing technology may not be appropriated to reward the development of it; smaller manufacturers lack the funding to do so, and larger multinationals are already committed to low-cost production abroad. Apple, for example, is now locked into production in Shenzhen; it is not going to return any significant production to the United States anytime soon. There is a *collective action* problem because most of the small and midsize producers are undercapitalized, limiting their ability to absorb new manufacturing technology—they are simply not organized to do so. And there is a *governmental institutional activity* problem, where government is unprepared to take on the public-private organization of an innovation challenge of the complexity of a major sector such as manufacturing.

There is system failure here.[15] The problem is not the failure of a single component or even a group of components in the legacy manufacturing sector. A component failure can be addressed by reengineering the component that led to the system failure. Instead, the challenges for upgrading U.S. manufacturing to a much stronger, world-competitive posture appear broad enough that we need to treat the failure as systemwide. It could be called a system-of-systems failure, stemming from trying to impose new requirements on the legacy sector.[16] But a manufacturing system-of-systems needs to be envisaged not simply as a set of engineered technological systems but much more broadly, encompassing technological as well as related economic, political, and social systems. Applying a single model of innovation will not work for a system failure; instead, a full range of models may need to be applied.

Applying the Five Models of Innovation

As argued in a previous work, there are five basic models for the dynamics that drive innovation in different settings: the innovation pipeline, induced innovation, the extended pipeline, manufacturing-led innovation, and innovation organization.[17] These provide a framework for approaching the twin issues in U.S. manufacturing of furthering innovation and creating jobs. It must also be kept in mind that innovation does not happen entirely through an "invisible hand"; innovation introduction generally requires active efforts by change agents. Such agents are particularly critical for innovation in legacy sectors, given the significant barriers innovation faces in these sectors.

The *"pipeline" model* has long dominated U.S. science and technology thinking. It pictures invention and innovation as flowing from investments in research—predominantly from federal basic research support—at the "front end" of the innovation system. Thus, research is dumped into one end of the innovation pipeline, mysterious things occur in the pipe as industry picks up the development, then new products emerge at the pipe's end. Vannevar Bush is considered the author of this model, because he played such a central role in creating it in the early postwar period.[18] This model is frequently the origin for major breakthrough inventions. It is a "technology supply" or "technology push" model—government research support supplies the technology, which pushes into the innovation pipeline. Here the change agents are the researchers, inventors, and entrepreneurs who conceive the technology idea and hand it off to become a breakthrough new product. It serves radical innovation.

But most technology comes from private sector firms that respond to market opportunities by employing a second model, *"induced innovation."* Vernon Ruttan is the growth economist who elaborated on this model.[19] Here, the originator—the change agent—is typically a firm that spots a market opportunity or niche that can be filled by a technology advance, which is typically incremental rather than radical. It is a "technology demand" or "technology pull" model—the market creates the demand and pull to induce the technology. Here, the change agents primarily include firms, and entrepreneurs and inventors linked to them. Induced innovation in legacy sectors can also be affected by policymakers in government and standard setters in industry that can affect market signals and regulatory requirements.

The third model can be termed the *"extended pipeline,"* where certain U.S. R&D organizations, particularly the Department of Defense (DOD), support moving innovations through every innovation stage. This means support not just for front-end R&D but also for each successive "back-end" stage, from advanced prototype to demonstration, test bed, and often to initial market creation, where DOD will buy the first products. While the government's support role in the pipeline model is disconnected from the rest of the innovation system, in this model it is deeply connected. Most of the major innovation waves of the past three-quarters of a century have evolved from this system, including aviation, nuclear power, electronics, space, computing, and the Internet.[20] The extended pipeline facilitates the bridging of the "Valley of Death" between advanced research and implemented technology. Here, the change agent includes the governmental entity seeking the advance; the Defense Advanced Research Projects Agency (DARPA), for example, was a critical change agent for computing and the Internet.

The fourth model of innovation dynamics, *"manufacturing-led"* innovation, describes innovations in production technologies, processes, and products that emerge from expertise informed by experience in manufacturing. This is augmented by applied research and development that is integrated with the production process. It is typically industry led but often with strong governmental industrial support. While countries such as Germany, Japan, Taiwan, Korea, and now China have organized their economies around "manufacturing-led" innovation systems, the United States in the postwar period has not. It is a major gap in the U.S. innovation system.

The fifth model, *"innovation organization,"* is different from the others. It calls for improving the means, methods, and organization of innovation efforts, both on the front and back ends of innovation—it is an organizational model. In this innovation organization model, the innovation system supports the full innovation spectrum, each stage in the innovation process. While the pipeline model supports R&D at the front end, and the manufacturing-led model supports the back-end production stage, the innovation organization model contemplates all stages. It goes beyond the extended pipeline model to orchestrate the institutional and policy changes needed to facilitate innovation not just for a government customer. The other models describe the various existing approaches to innovation, but "innovation organization" describes a different approach, enabling and enhancing innovation by examining a sector's innovation environment, including the institutions and barriers within it, assessing their strengths, evaluating means for improvement, and crafting policies and steps to strengthen the system and overcome barriers. Arguably, the complexity and barriers in major legacy sectors, such as manufacturing, require this overall organizational approach; they will not yield to a single innovation dynamic.

As will be delineated in chapter 2, when the United States was constructing its innovation system in the postwar period, it paid little attention to manufacturing-led innovation. This had been the innovation strength of the United States since the nineteenth century; it had created the mass production system that had played a central role in winning World War II. Production was not the problem—the United States led in that area. Instead, it focused on its research system, the front end of innovation, which had emerged at scale during the war but needed to be retained and augmented. This was the system Vannevar Bush, as Roosevelt's and then Truman's science advisor, focused on. Germany and Japan, emerging from wartime chaos, had to concentrate on rebuilding their industrial bases, so they developed and extended their manufacturing-led innovation systems. Taiwan, Korea, and China needed to build their industrial bases as their economies emerged, and they also followed the manufacturing-led innovation path.

An innovation irony is now developing. Japan, Korea, Taiwan, and China, with strong manufacturing-led innovation systems, now see that this must be complemented by stronger front-end, R&D-based innovation. They are working hard to build their front-end capacity. Whereas the United States spends 2.73% of its GDP on R&D, Japan spends 3.47%, Korea 4.15%, and Taiwan 3.0%.[21] China has been rapidly accelerating its total R&D expenditures, which are now $336.5 billion, compared to $456.9 billion in the United States, a level that has been stagnant.[22] While these nations pursue the technology frontier, ironically, after a painful decline in its production sector, the United States now appears to be waking up to its weakness in manufacturing-led innovation through an advanced manufacturing effort, the subject of this work. Each region is playing catch-up on gaps in their innovation systems.

But if the "innovation organization" model is right, the United States will need to do more in manufacturing in addition to its new focus on including "manufacturing led." It will need to apply the other models to its production system as well. Historically, it has had a strong "pipeline" model, but it will need to move its R&D agencies to include advanced manufacturing in their research portfolios. Industry, if it starts to see new market opportunities in advanced manufacturing technologies—such as 3D printing or advanced materials—could be encouraged to apply further "induced innovation" to them. The Defense Department has long led the "extended pipeline" model. It has a major stake in the strength of the U.S. industrial base and needs to further apply its toolset to serve its own technology needs, including its procurement system. All of these steps will need change agents to provide leadership because technological innovation in legacy sectors requires them. The "innovation organization" model requires that these efforts have coordination and orchestration between the public and private sectors.

Some Core Ideas

A core idea in this book is that there could be new production paradigms that could transform the sector. We have seen these new production paradigms before: application of steam power to run textile factories in Britain, development of interchangeable machine-made parts and then mass production in the United States, and the creation of quality manufacturing in Japan. The United States is competing with low-wage, low-cost producers, particularly in Asia. Could it develop new production paradigms to drive up production efficiency and drive down costs so it could better compete? Innovation also carries its own rewards—production innovation can enable more innovative products. Scientists and engineers are now telling us that there may be breakthroughs—new paradigms—available from a series of fields that could significantly change the way we produce complex, high-value technologies and goods, enabling dramatic production efficiencies. New technology advances, in turn, must be accompanied by new processes and business models to implement them. Developing such new paradigms is the core behind advanced manufacturing. The concept of advanced manufacturing institutes as a means to nurture such paradigms is explored in depth.

Another core idea in this book concerns the next generation of production. Increasingly, the United States has turned to the entrepreneurship/start-up model backed by venture capital to launch new technologies. The system came into its own to support the information technology innovation wave of the 1980s and 1990s, starting with support for "hard" technologies around computing and semiconductors. In recent years, it has shifted significantly to software, which requires little capital or infrastructure and no production, and succeeds or fails quickly. Along with biotechnology and services such as media and entertainment, software now dominates venture funding. The system is simply not supporting technologies that require manufacturing, because these are longer term and higher risk. As will be delineated, this means that the next generation of innovative manufactured technologies and goods may not be produced in the United States. This has major implications for the longer-term future of U.S. innovation as well as production. Possible alternatives to venture support for start-ups that require scale-up are explored.

These are just two examples. There are many more building-block ideas in chapters 2–9, with other core concepts summarized in chapter 10.

We should also be clear at the outset: innovation is not the only issue facing American manufacturing. There are a series of major macro issues— trade, tax, and currency—that are quite significant. Countries around the world undertake various practices to advantage their producers. For example, a number of Asian nations have intervened to undervalue their currencies to enable their exports to be underpriced against foreign producers. This amounts to a subsidy for goods imported to the U.S.—some have estimated it may approach 25%. A number of foreign competitors provide investment incentives for their manufacturers by waiving taxes, providing free land for production facilities, reducing utility rates, or providing capital grants, all of which drive the cost of their goods down to shift comparative advantage. Some nations "dump" goods on the U.S. at prices below their actual production cost to capture markets and drive U.S. competitors down. While the U.S. has proceedings to challenge these practices—antidumping and countervailing duties[23]—these are often slow and deemed inadequate.

The current U.S. tax system is also commonly cited as harming the competitiveness of U.S. companies. The United States is one of only two nations in the world that taxes the overseas earnings of its firms, which in turn gives its firms a major incentive to invest these profits abroad not at home. The current tax laws also have loopholes that can result in an uneven playing field for manufacturers. A 2015 Tax Foundation study found the effective tax rate for capital intensive manufacturers varied by up to 15% between states,[24] although the tax rate on corporate income, profits and capital gains as a percent of U.S. GDP falls below the OECD average.[25] Value-Added Taxes have also become a contentious issue following the 2016 election. These tax the value added to a good at each production stage; they are rebated when the domestic manufacturer exports the good, and in turn imposed on imported goods increasing their cost. By not adopting such an approach, many argue the U.S., in effect, subsidizes imports and taxes its exports, giving imports favorable tax treatment and discouraging its exports. Proponents argue a VAT or a comparable border adjustment tax could readjust this balance, although a number of prominent economists dispute this primarily because the effect could be offset over time by a rise in the value of the dollar.[26]

In summary, various practices can amount to a significant burden on U.S. manufacturers, although the extent has been subject to longstanding debate. However, the focus of this work is not on these macro issues—which remain important—but on another foundational problem which has received almost no attention until recently: the failure to bring the still strong U.S. innovation system to bear on its manufacturing system. Innovation is the new story in American manufacturing.

The Story Ahead

A multisided manufacturing and innovation story is ahead, with the highlights as follows:

• Chapter 2 presents a series of pictures of critical developments in U.S. *production history*. It closes with the story just cited of the gap the United States allowed to enter its overall innovation system when it failed to place sufficient emphasis on manufacturing-led innovation.

• Chapter 3 reviews the sharp U.S. *manufacturing decline in the first decade of the twenty-first century*, examining this from a series of dimensions, including the critical relationship between the production stage and the other parts of its innovation system, a connection the United States has largely ignored. It has been moving from a system of "innovate here/produce here" to "innovate here/produce there." Because innovation is linked to production, particularly initial production of a complex new technology, it may be risking "produce there/innovate there," and corresponding damage to what has been its core capability: innovation.

• Chapter 4 examines *mainstream economics and its varied attitudes toward manufacturing over time*. It looks at growth theory and then trade theory, and notes the connections between New Growth Theory and New Trade Theory over the importance of productivity gains, an area where manufacturing appears particularly significant. However, forces in mainstream economics have still shied away from manufacturing. Given the growing social disruption explored by a rising group of economists, an innovation focus for manufacturing might now fit emerging economic perspectives.

• Chapter 5 looks at how the new policy focus on *advanced manufacturing* developed following the Great Recession. It examines a series of critical studies that began the effort to chart this course, evaluating the manufacturing problems identified and corresponding policy proposals. It places the reports and early policies in the context of how they emerged.

• Chapter 6 reviews the centerpiece of U.S. advanced manufacturing policies to date, the *advanced manufacturing institutes*. The questions of how these are organized, their missions, what lessons have been learned as the institutes have been started up, and what enhancements might be considered are all addressed.

• Chapter 7 looks at a new but related problem: *start-up scale-up*. Start-ups developing "hard" technology that they plan to manufacture have a growing problem in finding financing for production scale-up. Yet these start-ups represent the future of U.S. technology production. The venture capital start-up financing system is now heavily focused on software, with support still available for biotech and various service sectors. Support is minimal for hard technologies that must be manufactured, because they entail higher risk and longer development. New mechanisms to get past this financing barrier are reviewed in detail.

• Chapter 8 takes a deep dive into the *manufacturing workforce*. Without highly skilled workers, advanced manufacturing will simply not evolve. New training models that could fill this gap, including apprenticeships and new community college roles, are examined.

• Chapter 9 returns to economics. There is now a major focus on what economists term *"secular stagnation,"* a concern about a decline in innovation, growth, the middle class, productivity rates, and related investment. The chapter examines a role for manufacturing in addressing these issues. It further considers new debates about *technological displacement*—that the IT revolution is displacing employment—and manufacturing's place in job growth.

• Chapter 10 is the *wrap-up*, a summary of key findings. It walks systematically through the numerous new ideas in this work.

Manufacturing is now in a place different from the dark days of the Great Recession, with the auto sector collapse and 10% unemployment. The unemployment rate has finally improved, eight years after the official end of the recession,[27] but deep economic challenges remain. As will be discussed, particularly in chapter 9, the United States and other developed nations are facing "secular stagnation": what may be a prolonged period of lower productivity rates, more limited advances in technological innovation, lower capital investment, and correspondingly lower rates of GDP growth, which at its worst translates into falling GDP per capita. Overall U.S. productivity, for example, has fallen from the 2.4% rate of 1995–2008 to 1.2% in the 2008–2015 period.[28] Net private investment in capital equipment and software averaged around 2% of GDP in the 1990s, fell to 1.2% over the following decade, and is now in the 1.1% range.[29] Gross private domestic investment as a percentage of GDP has fallen from 20.2% in the second quarter of 2000 to 16.2% in 2016. This fall in investment, in turn, affects productivity, and it has not been counteracted by a significant drop in savings and a rise in consumption. In fact, savings increased from 4.2% of GDP to 5.7%, while personal consumption saw only a minor increase from 66% to 68.1% of GDP over the same period.[30] This excess of savings over investment helps explain why the federal funds rate has remained close to zero since the start of the recession. Growth in GDP is in the 2% range, not the historical 3% range. Economist Robert Gordon has argued that the information technology innovation wave of recent decades is less significant in providing enduring higher productivity and growth rates than the innovation waves of 1870–1970 (the internal combustion engine, modern communications, electricity, chemicals, pharmaceuticals, and other advances).[31]

Meanwhile, as noted, the median income for non–college-educated workers has been declining for a decade and a half, higher-paying manufacturing jobs have been replaced by lower-paying service jobs, and economic inequality has expanded to problematic levels. This list of big problems will not be solved simply by short-term economic stimulus measures or "pothole filling" infrastructure repairs. These are powerful structural problems and require a structural response. The United States appears to need productivity gains to restore growth and higher-quality jobs. Advanced manufacturing, with its potential for gains in productivity and employment (systemwide) and its core role in the innovation system, would seem to be a top target for addressing the nation's economic troubles. So, could it? What happened to U.S. manufacturing? What is advanced manufacturing? Where did it come from? What could it get us? And what are the tools we need to build it?

2 The Backdrop: Manufacturing's Economic History

Here are snapshots and lessons—pictures of critical moments for U.S. manufacturing history, drawing lessons for production policy. An eighteenth-century snapshot captures lessons from James Watt's famous "walk on the Green" of Glasgow. We then shift the lens to the nineteenth- century interchangeable machine-made parts paradigm in the United States, nurtured through early War Department technology policy. This technology advance snowballs through the nineteenth century into the blizzard of true mass production, leveraging the scale advantage of the world's first continent-sized market. The story then turns to the defense innovation system, where a powerful agency with immense funding and a national security rationale leads a series of major economic innovation waves; aviation in the early twentieth century is the case study summarized here. The defense innovation system subsequently birthed the foundational technologies behind the information technology (IT) innovation wave that evolved through the second half of the twentieth century. Importantly, this defense innovation role, which had its roots in production, by the mid-twentieth century had shifted almost exclusively to technologies, not the production systems behind them. This innovation/production disconnect had dramatic subsequent effects on U.S. manufacturing.

The Walk on the Green

Early steam engines had been around for some fifty years, pumping water out of English mines, before they became the focus of James Watt's profound attention.[1] Watt was raised in the growing seaport of Greenock on the upper Firth of Clyde in Scotland; when he was eighteen, his mother died and his father's health declined, so he was off to London to study the craft of instrument making. After a year, he returned to Glasgow to open a shop for brass instruments he would make and repair—parallel rulers and reflecting quadrants for navigation, scales, parts for barometers, and tele-scopes. But Glasgow's Guild of Hammerman got in his way; he could not do what he was doing, because he had not served a seven-year apprenticeship.

His livelihood was saved by the University of Glasgow, which needed an instrument maker for the new astronomical instruments required for its obser-vatory. So Watt entered the academy as a craftsman and was befriended by chemist Joseph Black and philosopher Adam Smith. The craftsman became schooled in the underlying sciences. In 1759, Watt began to study the New-comen steam engine, and although the formal laws of thermodynamics were still a century away, he began to understand topics such as latent heat and thermal energy. In 1763, he was called on to repair a Newcomen engine. He found that three-quarters of the thermal energy was being wasted dur-ing each piston cycle. Steam injected into the cylinder pushed the piston, but then cold water was sprayed into the cylinder to condense the steam, causing the piston to be sucked back to its original position by the result-ing pressure vacuum. Then more steam was pumped into the piston and it pushed forward again, and more cold water was added. This splash of cold water meant most of the engine's potential mechanical energy was being lost. It was very inefficient.

Then, just over 250 years ago, in 1765, Watt took a walk on the Green of Glasgow on a Sabbath spring day. Toward the end of his life, he gave an account of the resulting flash of insight. As he walked halfway across the green, he had the idea of a separate condenser. It would enable the vacuum to suck in the piston but would allow the cylinder to maintain its constant temperature—no splash of cold water would be needed. "I had not walked further than the golf house"—this was, after all, Scotland—"when the whole thing was arranged in my mind," he recalled in 1813.

He had to await the end of the Sabbath but promptly made a model of his device and four years later obtained a patent. It tripled the mechanical efficiency of the steam engine. Instead of a clumsy way to gradually pump out water from coal and tin mines, it became powerful enough to power the Industrial Revolution, an engine of growth. But there is more to the story of the insight on the Green. It took decades before networks of factories and coal mines linked by railroads spread across Britain, making it the first industrial power.

Watt needed capital, not just a working design, to turn the design into a large-scale working engine and scale up engine production. John Roe-buck, founder of the noted Carron Iron Works, backed him, but getting the precision fit for the piston and cylinder in an era of blacksmiths required Watt to work for eight years as a surveyor and civil engineer to support this work. After Roebuck went broke in the process, Matthew Boulton, who owned the Soho Iron Works near Birmingham and employed some of the finest ironworkers anywhere, came to the rescue; his team solved the precision problem. By 1776, the first working engines were in commercial enterprises, and Watt initiated continuing incremental advances—steam indicators, parallel motion, and centrifugal governors—that significantly improved his technology.

There are four important lessons for us here at the onset of the Industrial Revolution:

Lesson 1: "mind and hand." Watt was a blend of craftsman and academic: he was first a precision instrument maker and then added a formal science background. He had crossover expertise, which can be vital because creativity often comes from combining one field with another. Industrial Revolution historian William Rosen reminds us of philosopher Immanuel Kant's saying that the hand is "the window on the mind" and of theologian and physician Charles Bell's concept of the "intelligent hand."[2] Watt was equipped to do learning by doing, learning by making—mental gymnastics reinforced by physical applications. This relationship between learning and making is a vital part of the significance of the production stage.

Lesson 2: tinkering and science, the practical and the theory. A second lesson comes from the fact that Watt took the simple Newcomen engine, designed by an imaginative ironmonger—a tinkerer—and applied his hard-won academic learning to gauge the inefficiencies in the system and think through needed advances. This, too, presents a pattern—much of the Industrial Revolution was initiated by tinkerers and then perfected by the application of mathematics and science. This moving picture of the practical informing the science, which in turn informs the practical, lasted from the nineteenth century into the present: Edison's electric light bulb informed electron theory, and the transistor led to semiconductor physics. Science can form from technology, and technology can form from science—it is a two-way street. One of the most important aspects of making something is that it helps develop the scientific theory behind it; new technologies are on a continuum between technology and science, and a two-way street is needed.

Lesson 3: "expert performance." Watt began working on the engine six years before his "flash of insight" on the Green. This tells us that it was no quickie brainstorm but rather was founded on years of focused attention and learning. While Watt's thoughts may have come together in front of the Glasgow golf shack, there were years of the equivalent of musical practice or mental weightlifting before he saw the solution to the puzzle come together. As William Rosen points out, this was an "expert performance model"—the insight only came because it was trained to come, preceded by years of attentive practice.[3]

Lesson 4: industrial scale-up. An invention does not enter the economy on autopilot; it takes relentless effort to improve and perfect it through processes of advanced prototyping, demonstration, testing, feedback from testing, and finally pilot production. Watt's insight on the Green was in 1765; it took until 1776 for these preproduction processes to play out to enable the technology to start to scale. These processes require very complex and sophisticated efforts—the engineering and reengineering, and the application of new science, required all of Watt's effort. What we now call R&D is not enough.

We will see these rules in practice again and again as our production story unfolds.

Interchangeable Machine-Made Parts

A story of the economic history of manufacturing must begin with a snapshot of Watt, but we now fast-forward to a snapshot of 1800s America and an approach that led to a critical stage of mass production.

Enter George Washington, as he does in so many early American stories. In 1794, frustrated with unreliability and corruption in purchasing guns from abroad and from private contractors for his new nation's tiny army, he proposed the legislation that led to government-owned armories in Springfield, Massachusetts, and Harper's Ferry, Virginia (later West Virginia), to make muskets and ordnance, supplanting the private sector's role.[4] We don't think of Washington as an advocate of industrial policy, but here he is. At the time, guns were made largely by hand by skilled artisans, with metal parts filed to fit each weapon. No two guns were exactly alike, they were handcrafted, and their parts could not be interchanged, so each part was made anew. And they were very expensive. Arrayed in a vast circle on the ceiling of the great entry room of the governor's mansion in Colonial Williamsburg are over a hundred muskets. The display announced that the governor not only commanded power and might but also had access to startling wealth to be able to fund such a display. And armies had to be accompanied by armorer's trains: covered wagons with smiths, anvils, and heavy equipment to individually repair weapons that broke down by remaking the individualized part. These heavy trains slowed armies to a crawl.

Enter Eli Whitney, the canny Yankee inventor. He had been utterly frustrated in his attempt to earn profits from his 1794 cotton gin—the simple design had been stolen and replicated by hundreds of tinkerers across the south, his patent completely ignored. He was piling up litigation debts trying to get cotton planters and states to pay him for the cotton bonanza his invention enabled, and he was near bankruptcy. It looked hopeless. What could be done? Why not a government bailout? Facing an imminent undeclared war with France, John Adams's young government in Washington in 1797 began planning a frantic military buildup. Whitney, carefully following the war news and noted for his gin invention, decided to become an arms maker, applied some New England political connections, and proposed to the government that he make the muskets for the buildup. In mid-1798, he obtained a contract to manufacture ten thousand muskets within the incredibly short period of two years. He knew nothing about gunmaking, and it was a stunningly aggressive bid. No gunmaker in America had produced guns at this volume, including the two government armories.

How would Whitney take on this mission impossible? He proposed using water-powered "Machines for forging, rolling, floating, boreing, Grinding, Polishing, etc."[5] Alerted by fellow Connecticut resident Treasury Secretary Oliver Wolcott, Jr., to French ideas in this area,[6] he planned to make the muskets by using interchangeable machine-made parts. Whitney wrote to Wolcott, "One of my primary objects is to form the tools so the tools themselves shall fashion the work and give to every part its just proportion— which when once accomplished, will give expedition, uniformity and exactness to the whole. . . . In short, the tools which I contemplate are similar to an engraving on a copper plate from which may be taken a great number of impressions perceptibly alike."[7] He aimed to develop what his son later described as a "uniformity system—or making the similar parts of an arm or machine so near alike in shape that they can be used in assembling the piece without [hand] working."[8]

Whitney was unable to make the new system work. By 1801, he had not yet produced a musket and was called down to Washington before a group of officials, including President Adams and President-elect Jefferson, to justify his use of taxpayer monies. He put on a brilliant show, assembling muskets in front of them, choosing parts, apparently at random, from a parts pile he brought with him, snapping and screwing parts in place, and voila! A musket! Jefferson, in particular, was delighted by the presentation and saw its production implications. The show earned Whitney renewed federal support. However, he appears to have fudged the presentation; he had apparently marked the parts beforehand—they were not fully interchangeable.[9]

Whitney saw the technical challenge well: "A good musket is a complicated engine and difficult to make—difficult of execution because the conformation of most of its parts corresponds with no regular geometrical figure."[10] He had made progress with a strict division of labor in his factory workforce (a practice Adam Smith had expounded on as an engine for progress), developed important factory management practices, and may have made progress on a milling machine (a rotating cutter that removes metal).[11] But musket making was estimated to require some 195 separate steps, with the 29 required parts undergoing separate shaping, cutting, and heat treating[12]—there was still much handwork in his production process. It took Whitney eight years to deliver his ten thousand muskets; his parts were not fully interchangeable.

But the idea was there, and progress picked up elsewhere. Springfield Armory, starting around 1815, created one of the most advanced manufacturing facilities in the nation, using extensive division of labor to form over one hundred specialized occupations. For making gunstocks, it pioneered a lathe, a complex new machine that could produce irregular shapes and forms.

Enter John Hall, a Maine Yankee who ran a woodworking and boatbuilding shop in Portland. In his spare time, he developed a prototype for a breech-loading rifle, patented and improved it, and then brought it to the attention of the War Department, selling a few between 1813 and 1819. The department found that his rifles were not only superior to others but also that "the rifle's parts could be mutually exchanged with another, thus greatly simplifying the task of making field repairs."[13] In 1819, Secretary of War John C. Calhoun brought Hall to the Harpers Ferry Armory as assistant armorer to produce breech-loading rifles. The next year, he was put in charge of a separate rifle works at the armory, with independence from its Army bureaucracy, which had constantly sniped at him and tried to siphon off his funding. Hall was now free to pursue his development of machine tools and rifle production with government backing. He used waterpower to run belts and pulleys to power machines that could rotate at 3000 rpm, cutting metal with cutters and saws, making advances in the milling machine and using precise gauges to test size and fit.[14]

By December 30, 1822, Hall was able to write to Calhoun, "I have succeeded in establishing a method of fabricating arms exactly alike & with economy, by the hands of common workmen & in such a manner as to insure perfect observance of any established model."[15] His contract for one thousand rifles was completed in 1825, and Ordnance Department officials came up for a visit. They were astounded by his system. Hall's "system for manufacture of small arms [was] entirely novel" and could yield "the most beneficial results to the Country especially if carried into effect on a large scale."[16] The productivity gains were dramatic; Hall claimed, "one boy by the aid of these machines can perform more work than ten men with files, in the same time, and with greater accuracy."[17] Unskilled "common hands" could replace highly skilled but slower artisans. Because many of the workmen at the rifle works were also involved in developing the machine tools, Hall's Harpers Ferry rifles were higher in cost than rifles produced at the Springfield Armory. However, the Army's chief of ordnance strongly defended Hall's advances to Harpers Ferry management as an experiment that justified the higher costs and would enable potential future savings through fully machine-based production.[18]

In other words, just as with Eli Whitney's earlier experiment, the military was willing to invest long term, with sustained patient capital, to enable a critical technology and process advance—a vital pattern that recurs throughout U.S. technology history.[19]

Hall's technology advances in machine tools were transferred by the War Department to another innovative gunmaker, in Middletown, Connecticut, Simeon North. By 1834, North was able to produce rifle parts that were fully interchangeable with parts made at Harpers Ferry. So the machine-made parts made at two widely dispersed plants were functionally identical. Hall's production system was also introduced at the Springfield Armory, and it began to spread quickly to other early manufacturers of simple machines in the Connecticut River Valley as workers trained at Harpers Ferry and Springfield brought their skills to other firms.[20] By the 1850s, British and European officials were visiting these American manufacturing sites, wondering at the accomplishments of what became known as the "American System"[21] of manufacturing. Although the British had been the first to develop mass production machinery for their textile sector, they had not brought this conceptual design to other sectors.[22] They were startled—they had long dismissed Americans as errant colonists, and now these upstarts were taking them head-on. Alexander Hamilton, an admirer of British systems and an early advocate of American manufacturing, had thought that his new nation might pass Britain economically in a half century,[23] and now it was starting to happen. The key foundational step for mass production was now in place, which brings us to an additional lesson:

Lesson 5: the role of patient, long-term government support. Technology development is high risk and long term; it requires corresponding long-term perspectives and capital. Such support from the government, particularly from the defense sector, has been critical for U.S. technology advances, starting with the developments in the eighteenth century given here.

Economic Behemoth

The "American System" of manufacturing as it evolved in the early nineteenth century was not limited to simple machines such as clocks and guns. By the 20th century, it had also led to complex machines, such as automobiles. But, as Charles Morris has noted, the idea was stretched to characterize all forms of production, from processed food, to soap, to clothing, to railroads.[24] And the same approach was taken to create industrial-scale agriculture. It was about industrial organization as well as industrial machinery.

The relentless doubling of America's population every generation in the nineteenth century created the opportunity for mass consumption to spur mass production. Unlike European nations that had to evolve their large middle classes over time, America was settled largely by middle classes—it was predominantly middle class from the start, as Alexis de Tocqueville understood, and skipped the lethargy of a ruling class.[25] Middle class energy dominated every sector of endeavor, as Tocqueville was the first to expound. And the U.S. Constitution's commerce clause created, from 1789 onward, a common market, which in the nineteenth century rapidly became continent sized. Mass production and mass scalability applied to everything and were enabled by a mass-consumption economy. It was not only an American system of manufacturing but rather an American system of everything—a relentless scale-up of all.

The railroads were a crucial tool knitting this continental common market together. In 1840, America had 2700 miles of railroads; by 1860, 28,000 miles; and by 1890, 164,000 miles.[26] Steel production paralleled growth in railroads, buildings, civil works, and ships. Steel became the world's metric for industrial leadership; by the turn of the nineteenth century, U.S. steel production led the world. One steelmaker, Andrew Carnegie, controlled one-quarter of U.S. steel production; Carnegie's production alone amounted to half of Britain's steel production.[27] Energy resource production was another enabler; John D. Rockefeller's Standard Oil, an integrated monopoly that ran from oil production to refining, transport, and product, created the U.S. oil industry at huge scale and became the first truly global corporation.[28] The final piece in the American behemoth's economic leadership came during the First World War, when American lending to European powers enabled Wall Street to dominate world finance.

Mass Production

The story of interchangeable machine-made parts transitions into a story of true mass production through Henry Ford.[29] Like the IT revolution in the late twentieth to early twenty-first century, a production revolution was seeded by government technology development support early on and then completely absorbed by private sector market forces. By the time of Ford, the private sector was, shall we say, in the driver's seat.

Ford was a mechanic through and through, and had great insight into machinery and its workings. He developed, with a team of engineers and managers, new ideas for factory layout, production design, quality control, and parts and materials handling. It helped that a new production floor setup was enabled by tools that could be driven by new individual electric motors, which replaced tools driven by central shafts and the belts coming off them. Static assembly tied to fixed tool location could be replaced by sequenced production operations. Ford created his new factory with these ideas in Highland Park, Michigan, in 1909. Parts were distributed to work stations, with their delivery timed to arrive just before they were needed. A line of assembly moved the vehicles from work station to work station down the factory floor, with the next stage of components being added at each station until a fully completed product emerged at the end of the line. The assembly line had been deployed by innovative nineteenth-century production firms such as gunmaker Colt, but Ford automated it. Ford described his process: "Mass production is not merely quantity production. . . . Nor is it merely machine production." The essential mass production system entailed the progression of the product in a staged order through the factory, the delivery of parts to the work stations, where they could be snapped onto the product, and systematic breakdown of operations into constituent elements. Ford made it clear that "every part must be produced to fit at once" into the component that was to receive it, adding, "In mass production there are no fitters."

Ford's moving assembly line was enabled by technology advances, such as the electric motor, and by new process advances, including his staged operations in successive work stations. He joined his assembly line to a new business model as well: the productivity gains from his production system enabled production of a truly low-priced car highly accessible to the general public at commodity scale, as well as higher wages for employees. Early on, Ford's production plants had to provide huge parking lots so that its workforce producing the Ford had a place to park their Fords. This gives rise to a further lesson:

Lesson 6: join technology, process and business models. Production paradigms emerge by joining technology advances with process advances and with business models. It is not the technology advance alone that is needed; for transformative new production systems, you need process advances and new business models as well.

The Defense Innovation System

We glimpsed the defense-driven innovation system in the story of interchangeable machine-made parts, but it really began to emerge at scale in the United States in the years leading up to World War II. The Wright brothers' first customer for their flying machine was the U.S. Army; the evolution of the aviation industry is profoundly tied to the military.

Aviation

The pattern of military support for aviation would set a pattern for other sectors as well. The military supported research and development in aviation, it systematically sought and procured advanced aircraft designs, and it subsidized the early evolution of the sector.[30] In R&D, the mechanism for support was the National Advisory Committee for Aviation (NACA—which in 1958 was turned into the National Aeronautics and Space Administration, NASA). Founded in 1915 as an independent agency for research, it did for aviation what the armory model did for manufacturing, providing long-term, stable support for experimentation through basic and applied R&D for a wide range of aviation technologies. Its governing committee included representatives from the aviation branches of the military services as well as science and engineering experts. This was a talented group. For example, Vannevar Bush, one of the great twentieth-century figures in engineering, who led defense R&D in World War II for President Roosevelt and then created the model for postwar federal R&D support, received his training in government R&D as NACA's chairman in the 1930s.[31]

Following World War I, military aviation was led by exceptionally talented officers: General Billy Mitchell for the Army Air Corps and Admiral William Moffett for Naval aviation. Both pursued systematic industrial policies. Moffett, for example, built his annual appropriation funding requests around the need to build up and sustain an ever-growing industrial base of aircraft and engine makers.[32] He explicitly recognized that military aviation must have such a strong base of competitive but well-supported industries. Faced with global competition with Germany, Japan, and Britain for aircraft advances, the military, buttressed by NACA R&D, supported a relentless series of ever-improving prototypes. The United States was particularly effective in developing the first long-range, four-engine, all-metal bomber before World War II. Its military planes exceeded Germany's in capability by the time it entered the conflict in the European theater. Its aviation industrial base dominated all others and was able to surpass Japan's lead in fighter aircraft performance and dominate all other aircraft types within a year of the start of the Pacific war. Although Germany fielded the first jet aircraft, the United States, aided by British designs,[33] was able to launch a counterpart within months.

The third area involved support for an emerging civilian sector. Here, following World War I, the government directly subsidized air transport firms through sizable airmail contracts to get new civilian transport firms established. In the 1930s, the government, through the Civil Aeronautics Board (CAB), created a friendly regulatory structure to help assure emerging firms of profits, ensure their market share, and protect them from undue competition. Military support for technology development was also often transferred directly into civilian air transport designs. For example, U.S. development of long-range bomber technologies directly benefited civilian transport designs.

In aviation, then, the military performed the research and development to create the technology, supported the development and prototype stages, undertook the demonstration and testing, and its procurement support created and sustained initial markets. This was a new model for the governmental role in the United States, at least in the twentieth century. It not only offered support for production but also sustained a full spectrum of support for the evolution of a major new technology sector. Aviation was a technology the military had to have, but it was "dual use," not military only; it created a parallel civilian sector with mutual synergies. This model can be termed the "extended pipeline" model of innovation, offering defense sector support for every stage of the innovation process throughout the stages of the innovation pipeline.[34] The U.S. military applied the model to create what became a series of world innovation waves[35] with corresponding economic advances in the second half of the twentieth century in aviation, electronics, nuclear power, space, and computing and the Internet.

Lesson 7: The significance of Defense Department support at every stage of the innovation process. In the early twentieth century, the defense agencies played the central role in fostering aviation, a critical defense technology with massive spillover effects on the nondefense transport sector. The Army and Navy supported the research, the development, the prototypes, the demonstrations, the testing, and the markets for aircraft and their embedded technologies, both fostering and sustaining a new economic sector. The lesson from aviation is the potential importance of government support for every stage, from research through implementation. The resulting defense innovation system operates not from a single input, unlike research-only support from civilian R&D agencies such as the National Science Foundation or the National Institutes of Health, but is a comprehensive input system, with the ability to support innovation systematically at every stage.

As a result, the federal government has two parallel support systems for innovation. The first is the research-input-only model followed by civilian R&D agencies, which can be termed the "pipeline" model, where the government supports the research and trusts markets for the subsequent phases to evolve. The second is the comprehensive input system of the defense innovation system, which can be termed the "extended pipeline" model, with government support for every phase, including initial market creation.[36] It is this "extended pipeline" system that has led to the succession of major twentieth-century innovation waves: aviation, electronics, nuclear power, space, and, lately, computing and the Internet, supplementing the civilian agency R&D.

Computing and the Information Technology Revolution
Computing offers another prime example of this extended pipeline innovation model. The IT revolution amounted to the most powerful worldwide innovation wave of the latter part of the twentieth century and has continued into the twenty-first. Starting during and immediately after World War II, and continuing as the Cold War evolved, the Defense Department led the creation and support of electronic computing, semiconductors, supercomputing, software, personal computing, and the Internet. Because of its mammoth economic scope and the range of technology advances within it, it deserves particular attention. But it was different from its "extended pipeline" predecessors highlighted here—interchangeable parts and aviation. With one exception, Sematech, there was less focus on production technologies, processes, and industrialization. What follows is a dissection of the major elements of the IT innovation wave, and a summary of the role of government support in each.

The early *mainframe computers* were funded by and built to meet military needs. The Army supported the Electronic Numerical Integrator and Calculator (ENIAC) computer developed at the University of Pennsylvania by John W. Mauchley and Prosper Eckert, with conceptual contributions from

Princeton's John Von Neumann, to assist the Army Ballistic Laboratory in the massive calculations required for accurate artillery ballistics range and targeting tables. It was more than a thousand times faster than previous mechanical calculating machines. Development of the hydrogen bomb and then ballistic missiles required ever-greater computing capabilities and led to additional mainframe computing advances and models, following the "von Neumann architecture" of a central processing unit that was fed both stored memory and programs that processed data and returned it to the memory. These variants created massive calculators.

But computers also needed to operate in real time, not just serve as calculators. The Navy's Office of Naval Research at the end of World War II supported MIT's development of the Whirlwind computer to operate in real time to enable flight simulation. Just as the Navy was about to cut back funding, the Air Force was stung by the realization that the Soviet Union had developed a first-strike capacity with atomic weapons that could be delivered by new long-range bombers flying over the Arctic. There was no defense. The alarm was sounded by a science adviser, MIT professor George Valley, who successfully pressed the Air Force to organize a systematic air defense system. Valley knew he would need computing power at the heart of the system, and he enlisted Jay Forrester, who shifted the Whirlwind computer project he was leading to make it the center of the SAGE air defense mission.

Receiving transmissions from radar sets strewn across the Arctic and North Atlantic, transmitted over phone lines, analyzing them, and scrambling fighters and antiaircraft missiles in response, within a highly demanding time frame, mandated real-time computing. Forrester led the effort to create magnetic core memory, the first effective computer memory system and a critical enabler of real-time operations. It was through Whirlwind and then SAGE that computing began to assume its modern face, with operators sitting in front of cathode-ray tube (CRT) terminals typing input on keyboards and highlighting screen data with light guns—an early mouse. One computer was not enough; because MIT did not want to go into production of its prototype computer to outfit the whole SAGE system, it enlisted IBM to do so. The SAGE computer became IBM's first major computer product line, the 700 then 7000 series. The SAGE system thus became the initial driving force behind the development of the U.S. computer industry. During the critical first two decades of computing, a major National Research Council study found that the technical cutting edge of this critical new technology was supported by the military, through its support of university research, its labs and research organizations, and private sector firms engaged in its R&D and production.

Semiconductors and Sematech emerged in a somewhat different way, evolving from the transistor that was developed in 1947 by John Bardeen, Walter Brattain, and William Shockley at Bell Labs. The integrated circuit came in 1958 from Jack Kilby of Texas Instruments and at nearly the same time from Robert Noyce at Fairchild Semiconductor, and the third major advance, the microprocessor, was led by Noyce in 1969 at Intel, the successor firm to Fairchild. The military potential of the semiconductor was immediately understood, both for computing needs and for onboard guidance systems for missiles. For some four years after the development of the integrated circuit, the only customers were the Air Force and NASA. Demand for semiconductors continued to be dominated by military needs—for missiles, computing, space, and nuclear energy—well into the 1970s.

More was to come as the Defense Advanced Research Projects Agency (DARPA) emerged out of the Sputnik crisis in 1958 and addressed chip challenges. It was created to lead high-risk, revolutionary technology challenges and avoid "technology surprise." In the mid-1970s, Robert Kahn at DARPA saw that the then modest group of computer firms were only taking incremental steps to move from chips with thousands of transistors to chips with millions of transistors, a move needed to keep on the Moore's Law curve of relentless computer advancement and ever-lower costs.[37] In 1977, DARPA initiated the Very Large-Scale Integration (VLSI) project to transition chip design. An additional key step also emerged. Carver Mead of Caltech and Lynn Conway of Xerox PARC developed, with DARPA support, both a straightforward set of design principles and an accompanying "silicon foundry" model so that many chip designers could submit designs, which could be compiled onto a single chip, sent to a shared foundry, split apart, and shipped back in weeks, with costs shared across the network. DARPA's resulting MOSIS (the Metal Oxide Semiconductor Implementation Service) program spurred great creativity and experimentation in chip design, building a much larger community of designers across universities, companies and research agencies, which also greatly enhanced the integration process for chips of much larger scale. Microchip technology burst all barriers in the 1980s.

That was not all. The U.S. semiconductor industry faced a major challenge from a well-coordinated effort by Japanese firms to capture chip production (particularly memory chips). Offering higher quality and more efficient production, the Japanese firms were moving ahead in what the Reagan administration viewed as a critical defense technology sphere. In response, in 1987 the semiconductor industry, led by Robert Noyce, organized a collaborative, public-private partnership to dramatically improve semiconductor manufacturing quality and performance. DARPA cospon-sored and cofunded this Sematech project,[38] providing $500 million of funding over five years. The combination of major manufacturing improve-ments directed at semiconductor equipment makers and the emergence of microchips restored U.S. semiconductor leadership. Sematech remains an important industry collaboration but in 1996 transitioned out of govern-ment cofunding to industry leadership and funding and a global outlook. Sematech was a classic example of defense support for transformational production improvements and created a seminal collaborative partnership model for how this might be done. From a long-term policy perspective, creation of the working, large-scale, industry-wide collaborative model orga-nized around technology and process innovation in manufacturing may have been more important than the actual support.

Sematech, then, represents an iconic model for advanced manufactur-ing. When assembled, it was a consortium of small and large firms, semi-conductor fabricators, and semiconductor equipment makers, organized to meet a major technology challenge affecting the future of their industry—developing chips of much higher quality that would meet the relentless challenge of Moore's Law, which mandated ever-greater capability at ever-lower cost. It was allied with DARPA, an advanced technology agency, which cofunded the effort, and it also integrated the work of university research experts. So it was a cost-shared, industry-government-university collabo-ration organized around a technology challenge model. Its focus was on production technologies and processes, and these played a key role in the economic recovery and transformation of the industry.

Lesson 8: Sematech presents an important cross-industry/ university/agency man-ufacturing innovation organizational model for tackling complex, production-based challenges, optimizing the strengths of each. It was a public-private collaboration across small and large firms, government, and university research, which was cost-shared and organized to address a major pro-duction technology challenge, which demonstrated the ability to scale up across an industry relatively quickly. This combination of a *collaboration* model with a *challenge* model (discussed later) presents a clear approach to meeting advanced manufacturing needs. It is also a model for how to pre-vent needless loss of domestic industries to foreign competition.

Sematech, then, is an example of an innovation organization solution resolving an important set of manufacturing issues. It is a clear ancestor of the current generation of advanced manufacturing institutes discussed in chapter 6. Interestingly, despite its success and apparent relevance, DOD dropped the model for twenty years, returning to it only recently, through the manufacturing institutes.

Unlike the semiconductor field, *supercomputing* is still a government-dominated sector, meeting largely national security needs. In the 1950s, computers serving scientific needs were seen as a separate class from those serving data-processing business needs.[39] When IBM moved away from scientific computing to focus on the latter, led by its 360 series in 1964, which used the same programming across different sizes of computers, its leadership fell to others. Advances were led by a team within Control Data headed by Seymour Cray, then by his lab in Chippewa Falls, Wisconsin, and then in 1972 by his firm Cray Research, which developed the next generations of supercomputers. Cray had no interest in trying to serve two masters, both scientific computing and business data processing; he was only interested in the most advanced machines imaginable for the former. There were only five real customers for Cray's 1976 remarkable creation, the Cray 1: DOD, NASA, the nuclear weapons labs, the National Center for Atmospheric Research and the Weather Bureau. Los Alamos National Laboratory bought the first machine.

Cray Research built four generations of supercomputers and embraced massively parallel computing models, but it was not finding customers, and its successor went bankrupt in 1995. In 1996, Seymour Cray died from injuries sustained in an auto accident. Cray's name survived in mergers and spinoffs, and his company's successor built a successful new "Red Storm" model in 2005 for the Sandia energy lab, followed by new supercomputers for energy labs in 2009 and 2012. Induced by energy lab customers trying to model the status of the U.S. nuclear stockpile, IBM pressed forward again in supercomputing in 2004 with its Blue Gene models, which contributed new architectures. IBM's Sequoia and Cray's Titan operated at the 16 and 17 petaflop levels, respectively, as of 2012. Both Japan and China also have entrants competing for the world's fastest supercomputer. Concerned about U.S. supercomputing technology leadership, DARPA launched a series of new initiatives; in 2015, contemplating an exascale machine capable of a billion billion calculations per second, President Obama announced a strategic initiative to achieve this, a major technology challenge.[40] While interest in "big data" promises possible support from new fields such as health research, these market opportunities are still emerging. And, supported by security agencies, a very different approach, quantum computing, is also evolving. One underlying point remains central: government national security concerns have led supercomputing development.

Software presents yet another variant, but, again, initial defense support was crucial. While the first electronic computers were programmed by rewiring them, the processing required by the von Neumann architecture for computing mandated software.[41] Still, hardware and software remained tightly linked. The Whirlwind and SAGE computers, with their need for immediate entry and continuous updating, forced software evolution and led to the training of large numbers of early programmers. This may have begun the split between software and hardware, which was accelerated when IBM created its 360 family of computers and gave independent software service firms the opportunity to develop products and market them to users. The development of microcomputers expanded these opportunities, and when IBM launched its PC in 1981, it controlled the hardware but used a separate Microsoft operating system and allowed software vendors to supply products, and the software field blew wide open.

However, the early development of software was underwritten by defense needs, and even through the early 1980s, defense accounted for more than half of the software market.[42] Academic computer science departments were founded in the 1980s, often with DARPA support; through the mid-1980s, more than half the R&D they performed was for the Defense Department.[43]

Personal computing (or desktop or microcomputing) relied on an initially direct but later less direct, but still critical, DOD role. J. C. R. Licklider, an MIT psychology professor, acoustics engineer, and computing fanatic, who became the first director of DARPA's Information Processing Techniques Office (IPTO), was the critical initiator. Frustrated by the arm's-length, "hands-off" nature of the batch-processing, card-spitting, "big calculator" model of mainframe computing, in 1960 he wrote a seminal article that envisioned much of what was to come.

The article portrayed with remarkable clarity the computer as embodiment of what he called a "man-computer symbiosis" with interactive computing on a contributing, collaborative continuum with people, not computers superseding people. He foresaw personal computer workstations with rich graphics capabilities, time sharing and computer-aided collaboration, networks and an online community, online libraries of the world's knowledge and information with instant retrieval and universal access, computer languages enabling a new digital medium of expression, the evolution of information science into a new science of computing as a significant new scientific field, enabling new ways to portray and thus understand complex data, and shifting rote work and work preparation to computers.[44] He uniquely saw computers as potentially both exciting and a joy to play with.

In 1962, Licklider went to the Advanced Research Projects Agency (ARPA, which, with the word Defense inserted at the front in 1969, became DARPA) to create a new office to link behavior and computing to solve what DARPA was thinking of as "command and control" challenges.[45] It was the rarest of innovation moments—the technology visionary was given the resources to become the technology implementer. An early task was "time sharing." Computers were mainframes and very expensive, with ideas for minicomputers just starting to emerge through Digital Equipment Corporation (DEC) and a few other firms. Time sharing enabled groups of users to obtain slivers of a central computer's processing time so individuals could make the computer responsive to their own particular commands. It was an early version of interactive computing, with numerous users operating off a central utility. DARPA spawned Project MAC at MIT, where programming for time sharing enabled the first online community, online bulletin boards, email, sharing of software ("freeware"), early computer games, and—hackers.[46]

Under Licklider, DARPA funded innovation "great groups,"[47] personally selected, breathtakingly talented research teams from institutions around the country that would over time populate the personal computing field. DARPA, under Licklider and its other early leaders, represented a unique innovation architecture. Innovation ultimately is intensely personal and face-to-face, and at the level of complex technology required, it groups into "great groups." These groups require support from institutions within ecosystems of innovation. DARPA uniquely was able to join both strands— supporting great groups (and often it operated as a great group itself) at the personal level but also operating at the institutional level to evolve the innovations from the groups it supported.[48] One of the proudest great group examples was Doug Engelbart's team at SRI, which would develop the mouse, onscreen windows, hypertext, full-screen word processing, collaborative real-time editing, graphics, and videoconferencing, and demonstrate these at "The Mother of All Demos" in December 1968, an early computer conference.[49] Whereas SRI thought Engelbart was flaky, Licklider supported him from the beginning of his DARPA IPTO tenure. Bob Taylor, a Licklider team member at DARPA and a successor to him as director of IPTO, left for Xerox PARC in 1970 to assemble a great group. Meeting weekly on beanbag chairs, the group picked up ideas from Engelbart and other DARPA projects and created the first personal computer, the Alto.[50] Although Xerox famously failed to commercialize it,[51] Steve Jobs at Apple saw the Alto model and its concepts and created the Mac. DARPA did not create the personal computer but fostered and supported the great groups that systematically erected its foundations.

The *Internet* was the indispensable app that scaled personal computing. Licklider once again was present at the creation. In an April 1963 DARPA memo to the research community he was funding, addressed to "the members and affiliates of the Intergalactic Computer Network," he outlined the need to connect them all through their computers onto a single network that would bridge the continent. He wanted an electronic commons as "the main and essential medium of informational interaction for government, institutions, corporations and individuals." It would support electronic commerce, banking, digital libraries, the "dissemination of information in your field of specialization, announcement of cultural, sport, and entertainment events" and on and on and on.[52]

Licklider set the agenda and under another of his successors as IPTO's director, Larry Roberts, DARPA selected BBN (a Cambridge-based MIT spinoff where Licklider had earlier started its computer wing), with a team under Frank Heart, to launch the ARPAnet in 1969. It reached into the growing number of computer science departments that DARPA funding had initiated, and a user community started to scale as new Internet features were added, building on the foundational Internet protocol TCP/IP contributed by DARPA researchers Bob Kahn and Vint Cerf.[53] True scaling was enabled when DARPA shrewdly spun off ARPAnet to become NSFnet, with the growth of the Internet backbone guided there by critical decisions by Steve Wolff, NSF's manager for the Internet. He and his colleagues helped evolve the "Internet service provider" commercial model, multiply the backbone, and finally spin off NSFnet in 1995.[54] Then Tim Berners-Lee combined hypertext and browsing into the World Wide Web,[55] and then . . .

By 1990, at the time of Licklider's death, the revolution first launched by "Lick's kids" to make computing personal was in full force, and IT became an economic innovation wave, leading at the close of the twentieth century, as noted at the outset of this section, to one of the strongest sustained periods of growth in U.S. history. Not bad.

An important additional lesson emerges from the defense innovation system:

Lesson 9: the challenge model for technology innovation. The IT revolution led by DOD agencies did not evolve from curiosity-driven research; it evolved from systematically addressing at every stage of the innovation process a series of carefully posed technology challenges in a series of related sectors. This "challenge" model clearly led to very significant results, and it stands for a model of organizing innovation advances around challenges.

What does the DOD role behind the core strands of the IT revolution mean for manufacturing? Most importantly, the IT revolution was not about manufacturing. Digital technologies certainly affected manufacturing, but the great innovation engine of defense R&D (with the exception of five years of support for Sematech) was directed not at manufacturing but at a new generation of its products. It was assumed that manufacturing simply was not on the innovation agenda at DOD. The United States had achieved world production leadership by the close of the nineteenth century, and such leadership was simply assumed—the United States simply was not paying much attention to manufacturing.

So a great new engine for innovation had been created, coming out of institutions created for technology advancement in World War II, out of Vannevar Bush's postwar advocacy for a continued federal research role, which created federally funded research universities, and out of defense Cold War technology investments. But innovation, in the eyes of the United States, did not encompass production technologies and processes. Like the poor and taxes, the United States simply supposed manufacturing would always be with us; it was outside the innovation agenda. This is a critical point for understanding the subsequent history of U.S. manufacturing's decline.

To reiterate, when Vannevar Bush created the postwar system of postwar federal R&D focused on basic research, manufacturing was not on that agenda, because the United States already had a startling manufacturing lead; it had created mass production, and its global competitors were not close to its production scale. Instead, Bush wanted to keep building up early-stage research, a comparatively new project in the United States, which had rapidly scaled up (with the creation of the federally funded research university model and federally funded R&D centers, FFRDCs) during the war. Similarly, when the Defense Department created its parallel innovation system in the postwar period, which was far more connected to subsequent stages than were the civilian sector R&D agencies,[56] manufacturing was not the problem. The two sides of the federal R&D system—defense and civilian—focused on science and development of new technology fields; manufacturing was not on either agenda.

Dan Breznitz and Peter Cowhey have argued that the United States needs to better link its federal R&D, which is at the heart of the system of innovation it maintains, to innovation for production.[57] Its *novel and breakthrough product/technology innovation* system includes university research supported by R&D agencies—it is often known as the "pipeline" system—and it uses "technology push" to implement its advances.[58] Industry in the United States pursues a *process and incremental innovation system* that emphasizes engineering enhancements to products and technologies, including the way they are produced, distributed, and serviced; this is led and dominated by industry.[59] Both are vital, yet the current U.S. technology policy model pays great attention to the former and little to the latter; the first system rarely comes to bear to assist the second. Manufacturing has historically fallen into the second category, considered dominated by engineering/process and industry, although, as has been demonstrated repeatedly over the decades as discussed earlier, it can be novel and breakthrough as well. It has not been the focus of a major federal government R&D effort since the early nineteenth century. This is part of the reason why the United States continues to innovate technologies, yet the product evolution occurs abroad.

Lesson 10: production and innovation are linked. Grasping that production is a critical feature of innovation, and integrating it into the innovation system, constitutes the tenth lesson in our litany; it is the core topic of the remainder of this book.

Suppose the United States worked to unify these innovation and production systems and brought the remarkable innovation talent in the first to support the second as well as the first. This innovation organization reform arguably is an important part of what the United States must accomplish if it is to bring on new manufacturing technology paradigms.

3   International Competition and the Decline
of U.S. Manufacturing

The United States paid a price for the missing production focus in its innovation system. The profound challenge to U.S. production in the 1970s and 1980s from Japan's quality manufacturing model and its accompanying technology and process advances, which dramatically disrupted U.S. production practices, is the first issue that must be understood. This chapter then explores the rise of China's manufacturing economy; its innovative new production scale-up approaches knocked the United States into second place in world manufacturing output in a remarkably short period. Accompanying that rise was a parallel and related rise in distributed production by U.S. firms, with outsourcing of production stages and corresponding issues of "innovate here/produce there," which could lead to "produce there/innovate there." The chapter closes with a discussion of the significant hollowing out (and the factors behind it) of U.S. manufacturing, and the related social disruption, particularly during the 2000–2010 period.

Japan's Quality Manufacturing Model

Japan in the 1970s and 1980s did not make the disconnect between its innovation system and production that the United States had made. As Japan reindustrialized in the postwar period, it undertook major innovations in production, using manufacturing as a means to bring it to the frontier of international technology and economic competitiveness. This approach was not new: it was the same technique the United States had employed in competition with Britain in the nineteenth century on its way to industrial and then economic supremacy.

A New Quality versus Price Trade-off
In pursuing its mass production model, the United States had developed an approach to the "quality versus price trade-off." It developed statistical quality control—finding an acceptable level of quality based on production

cost considerations. It then applied those statistics at the end of the production line, with quality inspectors throwing out a set percentage of
the products to match the statistical requirement. Here quality control
meant ensuring that each unit was of equal quality. The vital thing was
to keep the production line moving to retain mass production efficiencies, and treat quality as the end step. No worker could stop the production line.

In Japan, influenced by writings of Edwards Demming,[1] Toyota and other
firms ended this quality versus price trade-off. The new approach was to
build quality into every step of the production process, not treat it as a statistical afterthought. Any worker could stop the production line to assure
that quality was being implemented at each step. This became known as
"total quality control" and was implemented through "total quality management."[2] This approach foresaw that customers will pay a higher price
for quality to obtain more reliable and enduring goods and will remain
customers. In turn, higher quality could actually be a lower-price strategy as
well. The approach reversed the old quality versus price trade-off away from
average quality and lower price to high quality, which would more than
offset a higher price, and, through relentless system-quality performance
improvements at every step, lead to a lower price. This was not the only
advance from Japan; it was joined with a series of other important steps:
quality circles (teams of employees working collaboratively to solve quality
problems), just in time inventory (increasing efficiency and reducing cost
exposure by receiving supplies and goods for production only as they are
actually needed in the production process, cutting onsite inventory), and
supply chain integration (rather than keeping suppliers at arm's length,
undertake close alignment and coordination between suppliers and producers to gain production efficiencies). Japanese firms grasped the importance
of the production floor; engineers would start their careers on the factory
floor, not in a separate product design shop, so that product design more
fully integrated production design.

Concurrent Design
This integrated production methodology was an important step toward
what became known as "concurrent engineering design." Time is a cost
of production, so eliminating time delays is key. Concurrent engineering
design means coordinating in parallel the participants who have input into
product design, including the production, software, marketing, and engineering design sides, using an integrated design team for what became a
new, concurrent design management system that could better account for

the mix of design, production, sales, and product life-cycle elements. As this new quality-based manufacturing paradigm enabled Japanese firms to move toward dominance in the auto and consumer electronics sectors, U.S. firms were left scrambling to catch up. Eventually they understood what the Japanese firms had accomplished with a new mix of exacting production technologies, new processes, and new business models to match and exploit them.[3] As these advances were understood, American firms copied them and responded with their own equivalent efficiency paradigms of "Six Sigma" (a systematic means to eliminate production defects initiated in the late 1980s and 1990s, initially by Motorola and General Electric) and "lean manufacturing" (a system for constant elimination of waste in production time and cost first posed in 1988 by John Krafcik at MIT's Sloan School of Management based on his experience on a joint Toyota-GM auto production venture in California).[4]

There is an important lesson here: economic innovation waves can stem from manufacturing technology and process breakthroughs. Japan's quality revolution in production amounted to an innovation wave that enabled it to capture major portions of critical economic sectors, particularly autos and consumer electronics in the 1980s. Although it had used this approach in the nineteenth century, by mastering mass production, the United States lost track of it in the mid- to late twentieth century and paid a significant price in economic disruption.

A Different Labor Model

Japan also developed a different labor versus employment trade-off, a step that U.S. firms did not emulate. Although this has eroded somewhat under the pressure of subsequent international competition, Japan treated workforce employment as a lifetime guarantee, and so made labor cost a fixed cost. In return for this employment guarantee, the workforce (and its unions) allowed management great flexibility in defining jobs, in changing work rules, and in introducing production efficiencies and productivity advances. Labor was collaborative. Manufacturing firms in the United States had evolved using the opposite approach: the workforce was treated as a variable cost, with employers controlling employment levels, using layoffs and firings to adjust to business cycles. In return, the labor force (especially in unionized firms) demanded control of the introduction of work rule changes and efforts to improve productivity, "protecting" workers from flexible work rules and efficiency introductions. Labor was adversarial. Japanese firms, by assuring employment by making employment a fixed cost, were able to systematically introduce productivity gains, whereas, by controlling and using hiring and firing as a flexible cost, large U.S. firms had to battle to introduce productivity gains.

The Role of Industrial Policy

Throughout the 1980s, as U.S. industries struggled to understand Japan's quality revolution and catch up, there was much grappling with Japan's "industrial policy" model. Its Ministry of International Trade and Industry (MITI, now renamed Ministry of Economy, Trade and Industry, METI) was held up as a symbol of an interventionist governmental support model, orchestrating industries and their technology policies in contrast to the more laissez-faire, noninterventionist U.S. governmental role in manufacturing. Japan's "keiretsu" model of integrating production, capital, trading, and supplier firms into interlocking networks with cross-ownership, organized around industry-leading firms in a series of sectors, also seemed daunting to U.S. firms, which were blocked from such groupings by antitrust laws. Keiretsu groupings were successors to the even more integrated pre–World War II system of "zaibatsu" family-controlled groups, which were only partially dissolved by U.S. occupation forces before the onset of the Cold War forced the occupation to accelerate Japan's economy. The keiretsu became a tool for rapid postwar reindustrialization. The keiretsu were shareholder controlled, not family controlled, but included elements of the predecessor zaibatsu in looser groupings. To the keiretsu, MITI added significant governmental technology support focused on industry (not research university) R&D, technology targets and strategies, and trade controls and import restrictions. The Bank of Japan used currency controls to keep the yen valued lower than the dollar to help assure a competitive trade advantage in manufactured goods. This combination, joined to the new quality production paradigm, presented a powerful juggernaut.

The U.S. Response

How did the United States get out of this box? Why didn't Japan's rapidly growing GDP continue on its trajectory toward passing that of the United States? In the 1980s, as the realization dawned on industrialists and policymakers that Japan had launched a new kind of manufacturing system, heavily innovation-oriented around quality in production, the U.S. political system was forced to react. As noted, Japan's quality revolution was built on new precision in production technologies, tied to new production processes and new enabling business models. U.S. industry took a long time to understand this revolution and to try to catch up, and meanwhile the United States lost innovation leadership in two major sectors: autos and consumer electronics. As Kent Hughes has described, the political system was affected by anxiety and frustration, particularly in the region most disrupted by Japan's new quality manufacturing system, the industrial Midwest—the origin of the term "rust belt."[5] There was a political outcry.

The Republican Party's response was around its traditional mantra of capital supply: Congressman Jack Kemp from Buffalo and Senator Bill Roth from Delaware proposed significant changes in marginal tax rates.[6] Traditional Democrats called for what was known at the time as "industrial policy."[7] Noting the interventionist industrial policies of Japan's Ministry of International Trade and Industry (MITI),[8] they called for sustaining failing firms and sectors, and their employees, to enable a turnaround. Labor retraining, education, and assistance were part of the proposals, essentially a labor supply approach, a long-standing Democratic mantra. It was classical economics all over again—each party locked in on one of the two major elements of classical economics' growth theory, capital supply and labor supply, solutions long embedded in their political philosophies. But classical economics, as Robert Solow has demonstrated, lacked a sound theory of economic growth.[9] Both parties, then, lacked workable growth policies. They had missed the advent of growth economics (often termed innovation economics), initially articulated by Solow, which found that technological and related innovation was the dominant causative factor in growth. Capital supply and labor supply remained significant factors but were not nearly as important as technological innovation.

There were glimmers of this recognition within the parties. President Ronald Reagan named John Young, CEO of Hewlett Packard, to lead the Commission on Industrial Competitiveness (the "Young Commission"), given the challenge posed by Japan. Young's commission argued for R&D growth and new public-private partnerships to accelerate technology advances.[10] Its recommendations, presented in 1984, were largely ignored by the Republican administration, but a number of the ideas were picked up in Congress's Omnibus Foreign Trade and Competitiveness Act of 1988.[11] A few "Atari Democrats," including Senators Gary Hart[12] and Al Gore,[13] began to focus on the importance to growth of "sunrise" industries. The House Democratic caucus adopted this "future" perspective, which led to the 1988 act and other legislation.[14] This included efforts to bring basic research closer to the market, and Sematech, which, as noted earlier, brought significant advances to semiconductor equipment production.[15]

In its catch-up to Japan's advances in production, the United States created a series of new federal programs in the 1980s to supplement its long-standing basic research emphasis:[16]

• The *Bayh-Dole Act* was passed in 1980 and was the first of the new generation of competitiveness legislation. Historically, the federal government had held the rights to the results of federally funded research. Since the federal government did not undertake technology implementation, this intellectual property sat on the shelf. The act shifted ownership of federally funded research results to the universities where the research had been performed, giving universities a stake in its commercialization, and spurring an entrepreneurship role for university researchers.

• The *Manufacturing Extension Partnership* (MEP) was authorized in 1988, based on the success of the long-standing U.S. agriculture extension program. It aimed to bring the latest manufacturing technologies and processes to small manufacturers around the nation—since small firms were increasingly dominating U.S. manufacturing—advising them on the latest manufacturing advances to foster productivity gains. It formed extension centers in every state, the costs of which were shared by the states, and the centers were backed up by a small Commerce Department headquarters staff charged with program evaluations and transmission of best practices to the centers.

• The *Small Business Innovation Research* (SBIR) program offered competitive R&D grant funding to small and start-up companies, administered by the 11 largest federal R&D agencies as part of their research programs. These grants aim to ensure that small, high-tech, innovative businesses are a part of the federal government's research and development efforts.

• The *Advanced Technology Program* (ATP) was formed in 1988 in the Department of Commerce's National Institute of Standards and Technology (NIST) program to fund a broad base of high-risk, high-reward R&D undertaken by industry. Although it had success nurturing later-stage development projects for new technologies, Congress gradually defunded the program in the first decade of the new century, viewing it as overly interventionist federal "industrial policy."[17]

• *Sematech* was formed by a consortium of semiconductor fabricators and equipment makers that by the late 1980s was facing its imminent demise because of strong competitors in Japan. As discussed in chapter 2, because semiconductor technology was key to many defense systems, the effort had national security implications, so industry funding was matched by the Defense Advanced Research Projects Agency (DARPA). The consortium focused on major efficiency and quality improvements in semiconductor manufacturing; after five years, production leadership was restored, and DARPA funding ended in 1996. Sematech continued as a key technology planning organization to keep the industry on a Moore's Law roadmap (although that effort is now coming to an end). The Sematech model is the closest to the organizational approaches that the Obama administration came to consider for manufacturing in the 2010–2012 period.

U.S. firms and government gradually pursued a policy of trying to match Japan in manufacturing quality. The federal government launched the various programs listed, but these were modestly funded and still of quite limited scale. Even Sematech addressed only one industrial sector. Nearly all of these government programs addressed the development stage of innovation, not production itself. And the overall attempt in the 1980s was only catching up to Japan; this alone was not enough for production leadership. Lurking underneath the quality manufacturing innovation wave that Japan launched in the 1970s and 1980s was the next innovation wave. The political need to respond with new manufacturing policies in the United States was swept away[18] by the success of the innovation-induced information technology innovation wave.[19] The IT wave, described in chapter 2, transformed the decade of the 1990s into one of the strongest growth spurts in recent U.S. history, with strong GDP and productivity gains. The lessons of the manufacturing challenge of the 1980s went largely unlearned.

Japan's government support for R&D was more focused on industry than on university research; the former typically produces incremental technology advances. In contrast, U.S. government support for basic research, through universities and other research institutions, and less industry focused, created more of an opportunity for radical technology advances. Although not a conscious U.S. competitive policy approach, this different pattern of R&D support enabled the United States to pursue a course toward disruptive innovations based on breakthrough research, which enabled the emergence of new technologies that could displace existing ones and allow greater entry of new business models. Whereas existing firms tend to pursue incremental advances, moving upmarket and abandoning less profitable lower-end markets, disruptive innovations bring in new firms that start up new markets, often in the lower ends and outside existing competitor and customer bases. These new markets evolve as once-dominant technology areas are disrupted by new ones. As discussed in the previous chapter on the IT revolution, this was the technology revolution the United States launched at scale in the 1990s, after decades of nurturing it through its defense innovation system. Japan largely missed this innovation wave, suffering from the bursting of an asset bubble starting in 1990 and an ineffectual government response. This led to economic stagnation, a period called the Lost Decade. In other words, the approach to the intense competition in production from Japan was to catch up on quality and, in parallel, launch a major new innovation wave built around computing and the Internet.

To summarize, when the United States missed the quality manufacturing wave Japan launched in the 1970s and 1980s, it saw a period of industrial decline, income stagnation, low GDP and productivity growth, and deep industrial resentment. The tables turned after the IT revolution. In 1990, when the IT wave began to scale, U.S. GDP was $5.9 trillion and Japan's $3.1 trillion; by 2005, after the U.S.-led IT innovation wave had moderated, U.S. GDP was $13.1 trillion and Japan's $4.7 trillion.[20] If you organize your economy around leading innovation waves at the frontier of technology advances and you miss an innovation wave, the consequences can be quite dramatic.

This wave in the United States evolved in significant part from its own "industrial policy," its defense innovation system, which, as discussed earlier, operated at every innovation stage from research through initial market creation.[21] After missing the 1990s IT wave, MITI itself had to evolve. As Glenn Fong has written, Japan, competing against the United States in the postwar era, went through stages of "pursuer after the pioneer," then "follower at the frontier," and then "world class competitor."[22] Although MITI's pragmatic technology initiatives initially had been selected directly by high-level government leaders, when Japan's industries arrived at the technology frontier, complex new technology advances could only be grasped by those doing "hands-on" work with them. So industry research leaders became the de facto developers of technology strategies. Whereas an early system of technology targeting led to a focus on just a few technologies, when it arrived at the frontier, Japan's institutions had to open the door wider, with less targeting and more basic research to enlarge the menu of technology options. Whereas MITI had once selected firm leaders for technology areas top-down, once at the frontier, this changed to more bottom-up collaboration between growing numbers of firm participants to ensure a more broadly based pursuit of breakthroughs. The complexity of frontier technologies required a more complex, more decentralized innovation system model. So after the advent of the U.S.-led IT innovation wave, Japan had to shift its previously highly centralized industrial policy model to take better advantage of its role at the innovation frontier.

The Emergence of China in Manufacturing

The United States got through the competitive manufacturing challenge from Japan and Germany of the 1980s largely because it changed the subject in the 1990s: it led the IT revolution. As the intensity of that innovation wave faded in the decade that followed, the United States awoke to see its manufacturing net output as a share of world output passed by China in 2011.[23] Part of this resulted from a shift in its geopolitical view of production.[24]

China and American Geopolitics of Production

Since Alexander Hamilton put the financial building blocks in place to transform the United States into the world's largest commercial economy, manufacturing has been central to U.S. geopolitical strategy. Barry Lynn argues that the United States has gone through three evolutionary phases. From the time of Hamilton until 1945, it pursued national self-dependence in manufacturing as key to its security.[25] Hamilton saw that in a world of dominant and colonizing European powers, the United States would retain its independence on the world stage only if it magnified its commercial power, with manufacturing as a critical component. The United States pursued Hamilton's basic strategy through World War II. From 1945 until the end of the Cold War in 1991, faced with a struggle with a Marxist economic model, the United States built a series of postwar agreements that entwined the United States, Europe, and Japan in a system of mutual economic dependence around Americentric consumer markets and manufacturing. The geopolitical concept in this period was that U.S. national security would be enhanced through an economic embrace of our Cold War allies—it was a system of mutual economic interdependence to build the economic strength to fend off Marxist geopolitical competitors.

The third period began in 1993 under President Clinton and involved the eventual entry of China into the WTO. The geopolitical concept was to bind the world, not just allies, into an interdependent economic system tied together by open trading, financial integration, and joint manufacturing. The aim was to integrate China into the world economy to assure peace in a way comparable to Jean Monnet's design for a postwar common market to assure future European peace. Clinton's perspective, in effect, embraced a completely laissez-faire perspective toward manufacturing. Integrated manufacturing was to assure an integrated world economy, and Hamilton's earlier concept of manufacturing assuring national security was set aside.

China meanwhile pursued a different approach, perceiving that innovation-based growth would be key to its ascendency as a superpower, and using neomercantilist policies[26] to get there. It has sought to build a rim of Asian economies increasingly dependent on China's economy for their exports and production facilities, and running a huge trade surplus in manufactured goods with the United States to generate the capital to finance internal growth and offset trade deficits with its dependent economies of the Asian rim. Economist Carl Dahlman has portrayed this strategy as a deliberate attempt to hollow out the economies of developed-nation competitors to finance its own geopolitical rise.[27]

Trade Effects

In 2004, Paul Samuelson asked how the United States could be an economic loser with a low-cost, low-wage competitor like China, despite David Ricardo's long-standing economic theory of "comparative advantage" in trade.[28] Samuelson noted that if China begins to make productivity-enhancing gains in its production, coupled with a low-wage advantage, it can capture some of the comparative advantage that previously belonged to the United States through its productivity dominance. Then, in Ricardian analysis, there is never any unemployment that lasts forever from trade, "so it is not that U.S. jobs are ever lost in the long run; it is that the new labor-market clearing real wages has been lowered by this vision of dynamic fair trade." In other words, U.S. wages will fall to a point where China's production price advantage is offset. The United States still benefits from lower-priced goods, but there are now "new net harmful U.S. terms of trade." He cited many historical examples of this phenomenon, from the shift of the U.S. textile sector from the northeast to the southeast in the early twentieth century, to the way midwestern agriculture surpassed eastern agriculture in the second half of the nineteenth century. Samuelson's analysis suggests, too, that nations like the United States that build their comparative advantage on innovation capacity as opposed to a resource advantage face a problem: an innovation advantage is not necessarily eternal—it can be captured by others as they build their own innovation systems.

Economists David Autor, David Dorn, and Gordon Hanson have validated Samuelson's concerns.[29] Studying labor markets in regions of the United States where Chinese-produced goods have captured markets, they found widespread patterns of rising unemployment and reduced wages, not only in the affected manufacturing sectors but also in a wide range of dependent and related job sectors in both services and production. They found that the gains from increased trade were offset by what they term "deadweight losses" to the economy, particularly through the rise in transfer payments for unemployment, health and disability insurance, and food stamps required to cope with declines in employment and real wages, which are compensatory, not immediately economically productive investments.

In a subsequent 2016 paper expanding on their earlier findings, these economists found that the trade relationship between the United States and China, formed in the 1990s and formally recognized with China's accession to the World Trade Organization (WTO) in 2001, affected a large number of labor-intensive industries in the United States, where significant numbers of those jobs shifted to China.[30] Their study found that this shift came with a heavy cost to U.S. workers, with many blue-collar jobs in particular disappearing, and the communities where they worked also being punished economically on a continuing basis. These findings about enduring adverse effects from trade ran counter to traditional economic assumptions about the size and scope of the offsetting net gains from trade. From 1999 through 2011, the study found that import growth from China cost the United States about 2.4 million jobs. About 985,000 of those were in manufacturing—a large portion of the 5.8 million manufacturing jobs that the United States lost in total in that time. Although trade can also add to employment, the data indicates that these job gains did not counter the employment losses in sectors that compete with imports. The net impact on workers in U.S. regions heavily affected by competition from China was particularly serious. The study examined the direct impact of Chinese industry on incomes in some seven hundred urban areas ("commuting zones") reviewed, comparing workers in heavily impacted areas (at the seventy-fifth percentile of exposure to Chinese competition) with workers in less affected areas (at the twenty-fifth percentile). They found a reduction in annual income of $549 per adult between the two, while per capita income from offsetting federal assistance only rose by $58. They found that the growth of trade with China has tended to make lower-skilled workers worse off on a sustained, ongoing basis. There was no relatively "frictionless" economic adjustment to other industries; little offsetting growth was found in industries not affected by this "China shock." Instead, workers do not make up lost wages, and their communities enter a slow decline.

A 2015 paper by Andrew Foote, Michel Grosz, and Ann Huff Stevens[31] found similar long-lasting effects on workers and their communities. Studying those affected by mass layoffs, they found few would or could leave and abandon family, friends, and communities, so they were saddled with long-term unemployment and lower-end jobs. We can speculate that job migration away from affected jobs may have been exacerbated by the Great Recession housing crisis but also by a decline in availability of comparable jobs. Danny Yagan, in a 2016 paper on regional effects, reported that in the wake of the Great Recession (including the manufacturing decline central to it), employment remained significantly depressed in heavily affected regions, with adjustment in those regions occurring at a glacial pace. The paper found a "'lost decade' of depressed employment for half the country," with these effects likely to extend into the 2020s.[32] While these two papers review broader economic issues than Autor and his colleagues did, they underscore the impact of the latter's findings.

As economics Nobel Laureate A. Michael Spence found, as previously noted, "Globalization hurts some subgroups within some countries, including the advanced economies. . . . The result is growing disparities in income and employment across the U.S. economy, with highly educated workers enjoying more opportunities and workers with less education facing declining employment prospects and stagnant incomes."[33] Just as manufacturing employment was a key to enabling less-educated workers to enter the middle class after World War II, the loss of manufacturing jobs has correspondingly been a key element in the decline in real income for a significant part of the American middle class in the past few decades.

Growth of China's Production Capabilities

The core issue is China's movement from 5.7% of global manufacturing output in 2000 to 19.8% in 2011, which, as noted, enabled China to pass the United States in output that year. The Manufacturers Alliance for Productivity and Innovation (MAPI) notes that China is now the largest manufacturing economy in the world, and by 2012 its share had grown to 22.4% of global manufacturing activity, with the United States in second place with a 17.4% share.[34] China has more than four times the population of the United States; although its manufacturing intensity of $1,856 value added per capita in 2012 is high for a developing economy, it is well behind advanced countries such as the United States (at $6,280). According to MAPI, based on economic data from the United Nations, manufacturing value added in China totaled $2.56 trillion in 2012 compared with $1.99 trillion for the United States.[35] The U.S. share of world manufacturing value added declined from 18.1% in 2010 to 17.4% in 2012—a decline that was primarily against China's growing share. Chinese global exports of $935 billion in manufactured goods in the first half of 2016 were 68% larger than the $555 billion of U.S. exports; this is striking because, in 2000, U.S. manufactured exports were three times larger than Chinese exports.[36]

What happened to lead to this stunning and rapid shift? MAPI found that China attained its number one output ranking through a combination of price increases, exchange rate advantages, and, particularly, an extremely fast growth rate in the physical volume of manufacturing value added. What is behind this latter characteristic?

Most have assumed China's rise is the result of low production costs from cheap labor and cheap parts. There is also an assumption in the United States that manufacturing must naturally migrate to low-cost producers and that the knowledge required for production processes is relatively trivial and readily replicable—neither is true. Further, there are assumptions that production knowledge flowed solely via multinationals from the outside into China, and that the IT revolution enables severing of manufacturing from R&D, product definition, design, branding, and marketing, which China has taken advantage of. Part of the story is China's neomercantilist policies to mandate technology shifts and to dominate markets with below-cost goods. Intellectual property theft has also played a role, and recent fiscal and market policies show how the West has underestimated China's nationalistic government economic controls. Yet, as Jonas Nahm and Edward Steinfeld argue, none of these adequately explains China's rise.[37] Instead, they find that China has undertaken a new link between process innovation and manufacturing.

They find that China's form of innovative manufacturing specializes in rapid scale-up and cost reduction. It has joined together previously unparalleled skills in simultaneous management of tempo, production volume, and cost, which enables production to scale up quickly and with major reductions in unit cost. This capability has allowed China to expand even in industries that are highly automated or not on governmental priority and support lists, despite limited labor cost advantage or government subsidies, respectively. So low labor costs and government subsidies and support are not sufficient to explain China's success in manufacturing.

China has also improved on production processes that developed nations previously considered fully mature and impervious to further cost reductions or technological improvements. The key to this ability to innovate new production processes has been the ability of Chinese firms to accumulate firm-specific expertise in manufacturing through extensive, multidirectional interfirm learning, taking advantage of international know-how from multinationals and building on it. For example, in wind turbine production, although also aided by government subsidies, Chinese firms rapidly absorbed lessons from international competitors and then modified them to create designs to fit their own markets, created production systems fully capable of established production capabilities, nurtured cutting-edge technologies such as advanced aerospace designs for blades, drew on materials science and systems engineering in production that could be both labor and capital intensive, and rapidly scaled up production.[38]

Nahm and Steinfeld conclude that the elements of China's emerging production model include: (1) backward design—the ability to take existing products and create cheaper models that can better fit low-cost Chinese markets; (2) partnerships that use foreign designs joined with Chinese production, which have enabled multidirectional learning about production; and (3) technology absorption and collaborative development across networks of regional production firms, allowing rapid scale-up.[39] Although subsidies, low wages, and neomercantile policies are factors, innovative capabilities cannot be discounted.

Manufacturing Competitiveness Then and Now

As noted, the United States faced an intense competitive challenge in the 1970s and 1980s as a result of Japan's growing production capability. That was a simpler and more straightforward competition between comparable economies, as opposed to the much more complex competition it faces with emerging nations like China and India. Table 3.1 illustrates some of the differences in competitive patterns the United States faces by comparing U.S. competition with Japan versus its competition with China.

To summarize, both Japan and China amount to advanced technology economies with industrial policy advantages and have used debt financing and subsidized currencies to compete. Trade with China, however, is complicated because of China's (1) lack of intellectual property protection, (2) limited rule of law, (3) status as a competitor regarding national security, and (4) low-wage, entrepreneurial economy, which has purchased U.S. assets. Competing with China, then, is much more complicated than the competitive pressures the United States faced in the 1970s and 1980s with Japan. At the same time, largely because of inattention or lack of understanding of its own historically successful model, the United States has departed from a geopolitical strategy that incorporates the concept of strategic economic advantage built around production and innovation leadership. The geopolitical issues behind innovation capacity and advanced manufacturing are profound and remain largely unexamined. Despite the current era of benign neglect, for a century these two interrelated factors largely determined the national security advantage of the United States. They remain a significant element in understanding the U.S. manufacturing challenge.

Table 3.1.
Competitiveness Then and Now

JAPAN vs. United States 1970–1990	*CHINA* vs. United States today
Became a high-cost, high-wage, advanced technology economy—comparable to the United States	Low-cost, low-wage, increasingly advanced technology economy
United States had entrepreneurial advantage; Japan had industrial policy advantage	Entrepreneurial *and* pursuing industrial policy
Rule of law	Limited rule of law
Intellectual property protections	Extensive intellectual property theft
Trade: limited imports to create export trade surplus; used protected domestic markets to cross-subsidize exports	Trade: applies a series of neomercantilist policies
Subsidizes currency and buys U.S. debt to limit U.S. opposition to trade and currency protection	Following Japan's model: has subsidized currency and is largest holder of U.S. debt; uses foreign currency reserves for sovereign wealth funds to acquire U.S. assets
National security ally for seventy years	National security potential peer competitor

Eroding Advanced Technology Sectors

Although many economists in the past have preached that the United States should cede lower-end manufacturing sectors and offset these losses with success in high-end, high-value goods emerging from its leading innovation system,[40] the picture in this advanced technology sector is so unsettling that this standard thesis now looks misleading. Gary Pisano and Willy Shih[41] have examined the advanced IT sector and found, for example, that the most recent edition of Amazon's Kindle could not be made in the United States. The flex circuit connector, controller, lithium polymer battery, wireless card, and injection-molded case are all produced in China, and the electrophoretic display is made in Taiwan. Every brand of U.S. notebook computer, except Apple, and every mobile/handheld device are now designed in Asia. Reviewing advanced technology sectors innovated in the United States and in danger of shifting abroad, Pisano and Shih conclude that major erosion has already occurred in advanced materials, computing, communications, renewable energy technologies and storage, semiconductors, and displays, and that the next generation of technologies in each area is facing an imminent shift. This is the reason why the United States has run a trade deficit in advanced technology goods every year since 2002, and that deficit is reaching $100 billion annually.[42] Given the experience of the past decade, continuing to contend that the United States will make up for its manufacturing decline by assuming it will always capture high-end manufacturing can only be considered a game of "let's pretend." Our problems are deeper than we have acknowledged, and the emerging contender in this space is China.

Clayton Christensen has argued that, faced with disruptive innovation, established production firms typically cede low-margin production and work to retain leadership through incremental ("sustaining") advances in high-margin production. But the established firms end up ceding these as well because the disruptive advances that allowed capture of low end production, through lower costs and expanded customer bases, mature over time and improve to enable capture of the high end.[43] The argument may prove relevant to U.S. manufacturing strategy—the United States may be facing disruptive innovations it has not recognized as such. China, as noted, appears to be not simply pursuing its low-cost production advantage but also innovating in rapid production scale-up through process advances that are integrated across regional firms. It is also accelerating production tempo and volume tied to cost savings.[44] In other words, it is pursuing a very innovative production strategy, using "manufacturing-led" innovation for competitive advantage. While China is following this manufacturing-led model step-by-step up the innovation value ladder, at the same time the United States has allowed its historical production leadership to slip, endangering its innovative capacity in important areas of technology.

American Manufacturing in Decline

The Decade of the 2000s

The U.S. manufacturing sector had a devastating decade between 2000 and 2010 and has only partially recovered since then. The decline in this sector is illustrated by four measures: employment, investment, output, and productivity.[45]

Employment. Over the past fifty years, manufacturing's share of GDP has shrunk from 27% to 12%. For most of this period (1965–2000), the number of people employed in manufacturing generally remained constant at around 17 million, but in the decade from 2000 to 2010, it fell precipitously, by almost one-third, to under 12 million.[46] Manufacturing employment in 2000 was 17.3 million, but by 2010 it was down to 11.5 million, a loss of 5.8 million jobs, and by the beginning of 2015 had only recovered to 12.3 million, still 5 million jobs below the 2000 level.[47] All manufacturing sectors saw job losses between 2000 and 2010, but lower-value sectors readily subject to globalization, such as textiles and furniture, were most adversely affected, losing almost 70% and 50% of their jobs, respectively.[48]

Investment. Fixed capital investment (plant, equipment, and IT) in manufacturing grew in the first decade of this century at its lowest rate as a percentage of GDP (below 1.5% annually) since such data began to be compiled at the end of World War II.[49] If this number is adjusted for cost changes, fixed capital investment in manufacturing actually declined during the period (down 1.8%)—the first decade in which this has occurred since data collection began in the 1950s. In contrast, manufacturing investment grew at an average rate of 5.5% annually in the 1990s. Investment in the following decade declined in 15 of the 19 industrial sectors measured by the Bureau of Economic Analysis.[50] As a share of GDP, through 2012, overall business investment had declined by 3% since 1980.[51] Some 64,000 manufacturing plants closed between 2000 and 2013, with only very slight recovery since then.[52]

Output. Based on published government statistics, analysts had been assuming that U.S. manufacturing net output as a share of world output had been stable, not passed by China until 2011,[53] but the assumption appears inaccurate given stagnating U.S. output in the period. Analysis based on Bureau of Labor Statistics data shows U.S. manufacturing output growth of only 0.5% per year between 2000 and 2007 (before the Great Recession hit), and zero output growth per year between 2007 and 2014 despite the gradual overall economic recovery after 2008.[54] In the Great Recession itself, manufacturing output fell dramatically, by 10.3% between 2007 and 2009, which was followed by the slowest recovery in total GDP in sixty years. Manufacturing was clearly a leading victim of the Great Recession, and its weakness was a leading culprit in the slow recovery. The sharp drop in the rate of growth of manufacturing output between 2000 and 2007 was in significant part responsible for the massive decline in manufacturing employment; if output had grown at the same rate of 3.7% per year that it did in the 1990s, employment would have been stable during the period from 2000 to 2014.[55]

An ITIF report[56] and other economic evaluations[57] suggest that, when examining production by sector, the output data for the first decade of the twenty-first century was significantly overstated. The official government data indicates that net output in 13 of 19 manufacturing sectors declined during the period, in many sectors significantly, and three more grew at below the rate of overall GDP growth; it shows that these declines were offset by two sectors, computing and energy.[58] ITIF and other economists make three arguments why output has been overstated. First, the number of foreign components in U.S. manufactured products has risen sharply, and these have not been adequately accounted for, overstating U.S. output. Second, although employment in the computer production sector declined by 43%, a significant amount of computer production moved offshore, and nominal U.S. industry shipments in this sector barely grew, government data included an inflationary output factor for increased computer quality and performance that caused the computing sector's output to be significantly overstated during the period. Third, output in the energy sector similarly was significantly overstated. Adjusting for these factors, ITIF found that net U.S. manufacturing value, when reviewed by sector, actually fell by 11% in the first decade of this century.

Productivity. As MIT political economist Suzanne Berger has pointed out, economists have been mixing up manufacturing with agriculture.[59] The story of agriculture has been of major productivity growth; it has had ever-increasing production using an ever-smaller labor force. Many economists thought the recent decline in manufacturing employment was the same story, but it was not. Since output is a factor in calculating productivity, previous assumptions about strong productivity growth in manufacturing must be scaled back as well, although, historically, manufacturing productivity has significantly exceeded service sector productivity.

Recent analysis based on Bureau of Labor Statistics data shows that while the rate of productivity growth in manufacturing averaged 4.1% per year between 1989 and 2000, while the sector was absorbing the gains of the IT revolution, it fell to only 1.7% per year between 2007 and 2014.[60] Because of the relationship between productivity and output, the decline and stagnation in output cited was a major cause of the decline in the productivity rate in that period. Adjusted against 19 other leading manufacturing nations, the United States was tenth in productivity growth and seventeenth in net output growth.[61] So productivity increases are not the significant cause of the decline in manufacturing employment that many thought.[62] And a Brookings study contends that the historical pattern of productivity gains leading over time to overall job growth remains in effect.[63] This means we have to look at an overall decline in the sector itself for reasons why manufacturing lost nearly one-third of its workforce in a decade.

To summarize, U.S. manufacturing employment is down, manufacturing capital investment is down, manufacturing output is down, and manufacturing productivity is lower than previously assumed. Overall, the argument that the U.S. manufacturing sector has been hollowing out appears strong. The recovery since the Great Recession has not been strong enough to reverse this conclusion. This manufacturing recovery has been the slowest in history. Although there has been some recovery in manufacturing jobs and output, they remain below prerecession levels.[64] The underlying structural problems in the sector still need addressing.

Manufacturing and Trade

Success in a highly competitive world rewards nations and regions that produce complex, high-value-added goods and sell them in international trade. Although world trade in services is growing, world trade in goods is still four times larger.[65] Complex, high-value goods (including capital goods, industrial supplies, energy technologies, communications and computing, transport, and medicines) make up over 80% of U.S. exports and a significant majority of its imports. The currency of world trade is in such high-value goods, and will remain so indefinitely. Yet, in 2015, the United States ran a trade deficit (balance of payments in imports over exports) of $832 billion in manufactured goods,[66] a total that included a $92 billion deficit in advanced technology products.[67]

Will services offset our manufacturing decline? After all, since services are 80% of our economy, why can't we just continue this trend? The problem is that the modest and gradual growth in our services trade surplus ($227 billion in 2015)[68] is dwarfed by the size and continuing growth of our deficit in goods; the former will not offset the latter anytime in the foreseeable future.

Given the net transfer of wealth out of the country represented by the trade imbalance, it is hard to avoid the conclusion that the United States has been shifting to a consumption-led versus a production-led economy. We now arguably have an imbalance between consumption and production, with significant long-term economic consequences regarding our ability to generate higher growth. U.S. policymakers, under the influence of standard macroeconomic theory, were largely content to allow U.S. manufacturing capacity to erode and shift offshore because they were confident that the knowledge and service economies would readily replace jobs and salaries from lost manufacturing. One could reasonably speculate that the Donald Trump candidacy, and the deep economic discontent it exposed in U.S. society, is one consequence of this approach to national innovation policy.

Macroeconomic Factors

As suggested, the argument that advanced economies essentially become so productive that the number of manufacturing jobs goes down while output goes up—the agriculture story—is not an adequate explanation of

the decline in U.S. manufacturing employment. Manufacturing employment peaked in 1979, when it reached 22% of nonfarm employment, with
over 19 million jobs.[69] It now employs 12.3 million. Macro policies are
part of that story. There have been extended periods in recent decades (in
1982–1987, 1998–2004, and 2014–2017) where the dollar had a high value
against leading foreign currencies,[70] with Treasury secretaries and Federal
Reserve chairs generally supportive of a strong dollar.[71] Correspondingly,
U.S. manufactured goods became less competitive in foreign markets. In
parallel, from 1981 on, U.S. personal consumption as a share of GDP began
a continuous rise, reaching 69% in 2011, higher than in other developed
economies.[72] The stronger dollar helped push the country toward what
many consider overconsumption compared with saving and investment;
there was a growing production/consumption imbalance. The combination
of an open trading regime, generally strong dollar, high consumption rates,
open financial markets, and, lately, the role of oil and gas assets in inflating
the U.S. currency, created advantages for competing nations' exports.

This created a particular advantage for nations that chose to practice
financial repression—such as Japan's and then China's efforts to undervalue
their currencies and increase savings and investment. Germany, too, has benefited, from being part of the Eurozone. The euro is likely undervalued in
relation to the value of a stand-alone German currency (although Germans
argue that prior to the euro, it purposely kept its Deutschmark high to force
its production firms to innovate). U.S. policy, as noted, further opened an
opportunity for export-led growth by its international competitors because
of continued U.S. support for free trade policies despite the neomercantilist
policies used by trading partners such as China. The data for manufacturing
job loss after 2000, when China joined the WTO, tends to support this case.

So, in assessing the U.S. manufacturing decline, part of the story is trade
policy. Accordingly, this argument suggests that there does not appear
to be an inherent and inevitable manufacturing employment or sectoral
decline in advanced economies. Germany, with its continuing very strong
manufacturing sector and major trade surpluses in goods,[73] appears as the
obvious counterexample. In fact, Germany now has a larger trade surplus
than China's, led by its high-value manufactured goods. The situation
between China and the United States substantiates the point: the United
States runs a deficit-ridden but conservative fiscal policy while China has
been able to force savings rates and investment to record levels and subsidize and grow exports. The policies that led to a strengthening of the dollar,
which helped finance fiscal deficits, while maintaining an open trading
regime, are clearly factors. But these are macro factors; they do not appear

to be a complete explanation for the U.S. manufacturing decline—we must also look at what was happening at ground level, at the innovation level.

The "Innovate Here/Produce There" Assumption

Since World War II, the U.S. economy has been organized around leading the world in technology advancement. It developed a comparative advantage over other nations in innovation, and as a result, it led all but one of the significant innovation waves of the twentieth century.[74] The United States led innovation waves in aviation, electronics, space, computing, the Internet,[75] and biotech, although it played catch-up on quality manufacturing. Its operating assumption was that it would innovate and then translate those innovations into products. By innovating here and producing here, it would realize the full spectrum of economic gains from innovation at all stages, from research and development, to demonstration and test beds, to initial market creation, to production at scale, and to the follow-on life cycle of the product. This "full spectrum" worked—the United States became the richest economy the world had ever seen. For the past two-thirds of a century, it has been playing out economic growth theory—that the predominant factor in economic growth is technological and related innovation—and demonstrating that it works.

But, in recent years, with the advent of a global economy, the "innovate here/produce here" model has no longer held. In some industrial sectors, firms can now sever R&D and design from production. Codable IT-based specifications for goods tied to software-controlled production equipment have enabled this "distributed" manufacturing.[76] Whereas manufacturing once had to be integrated and quite vertical, firms using the distributed model can *innovate here/produce there*. It appears that this distributed model works well for many IT products, as well as for commodity products. Apple is the standard-bearer for this model, continuing to lead in dramatic IT innovations but distributing virtually all of its production to Asia. As of 2012, imported content was about 21% of the value of output for the typical U.S. firm.[77] Overall, only 53% of U.S. domestic demand for manufactured goods is met by goods made in the United States. Most computer and electronics products are not "Made in the USA": 72% of domestic demand for these products is met by imports, including Apple iPhones.[78]

However, there appear to be many sectors where the distributed model does not work, which still require a close connection between research, design, and production. Supply chains for domestic firms remain largely domestic.[79] Capital goods, aerospace products, energy equipment, and complex pharmaceuticals appear to be examples of this phenomenon. In these sectors, production and R&D/design are the yin and yang of innovation. Here, our production infrastructure provides constant feedback to our R&D/design infrastructure. Product innovation—incremental advance—is most efficient when tied to a close understanding of and linkage to manufacturing processes. However, if R&D/design and production must be tightly linked, the innovation stages—R&D and design—may have to follow production offshore. *"Produce there/innovate there"* may be even more disruptive than "innovate here/produce there." The high percentage of U.S. demand for manufactured goods that is being met by foreign production suggests this evolution. These twin developments bring the economic foundations of U.S. innovation-based economic success into question. It means that innovation investments will not lead to "full spectrum" economic gains. Taxpayers might ponder, what good is a world-leading innovation system if much of the gain flows elsewhere?

The Innovation Perspective

If the picture on the production side is problematic, what of the innovation side of the equation? The United States has been maintaining the same national innovation intensity (R&D relative to GDP) it developed in the 1960s, while other competitive economies have steadily increased theirs.[80] A group of Asian nations have now collectively passed the United States in total R&D investment as well.[81] National Institute of Standards and Technology (NIST) former senior economist Gregory Tassey suggests that "input/output" theory in economics applies: if you freeze a major input, which the U.S. has increasingly been doing through stagnated R&D intensity, then your growth rate is limited.[82]

The intensity of federal R&D investment to GDP has been in decline for decades, falling from 1.8% of GDP in 1965 to 0.7% of GDP in 2013; it has been offset by a numbers flip—a rise in industry R&D from 0.8% to nearly 1.8% of GDP in that same period.[83] However, industry R&D only increased by a total of 9% over the six years from 2008–2013, during the recovery from the recession.[84] One reason for this stabilization is that U.S. manufacturing firms have dramatically shifted their R&D investment strategies during the last decade and a half toward an increasingly global perspective. Their offshore R&D investment has increased at three times the rate of domestic R&D spending. Tassey further argues that, in addition, U.S. manufacturing firms have shifted the composition of their R&D portfolios toward shorter-term development objectives[85] in an increasingly competitive international marketplace. He argues that the "Valley of Death" barriers between R&D and later-stage development are actually widening in the

United States as firms pull back from investment in radical or breakthrough innovation and focus more on shorter-term incremental advances.

Nonetheless, the United States retains the world's strongest innovation system, in the face of growing competition. Any advanced manufacturing strategy must seek leverage from this comparative advantage. However, it should be recognized that U.S. R&D in the past has had only a very limited focus on the advanced technologies and processes needed for production leadership; this is in sharp contrast to the approach to manufacturing R&D taken by Germany, Japan, Korea, and China, which have what we have termed "manufacturing-led" innovation.[86] Although the major U.S.-based multinational manufacturing firms fund most of the nation's technology development stage and thus have the capacity to keep up on the innovation front, the majority of the U.S. manufacturing sector belongs to the 250,000 small and midsize firms lacking this capacity. The base of small and midsize enterprises (SMEs) that manufacture represents 86% of our manufacturing establishments and employs more than half of our manufacturing workforce, and SMEs overall produce some 46% of private sector non-farm output, and contribute a third of goods exported (valued at $482 billion),[87] but these firms are largely outside our innovation system. Extending the innovation system to reach this sector would help fill a serious gap in manufacturing capability. It is therefore a key element in an advanced manufacturing innovation strategy.

Significance of Manufacturing in the American Economy

Manufacturing remains a major sector of the U.S. economy. Official statistics tell us it is approximately 12.1% of U.S. GDP,[88] contributes $2.09 trillion to our $17.3 trillion economy,[89] and employs 12.3 million[90] people out of a total employed workforce of some 150 million. Manufacturing workers are paid substantially more than service sector workers: 20% more.[91] Growth economists tell us that 60% or more of historical U.S. economic growth has come from technological and related innovation.[92] Although the United States does not usually see this perspective, manufacturing is the predominant stage for implementing innovations, so is a critical element of the innovation system. Industrial firms employ 64% of our scientists and engineers, and this sector performs 70% of industrial R&D.[93] Thus our manufacturing strength and the strength of our innovation system are directly linked.

Another way to understand the significance of production firms is to place them within an overall industry context. A Brookings study has shown the importance of advanced industries in the United States, those that conduct large amounts of R&D and employ a disproportionate share of science, technology, engineering, and mathematics (STEM) workers.[94] These firms, which fall into 50 identified sectors, conduct 89% of the nation's private sector R&D and generate 80% of the nation's patents, so they represent the main source of the kinds of technical advances that lead to productivity improvements.[95] They also create 60% of the nation's exports and pay a major wage premium over other sectors. Within the 50 sectors, 70% of the firms are manufacturing firms.[96]

Despite the decline in the manufacturing employment base, manufacturing remains a major employment source for the economy (official statistics say over 8%), measured largely by workers at the production stage. But the official data is collected at the factory level. Should we limit the view of manufacturing to the production moment? Why is manufacturing just measured at the factory? This arguably provides only a partial perspective on the role of this sector.

The manufacturing sector can instead be better viewed as an hourglass (figure 3.1). At the center, the narrow point of the hourglass, is the production moment. But manufacturing employment cannot be looked at as simply the production moment. Pouring into the production moment is a much larger employment base, which includes those working in resources, those employed by a wide range of suppliers and component makers, and the innovation work force, the very large percentage of scientists and engineers employed by industrial firms. Flowing out of the production moment is another host of employees: those working in the distribution system, retail and sales, and on the life cycle of the product. The employment base at the top and bottom of the hourglass is far bigger than that of the production moment itself.

Arranged throughout the hourglass are lengthy and complex value chains of firms involved in the production of the goods—from resources to

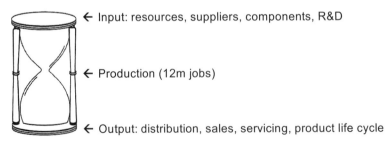

Figure 3.1
Notional Figure of Manufacturing Employment as an Hourglass.

suppliers of components to innovation, through production, to distribution, retail, and life cycle—a great array of skills and firms, and many we would count as services. But they are tied to manufacturing. If we removed the production element, the value chains of connected companies are snapped and face significant disruption. While the lower base of the hourglass, the output end, may be partially restored if a foreign good is substituted for a domestic good, the particular firms involved will be disrupted. The upper part of the hourglass, the input end, with its firms and employees, does not get restored.

When these complex value chains are disrupted, it is very difficult to put them back together. That is why, historically, once the United States loses an economic sector, it is so hard to resurrect it—it does not come back. It also loses the potential to innovate in the sector. We do not collect data on value chain effects on our industrial sector; the closest data we have is job multiplier data, which does not tell the full story. Understanding manufacturing in terms of the hourglass and the value chains within it may provide part of the explanation for the economy's current predicament over loss, and creation, of quality jobs, and declining median income.

However, a new MAPI Foundation study develops new data perspectives to tell more of this value chain story. The study makes a number of key new findings:[97]

• The manufactured goods value chain, plus manufacturing for other industries' supply chains, accounts for about one-third of GDP and employment in the United States.
• The domestic manufacturing value-added[98] multiplier is 3.6, which is much higher than conventional calculations. For every dollar of domestic manufacturing value added destined for manufactured goods for final demand, another $3.60 of value added is generated elsewhere in the economy.
• For each full-time equivalent job in manufacturing dedicated to producing value for final demand, there are 3.4 full-time equivalent jobs created in nonmanufacturing industries; this job multiplier is far higher than in any other sector.
• Most (54%) of the value added in manufactured goods destined for final demand is from the downstream sales chain; the upstream supply chain accounts for the remaining 46%.
• Domestic manufacturing accounts for only 22% of the value chain of manufactured goods for final demand. Nonmanufacturing value added is 53% (imports supply another 25%).

• Relative to other industries, manufacturing is efficient in delivering value added. It takes about 5.8 full-time equivalent manufacturing jobs to achieve $1 million in value added, compared with 7.7 jobs for both transportation and services and 16.9 jobs for retail trade.

The report's central finding is that the current estimates of manufacturing's share of the GDP are partial and seriously understated; when the full scope of the manufacturing footprint is examined, it amounts to around one-third of the U.S. economy, not one-tenth.[99]

There are of course issues in this analytical approach: if manufacturing is performed abroad, some of the downstream system (the lower part of the hourglass) is restored, as noted and as the MAPI study recognized; there are downstream jobs from manufactured imports. Consumers can and do shift some spending from manufactured goods to services as well (for example, they can buy less processed food and eat more at restaurants serving locally raised food). Long-standing economic theory suggests that economies tend toward full employment, and lost demand from complex goods in complex value chains can be redeployed over time—in the United States that has tended to be in services. However, if economists are now seeing a period of "secular stagnation"—permanent lower demand and employment—then if demand shifts this way, it would be economically problematic.[100] The studies by Autor, Foote, Yagan, and their colleagues about long-lasting adverse effects on workers and their regions tend to bear out the MAPI conclusions on the breadth of manufacturing's reach and the corresponding depth of this economic concern.

The United States did not take manufacturing seriously in recent decades because the series of well-established economic views examined here reassured us that declines in manufacturing were more than offset by gains elsewhere in the economy.[101] The nation was losing manufacturing jobs because of major productivity gains; the production economy would naturally be replaced by a service economy; low-wage, low-cost producers must inevitably displace higher-cost ones; do not worry about the loss of commodity production, because the country will retain a lead in producing high-value advanced technologies; the benefits of free trade always outweigh any short-term adverse effects; and innovation is distinct from production, so innovation capacity remains even if the production is distributed worldwide. Unfortunately, none of these arguments proved correct. Chapter 4 looks in depth at how economics has handled manufacturing, including the developments in mainstream economics that helped us down this path.

There is a lurking story of social disruption here. In the past, manufacturing was a major way for males with a high school education—particularly white males—to reach middle-income levels. Yet for white male high school graduates, earnings per person between 1996 and 2014 fell by 9%.[102] In contrast, for white male college graduates, earnings rose more than 22% over the same period. In 2014, income per cohort member for high school graduates was only $36,787, compared to $94,601 for college graduates.[103] Not only white males were affected. The African American diaspora from the South in the last century often focused on manufacturing jobs in the North; these jobs were an important route into the middle class for this community, too.[104] With the manufacturing sector in decline, this important way out of poverty in urban production centers was curtailed as well; the current hollowed-out shell of urban Detroit is largely this story. And for African Americans in the South who escaped from poverty through production jobs in sectors like textiles and furniture, these sectors have been particularly devastated. African Americans make up 10% and Hispanics 16% of the manufacturing workforce. These are all signals of a working-class decline and growing social inequality, not the assured progress of the American Dream.[105]

For example, the ratio of the average income of the top 20 percent of Americans to the average income of the bottom 20 percent has grown to eight to one; in Germany, it is four to one.[106]

Part of the disruption represented by the 2016 presidential election appears to be the result of a working class that increasingly understands it is being left behind. Recent studies confirm that trade disruption in historically manufacturing-dependent areas has led to anti-incumbent voting patterns and a growing ideological split.[107] The threat of social disruption has become another key reason to address manufacturing decline.

But to return to our manufacturing innovation theme, there is a macroeconomic story here but also an innovation system story, which will be the focus of this work. The failure of the U.S. innovation system to consider the production stage as an important element of that system is problematic enough when the scope and role of manufacturing is judged according to current estimates; if manufacturing is viewed through a larger value chain lens, the consequences really must be reckoned with.

4 Economic Perspectives on Manufacturing

Introduction

We have reviewed historical developments in U.S. manufacturing and its subsequent decline in the first decade of the twenty-first century. We now turn to an overview of how economic theory explains manufacturing. General readers should be aware that this chapter focuses heavily on economic theory, which may not be of interest to those with a disinclination towards economics. However, economics and manufacturing have been linked since at least the work of Adam Smith in the late eighteenth century. An in-depth, longitudinal analysis is mandatory to fully contextualize and understand the current opportunities and challenges in manufacturing. So addressing manufacturing policy requires addressing its treatment in economics. Although key concepts, such as productivity, have persisted for well over two centuries, the discipline as a whole has evolved in tandem with global changes. More recently, discussions of manufacturing's decline have centered on either economic growth resulting from productivity gains or on trade. There is a widespread consensus that innovation and new technologies are primary drivers of growth. However, modeling how new ideas and technologies are generated in and enter the economy is far from complete. This gap has created significant problems for understanding manufacturing. The gap has significant policy implications, especially if production is viewed separately from the innovation process. As we argue here, manufacturing is in fact deeply embedded in the innovation process, which means that the economic losses are generally underestimated by mainstream economic models.

Aside from growth, trade has been central to political discussions in recent years. Theories of trade have changed significantly since Ricardo first wrote about comparative advantage in the 1800s. There has been a growing level of specificity regarding which people and firms benefit from or are hurt by trade. Work on firms of varying sizes helps explain why small manufacturers have struggled more than large firms in international markets. Ultimately it is those larger firms that are more productive, likely as a result of a greater ability to invest in research and development, which can lead to success while smaller firms falter, as they are unable to make productivity-enhancing investments that allow them to compete internationally over the long term. It is at this point that policy discussions aiming to support U.S. manufacturers come to a standstill, hung up on arguments about industrial policy. For example, should there be, and what is the right amount and type of, federal investment in research and development in support of manufacturing? Understanding the innovative nature of manufacturing can help bring together innovation theory and economic theory that has focused on firm-level productivity to form a stronger set of policy options.

This chapter provides an overview of manufacturing in the early foundations of economics before moving into a relatively short, but admittedly complex, application of both economics and trade theory to the manufacturing sector. A firm grasp of these theoretical underpinnings, however, is needed to provide a framework to inform future manufacturing policy. The review focuses first on growth theory, including New Growth Theory and its efforts to better model growth. Because these models remain imperfect, manufacturing's role is still not adequately understood. But productivity concepts offer another analytical strand: theories of nonbalanced growth between sectors with varying productivity levels help us see the role of manufacturing in growth. The discussion then turns to trade theory. New Trade Theory has led to a focus on the innovative and competitive capabilities of firms; the weaknesses of smaller firms in developing innovation capability have affected the manufacturing sector overall. But these developments in growth, productivity, and trade theory and their application to manufacturing have been largely missed by mainstream economics. The analysis then turns to a discussion of some of the shortcomings of mainstream economics as it has applied to manufacturing. This is followed by a presentation of the case for policy to focus on strengthening the country's manufacturing innovation system.

The Role of Manufacturing in Early Economics

The discipline of economics began to take shape during the Industrial Revolution, a period of history when economic growth first became perceptible through a rising standard of living. For most of recorded history, improvements in living standards were measured in generations. It took four hundred years, from 1300 to 1700, for GDP per capita to double in Great Britain. By the eighteenth century, improvements in living standards became noticeable within a person's lifetime. In fact, starting in 1700, it would only take a little over 160 years for GDP per capita to double again, an incredible acceleration in growth.[1] During this period, the first seminal texts on economics were written, laying down the theoretical concepts that showed the importance of competition, free trade, and productivity, which remain the mainstay of the discipline today. Industrialization, driven by advancements in manufacturing, was at the core of this historically unprecedented period of growth, which has persisted to the present day.

The birth of economics as a discipline is associated with British scholars, such as Adam Smith and David Ricardo, toward the end of the eighteenth century. However, it was in France, a few decades earlier, that the Physiocrats, led by François Quesnay, began to push back systematically against the prominent ideology of the day, mercantilism. Although their idea that agriculture was the source of a nation's wealth has disappeared from the mainstream of economics, their maxim *laissez faire, laisser passer* (roughly, free competition and free trade) has remained a mainstay in discussions on economic policy.[2] Adam Smith was well acquainted with the Physiocrats, having met them in Paris, but was less uncompromising in his advocacy of free markets. Famous for introducing the idea of the invisible hand, he also warned, "People of the same trade seldom meet together, even for merriment and diversion, but the conversation ends in a conspiracy against the publick, or in some contrivance to raise prices."[3] In addition to this indictment of the tendency for oligopolies to form at the expense of the public, Smith also suggested that, in some cases, it might be necessary for the government to intervene. One example is his support of government involvement in education "to prevent the almost entire corruption and degeneracy of the great body of people."[4] Smith left open a place for government intervention when markets failed the public good, which was broader than the view of the Physiocrats, while still remaining highly critical of mercantilism. Adam Smith is typically considered to have founded the school of classical economics with the publication of his famous *An Inquiry into the Nature and Causes of the Wealth of Nations* in 1776.

Perhaps the best-known example in *The Wealth of Nations* is that of the pin factory. Surprisingly, as noted by Sandmo, the pin factory is the only direct reference to any of the technological advances of the Industrial Revolution in Adam Smith's writings.[5] It hardly diminishes the importance of the idea; the "invisible hand" is also only referenced once in the entire book. Smith puts forward the example of a pinmaker to highlight the division of labor. One person may only be able to make 20 pins, or maybe even just one each day, by themselves, but when the manufacture of the pin is divided up into 18 different steps among ten workers, they could make 48,000 pins in a day, or 4800 each.[6] The productivity gains are a result of reducing the work to one or two simple tasks and eliminating time lost switching between multiple tasks. What has proven to be even more important are advancements in machinery, of which, Smith said, "Every body must be sensible how much labour is facilitated and abridged by the application of proper machinery. It is unnecessary to give any example."[7] Interestingly, Smith credits the laborers for altering or inventing new machines that increased productivity[8]—early recognition of the innovative nature of manufacturing itself.

The pin factory highlights some important ideas that underlie most economic models today. The division of labor or the specialization on a narrower range of tasks is a straightforward example of an increase in labor productivity. The inputs remain the same (i.e., materials and labor hours), but the combined output increases. In this case, an increase in human capital, the skills or knowledge of the workers, was the cause. Of course, this is not the only way to increase labor productivity; an increase in capital— machinery, for example—can lead to the same result and, as we will address more fully later on, the role technology plays. Interestingly, in Smith's work, he differentiates between productive and unproductive work. He specifies manufacturers as the former and menial servants as the latter.[9] Although such a distinction is no longer made, it highlights the difficulty of observing and calculating productivity in services as opposed to the production of physical goods.

One tenet of mercantilism that Adam Smith argued against was protectionist trade policies. These policies, to ensure more exports than imports and thus an inflow of gold specie, did not in fact make the country wealthier. Smith notes that, in particular cases, the natural endowment of a country gives it an absolute advantage over another. He asked rhetorically whether foreign wine should be banned to encourage the production of wine in Scotland, where it would require the construction of greenhouses to grow the grapes.[10] It would take another four decades before the most enduring conceptual model of the gains from free trade was published. David Ricardo, building on Smith's work, released *On the Principles of Political Economy and Taxation* in 1817, introducing the concept of comparative advantage.

The idea that France has an absolute advantage over Scotland in the production of wine, and therefore Scotland should buy its wine from France, is intuitive. Comparative advantage, on the other hand, is less so. Ricardo lays out his example, famously using two goods, wine and cloth, and two countries, England and Portugal. In Portugal, it requires less labor to produce both cloth and wine than it does in England. However, England is relatively better at producing cloth and Portugal better at producing wine. If each country focuses production on what it is relatively better at, the total amount of wine and cloth will be higher than if each tried to produce both.[11] Then, through trade, both countries are better off than they could have been without trade. Importantly, Ricardo's theory is premised on the idea that there is no free flow of capital and labor between the two countries. Ricardo's theory of comparative advantage remains a mainstay in neoclassical economics.

In the centuries since Adam Smith laid out the framework for economics, the field has grown exponentially. A wide variety of theoretical models have been created that describe all different facets of the market. As Dani Rodrik has written, "The correct answer to almost any question in economics is: It depends. Different models, each equally respectable, provide different answers."[12] In many of today's policy debates, the same concepts Smith and Ricardo laid out still dominate the discussion. However, today the data and models that are available to economists allow for a more nuanced understanding of market mechanisms, even if this does not find its way into the political sphere. In the last few decades, whether mainstream economics can account for the critical role manufacturing plays in the U.S. economy has come into question with increasing frequency.[13] The following sections provide an overview of some well-known economic models and empirical studies to examine whether the shrinking manufacturing sector threatens the long-term health of the U.S. economy.

Technology, Productivity, and Economic Growth: A Snapshot

Classical economics seemed to have hit a wall by the middle of the nineteenth century because of an approach that assumed the value of a product was the result of the costs incurred to produce it. By the 1870s, a number of economists, including William Stanley Jevons and Leon Walras, began looking at the problem from the consumption side rather than the production side. The value of goods, they theorized, was based on the marginal utility, which in a sense was the value of one additional unit of a product to the consumer. The "marginal revolution" started the neoclassical school of economics, now considered mainstream economics. However, neoclassical economics mostly set aside the issue of growth until the 1950s. In 1956, two papers were published that raised the issue of long-term growth, one by an Australian economist, Trevor Swan, and the other by Robert Solow, an American, which received and continues to receive significantly more attention.

Solow's article, "A Contribution to the Theory of Economic Growth," was written as a response to the Harrod-Domar model of growth, an attempt to extend English economist John Maynard Keynes's thinking into a long-term model for growth.[14] Solow set out to create a model without the assumptions in the Harrod-Domar model of fixed capital and labor supply that required the economy to balance on a knife's edge in order to grow.[15] In addition to the substitutability of labor and capital, as well as the flexibility of factor prices, the model also included a variable for technical progress. The use of a Cobb-Douglas function in his model meant it had what Solow has called "Santa Claus properties." Among the "Santa Claus properties" are not only the evaporation of the distinction between labor augmenting (Harrod-neutral), capital-augmenting (Solow-neutral), and output-augmenting (Hicks-neutral) technical progress but also the constancy of the income shares of the factors of production.[16]

Solow's point is that it can hardly be assumed that the majority of technological advancements are simultaneously Harrod-, Solow-, and Hicks-neutral. Another interesting conclusion that arises out of Solow's model is that long-term growth is independent of savings and investment rates. In the short term, for example, higher saving and investment can increase the speed of growth, but the capital-to-labor ratio increases as a result, and diminishing returns to capital restore the economy to the same long-term growth rate.[17] Technology, although little discussed in this early paper, is the key to economic growth in this model.

Solow returned to the issue of technology and growth in a paper a year later. He employed a model where technical change was neutral, meaning it would lead to higher output without causing capital or labor to be substituted for one another.[18] Using data on labor, capital, and total output, from 1909 to 1947, Solow calculated the relative effect of technical change as the remainder of output after accounting for labor and capital. This concept of technical change is often referred to as the Solow residual, total factor productivity, or multifactor productivity. This means technological change is not being directly measured, all factors other than capital and labor are also captured by the residual. Solow concluded that 87.5% of the increase in gross output per man hour, which doubled over this time, resulted from technical change (an increase in capital accounted for the rest).[19] This challenged the view that capital accumulation was the primary driver of growth. Solow's model continues to be widely used, at times with modifications, such as those from Mankiw, Romer, and Weil; their work found that the addition of human capital to the production function enables the model to better account for variations in living standards among countries.[20] As a result of the simplicity, adaptability, and explanatory power of Solow's model, it is widely taught in macroeconomics courses, but it is not without its challenges.

The measurement of total factor productivity has been a topic of debate since Solow's paper was published. A wide range of measurement issues came up, including whether two products that cost the same but have different levels of performance should be counted the same. Two prominent economists, Dale Jorgenson and Zvi Griliches, ended up on one side of the debate, that the technology residual is in fact smaller, with John W. Kendrick and Edward F. Denison on the other.[21] The development of productivity accounting is useful for determining the health of an economy. However, it is measured as an exogenous variable, meaning it is independent from both the capital and labor variables. On this issue, Robert Gordon noted: "For decades economists have debated the relative importance of capital accumulation and technical change as sources of economic growth. But this is a false dichotomy if capital accumulation is not an independent source of growth but rather a by-product of technical change."[22]

The placement of Solow's technological change into an exogenous "black box," entirely external to the economy, prompted a wave of new models that attempt to bring technology, learning, or human capital back into the models.

While recognizing the importance of Solow's growth model, Kenneth Arrow sought to address some of its crucial shortcomings, including the absence of policy variables that would give the theory a practical application.[23] Instead of an exogenous factor for technology, Arrow uses an endogenous variable for learning. Because of some exogenous parameters, the model is not usually considered entirely endogenous.[24] The stock of learning grows over time, and new products incorporate the advancing technology, leading to increasing returns to scale.[25] The model only accounts for learning in the process of production and excludes the learning that occurs in educational institutions.[26] Perhaps the most commonly used example of learning by doing is of the construction of 2699 Liberty ships during World War II. Over the course of three years, production time for one Liberty ship dropped from six months to thirty days.[27] Famously, production of one such 10,000 ton ship was even cut to four days and fifteen hours.[28] Although it was believed that the majority of this improvement in construction was the result of learning by doing, Peter Thompson suggests that earlier studies failed to account for capital deepening, thus mistakenly doubling the productivity gains from learning.[29] The productivity gains are nonetheless enormous, demonstrating the gains from learning that can accrue during the manufacturing process.

Endogenous growth models remained in the background until a wave of new models, often called "New Growth Theory," were developed beginning in the 1980s. Paul Romer's models are some of the most well-known, demonstrating a much higher potential for growth. This becomes possible when the underlying assumption of diminishing returns is discarded. This is possible when there is no limit to new knowledge (considered a form of capital good), and since the firms that invest in research are not able to capture all of the gains, knowledge spills over into the economy, enabling broader gains.[30] To prevent unrealistic levels of growth, Romer specifies that while new knowledge increases output, there are some diminishing returns in the production of knowledge itself. If this were not the case, growth would accelerate faster as the investment in research increased, without limit.[31] Many models similar to Romer's replace the stock of knowledge variable with human capital, which typically has similar positive externalities.

There are clearly a multitude of ways for an individual to acquire human capital. In a 1988 paper, Robert Lucas considered two of these ways in two different models. In one, human capital is acquired through education, necessitating that the individual leave the workforce. In the other model, learning by doing is the source. In both models, the outcome is not efficient, the growth rate is too low, and there is a loss of welfare. There is a policy solution for each: subsidize education and subsidize production—industrial policy.[32] Although Lucas notes the theoretical possibility for industrial policy to be welfare enhancing, he rules it out as practically infeasible. Lucas, as well as Stokey and Rebelo, also find in their endogenous models that taxes may have no effect on growth.[33] In essence, in their view, the issue at stake for policy consideration is to determine the underlying assumption about knowledge or human capital.

Paul Romer, in his project to make growth theory in economics endogenous, applied traditional economic ideas of rivalry (does the use by one person limit that of others?) and excludability (is it possible for someone to prevent someone else from using a good?—this is the idea underlying a patent system) of technological knowledge. For instance, models that use learning by doing typically consider knowledge to be a public good, nonrival and nonexcludable. However in this model intentional investment in R&D by firms is ruled out because firms are unable to capture the gains. Another possibility is that knowledge is both nonrival and at least partially excludable,[34] which means moving away from the model of perfect competition to one where firms have some market power. This implies that firms invest in research for a product that can then be sold for more than marginal cost. In an environment of monopolistic competition, knowledge can be both nonrival and excludable, meaning firms will invest in R&D.[35] In this case, like that of Lucas's earlier, the accumulation of knowledge has higher social returns than just the private returns, because the firm that invests in research cannot prevent some of their knowledge from spilling into the economy at large. Romer suggests that one possible policy to partially remedy this would be to incentivize research by using a subsidy.[36]

There is another area of growth theory along lines similar to Romer's later models: Schumpeterian growth. Joseph Schumpeter was a noted Austrian-born economist who wrote extensively on the dynamics of capitalism. He is best known for introducing the term "creative destruction," which describes the process by which new technology replaces the old, or technologically advanced firms push lagging firms out of the market, resulting in growth. According to Aghion, Akcigit, and Howitt, there are three defining features of Schumpeterian growth. These are innovation, ability to secure monopoly rents, and creative destruction.[37] These models are based on quality ladders. Each new product attempts to improve on its predecessor, and if it is of higher quality, the lower-quality products get pushed out of the market.[38] Competition is central to this model, because if there are strong intellectual property laws, this will increase research and development (R&D), but if there are no enforceable rules in place, there will be no corresponding increase in R&D.[39] This is another model and, not surprisingly, presents an additional possible policy option regarding intellectual property protection to stimulate growth.

What emerges from this brief overview of a series of economic growth models is the primacy of technology and complementary technological learning from human capital. Manufacturing is clearly embedded in these models. However, the role the government plays varies widely, depending on the market structure and the nature of knowledge. Agricultural, manufacturing, or service sectors can generally be looked at singly or with all three aggregated together. In Solow's calculations of the role of technology in growth, agriculture is excluded. A multisector model is necessary to offer insights into the ongoing structural change in the U.S. economy: loss of manufacturing jobs, which are replaced by seemingly lower-productivity service jobs. Between 1972 and 1996, average manufacturing labor productivity increased about two times faster than in the nonmanufacturing sector, and continued to increase at a faster rate through 2011.[40]

To summarize, Solow and his growth economics colleagues keep pointing us to the significance of growth of technological advancement supported by corresponding technological learning. Historically, as Adam Smith first suggested with the pin factory, that has been implemented predominantly through the production side of the economy. It has been largely through the manufacturing process that technological advances and productivity gains scale. As discussed in earlier chapters, this means that manufacturing along with R&D must be seen as inherent in the innovation system, not as separated. In other words, growth economics made technological innovation—and supporting advances in technological learning, achieved in major part through manufacturing—the dominant factor in economic growth. But neoclassical economics had difficulty incorporating the systems around innovation—including manufacturing—as "endogenous" factors. "New Growth Theory" economists have made strides toward making innovation endogenous, but this effort is incomplete. So far, economists have not been able to model the innovation system, and this includes its manufacturing component. This has meant that economics continues to have an imperfect understanding of manufacturing. Productivity concepts, however, offer a supplementary framework to growth theory for considering manufacturing.

So let us compare productivity levels—how do different sectors perform differently? And then, let us look at employment—does productivity gain inevitably lead to a lower employment base? Is manufacturing the same as agriculture, where rising productivity has been accompanied by declining employment? Theories of nonbalanced growth (or structural transformation) attempt to explain why this happens.

Productivity and the Theory of Nonbalanced Growth: Manufacturing vs. Agriculture

Between the nineteenth century and the twenty-first, agriculture's share of employment fell dramatically. Initially, these jobs were replaced by those in the service and manufacturing sectors. More recently, manufacturing jobs peaked and began to fall, while services continued to employ a larger and larger share of workers.[41] Daron Acemoglu and Veronica Guerrieri present a fairly straightforward two-sector model that provides a theoretical explanation for structural shifts. If the two sectors have different proportions between labor and capital—for instance, capital intensive versus labor intensive—then capital deepening will cause output to increase more in the sector that is more capital intensive. Even though this sector sees its output grow faster, its value will grow more slowly than that of the labor-intensive sector. Essentially, there are diminishing returns to that sector, which result in both capital and labor moving to the labor-intensive sector.[42] Acemoglu and Guerrieri present a theoretical model, but they do not use it to explain sector shifts in agriculture, manufacturing, and services. However, the model seems to provide an economic rationale for the movement of jobs from manufacturing, typically more capital intensive, to the service sector, although it does not account for the increase in the relative prices of services.[43] Acemoglu and Guerrieri's theory of nonbalanced growth may be better aligned with the shift of labor out of agriculture than that of manufacturing.

Four decades earlier, William Baumol had introduced an idea along similar lines. Baumol posited that low productivity or stagnant sectors would see rising costs and only a relative increase in output. With an increasingly large share of the economy being commanded by a stagnant service sector, economy-wide growth would ultimately slow.[44] This is known as Baumol's cost disease. William Nordhaus examined industry data from 1948 to 2001, looking for signs of Baumol's disease. Although Nordhaus acknowledged imperfect data, there was substantial evidence of low productivity dragging down growth.[45] Another interesting finding was that for manufacturing industries, unlike the others included in the study, when productivity increased, so did the number of hours worked.[46]

Following the increase in growth in the 1990s resulting from the information technology (IT) revolution, there has been a discussion about whether Baumol's disease has been "cured." Some service sectors, including financial and wholesale/retail services, saw substantial increases in productivity, but there was certainly not a uniform increase across the board.[47] Thus, Baumol's disease does not appear resolved, so a "cure" cannot offer a full explanation of the changes in employment in manufacturing in the United States in the postwar period. Between 1948 and 1972, manufacturing productivity growth was on average 0.5% higher than that in nonmanufacturing sectors. Since 1972, manufacturing productivity has on average been over 1% higher, with a spike up to 2% between 1996 and 2004.[48] The average decrease in the share of manufacturing employment per year remained stable for the first two periods. Starting in 1996, the rate of decline increased, and from 2004 until today, the rate increased further.[49] Although Baumol's finding offers a compelling explanation for the sectoral shifts during the postwar period, a number of other factors need to be included in the analysis before any final conclusions on the usefulness of policy changes can be reached.

However, despite the variations over time noted here, Baumol's overall approach to looking at productivity, an approach that originated with Adam Smith, as well as the supporting data, suggest that the manufacturing sector plays an important economic role. If productivity gains are tied to the ability to introduce real economic gains into society, then a dominant service economy will tend to produce less gain than a manufacturing sector that is stronger, with consistently higher productivity. It is a theory of nonbalanced growth.

There is another key question: what is the relationship between productivity gains and employment? Again, is agriculture a stalking horse that can tell us about this relationship in manufacturing? Let us examine a model to account for an enormous drop in the number of people employed in the agricultural sector. The change is quite dramatic: between 1900 and 2000, the percentage of the workforce employed in the agricultural sector dropped from 41% to 1.9%.[50] The most important contributing factor was the rise in productivity as a result of technological advancements. Initially, these were from advances like the tractor and the Haber-Bosch process, which enabled the industrial production of nitrogen-based fertilizers and corresponding increases in crop yields. Advances in genetics and plant breeding, along with applications of chemical advances made during World War II to herbicides and pesticides, led to further acceleration in productivity resulting from technological advances. If the decline in agricultural employment was only a matter of productivity, we would expect to see the same pattern in the manufacturing sector. However, the model is premised on the idea that as people become wealthier, their consumption patterns change and their consumption of services increases in proportion to their consumption of agricultural products. Employment and value added in agriculture decrease while rising in services, leading to a sectoral shift where agricultural jobs are replaced by new service jobs.[51] This idea is in line with Engel's law that as income increases, relative expenditure on food falls. The data supports this idea. Between 1909 and 2009, the U.S. per capita consumption of food remained almost unchanged.[52] Real personal consumption expenditures on durable and nondurable goods, in contrast, increased approximately 139% and 40%, respectively, between 1999 and 2016 alone (in chained 2009 dollars).[53]

Some economists have suggested that the sharp decline in manufacturing employment in the first decade of this century should not be an object of concern because it was simply akin to the productivity-driven decline in agricultural employment—fewer jobs but growing productivity.[54] Based on the very different food and manufactured goods consumption patterns, however, sectoral changes in the manufacturing sector should not be equated with the historical changes in agriculture.

To summarize, the exogenous growth models developed by Swan and Solow were both simple and offered a high degree of explanatory power. The problem with the models is that if the single most important factor for economic growth is technological progress, why is it an exogenous variable? The new endogenous models sought to remedy this, and a proliferation of models followed Romer's groundbreaking work in 1986. Although endogenous growth models seem particularly relevant for examining U.S. economic growth, they have been criticized for their failure to explain conditional convergence;[55] that is, the explanation for the higher growth rates in poorer countries than in wealthier ones. However, the preliminary conditions that poorer countries need to meet for this to occur tend to depend on the economist. To reiterate, this highlights the general problem economics has had when trying to model innovation. Another criticism of mainstream growth economics is that the models are ahistorical. Carlaw and Lipsey argue that economies are in fact path dependent: we are constrained by past decisions, especially with regard to technology. Innovation occurs in an environment of fundamental uncertainty, not calculable risk, which means there is no unique set of decisions that maximizes profit.[56] Economic models attempt to simplify complex problems so we can make sense of them, and growth models, although a work in progress, have brought to the forefront the importance of human capital and technology. Although the limits to the models mean manufacturing's role is less than clear, it is clearly an enabler in this regard. The additional focus on productivity discussed earlier, a long-standing element in economics that is understood to be driven by technological advancement and is key to growth, helps here. This line of thought enables us to differentiate between higher- and lower-productivity sectors; as a high-productivity sector, manufacturing may be a sector particularly worthy of focus.

There is one further strand in economic growth thinking that should be accounted for: innovation organization. The role of innovation organization in growth theory was anticipated in the "evolutionary" approach of economists Richard Nelson and Sidney Winter.[57] They examined innovative large corporations of the 1970s and found that their success in evolving innovation was based on the effectiveness of their organizational routines for R&D, management organization, product commercialization, and efficient production. Although they focused on what was going on inside a company rather than on the larger innovation system, they argued that innovation organization and the routines that connected organizational elements were key to a firm's ability to innovate. Nelson took these considerations to the next level in a 1993 book[58] examining not simply firms but innovation systems. He argued that there were national systems of innovation with innovation actors interacting in those systems. The actors included government support for R&D, government-funded research universities, government laboratories, and educational institutions, as well as strong firms, both small and large, and their R&D laboratories. Nelson saw the firm as the most critical element in this system, but he saw innovation as occurring within a larger institutional system, in which a series of connected and interacting actors influenced the innovation that could occur in firms.

Nelson's focus on innovation organization at both the firm and national levels, with government, university, and business actors in interactive relationships, provides an additional element in innovation theory for our analysis. Although growth economists make clear that innovation drives growth, innovation does not just happen; it requires innovation organization and the resulting innovation systems. As argued in previous chapters, manufacturing is part of the innovation process. Therefore, treating manufacturing as part of the innovation system and optimizing institutional and organizational linkages in that system, as Nelson suggests and emerging advanced manufacturing policies propose, become an important task for advancing innovation, productivity gains, and therefore growth.[59]

Up to this point, the discussion has centered on economic growth, as well as structural transformations that can accompany differentiated productivity growth. As the 2016 presidential election illustrated, much of the discussion on manufacturing in the public arena centers on the issue of trade. Since the end of World War II, trade has played a growing role in the U.S. economy. In 1950, total trade was a mere 6% of GDP, but by 2010 it had grown to over 29%, though political uncertainty makes it difficult to tell whether this trend will continue.[60] Based on GDP per capita, the United States is one of the wealthiest countries in the world; most of the countries that are ahead of the United States are rich in natural resources. Looking at exogenous and endogenous growth theory, this is the result of the United States leading on the technological frontier and having large stocks of human capital engaged in R&D. When broken down into sectors, the United States has high levels of productivity in both agriculture and manufacturing, with the service sector lagging behind. Why then does the United States have a large trade deficit in manufacturing and a small surplus in services? Next, we turn to trade theory to broaden the picture of what is happening to manufacturing in the United States.

A Brief Look at Trade Theory

By necessity, our discussion of the vast scope of trade theory must be short and incomplete. However, trade is an issue of special importance for manufacturing and needs to be thoughtfully considered along with growth theory. It is also timely, with the global rise of nationalistic and protectionist politics evidenced by Brexit and the 2016 U.S. presidential election. In 2016, the U.S. exported around $1.46 trillion worth of goods, around 66% of all its exports, and imported around $2.21 trillion worth of goods, or nearly 82% of all imports.[61] As noted in chapter 3, the volume of trade in services is still quite small in comparison to the trade in goods. Although the bulk of trade occurs in manufactured goods, the manufacturing sector has declined as a part of the economy, now accounting for 11.8% of value added to U.S. GDP according to the current measurement system. Corresponding trade deficits ensure that trade and manufacturing concerns are tightly linked policy concerns.[62] The consensus among economists on free trade is nearly unanimous, with 93% of economists, in a survey by Gregory Mankiw, supporting a statement that trade barriers lower the general welfare of an economy.[63] Theory tends to support the idea that the economy as a whole gains from trade, although not every individual or sector will benefit.

Ricardo's comparative advantage shows up in a number of different trade models. One of the most common presentations of the model points to technological differences between countries as the underlying reason for trade. In essence, labor is the only factor of production, so productivity differences between countries drive trade. The relative prices also have to fall into a certain range; otherwise, it would be more productive for a country to only produce for the domestic market. Ricardo's theory of trade faced no serious challengers in the century after its publication. By 1919, a new theory began to take shape, led by Eli Heckscher and Bertil Ohlin.[64]

Heckscher and Ohlin's theorem changed some basic assumptions that underlie the Ricardian model. First, they assumed that countries tend to have equal access to technology, essentially ruling out technology as the major factor driving trade. Instead there are two factors in the Heckscher-Ohlin theorem, labor and capital. Two conditions have to hold or there will be no trade in this model. Countries must have different factor prices, and the proportion of capital and labor used in goods cannot be identical in all countries.[65] At its simplest, the theory suggests that a country that can produce capital-intensive goods, because of its relative abundance of capital, can trade with a country that produces labor-intensive goods, to the benefit of both. It is a straightforward idea and seems to make intuitive sense; for example, the United States' top export to Indonesia is aircraft, and its top import is clothing, as was the case in 2012.[66] The United States will have higher levels of consumption by continuing to build aircraft rather than diverting workers to produce clothing. However, although the country is better off as a whole, it is not necessarily the case that each individual or certain groups of people will be better off.

In 1941, Wolfgang Stolper and Paul Samuelson published a paper addressing the issue of winners and losers from trade within a country. Their theorem builds on the Heckscher-Ohlin theorem and examines the changes to factor prices as a result of trade. What the Stolper-Samuelson theorem demonstrated was that the abundant factor gains from trade, whereas the scarce factor loses in real terms, not just relatively.[67] As with any economic theorem, there is no shortage of criticism, with Donald R. Davis and Prachi Mishra titling a paper "Stolper-Samuelson Is Dead."[68] In the years since Stolper and Samuelson published their paper, a range of different trade models have reinforced the finding that the factors in the exporting sector gain while those in the sector facing import competition come out worse.[69] Although there is strong theoretical support for the Heckscher-Ohlin theorem, it has not fared as well when tested empirically. It has tended to over-predict the actual amount of trade, what Daniel Treffler has called "missing trade." One component of this is a home bias among consumers, who tend to pay more for a domestically produced good than an identical foreign good, reducing the level of trade.[70] Mitchell Morey's finding that consumers in Madagascar pay 8% more for domestically grown rice, which theoretically should lower their consumption by 5%, is compelling evidence of a home bias.[71] If this bias appears in consumption of basic food staples, it suggests it is deep seated.

Accounting for home bias alone does not explain the model's poor fit to the data. Davis, Weinstein, Bradford, and Shimpo have shown that when some of the underlying assumptions are relaxed, the model does a much better job of describing the data. One assumption they do away with is universal factor price equalization, only applying the model to regions where there was evidence of factor price equalization.[72] The factor price equalization theorem, for which we also have Paul Samuelson to thank, shows that, if the assumptions of Heckscher-Ohlin hold, even in the absence of labor and capital mobility between countries, the trade of goods will lead to the same returns to capital or wage rates in the two countries. There appears to be some evidence supporting factor price equalization, though the wide variety of industries, goods, and technology adds a degree of complication that obscures the simplicity of the theorem.[73] Two areas where factor price equalization has tended to enter the public debate are around the expected convergence of wages resulting from the North American Free Trade Agreement (NAFTA) and some narrowing of the manufacturing wage gap between China and the United States.

Trade results from differing intensities of factors of production in Heckscher-Ohlin. An example of this might be trade between the United States and Kenya. In 2014, construction vehicles made up the largest share of U.S. exports to Kenya, while Kenya's leading exports to the United States were textiles, specifically women's suits that year.[74] This seems in line with the theories previously discussed—the United States is capital abundant, so it exports capital-intensive goods, whereas the opposite holds for Kenya. While the predictions of Heckscher-Ohlin are corroborated in some of the data, what stands out is that most trade actually occurs between advanced countries and in similar products. The Observatory of Economic Complexity, at the MIT Media Lab, provides visualizations of international trade along with bilateral trade, which makes it easy to see these trends. While U.S. exports to Kenya totaled $344 million, exports from the United States to Germany totaled $61.6 billion. The United States exports vastly more to a country with factors of production more similar than different from its own. At the Harmonized System two-digit level, the most general grouping of similar products, the top three U.S. exports to Germany, comprising 65% of all exports, are machines, chemical products, and transportation, respectively. Germany's top three exports to the United States, totaling 75%, are transportation, machines, and chemical products.[75] An effort to better account for this intra-industry trade, as opposed to the traditional inter-industry trade, took off in the 1980s and is often referred to as New Trade Theory.

Looking back on the development of New Trade Theory in his Nobel Prize lecture, Paul Krugman notes that it took the development of new models of monopolistic competition, most notably by Avinash Dixit and Joseph Stiglitz in the late 1970s, to enable the development of new trade models.[76] The key difference between monopolistic competition and perfect competition is the differentiation of products. Different brands are not viewed as perfect substitutes for one another, giving producers a small degree of market power. Increasing returns to scale are also a factor. Increasing returns can be internal to a firm, meaning it becomes cheaper as more of a product is produced, or external to the firm and in the industry as a whole, such that as the industry's output grows, production costs for firms decline. Intra-industry trade is the result of monopolistic competition, with internal returns to scale, and consumers in multiple countries who demand a variety of differentiated products, which are produced in more than one country.[77] It is worth noting that New Trade Theory was not covering entirely new ground. Jan Tinbergen proposed a gravity equation for trade in 1962, where the volume of trade between countries was based on their GDP levels, though there were obstructions such as transportation costs. Elhanan Helpman later found that Tinbergen's gravity equation was applicable to an extreme case of product differentiation.[78] Just as Heckscher-Ohlin failed to explain intra-industry trade, the first monopolistic competition models did not explain inter-industry trade.

Work by Paul Krugman, Elhanan Helpman, and others in the early 1980s presented a fuller view of trade. One way they were able to reconcile inter-industry and intra-industry trade was to assume that similar goods, just as with different brands, would be produced using the same factor proportions. Developed and undeveloped countries would specialize based on their factors of production, leading to trade, whereas developed countries would trade differentiated products with each other. Krugman's work also suggested that intra-industry trade would benefit both countries if trade barriers were eliminated, although the conclusions of Heckscher-Ohlin were still relevant for trade liberalization between developed and undeveloped countries.[79] An important factor that underlies brand and product differentiation is that economists consider them welfare enhancing—people benefit from choice. One other early finding by Krugman was that the result of scale effects and monopolistic competition was the home-market effect. Firms will produce a differentiated good in a larger country if transportation costs are factored in. The firm is choosing to manufacture in the market where it can sell the most goods without additional costs, and then export to the smaller countries.[80] New Trade Theory opened the door for a much more nuanced understanding of trade.

First and foremost, however, these models have not factored in that firms are not homogeneous and vary widely in both size and productivity. Work by Bernard, Redding, and Schott finds that trade increases industry's total factor productivity. This results from the least productive firms going out of business, raising each industry's productivity as a whole. The industry in which the country has a comparative advantage should also see higher productivity gains. This model blurs the distinction between comparative advantage in productivity and factor abundance.[81] The world in these models so far has been one where trade in goods and services is the focus but firms themselves are stuck within national borders. In today's world, companies have the option to outsource or produce offshore; in 2015, global foreign direct investment (FDI) net inflows totaled $2.1 trillion. These important factors are not addressed.[82]

The role of multinational firms in trade has grown substantially in the postwar period, and correspondingly their role in trade theory has likewise now risen substantially. Multinationals play an oversized role in the U.S. economy. They accounted for less than 1% of companies but 25% of profits in 2007. Analysis by McKinsey found that, between 1990 and 2007, multinationals accounted for 31% of real GDP growth and 41% of the increase in labor productivity. Also of significant importance is that 74% of private sector R&D is done by multinationals.[83] Multinational firms can operate in a number of different ways. Models of horizontal FDI weigh the costs of producing at home and exporting or acquiring a subsidiary in the other country. There is a large fixed cost for a firm to set up a foreign subsidiary, but there are also variable costs for exporting, such as tariffs and transportation costs. A simple model shows that as sales increase, eventually it will be more profitable to set up a subsidiary. Elhanan Helpman notes that an example of this model is Japanese car manufacturers opening factories in the United States after 1973.[84] Models like this can be extended further to differentiate firms between those that only produce for the domestic market, those that export, and those that set up subsidiaries.

Including heterogeneous firms in trade models brings productivity back to the forefront of the discussion. One simplified model by Helpman deals with three countries, a home country and two foreign countries, one of them high-wage and high-skilled and the other smaller, low-wage, and low-skilled, with firms that range in productivity, and high transportation costs, which produces a range of outcomes. The least productive firms in the home country export to both countries. In the next segment, more productive firms manufacture intermediate goods in the low-wage country and import them back for final assembly. Even more productive firms will continue to manufacture in the low-wage country, but final assembly will take place both at home and in the high-wage country. Finally, the most productive firms also manufacture in the low-wage country but assemble in all three countries.[85] This kind of firm-level review shifts trade analysis to a range of outcomes for a range of firms. The biggest trend in trade theory, then, seems to be a movement toward smaller units of measure, from generalizations about factors of production to the industry level and finally to the firm level.

The differences between growth theory and trade theory, then, have diminished substantially with the development of New Growth Theory and New Trade Theory. Productivity is the key factor in both, although the use of monopolistic competition in the models remains important. Perhaps most important is that trade effects are now seen at the firm level. Trade increases competition, which leads to different responses by firms. Large firms tend to be more productive than smaller firms and in turn tend to benefit more. Philippe Aghion has noted that competition propels firms near the technological frontier to innovate and increase productivity. In the simple U.S. export statistics, the relationship between the technological frontier and firm size shows up. Excluding petroleum, the three largest exporting industries are the aerospace sector followed by pharmaceuticals and integrated circuits.[86] All three of these industries are dominated by massive firms. One new semiconductor fabrication plant in Oregon may cost in the area of $14 billion.[87] At Boeing's Everett, Washington, site, the assembly building covers 98.3 acres, with a volume of 472 million cubic feet.[88] However, in 2013 there were only 2801 large manufacturers with over 500 employees, whereas there were over 250,000 small manufacturers with under 500 employees.[89] Smaller, less productive firms are more likely to be hurt by increases in competition, which constrains them from investing in research and development, affecting their ability to grow, and instead focuses them on remaining as efficient as possible.[90]

It may also be the case that large firms just don't face the same level of competition as smaller firms, due to high barriers to entry. As of now, there is no theoretical consensus on the effect competition has on innovation. The most recent empirical study to address this issue, at the time of this writing, by David Autor and a group of colleagues, examined the effect of import competition from China on U.S. firms' R&D funding and patent production. The paper found there was a decrease in patent production and R&D as firms faced increasing import competition. The authors noted, "The decline of innovation in the face of Chinese import competition suggests that R&D and manufacturing tend to be complements, rather than substitutes. That is, when faced with intensifying rivalry in the manufacturing stage of industry production, firms tend not to substitute effort in manufacturing with effort in R&D."[91] The paper's point reinforces the premise in this and earlier chapters about the important linkage between manufacturing and innovation. However, this study does not provide insight into the effect of trade competition on heterogeneous firms that would allow us to draw more specific policy implications. However, given that the majority of manufacturers employ under 500 people this finding may fit with some theories of the effect of trade on heterogeneous firms.

New Trade Theory, then, has moved us from a notion that trade is a positive for all to a more sophisticated notion that trade has to be understood at the level of firms, and that innovative firms may be trade winners and less innovative firms losers. It therefore may give us a signal about what has been happening in the U.S. manufacturing sector: innovation leading to higher productivity and competitiveness has been lacking in small and midsized firms, dragging down the sector overall.

In a number of ways, the work by Aghion, Helpman, and others confirms beliefs about a dynamic economy. Growth occurs as productive firms continue to innovate, whereas firms at the other end of the innovation curve go out of business. As Schumpeter said, "The fundamental impulse that sets and keeps the capitalist engine in motion comes from new consumers' goods, the new methods of production or transportation, the new markets, the new forms of industrial organization that capitalist enterprise creates."[92]

As trade theory has moved more to the level of firm analysis, centering on productivity, the economic mainstream is still focused on trade effects at the macro level, as Mankiw's poll of the profession, cited at the outset of this section, indicates. The policy implication of New Trade Theory as it has evolved is to focus on strengthening firms, their technological advancement, and their corresponding productivity advantage. This seems to fit with a policy focus on improving the manufacturing sector's performance across all firm sizes. The mainstream arguably has not kept pace. The following discussion of the positions of two leading economists on manufacturing illustrates the problem economics is having in confronting manufacturing and its economic role.

The Manufacturing Policy Implications of Mainstream Economic Theory

This short overview of economic growth and trade theory is not close to comprehensive. The intent is that it illuminate some accepted approaches for interpreting trends in the economy that can inform manufacturing policy. Economics has been a powerful driver of policy since the end of the Second World War, with policy arguments based on Keynesian economics giving way to neoclassical economics. For the last few decades, there has been a consistent discussion over what is generally called industrial policy, which has faced systematic attacks from mainstream economists. This has tracked closely with the decline in manufacturing jobs from 19.5 million in 1979 to 12.3 million in 2016.[93] At issue is whether the government should intervene to support a declining manufacturing sector. For a variety of reasons, the economic consensus since at least the 1980s is that deindustrialization is a sign of economic health rather than decline. However, there are some signs this may be changing.

Arguments tend to focus on the two issues discussed in the previous sections—that some combination of trade and technological advancement accounts for the loss of manufacturing jobs. In response to the argument that the loss of high-wage manufacturing jobs because of trade reduces the welfare of the United States, Paul Krugman in 1996 calculated that trade could only account for 0.5% of income loss.[94] Krugman suggested that productivity gains drive job loss. An interesting side point from Krugman's article is his note that whenever trade deficits in goods are matched not by service exports but rather by capital inflows, this will "imply a future in which the United States will run manufactures trade surpluses . . . in which trade will presumably lead to a larger number of manufacturing jobs."[95] This suggestion about a future with more manufacturing jobs has largely disappeared from the discourse. This is likely because the U.S. deficit in goods increased from about $191 billion in 1996 to around $750 billion in 2016.[96] The surplus in services only increased from about $87 billion to $250 billion over the same period.[97] This suggests that capital inflows cannot be assumed away as a temporary phenomenon when discussing international trade.

Jagdish Bhagwati has played a prominent role in policy discussions, especially in criticizing what he calls "the manufacturing fetish." The view that manufacturing is more productive than services goes back at least to Adam Smith, who differentiated between nonproductive and productive labor, giving the example that a manufacturer's labor adds to value but a menial servant's labor does not.[98] Ricardo followed Smith in attempting to create a labor theory of value, which ended up underlying much of Marxist theory. The idea of marginal utility as a way of determining price essentially sidestepped this debate. Bhagwati has called the emphasis on production as opposed to consumption a "quasi-Marxist fallacy." It is worth noting that while marginal analysis of consumption developed in the 1870s it took some twenty years before it was applied to production. In a number of ways, the neoclassical production function has yet to catch up with the explanatory power of the consumption function, as can be seen in our earlier discussion of growth models.[99] In his view, trade enables the focus to shift to consumption rather than production. Whether you make potato chips or semiconductor chips[100] is irrelevant because it is not determinative of consumption. An example of this Bhagwati cites is the transportation industry, a service sector in Australia, New Zealand, and Chile without a corresponding manufacturing sector but still a vibrant sector.[101] The modern neoclassical mainstream argument against manufacturing relies on that school's theory of value. Outside of the mainstream there is still disagreement about completely ruling out the labor theory of value, which has largely followed the work of Piero Sraffa.

Perhaps the most relevant critique of the significance of manufacturing for this book's perspective is that of Christina Romer. She was President Obama's chair of the Council of Economic Advisors for the first year and a half of his administration. Following the 2012 State of the Union address, it was clear that the administration intended to move beyond the auto sector bailout to help restore manufacturing, prompting Romer to publish an op-ed in the *New York Times* in opposition.[102] Like Bhagwati, she argued that goods are not inherently more important than services. Romer also addresses three common areas of argument in favor of intervention in manufacturing because of market failure that she deems unconvincing. The market failure argument falls short, she argues, because while there may be positive economic spillover effects where clustered industries would stand to benefit most, she argues there does not seem to be evidence that clusters are particularly common. Also, she asks, why would this mean that policy should favor manufacturing clusters over software or entertainment clusters on the services side? Additionally, learning by doing, a manufacturing strength, appears not to result in significant positive externalities. Generally, Romer does not see any reason why a policy focusing on manufacturing would greatly increase jobs, especially when more demand stimulus would be more effective. The third common argument for manufacturing she takes on is based on income inequality, linking the loss of jobs to rising inequality. Educational requirements have risen for manufacturing, so she argues that supporting education, or supporting low-skilled jobs like construction by rebuilding U.S. infrastructure, would have a greater impact. Ultimately, Romer sees manufacturing policy arguments as relying on mere history and sentiment.

It is important to note that when Bhagwati and Romer wrote their pieces the U.S. unemployment rates were 9.5% and 8.3%, respectively. In the summer of 2016, the unemployment rate fell below 5% for the first time since the beginning of 2008.[103] This is around the estimate for the natural rate of unemployment (although issues remain over long-term, structural unemployment not reflected in the statistics). As a result of the recovery, which took almost a decade to evolve, short-term economic stimulus no longer has the same urgency, but instead long-term economic growth and issues around income inequality are becoming increasingly important. This does not change what appears to be the consensus of mainstream economics that the loss of manufacturing jobs, which is indicative of high productivity in the sector and part of the transition to a service economy, is a net positive.

Of course, there have been dissenting voices to this consensus. Gregory Tassey has argued that neoclassical economic theory fails to "understand the complexity of the typical industrial technology and the synergies among tiers in high-tech supply chains," so it misses the significance of the production sector to innovation and growth.[104] Susan Helper has gathered data to show that, "Improving manufacturing's performance is a crucial part of the solution to America's trade, innovation, and income distribution problems."[105] In the post-Keynesian school of thought, Kaldor's focus on manufacturing as the engine of growth has also resurfaced.[106] But these have remained dissents to a mainstream consensus.

Could the Economic Consensus on Manufacturing Be Wrong?

The discipline of economics has secured a dominant position that looms over the rest of the social sciences. As a result, it frames most policy discussions; there is no Council of Sociologic Advisers. Part of the reason is that economics builds on what Robert Heilbroner called "something resembling the lawlike inner structure of scientific explanation."[107] Starting from the idea that individuals are utility maximizers, it is possible to construct mathematically elegant models. This has enabled the discipline to present itself as a social science that is closer to the mathematical exactitude of physics than it is to, say, jurisprudence. In large part, this has tended to obscure the role of ideology in economics. Karl Polanyi noted that an ideal self-regulating free market economy is as utopian in vision as communism.[108] Economics analyzes social orders; because economists themselves are members of these social orders, like all of us, they are unable to fully extract themselves from their analysis.[109] However, the assumptions economists make play a significant role in informing the outcome of the models. Looking at a market structure, they may apply a model of perfect competition instead of attempting to account for market distortions. Doubts about perhaps the single most important assumption in microeconomics, that people are rational actors, have resulted in the creation and growth of behavioral economics.[110] Paul Romer has noted that economists tend to conform to a norm of declining to openly critique work done by the most influential economists.[111] This helps explain why microfoundations for macroeconomics grew to dominate the mainstream starting in the 1980s, even though starting in 1973 Hugo Sonnenschein and others showed flaws in the idea that individuals' behavior can be simply aggregated.[112]

The failure of economists prior to the Great Recession not only to foresee but to even consider the possibility of structural catastrophe in the market economy led at least some in the profession to a more objective appraisal. In a 2009 piece titled, "How Did Economists Get It So Wrong?"[113] Krugman charged that his profession "mistook beauty, clad in impressive-looking mathematics, for truth." As he put it,

> As memories of the Depression faded, economists fell back in love with the old, idealized vision of an economy in which rational individuals interact in perfect markets, this time gussied up with fancy equations. The renewed romance with the idealized market was, to be sure, partly a response to shifting political winds, partly a response to financial incentives. But while sabbaticals at the Hoover Institution and job opportunities on Wall Street are nothing to sneeze at, the central cause of the profession's failure was the desire for an all-encompassing, intellectually elegant approach that also gave economists a chance to show off their mathematical prowess.

The messiness of actual economies necessitates taking into account thinking and disciplines beyond just mainstream economics when making policy.

One place to start is to look at trade theory. The accession of China to the World Trade Organization at the end of 2001 has become the most salient trade issue in recent years. Based on a very basic Heckscher-Ohlin model, one would expect to see Chinese gains in labor-intensive sectors and U.S. gains in capital-intensive sectors. This is in line with Chinese manufacturing employment, which increased from about 86 million in 2002 to 99 million in 2009.[114] However, in the United States, manufacturing jobs declined from 15.6 million to around 12 million over the same period (assuming a large percentage of American manufacturing was in fact capital-intensive).[115] Economists David Autor, David Dorn, and Gordon Hanson, as noted in chapter 3, have labeled this steep decline the "China Shock." The general consensus around 2000 was that workers displaced by trade would move to another sector.[116] However, as the scale of the numbers here indicates, this "shock" was much larger than previous ones that empirical studies had examined.

The empirical evidence shows that simple models are unable to describe the true impact. Not only were jobs lost in industries that now had to compete with China, but the communities in which they were located also saw significant employment declines. At the same time that these jobs were lost, there was no significant offsetting increase in employment in capital-intensive export industries, such as aviation, or in the nontradable sector. As discussed earlier, Autor, Dorn, and Hanson's work also touches on the distributional impact of trade. While high-skilled labor in the United States tends to see gains, as you move down to lower-skilled positions, lifetime earnings decrease proportionally more.[117] The cost to these individuals and communities as a result of trade is high. It is for this reason that Bhagwati's critique that it is not what you produce but what you consume runs into practical policy problems. Over the previous quarter century, there has been a polarization of wages, which typically has been explained by technological advancement.[118] But trade has also caused the loss of jobs in industries facing competition from imports, generally manufacturing, which has contributed to this polarization. Typically, the recommended theoretical economic solution is to redistribute some of the gains, preferably through a lump-sum tax that will not create market distortions. In a world of imperfect information, the lump-sum tax is in all likelihood impossible; however, it is theoretically possible to devise a tax that is Pareto optimal, a situation where no one can be made better off without making someone else worse off.[119] These theoretical possibilities suggest there is room for optimism but fail to address questions of what is possible practically—politically this seems very implausible.

The recognition that trade can displace a subset of workers is not a new idea in economic theory and has not been ignored by policymakers. Trade Adjustment Assistance (TAA) was first enacted in President Kennedy's Trade Expansion Act of 1962. It was originally proposed to gain congressional support for further trade liberalization with the European Common Market.[120] During the first years of the program, relatively few workers were approved to receive assistance: 53,899 between 1962 and 1975, at a total cost of $75.6 million. The Trade Act of 1974 increased the number of workers eligible for the program and the cash benefits they received; in 1976 alone, 131,765 workers received $162.5 million in assistance.[121] By 1981, the program had expanded to aid over half a million workers, at an annual cost of around $1.6 billion, prompting Congress to reverse course and restrict eligibility, with only 30,000 laborers receiving $103 million in 1982.[122] By 2007, the program was still substantially smaller than its 1981 incarnation, assisting around 150,000 workers, almost exclusively in the manufacturing sector, at a cost of $855.1 million.[123] This was a fairly high percentage of coverage, since the total number of manufacturing jobs lost in 2007 was around 262,000,[124] although these losses subsequently accelerated. Unfortunately, the outcomes for people that participated in the program were not particularly positive.

Part of the issue is that the jobs lost tend to be in concentrated sectors of lower-skilled manufacturing jobs, as discussed further in chapter 8. These firms tend to employ older workers who require new skills to enter sectors where they have not previously worked.[125] Analysis suggests that while TAA provides a small income safety net, on average it does not increase the likelihood that a participant will receive a new job that provides an income similar to that of the position lost.[126] The development of a long-term unemployment insurance system could be a better solution than TAA. In theory, workers being displaced in sectors pressured by imports could move into growth sectors, but as Autor and Dorn suggest, they are more likely to move to a low-skilled service industry. This suggests that we need a more comprehensive approach than unemployment insurance to assist trade-displaced workers.

Displaced workers who see their incomes decline because of trade are part of a much larger problem of inequality. Real median family income in the United States was $32,101 in 1954, and by the end of 2015 it had grown to $70,697. However, it must be noted that in 2000 median income was $69,822, indicating nearly a decade and a half of income stagnation.[127] During this same period, the share of income going to the top 1% and 10% increased from 9.39% and 32.12% to 18.39% and 47.81%, respectively. This corresponds to an increase in the average income for the bottom 90% of the population from $21,852 to $33,218, while the top 10% saw their average income increase from $93,095 to $273,843.[128] Although median household income in one 2015 Census survey at last showed larger returns for lower- and middle-income earners, it is not clear if this is just a statistical outlier or that income is still at the 2007 and 2000 median income levels.[129] So it is too early to see if this is a modest trend, and it still stands against more than a decade and a half of stagnation. The list of possible policies put forward is extensive. Standard proposals include raising the minimum wage; rewriting the tax code to help low-wage workers, which would be offset by increasing revenue from high-income taxpayers; increasing support for education; improving the social safety net; and restoring collective bargaining rights to workers.[130] There are a variety of arguments that attempt to explain the increase in inequality over the last half century; the most commonly cited, and the one we will focus on, is technological advancement.

As detailed earlier, Claudia Goldin and Lawrence F. Katz point to the education level of the U.S. workforce as the main driver of income inequality. To briefly recap, technological advancement, which as we have seen was rapid in the twentieth century, results in increased demand for skilled labor. Until the 1970s, economic growth was shared to a much larger degree than it had been in the nineteenth century. Goldin and Katz look at two educational attainment levels, high school and college. Essentially, when the supply of skilled workers is higher than the demand, the wage premium decreases, shrinking inequality. The rapid increase in the percentage of high school and college graduates explains the increasing equality pre-1970, but the supply (as college graduation rates stagnated) fell behind the demand in the decades since, with wage premiums going to the skilled, so inequality increased.[131] Along with the findings from analyses of Trade Adjustment Assistance programs, new skills and education become very important issues, to which we will return in more depth in chapter 8, on workforce development.

In a roundabout way, we have come back to the problem of nonbalanced growth. Manufacturing productivity increases, so high-skilled jobs are maintained and lower-skilled jobs are lost. These displaced workers will end up in the service sector, where there is a dearth of middle-skilled jobs.[132] Is it possible to increase college graduation rates, given the premium that the highly skilled have captured? In 2015, 91% of those 25 to 29 years old held a high school diploma, 46% had an associate's degree or higher, 25% had a bachelor's or higher, and 9% held a master's degree or higher.[133] This suggests that there are still opportunities to increase access to higher education. Indeed, the implementation of the Federal STEM Education 5-Year Strategic Plan as a cross-agency priority goal in the Obama administration focused on this goal in areas with direct relevance to manufacturing.[134] But it is also far from clear that even if the skill level of the workforce increases it will keep up with technological change so that wage polarization will decline to the point that there will be strong growth in middle-income jobs. This is predicated on keeping innovation moving ahead to drive growth, without being impacted by the structural changes taking place in the economy.

Another large issue is that the manufacturing process is detached from research and development in most economic models. This can be seen in a model created by Gene Grossman and Elhanan Helpman. It is arguable that Grossman and Helpman may have done more than any other economists in the last two decades to keep innovation embedded in the larger discourse of the discipline. In effect, their model shows how an economy with two sectors, research and development and manufacturing, with workers of varying skills sorted between the two, will lead to inequality, which only increases further when the country opens up to trade.[135] Models of the exchange of goods tend to address spatial questions in a concise, straightforward manner, simply adding in transportation costs. But are there costs to transmitting technology, ideas, or concepts across distances? One reasonable response would be that there used to be, but information technology has advanced to the point where not only is it cheap but it is also possible to transmit knowledge in a variety of formats. Computer-aided design (CAD) allows for rapid digital transmission, significantly reducing the cost of locating design and production far apart. The issue is that there is interplay between design and production: there are still constant judgments that need to be made that affect a variety of factors, such as speed, competitiveness, and cost. In certain situations, there may be no efficient optimal algorithms, problems of intractability may arise, and heuristic approaches need to be relied on.[136] Complexity places limits on the degree to which certain problems can be solved or information can be fully codified. There may still be a premium on proximity between production and design in many cases.

In his book *The Tacit Dimension*, polymath Michael Polanyi explores the idea of tacit knowledge. He notes, "I shall reconsider human knowledge by starting from the fact that *we can know more than we can tell*."[137] The spread of tacit knowledge within a business is most commonly the result of direct contact and personal relationships. Information technology allows for collaboration across distance but does not appear capable of playing the same role as direct contact. One interesting finding is that for organizations that have not developed strong cultures of trust and cooperation, much less tacit knowledge is shared.[138] There does seem to be evidence that more advanced communications technology—videoconferencing versus email—impairs the ability of people to communicate less than thought, but it is still less effective than face-to-face interaction.[139] Physical proximity plays an important role in the development of human capital, knowledge, and technology. These have historically been the key determinants of economic growth.

Manufacturing is not a process distinct from the rest of the innovation system. The development of manufacturing processes in the semiconductor industry is an interesting example. In some cases, there are separate development and production facilities, so when a new process is developed, it is transferred to the production facility. However, learning by doing takes place during the development phase, and much of this learning is lost when it is transferred. Hatch and Mowery found that if the two facilities are close together and have duplicate machinery, it is much more efficient to introduce new technologies. Bugs in new processes also require a shift in engineering to the production facilities.[140] Feedback loops are created between the two facilities because of the interplay of product and process innovation.

As explored earlier, simply relying on the idea of an innovation pipeline, a linear process where government funds basic research, which leads to corporate R&D followed by design and production, is an oversimplification. There can also be induced innovation, typically led by industry, which follows market signals or government regulations. Extended pipeline innovation, where the government, usually the military in the United States, supports not only research but also development, and creates test beds and initial markets, pushing products across the "Valley of Death," appears more efficient in hastening advancement. In other words, the proximity of the innovation actors across sectors and their connecting links appear important. Advances in manufacturing technologies and processes can also lead to a variety of innovations, with impacts throughout the chain of innovation. A collaborative model where business, government, and other stakeholders can systematically move an innovation all the way through production[141] has been particularly successful in the German production system, as explored in chapters 6 and 8. Nelson's work on the importance to innovation of effective innovation organization and systems, discussed earlier, underscores the significance of this approach. The point is that we need to treat production as part of the innovation system, as we will discuss in chapter 6. In effect, we need to go beyond a mechanistic, linear economic model; in this linear model, there is basic research funded by the government, because it can be considered a public good. Then market incentives take over, creating and bringing products to market, with at most a federal patent system, so companies can recoup the costs of their research. This model inherently limits the collaborative proximity that can further technological advances.

With universities, federal research labs, and private industry all participating in the process of innovation, it should not be surprising that there tend to be geographical concentrations of advanced jobs. These concentrations of firms and people result in agglomeration economies. There are three common theories on why industrial agglomeration occurs. If there are enough firms in one area, they are likely to share suppliers, specialized business services are more likely to locate in the area, and there is likely to be a substantial number of workers with experience. Specialized workers are more likely to locate in an area where there are multiple employment opportunities; switching jobs is easier if you do not have to move somewhere new. Finally, tacit knowledge is more likely to spread when people are concentrated in one location.[142] There also appears to be evidence that the agglomeration of small firms results in far more job creation than in large firms.[143] As Edward Glaeser notes, agglomeration occurs as a result of transportation costs. While shipping costs have come down, the cost of moving people has not.[144] Agglomeration can occur in service sectors as well as in mixed service and manufacturing sectors; there is no inherent reason it would be limited just to manufacturing firms.

The purely theoretical rationales for why policy should not favor manufacturing over the service sector also seem to fall short when one looks at the data on innovation. In 2013, just over $450 billion was spent in the

United States on research and development. Of this, about $322 billion came from the private sector.[145] While the federal government is the primary funder of basic research, the private sector undertakes later-stage applied research and particularly development. These combined investments lie at the heart of the country's innovation system. Again, just as productivity and firm size are connected, research is dominated by large firms (those with over 500 employees) that spend 83.6% of private sector research money.[146] It should come as no surprise that manufacturing industries account for 68.7% of all business R&D.[147] A possible explanation for this is that manufacturing firms typically have a formalized process to bring innovation to market. Services, which have historically invested very little in R&D, do not have the same formal structure as manufacturing and tend to be more reactive to customer demands. One explanation for this is that innovation in products and processes is more difficult to standardize in the service sector. Part of the concern about the far less formalized innovation system in the service sector is that it is less consistent. In 2002, at the end of the "dotcom" bubble, R&D spending by services accounted for nearly 43% of all private sector R&D. By 2005, it had fallen to 30%, nearly the same level it is at now, according to the most recent data.[148] This highlights the close relationship between information and communications technology (IT) and service sector innovation.

The integrated circuit is the backbone of the IT revolution. The worldwide semiconductor industry is responsible for continuously pushing the industry forward. In 2013, worldwide sales reached $305.6 billion, while the industry as a whole spent $50.3 billion on research and development.[149] It is the constant innovation in this industry that helps enable innovation in a wide range of products using this core technology, whether the next iPhone or software apps. A look at computer operating system minimum requirements from the last few decades provides an interesting reminder of this. Windows 95 required a minimum of 4 MB of memory; Windows XP, released in 2001, required 64 MB of memory; and this had increased to 1 GB for Windows 7 and then 2 GB for the new operating system Windows 10. Over twenty years, the amount of memory needed to run the current operating system increased five hundredfold. This incredible progress has been driven by Moore's Law, Gordon Moore's 1965 observation about doubling the number of transistors on an integrated circuit wafer, with a corresponding reduction by half in the price per transistor, every two years, increasing the number of transistors from about 1000 to 20 billion over fifty years.[150] In 2015, more transistors were produced than there were leaves on the world's trees, some 400 billion billion, or 13 trillion produced every second.[151] This is a triumph in manufacturing innovation as well as in technology innovation; the two are deeply linked. So, production advances were critical to enabling semiconductor advancement, boosted at a critical period, as discussed in chapter 2, by a government-industry collaboration, Sematech. It now appears that the steady pace of semiconductor progress that has driven the IT revolution has reached its end.[152] So while the performance of integrated circuits will continue to advance, other technologies will need to be developed if computing power is going to continue as rapidly. As Jorgenson has shown, semiconductor technology advances were the core driver of the IT innovation wave.[153] The manufacturing advances were as critical as the technology advances and, combined, spawned a massive new economic sector. Computer chips truly are not the same as potato chips. What will replace semiconductor advances as an innovation driver?

As with semiconductors, the next generation of products, both goods and services, will depend on advancements in manufacturing. The question is whether this will occur in the United States. Remaining on the technological frontier is key to productivity and economic growth. As argued earlier, colocation plays an important role in innovation, and manufacturing provides an outsized share of the funding for research and development. A strong indicator of this preference for colocation can be seen in the development of the Chinese manufacturing sector. One estimate of this growth is the change in employment in urban manufacturing, which increased from about 40 million in 2003 to just under 80 million in 2014.[154] From 2003 to 2012, majority-owned foreign affiliates of U.S. companies increased their R&D expenditures in China from $565 million to just over $2 billion.[155] Multinational corporations had set up fewer than 200 research and development centers in China in 2000, but this grew to more than 1300 as of 2013.[156] The idea that manufacturing can be moved to the locations with the cheapest labor and that high-value research, development, and design can remain at home ignores a number of important factors. Apple is often cited as a successful example, with high-value design taking place in the United States while much-lower-value manufacturing and assembly occurs in China. As Apple has faced political hurdles and growing domestic competition, its strategy has begun to change. From 2012 to 2016, Apple opened over 20 new corporate offices in China. The company has also announced that it will open its first four R&D centers and invest $507 million in research in China by the end of 2017.[157] While the world is more connected than ever because of IT, distance still matters when production and innovation are separated, even in the IT sector.

Closing Thoughts: Innovation Economics

Globalization has had an interesting effect on inequality both between individuals and between firms. While growing income inequality is discussed in the media, the same is not true for firms. If we go back to models with both heterogeneous firms and trade, there is a similar trend between the two. Large firms with high productivity and highly skilled workers have benefited disproportionately over the last few decades. Recent work suggests the two are related. In 2014, there were an estimated 288 manufacturing firms in the United States that employed more than 10,000 people out of a total of 251,901 firms.[158] In U.S. firms with less than 10,000 employees, 84% of the increase in inequality can be explained by growing differences in wages between firms, not by increasing inequality within firms. The authors of this study also found workers were segregating into high-wage or low-wage firms, decreasing the variance within firms.[159] Globalization and increased competition over technological advances would seem to have had a very polarizing effect on the United States.

This should raise questions about whether the current policy discussions based on leading economic theories offer a way forward. We live in a world where the theory of second best dominates. An optimal outcome may simply be impossible or, as is often the case, simply not politically feasible in a democratic country. We need to begin to acknowledge that a free market policy that leaves some members of the community worse off is not acceptable if no policies are put forward that would ameliorate the situation have any chance to be implemented. The political discussion about manufacturing over the last few years has highlighted this. In the 2016 election, not only did one major party candidate move away from support for free trade, but the other candidate went so far as to advocate for a complete reversal of U.S. policy from the postwar period and use tariffs to address domestic issues. Because of the complex nature of modern supply chains spread across boundaries, it is very difficult to see an outcome where large portions of the population would not end up worse economically by using tariffs.

While one could argue that public support of policies like this occurs either because large segments of the population are uninformed or just not rational, odds are that it is in fact a rational reaction. Work is central to the identity of most people, and the workplace situates people within a certain set of norms and a workplace culture.[160] The loss of a job or an industry in a small town can threaten its identity. For many people, this raises the attractiveness of a policy that promises to replace lost industries. One question is, why is it that more of the public does not agree to compensate those who lose from trade? Neoclassical economics and neoliberalism have provided the rationale for market liberalization, but at the same time, by underestimating trade effects, undercut the most efficient means to address the distributional issues that arise. Adjustment costs get pushed out of the policy picture by these perspectives, so the idea that government should support people financially while they transition to new jobs because of economic shocks and shifts becomes the view that the failure to find a new job quickly is an individual shortcoming rather than a societal one. Given this long-standing reality, it would seem that one sound way forward is to focus on an innovative, inclusive economy.

As suggested earlier, inequality problems will likely fester unless skills are raised more systematically by expanded education. But this approach will be undercut unless there is corresponding innovation-based growth. While manufacturing innovation policies certainly do not solve all of the economic problems facing the country, they do present a feasible way forward. Small manufacturers that have been squeezed because of competition could have the opportunity to gain access to results of research and development, with corresponding advances in efficiency and competitiveness, that they could never afford by themselves. Large manufacturers benefit from participation by university research in manufacturing, an area where it has not focused in the past. Workforce education and development efforts give employees at all levels the opportunity to develop skills that are in demand from manufacturers moving up the production value chain. The aim is to increase the skills of the workforce, which in turn should raise wages. By incorporating innovation for smaller manufacturers, these could have an opportunity to move toward the technological frontier, increasing their productivity and hopefully narrowing the gap with large firms, which could lower inequality between firms, and corresponding wage rates.

Summary

This chapter has provided an overview of how manufacturing has informed the development of economic theory over two and a half centuries and, in turn, how economics has considered manufacturing. While Adam Smith clearly saw its economic significance, the story has become more complex in recent decades. Growth economics elevated technology-based innovation (and the related advances around it) as the dominant factor in economic growth, but neoclassical economics had difficulty treating the complex systems around innovation—including the production phase—as "endogenous" to economics. "New Growth Theory" economists have tried to make innovation endogenous, but this is an ongoing effort. So far, economists have been unable to model the innovation system, including its manufacturing elements. This has meant that manufacturing continues to be imperfectly understood in economics. Productivity concepts have offered a supplementary framework, however; they raise issues about low-productivity sectors, such as services, which could drag down economy-wide growth—Baumol's cost disease. Lessening this drag on the economy requires an effective innovation system to boost productivity across the economy, including in manufacturing, historically a leading source of productivity advancement. Nelson's work on the importance of sound innovation organization and systems to innovation and corresponding productivity provides a supporting pillar for this point. Innovation gains can play an important role in offsetting inefficiencies in manufacturing and some services. Information technology is an example of innovation interdependence, where the productivity gains can enter both the manufacturing and service sectors. Chapter 3 argued, however, that without a healthy manufacturing sector, much of the innovation system, and corresponding productivity gains, breaks down.

Although most economists still assume gains from free trade for all participants over time, Paul Samuelson has noted potential long-term adverse consequences of trade for trade losers, and David Autor and his colleagues tracked enduring adverse consequences from trade in U.S. manufacturing communities. Recently, New Trade Theory has been focusing on productivity as a core competitive factor in trade. This theory has been moving away from a national competitive perspective to a more focused, competitive firm perspective, taking into account heterogeneous firms. With increased trade competition, innovative firms, which disproportionately are larger firms, can thrive, while smaller, less productive firms cannot afford the requisite R&D investment for innovation so they run into difficulty. Advanced manufacturing innovation policies, organized to improve production efficiency across firms of various sizes, arguably could be seen as consistent with the direction of this theory. However, mainstream neoclassical economics seems a step behind these developments, not fully addressing New Growth Theory, New Trade Theory, productivity perspectives, innovation organization, and their possible implications for the new economic look at manufacturing suggested here.

Of course, there is no guarantee of the outcome, but the real economic world is not full of perfectly competitive markets or information. In fact, most of the growth models we have looked at are not set in a framework of perfect competition; they have leaned heavily on the work of Joseph Schumpeter. While discussing the role of imperfect markets in growth,

Schumpeter wrote that "perfect competition is not only impossible but inferior, and has no title to being set up as a model of ideal efficiency. It is hence a mistake to base the theory of government regulation of industry on the principle that big business should be made to work as the respective industry would work in perfect competition."[161]

Pareto optimal outcomes are not the norm but the exception, so arguing from the standpoint of perfect markets against intervention in the markets to strengthen the innovation system, including manufacturing, does not mean the outcome will always be efficient or desirable. In chapter 5, we turn to the recent history of the introduction of innovation policy into manufacturing and the role the U.S. government has played in attempting to foster innovation in the sector.

5 Advanced Manufacturing Emerges at the Federal Level

"Half the people I talk to say 'This is the most important thing for the nation,' and the other half look at me quite quizzically, as if to say, 'Didn't you get the memo? America doesn't do manufacturing anymore'—a very worrying response. After more than a century of industrial success, America needs to revise its economic assumptions once again."

—Susan Hockfield, President, MIT, Co-Chair, Advanced Manufacturing Partnership, September 15, 2011

"The political reality is that manufacturing serves as a proxy for the American people for our economic might. And its decline serves as a proxy for the decline in our economic might."

—Ron Bloom, Senior Counselor to the President on Manufacturing Policy, September 15, 2011

Barack Obama was sworn in as president on January 20, 2009, and that winter day, with the nation in economic crisis, had something of the feeling of Franklin Roosevelt's inauguration in 1933, with the nation caught in the Depression. Obama faced the Great Recession, the first economic crisis since the 1930s to approach Depression levels of economic decline, with a 10% unemployment rate, the highest long-term unemployment rate since the Depression,[1] and over fifteen million unemployed.[2] In particular, the auto industry had collapsed, with General Motors and Chrysler in bankruptcy, smashing a large part of the manufacturing supplier sector, and a reeling financial sector was simply not lending. Frantic government efforts to return to tolerable growth levels were relying almost exclusively on short-term stabilization policies. Neoclassical economists were at the helm, pressing their menu of fiscal and monetary plans, including "shovel ready" economic stimulus efforts, to coax the price signals that could restore investment to nurture positive rates of growth.

The problem was that these stabilization policies were limited in their ability to offset long-term underinvestment in the economic assets and factors that create the larger growth multipliers needed.[3] For a significant period, as NIST's former chief economist Gregory Tassey has argued, this longer-term underinvestment had led to declining U.S. competitiveness and slower rates of growth. In other words, short-term stabilization was simply not enough; the problems were deeply structural and required a structural response. As Tassey put it: "Thirty-five years of trade deficits in manufactured products cannot be explained by business cycles, currency shifts, and trade barriers, or by suboptimal use of monetary and short term fiscal policies. High rates of productivity growth are the policy solution, which can be accomplished only over time from sustained investment in intellectual, physical, human, organizational, and technical infrastructure capital. Implementing this imperative requires a public-private asset growth model emphasizing investment in technology."[4] It was not that the stimulus was unnecessary, but alone it was insufficient.

Ron Bloom and the Restructuring of the Auto Industry

In 2009, President Obama named Ron Bloom as senior advisor on the President's Task Force on the Automotive Industry. As deputy on the Auto Team at the Treasury Department, he played a dynamic role in the government takeover of most of the auto industry and the subsequent restructuring of two of the "big three" auto firms, General Motors and Chrysler. Bloom's background fitted him for the task. He held union jobs after college, but he then decided unions lacked financial sector knowledge so he went to Harvard Business School. He then worked at Lazard Freres, a major investment banking firm, before going on to create his own firm to represent unions and employee groups, advising the Steelworkers Union and facilitating the restructuring of a series of manufacturing firms—LTV, Bethlehem Steel, Goodyear Tire and Rubber, and Wheeling Pitt. A veteran negotiator and restructuring expert, he was trusted by labor but could talk finance to management—he was ideal for the job. Bloom played a particularly central role in Chrysler's restructuring, as well as a major role in GM's. The firms had been taken over by the government, but by April 21, 2010, GM had paid back its last outstanding federal loan, leaving the government with 60% of its common stock and $2.1 billion in preferred stock, which were redeemed over time. Four months earlier, on Labor Day 2009, Bloom took on a new role for the president, senior counselor for manufacturing policy, assigned to revitalize the manufacturing sector. This shifted Bloom from a fiscal restructuring role directly into the technology policy space Tassey deemed so critical. This technology focus did not spring up entirely on its own;

in addition to Tassey, it was buttressed by an ongoing series of significant policy articles that helped it gain momentum.[5] Meanwhile, two projects, at the Massachusetts Institute of Technology (MIT) and at the White House Office of Science and Technology Policy, were progressing that would help inform a new manufacturing technology strategy.

MIT's Production in the Innovation Economy Study Begins

MIT, a land-grant university founded in 1861 with a practical outlook and an orientation toward industry and science in the public service, had created an informal expectation that its presidents should serve on the board of an industrial firm to stay fluent with industry needs and currents. MIT president Susan Hockfield was therefore serving on the board of General Electric (GE), giving her a catbird seat to observe the sharp decline of American manufacturing during the Great Recession. At GE, CEO Jeff Immelt was in the process of reorienting his massive company away from a tilt toward financial services and back toward technology and product innovation, and Hockfield was a keen observer. With alarm bells going off around the country because of massive unemployment levels, she and her staff began convening a group of MIT faculty to discuss whether a new innovation-oriented strategy around manufacturing should be developed.[6] On March 1, 2009, she convened a roundtable of 11 MIT faculty, open to the campus, to consider innovation policies, calling on the United States to innovate its way out of the recession.[7] Robert Solow, winner of a Nobel Prize in Economics and the founder of growth economics theory, introduced the discussion, arguing that to offset its enormous current account deficit, the United States must improve the productivity of its industrial economy through technological innovation, targeting sectors with growing markets as opposed to shrinking ones.[8]

A follow-on MIT roundtable was held on March 29, 2010, focusing on advanced technologies for manufacturing.[9] Recalling MIT's history in the late 1980s in formulating policy to contend with manufacturing competition with Japan and Germany through the books *Made in America* and *The Machine That Changed the World*,[10] President Hockfield noted that the United States needed to create some 20 million jobs in the coming decade to recover from the current downturn and meet upcoming job needs: "It's very hard to imagine where those jobs are going to come from unless we seriously get busy reinventing manufacturing. No matter how brilliant our innovations, they are not going to translate into strong, durable job growth unless a substantial fraction of these new technologies really is made in America."[11]

Professor Suzanne Berger (author of the 2006 book *How We Compete,*[12] which explained how U.S. firms used IT-based technologies to enable distributed manufacturing) made a case for the problems in store for the United States if it continued to treat manufacturing as a "sunset" sector, noting the important connection between the innovation system and production. She argued that, "Above all the U.S. needs to think about the new technologies, new products and new processes that could already be identified in MIT labs: Can they be brought to the market if new manufacturing industries cannot be developed?"[13] DARPA deputy director Ken Gabriel was the visiting keynote speaker and discussed a deep production problem faced by the Department of Defense (DOD) where even its more complex platform technologies required ever longer development times at ever greater expense, arguing that DOD needed a new production approach to "cut across the seams" of the development and production stages with a systems approach to the entire manufacturing process.[14] MIT faculty at the roundtable then discussed possible new production strands: advanced materials, bioinspired materials, nanomanufacturing, robotics and AI in manufacturing, production using RFID and sensors, and sustainable production. Already, we can see the concepts that would lead to a new manufacturing strategy: it would focus around "advanced manufacturing," aimed at innovating in the production system, with new production technologies plus new technologies that would require new means of production. It was an innovation response to manufacturing decline, not a fiscal signal response.

Hockfield soon commissioned a group of MIT faculty and researchers to focus on innovation and its relation to manufacturing, and determine whether and how a robust manufacturing sector was critical to the U.S. innovation economy. The project was named "Production in the Innovation Economy." "PIE" launched an MIT-style, data-driven investigation that commenced a two-year study with interviews of over 250 firms and surveys of over 1000 more, across the nation and the world, with case studies of manufacturing in four U.S. regions and in China and Germany.[15] Throughout the PIE project, the MIT project kept the White House, agency officials, and other policymakers informed about the policy ideas and findings that were emerging from the study.

White House 2011 Advanced Manufacturing Report

In parallel to MIT's project, a small group in the White House Office of Science and Technology Policy (OSTP) had been developing a report urging a strong new commitment by the administration to manufacturing. Led by

Sridhar Kota, previously a mechanical engineering professor at the University of Michigan, the report had been delayed because of questions from neoclassical economist Richard Levin, president of Yale and a leader on the President's Council of Advisors on Science and Technology (PCAST), which had to issue the report. Levin had been in communication with Lawrence Summers, the director of the White House National Economic Council and former president of Harvard. It was a classic economist versus engineer exchange—what justification could there be for according manufacturing economic or policy priority over other sectors?

The tenor of this internal debate can be sensed from an op-ed a few months later, noted in chapter 4. Christina Romer, chair of the President's Council of Economic Advisors in 2009–2010, wrote her *New York Times* op-ed titled "Do Manufacturers Need Special Treatment?" at the beginning of 2012.[16] The analytic elements were discussed in chapter 4, but two more subjective comments were particularly problematic to observers of the manufacturing decline: she suggested that Americans valued services like "haircuts" as much as manufactured goods, and she insisted that "public policy needs to go beyond sentiment," denigrating a policy focus on manufacturing. She was directly attacking her recent boss Obama's manufacturing policies extolled in his State of the Union speech ten days earlier, and her comments tended to be a lightning rod, attracting the damaged manufacturing sector's lightning.

Romer's argument that manufacturing jobs are economically equivalent to service jobs missed key points. As discussed earlier, manufacturing jobs have the highest job multiplier effect; that is, they lead to more jobs throughout the economy than do jobs in other sectors. Manufacturing is also an innovation driver, so critical related sectors, research and design, are also vital to technological innovation and therefore growth. But as Stephen Ezell of ITIF pointed out in rapid response to Romer, the top reason that manufacturing should be a preferred sector is that it is still America's largest "traded sector." In other words, much of its sales occur abroad, so it spurs exports and the accompanying positive trade gains and national wealth. Since trade in goods completely outweighs trade in services, Ezell noted that manufacturing will be the leading traded sector "for a long time, and it is simply impossible to have a vibrant economy without a healthy traded sector."[17]

In the final version of the 2011 manufacturing report, issued through PCAST, wording to accommodate traditional economists was included by incorporating a market failure rationale and national security justification.[18] It asserted that the report's proposals were not heavy-handed "industrial policy," where government invests in particular sectors or firms, but simply an extension of long-established government support for "innovation policy."[19] All politics tends to be local, as Tip O'Neill observed, and the President himself was fluent with what the manufacturing sector in his home state of Illinois had been going through. For example, in his 2004 speech to the Democratic National Convention, which was so critical to his emergence as a presidential candidate, then Senator Obama spoke of "the workers I met in Galesburg, Illinois, who are losing their union jobs at the Maytag plant that's moving to Mexico, and now they're having to compete with their own children for jobs that pay 7 bucks an hour."[20] Obama in turn was moving more toward economic policy pragmatists like Gene Sperling, who became chair of the National Economic Council in January 2011 and was a strong supporter of advanced manufacturing policies.

The final OSTP report, titled "Ensuring American Leadership in Advanced Manufacturing," defined advanced manufacturing as the manufacture of conventional or novel products through processes that depend on the coordination of information, automation, computation, software, sensing, and networking, and/or make use of cutting edge materials and emerging scientific capabilities.[21] The report argued that federal investments in such manufacturing could enable the United States to regain its status as a global leader in manufacturing, which would retain high-paying jobs, support domestic innovation, and enhance national security. However, the failure to lead in production would potentially jeopardize the nation's ability to develop the next generation of advanced products. Retention of manufacturing would enable new synergies, whereby design, engineering, scale-up, and production processes provide the feedback for the conception and innovation sectors to generate both new technologies and new later-generation products.

The report proposed "shared facilities and infrastructure," where small and midsize manufacturing firms could develop new production approaches embodying productivity gains, allowing these firms to more rapidly prototype, test, and make new products.[22] It recommended federal applied research support of "advanced manufacturing" processes that cut across a range of production sectors to enable producers to more rapidly develop new U.S.-made sectors. This included, interestingly, "Supporting the creation and dissemination of powerful design methodologies that dramatically expand the ability of entrepreneurs to design products and processes."[23]

It further recommended partnerships between industry, universities, and government, with government and industry co-investment, that could develop emerging technologies, such as "nanomanufacturing, flexible electronics, electronics, information technology-enabled manufacturing, and advanced materials," that could lead to the transformation of U.S. manufacturing.[24] Included in the recommendations was a proposed "Advanced Manufacturing Initiative" across government agencies that could link industry-university collaborations to develop more detailed approaches.[25] The report was released in June 2011 and provided initial material and perspectives for the next stage to work from. The strands identified, then, included "shared facilities" for small and medium-sized enterprises (SMEs), industry-university partnerships around manufacturing technologies, R&D on new processes, developing new manufacturing design methodologies, and a cross-agency government effort. Most importantly, the report and the parallel announcement of the Advanced Manufacturing Partnership (AMP) locked in a White House commitment to a manufacturing innovation strategy.

The Advanced Manufacturing Partnership Begins

Now, back to Bloom—and friends. Ron Bloom completed his dual-hatted role, where he was both the Treasury official in charge of the Auto Task Force and the president's adviser on manufacturing policy, and moved over to the White House at the beginning of 2011 to do exclusively the second job, with his deputy Jason Miller. Bloom and Miller engineered the White House announcement on June 24, 2011,[26] at Carnegie Mellon University in Pittsburg, of an "Advanced Manufacturing Partnership" (AMP), which named Dow Chemical CEO Andrew Liveris and MIT president Susan Hockfield as cochairs of a consortium rounded up by Bloom for President Obama.

Liveris, a forceful man with a graying moustache, was the author of a highly practical and personal new book on the central economic importance of manufacturing.[27] Australian-born to a family of Greek immigrants, he retained the Aussie accent, spoke with authority, and, like many foreign-born Americans, cared deeply where his adopted nation of four decades was heading. Dow was headquartered in Midland, Michigan, a company town, and its leaders were anchored in the hard-working, plainspoken industrial Midwest. Hockfield was a natural because she and MIT's PIE team had been providing Washington officials with their developing insights. She was a sharp and determined neuroscientist who did her science at the elite Cold Spring Harbor medical research center before becoming a dean and provost at Yale. She became MIT's president in 2006. What was of interest about her at MIT was not so much that she was its first woman president but that she was its first life scientist president—demonstrating to MIT that its powerful life science researchers and the thriving biopharma cluster they helped build around the campus had reached a critical leadership stage. At MIT,

Hockfield developed the idea that a university could launch major, cross-disciplinary, cross-school policy initiatives, joining strong MIT scientists and engineers with strong economists, management analysts, political scientists, and international affairs experts. She announced the first initiative around energy at her inauguration, where MIT served up a rich series of technology reports that began to influence energy policy and legislation, led by physics professor Ernest Moniz, who later became the nation's secretary of energy. The next initiative was around "convergence," the merger of the health sciences with the physical and engineering sciences for a new breakthrough research model. Then, while the country was still reeling from the 2008 economic crash, came advanced manufacturing. As noted, Hockfield served on General Electric's board and observed its CEO Jeff Immelt change the direction of the company toward a reengagement with technology development and production. Liveris and Hockfield brought to AMP the same intensity they brought to their day jobs; AMP had a mission.

On the industry side, AMP included CEOs from a diverse group of major companies, spread across a landscape of industrial sectors. Dow was from the chemical sector, Northrup Grumman and United Technologies from aerospace, Procter and Gamble from consumer products, Ford from automotive, Intel from semiconductors, Caterpillar from heavy construction equipment, Corning from fiber and advanced materials, Johnson and Johnson from pharmaceuticals and medical products, Honeywell from systems and software for hard technology sectors, Allegheny from energy, transport, and insurance, and Stryker from medical technologies. On the university side, it included presidents of six schools with very strong engineering and applied science programs: MIT, Carnegie Mellon, the University of California at Berkeley, Stanford University, the University of Michigan, and the Georgia Institute of Technology.[28] On the government side, the chair of the National Economic Council, Gene Sperling, an activist lawyer with a sharp understanding of the economic role of technology, and acting commerce secretary Rebecca Blank, an economist and a student of the interaction between economic and labor markets, co-led a cross-agency effort. Within the White House, Jason Miller at the National Economic Council (NEC) and David Hart and Charles Thorpe at OSTP provided leadership. The agencies deeply involved in supporting the effort, and some of their involved personnel, were NIST (led by Pat Gallagher, Phillip Singerman, and Michael Molnar), NSF (through its Engineering Directorate, led by Thomas Peterson, Steven McKnight, and Bruce Kramer), DOE (at first through its acting undersecretary, Arun Majumdar, then through its Energy Efficiency and Renewable Energy office, led by David Danielson and Mark Johnson), and DOD (through its Manufacturing and Industrial Base Policy office's Mantech program, led by Brett Lambert, Neil Orringer, Adele Ratcliff, and Steven Linder). The President's Council of Advisors on Science and Technology (PCAST), based in the White House Office of Science and Technology, provided an administrative home for the effort; it formally issued the reports written by AMP.

In launching the new partnership, the President highlighted the need to "reinvigorate" American manufacturing, once "the ticket to a middle-class life." He called for "developing new technologies that will dramatically reduce the time required to design, build, and test manufactured goods," with leading universities and companies complementing federal efforts "to invent, deploy and scale these cutting-edge technologies." He argued that, "With these key investments, we can ensure that the United States remains a nation that 'invents it here and manufactures it here.' "[29] "We have not run out of stuff to make," he said, citing robotics, materials, solar energy, and automobiles as examples of fields where new technology may prove revolutionary; he argued that inventing and commercializing this technology will create jobs and export opportunities for the United States.[30] The OSTP report on "Ensuring American Leadership on Advanced Manufacturing" was released on the same day that AMP was announced, to help buttress the rationale for a new partnership.

Setting up AMP was Ron Bloom's parting shot. Bloom aimed to form a strong public-private partnership to design an enduring innovation policy effort for manufacturing with industry and university buy-in; once its formation was assured, he left the stage, stepping down from his White House job and leaving day-to-day oversight in the hands of his deputy, Jason Miller of the NEC and special assistant to the president for manufacturing. The firms and universities organized and staffed the effort with support from agency staff, forming a series of topical task forces; the two supervising "technical co-leads" were Theresa Kotanchek, a vice president at Dow (who later led a big data/analytics start-up) and Professor (later Provost) Martin Schmidt of MIT. Both were deeply grounded in technology development and were astute analysts of the organizational challenges presented by transforming manufacturing. Kotanchek was assisted by Carrie Houtman of Dow.[31]

Speaking at MIT on September 15, 2011, at a PIE-sponsored forum on "Rebuilding the American Economy," Ron Bloom, who had left the White House the previous month, was introduced by MIT president Hockfield.[32] She noted (in the quotation at the outset of this chapter) that in discussions around the country about the state of U.S. manufacturing, she had been hearing from two divided camps. "Half the people I talk to say 'This is the most important thing for the nation,' and the other half look at me quite quizzically, as if to say, 'Didn't you get the memo? America doesn't do manufacturing anymore'—a very worrying response," she stated. "After more than a century of industrial success, America needs to revise its economic assumptions once again," she said. Bloom cited a then recent poll in which only 40% of Americans believed the United States was the world's top economic power. He said people simply responded that it was China, "because China makes everything." He said that while this was not correct, China's major manufacturing role makes it synonymous with economic power in the minds of many Americans: "The political reality is that manufacturing serves as a proxy for the American people for our economic might. And its decline serves as a proxy for the decline in our economic might" (as quoted at the beginning of this chapter).[33] Bloom closed his talk with a stark reminder of the social cost of manufacturing decline, a plea for workers, largely men in late middle age, who were trapped, jobless after a life of hard work, unable to support their families, and unlikely to ever again find comparable work at comparable pay. His point clearly touched the MIT audience; in retrospect, it was a preview of the 2016 election.

With few exceptions, the companies and universities that were part of AMP committed significant time from at least one senior employee, and often teams of them, to help staff the AMP effort. The participating government agencies likewise made parallel staff commitments. Ambitious working groups jointly led by industry, universities, and government were created around key topics, including technology development, shared infrastructure and facilities, education and workforce, business climate policy, and outreach, with industry and university co-leads for each.[34] Frequent live meetings, extensive prep work, and nearly constant group calls were the standard. Dozens of outside organizations and experts were consulted, and their ideas were brought into the process. The universities on the Steering Committee, in cooperation with committee companies, hosted four major regional meetings, each with hundreds of participants from small and large area firms and other organizations. These meetings featured discussions of AMP ideas and sought new ones.[35] The AMP group was outcome oriented, not simply report oriented, aiming for "actionable recommendations" that the agencies and participants were prepared to help implement. The level of commitment was highly unusual, and the one-year project kept to an intense schedule, pushed hard by Kotanchek and Schmidt. The Steering Committee of CEOs, university presidents, and top government officials, including the president, met periodically to review progress and ideas.

An early administration and AMP concept was to create "Advanced Manufacturing Institutes" similar to the Fraunhofer Institutes to creatively bring together into single public-private entities the technology development ideas being evaluated by AMP work groups. There are 60 Fraunhofer Institutes, operating in every region of Germany, fostering collaborations between the "mittelstand" (Germany's SMEs), larger firms, and engineers from academic institutions to foster technology and process advances. Although there were U.S. government programs related to manufacturing,[36] a Fraunhofer model was a dramatic new thrust. It was snapped up as an idea for implementation by the administration long before AMP submitted its final report containing this recommendation. The president strongly backed manufacturing in his February 2012 State of the Union address[37] and then in March called for creating 15 manufacturing institutes at a visit to an aircraft engine facility.[38] He reiterated that call in his February 2013 State of the Union address.[39] What was going on behind all this?

In working closely with AMP, it was clear that the president and his team wanted to move forward on announcing a plan in the FY2013 budget that included the institutes.[40] But the full plan—15 institutes supported by some $1 billion in federal funding—would likely require support from a deeply divided Congress. Following up on what would be the strong manufacturing focus in the 2012 State of the Union address, the president's economic team, led by Gene Sperling and Jason Miller, wanted to promote the institutes as something the president could announce to follow on the legislative requests he made in the State of the Union speech. But Sperling and Miller decided that the "vision" would be more powerful and would only be fully understood if the administration could create a pilot institute as a concrete example. Getting the funding for a pilot institute would mean that a mission agency with a technology need—Defense or Energy—would have to be willing to step forward.

Miller set up a dinner in late 2011 and invited the manufacturing leaders from four different agencies—Arun Majumdar (DOE), Subra Suresh (NSF), Pat Gallagher (Commerce/NIST), and Brett Lambert (DOD)—to convince them that it would be worthwhile for their agencies to jointly fund an institute. During the meal, after much back-and-forth, Brett Lambert forcefully announced that he and DOD would take the lead—and he would personally find the funds needed so long as each of the three others would do what they could to provide additional funding and technical support. It was with that dinner that what became America Makes—the first institute, organized around 3D printing, a field the military services saw as critical—came to be. DOD then ran an institute competition that elicited widespread interest, results were announced in March, and the institute was formed in August 2012. America Makes also received funding and support from DOE, NSF, NIST, and NASA.

The institute model was an early example of the dynamic of close interaction between AMP, a committed White House, and key agencies. AMP came to represent a new innovation model—a deep public-private collaboration bringing together linked industries, universities, and government agencies for policy design and implementation at a major scale. No one had seen anything quite like this intense collaboration in recent years.

AMP1.0 July 2012 Report—"Capturing Domestic Competitive Advantage in Advanced Manufacturing"

Shortly after AMP was created by the administration, it moved, as noted, to create five work groups, co-led by industry and university leaders, around key manufacturing topics: (1) "Technology Development," to identify a mechanism for evaluating manufacturing technology priority areas and nurture these key manufacturing technologies; (2) "Shared Infrastructure and Facilities," to assess derisking and scaling new technologies through the production stage via joint facilities serving the manufacturing community, particularly small and midsize firms; (3) "Workforce Development," to identify ways to better supply the talent needed for advanced manufacturing; (4) "Policy," to recommend economic and innovation policies to improve research collaboration on manufacturing; and (5) "Outreach," to link to manufacturing firms and organizations for input, and to help organize regional meetings around the country.[41] The work group assignments provide a good picture of the tasks and policy directions AMP pursued.

The focus of AMP was on "advanced manufacturing," which the report defined as encompassing "all aspects of manufacturing, including the ability to quickly respond to customer needs, through innovations in production processes and innovations in the supply chain," which are increasingly "knowledge intensive, relying on information technologies, modeling, and simulation." It noted that manufacturing "creates more value across the economy per dollar spent than any other sector" and that manufacturing was an enabler to "fundamentally change or create new services and sectors." However, it found that the United States was losing its ability to adequately use manufacturing for these ends: "The hard truth is that the United States is lagging behind in innovation in the manufacturing sector."[42] While manufacturing trade associations and firms had long focused their agenda with the federal government on tax and trade policy, AMP's focus on advanced manufacturing through an innovation agenda marked an entirely new policy approach for this sector. It called out the deep, interactive relationship between manufacturing and innovation.[43]

The report called for an "advanced manufacturing strategy" based on a "systematic process to identify and prioritize critical cross-cutting technologies."[44] That process should lead to an ongoing strategy, which in turn could be translated into more detailed technology roadmaps for each of the new technology paradigms, and the report developed a framework for prioritizing federal investments in such technologies based on factors such as national need, global demand, U.S. manufacturing competitiveness in the field, technology readiness, and an assessment of industry, university research, and government commitment to the technology (such as whether, in the case of government, it could serve national security needs).[45] Polling groups of manufacturers and university experts, the report developed a preliminary priority list of technology areas to be pursued:[46] advancing sensing, measurement, and process control; advanced materials design, synthesis, and processing; visualization, informatics, and digital manufacturing technologies; sustainable manufacturing; nanomanufacturing, flexible electronics manufacturing, biomanufacturing, and bioinformatics; additive manufacturing; advanced manufacturing and testing equipment; industrial robotics; and advanced forming and joining technologies. Again, strategies for these areas were to be developed over time into true technology roadmaps that were to be coordinated across technologies and periodically updated.

To nurture these technologies, the report called for building R&D efforts around them. Significantly, it also called for manufacturing innovation institutes (MIIs) of small and midsize firms linked to larger firms, backed by multidisciplinary university applied science and engineering, with cost-shared funding support from government (federal and state) and participating industries.[47] The U.S. institutes were to operate at the regional level to take advantage of area industrial clusters but still be able to translate their technology and process learning to manufacturers at a national scale. To facilitate this national translation and to tie together the MIIs around joint lessons learned, the report proposed National Network of Manufacturing Innovation (NNMI) institutes. These policies were guided by a vision that there was a gap between R&D supported by government and the product development role of industry, where a support system for the stages of technology development, technology demonstration, and system/subsystem development—technology readiness levels 4 through 7[48]—was simply missing in action. The institutes' role was to fill that gap, as figure 5.1, reproduced from the report, illustrates.

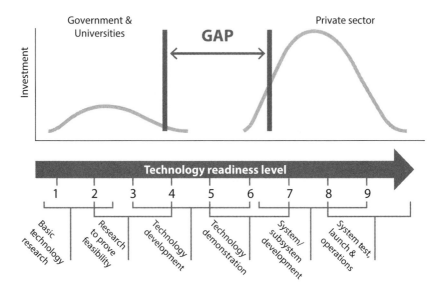

Figure 5.1
Gap in Manufacturing Innovation.
Source: AMP1.0 Report (2012), 21.

The institutes were to support the technology's development, offer shared facilities where firms could experiment with and adapt the evolving technologies, and train their workforces around it in coordination with area community colleges and universities. No one expected there to be a single "place" with everything present; networks of such shared facilities in multiple support nodes were understood to be required. The facilities, then, would primarily serve collaborative advanced prototyping, testing, and workforce training—a new kind of facility by now missing from the U.S. industrial landscape except perhaps in the largest firms. The idea was that these new institutes would recreate an industrial ecosystem missing since pressures of global competition, information technologies and the distributed production they enabled, and a financial services model of core competency that made firms less vertically connected, slimmed it down. Figure 5.2, reproduced from the report, illustrates the manufacturing innovation institute model.

AMP also looked closely at the talent base required for advanced manufacturing. It noted public surveys for the Manufacturing Institute by Deloitte that found that 86% believed manufacturing was critical to American

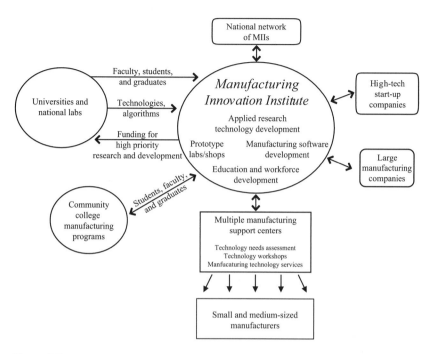

Figure 5.2
Source: AMP1.0 Report (2012), 23.

economic prosperity, that 85% believed it was key to the standard of living, and that of the types of new facilities that could be located in their communities, manufacturing plants ranked number one.[49] AMP made a series of workforce recommendations; the two with the broadest potential effect were to improve the links between manufacturing firms and community colleges to significantly expand advanced manufacturing training, and to develop partnerships between industry and community colleges to develop nationwide systems for highly marketable and transferable skills certification. After all, if there was no available talent base educated to use advanced manufacturing, it could never be implemented.

Could the AMP proposal for networked manufacturing institutes and new training models work? Could it help restore production leadership and help reconnect innovation and production? The AMP report did not elaborate on these questions, but by creating and enabling new production technologies and processes, the core notion was that U.S. producers would be better able to compete, through new efficiencies, growing productivity, and improved quality, against low-cost producers abroad, offsetting a wage advantage. Would these new technologies and processes emigrate abroad over time? Of course, but there would be three reasons why an innovation-based lead could continue: (1) there would be a "first mover" advantage that would endure for a time for the developer of the new approaches; (2) low-wage economies needing high employment levels for social and political reasons would have more difficulty shifting to a high-productivity model; and (3) once a strong process was put in place for creating and implementing these new manufacturing systems, the lead in oncoming new developments might continue.

MIT's "Production in the Innovation Economy" Study

Now, back to MIT. Its "Production in the Innovation Economy" (PIE) study emerged in 2013, after the AMP's 2012 study. It was funded by foundations and gifts, and engaged a "commission" of 20 senior faculty and nine graduate student researchers, with frequent meetings on campus and investigative studies in Europe, Asia, and the United States.[50] The group, starting in 2010, focused on regional industry case studies in Ohio, Georgia, Arizona, and their own neighborhood, Massachusetts, as well as in China and Germany. Throughout, the group was informing government officials and AMP participants of its findings. While the final study was not released until 2013 and early 2014, in two volumes published by MIT Press, its ideas were in circulation throughout the period. One high point was when Professor Suzanne Berger directly briefed the President on the findings; this clearly was not a typical academic exercise. The first volume, *Making in America*,[51] was drafted by Berger, who led the project, as an overview of the report; the second volume, *Production in the Innovation Economy*,[52] contained in-depth backup chapters drafted by faculty and researcher teams. These were rich and detailed volumes amounting to a historic and influential study of U.S. manufacturing. They told a complex story of what had happened and why it was not fully glimpsed elsewhere. The summary of its core findings presented here can only capture the surface of the story.

The research group examined a series of industrial actors and areas.[53] First, U.S. multinationals were reviewed; these firms had moved from predominately U.S. to global operations in three decades. Interviews with senior managers and reviews of firm data evaluated strategies for locating R&D, testing, pilot production, and full-scale manufacturing in the United States and overseas. Next, the other end of the industrial chain was examined.[54] Tracking a group of start-ups in the Boston area from lab idea to production, the study looked at the barriers these new firms faced in getting to the production stage, particularly in financing scale-up. Third, the study looked at "Main Street manufacturers"—small and midsize manufacturers—and the problems they faced in innovating in product, process supporting services, and business models.[55] This work was undertaken in four representative U.S. regions, as noted. There were also in-depth studies of firms in Germany and China and the innovations they have introduced in scaling up to production and in production itself.[56] Each worked off different models, but both offered important lessons. Fifth, the group undertook research on advanced manufacturing technologies and the potential role that innovation in the production process could play in reviving U.S. manufacturing.[57] Finally, there was research on skill training, which examined the extent of a manufacturing skills shortage, and the needs of advanced manufacturing for improved skills education.[58]

At heart, the PIE study asked "one big question": what production capabilities are needed to support innovation and to realize its benefits in quality jobs, strong firms, new business creation, and sustainable economic growth?[59] Assuming what economists had long accepted, that innovation is required for economic growth and a corresponding productive economy, the study examined "what it takes to sustain innovation over time and what it takes to bring innovation into the economy,"[60] reviewing innovation in products, processes, types of firms, and in other nations, through technology advances and workforce improvements. The focus that PIE helped initiate, starting in 2010, was the application of innovation theory to production. While such theory had been applied many times to particular new technologies, it had not been systematically applied to the U.S. production system. It was a new look.[61] The five overall areas it examined in turn led to a series of new policy approaches for each.

The PIE report found that a globalized world economy of distributed production—research, development, production, and distribution—had become fragmented and dispersed. Enabling this was a shift in U.S. corporate ownership and control, where major vertically integrated corporations began to divest many of their attributes, from R&D, to production, to postsale services. Few fully vertically integrated firms remained. They had been reorganized under pressure from a financial services sector that beginning in the 1980s required firms seeking capital to reorganize around "core competency"—leaner, "asset light" firms received higher stock valuations by weeding out their less profitable divisions.[62] At many firms, one of the first functions to go outside corporate boundaries was manufacturing, which reduced capital obligations and "headcount" commitments—it was often shifted abroad. IT advances helped enable this development—computer-driven equipment using digital specifications allowed firms to produce goods without the vertical linkages previously required. The reduction of trade barriers worldwide and China's entry into the World Trade Organization were further enablers.

The shift to core competency plus competition from abroad thinned out the manufacturing ecosystem. Support for training systems, inducements for suppliers to adopt best practices, and the depth of supply chains all declined. While major firms had once supported strong industrial labs that undertook basic and applied research, basic research at the industrial level dropped, and applied work became much more focused on incremental development that could translate to the bottom line. Expansion was more frequently accomplished through mergers and acquisitions, not through in-house innovation. While large, vertically organized firms had created numerous "public goods"—in research, training, and transfer of technology and expertise to suppliers—which populated the ecosystem with spillovers that helped small and midsize firms, these declined.

The growing gaps in the ecosystem could be characterized as "market failures" because the declining network of "complementary capabilities" made firms less capable as they found it harder to access the former industrial commons. So larger firms dropped a vertical model, hunkered down to "core competency," went "asset light," and distributed production. Small and midsize firms were increasingly what the study termed "home alone,"[63] operating in a thinned-out industrial ecosystem. The end of local banking hit them as well; as financial services pursued national and international investment models, the hometown banker with personal knowledge of those he or she was lending to was disappearing. Capital became harder to get, so small and midsize firms had more difficulty getting resources to scale up production of new innovations. The industrial ocean the Main Street manufacturer used to swim in began to dry up.

The researchers who studied German firms found a very different story. Its mittelstand firms were not home alone—they were swimming in a rich ocean of trade associations, shared institutions for developing new technologies across collaborating firms, supportive engineering centers, strong technical education and training systems producing highly qualified employees, and readily available local financing for scale-up. The Fraunhofer Institutes in particular created ties between small and large firms with expert engineering from academic and technical institutions for technology and process development. The apprenticeship system the small firms were part of provided highly skilled workers.

The researchers studying China found a production system that was increasingly innovative in its ability to rapidly scale up production levels to remarkable levels through methods for regional, cross-firm collaboration.[64] And there was a strong prototyping capability for redesigning and reengineering goods to cut costs to make them affordable to Chinese markets. Too many American firms, increasingly home alone in the case of smaller firms or dispersed in the case of larger firms, seemed to have lost these rapid scale-up and rapid prototyping strengths.

There was an additional challenge. Examining a wide range of firms, the study noted that small and midsize firms had to find ways to be innovative in order to survive in the first decade of the new century and get through the Great Recession. This usually was not innovation in the sense of taking advances from lab to product through R&D but rather in modifying existing product lines to fit new needs and market niches or finding new functions and therefore new markets for existing components.[65] In particular, the PIE study found that successful manufacturing firms were increasingly blending products and services, offering customers solutions to their problems through products and the related services to install and apply them.[66] Large firms—IBM and Apple were good examples—were also merging products and services as a new way of creating value for customers. Blending these two usually disparate worlds, which looked to be the future of most firms, was an additional new challenge.

These were the stories for major and Main Street manufacturers, but what was going on with start-ups, which had become key to the dynamic, innovation-driven part of the U.S. economy, starting with the IT revolution and backed by a new venture financing system? Start-ups tend to cluster in a few areas where there are institutions and mechanisms to support them, including San Francisco, Boston, and Austin. The researchers studied a group of Boston-area start-ups that had survived for a decade or more.[67] Boston was an ideal cluster for start-ups, with strong university research, great talent, great science, and capital support. If they could not make it there, it would be harder elsewhere. If the start-ups were not in the IT or biotech space, which had well-established development timetables and pathways, they had trouble scaling up. Their time frame was not the five to seven years of IT firms but instead a decade or more. These firms would go past the five-year period that venture firms were organized around to recoup their investors' funding; if they were promising, the venture firms would remain in because they did not want to dilute their holdings but would put the start-up on what could be termed "income maintenance."

When the non-IT start-up was finally well through product design, the following kind of conversation with the venture firm would generally occur:

Newtechco: "Hi, Ventureco, we're almost through design, we're ready to produce, send us a check for $30 million for the production facility to make our gizmo."

Ventureco: "That's nice, Newtechco, but we don't have that kind of money, we don't do this, the risk is too high, so call our contract manufacturer in [fill in the blank—China, Taiwan, etc.]."

There was good news here for the start-up—it could start to scale up. But its innovation team would have to start living for months at a time in, say, Shenzhen, educating the contract maker's engineers on the new technology as they designed it for production. The locus of innovation began to shift abroad, and if there were incremental advances in the product, they tended to be developed by the contract manufacturer. Sometimes the venture firm sent the start-up to a foreign sovereign wealth fund, but the effect was similar. The problem for the United States is that if its start-ups represent the next generation of technology advance, their scale-up and production may well shift outside the United States. (More on this start-up scale-up problem follows in chapter 7.)

The PIE study also told a technology story. A major example was studied in depth to evaluate the possibilities of innovation for production: a case study on a mix of very challenging technologies to enable "mass customization."[68] This entailed small-scale, local production using 3D printing and computer-driven standard equipment that could make small lots of uniquely designed products as cost-efficiently as uniform mass production. The case study elaborated on the technologies to enable this and found this model possible. It would mark a dramatic turn in the history of production. Manufacturing had always involved scale-up of ever-increasing production levels; the new technologies meant not scale-up but scale-down of production. Just as there was a local food movement, there could be a local production movement. And consumers could participate in design to match their precise needs and taste. If production were local, small-scale, and highly efficient, then the overseas production advantage would be erased. An innovation in production could be transformative. Obviously, this would only work for some goods, and obviously there were other technology paradigms aside from mass customization that awaited development. But the "advanced manufacturing" innovation model for production was found promising, an organizing principle for restoration of the manufacturing ecosystem.

Finally, PIE examined workforce needs. Earlier reports tended to query manufacturing senior management, who unfailingly complained that they were not able to find skilled workers.[69] But if this sector had shed one-third of its workers in the first decade of the twenty-first century, was there really a shortage? As will be discussed in more detail in chapter 8, the PIE study queried firms' hiring officials not about availability of skilled workers but more pointedly about how long it took to fill jobs; the answer was that open positions were being promptly filled in 76% of cases.[70] There was no skills emergency. Why did managers assert the opposite? Perhaps it was in the interest of all managers to beat the drums on skill shortages so educational institutions would respond to their needs? Or perhaps managers were unwilling to pay for the skill levels they desired?

But there were still the 24% of manufacturing establishments that reported some level of long-term vacancies—what was their story? This is where the story got more interesting. A subset in this group tended to include newer firms, working in fields of more advanced technologies; these firms did face skill needs. So if PIE was proposing the adoption of advanced manufacturing driven by new technologies and processes, it was clear that the training system would need work to meet this challenge. The recommendations called for "a new skill production system" requiring employers to engage with community colleges, supporting government programs at the federal, state, and regional levels, and intermediary organizations to help manage the linkages and communications.[71]

Overall, the PIE study called for rebuilding a thinned-out industrial ecosystem.[72] New shared facilities and capabilities across firms and industrial sectors were required, and larger firms and government could perform a convening function, comparable to what Sematech achieved in semiconductor production in the late 1980s and 1990s. Examples of this were cited in Upstate New York and in Ohio. A similar collaboration across firms, educational institutions, and public intermediaries could also work in the skills training context.

AMP2.0 October 2014 Report—"Accelerating U.S. Advanced Manufacturing"

The President "rechartered" the Advanced Manufacturing Partnership in September 2013 to work on implementation of the 2012 report and to identify new strategies building on the earlier AMP1.0 report. This project marked the next major step in advanced manufacturing policy development.

Most of the participating firms and universities from AMP1.0 became part of "AMP2.0," with presidents from two community colleges, a regional state university, two small firms, and the Steelworkers Union added to the team.[73] Andrew Liveris, CEO of Dow, was joined by MIT's new president, Rafael Reif (who succeeded Susan Hockfield), as co-chairs of the AMP2.0 Steering Committee; Reif had highly relevant experience with industry as a former director of a major MIT technology lab and from extensive work with the semiconductor industry on Sematech and the system of supporting research and development programs that sustained it. Ravi Shankar, Dow's global business advisor, and Professor Krystyn VanVliet of MIT served this round as the "technical co-leads" very effectively coordinating the highly active work groups, with Carrie Houtman of Dow again being very involved. On the administration side, Jason Miller and J. J. Raynor of the National Economic Council provided agency coordination and overall guidance.[74] As with AMP1.0, heavily attended workshops were held in Georgia, Ohio, New York, Massachusetts, and Michigan to develop and share policy ideas.

Since the administration was in the process of creating manufacturing institutes, the AMP2.0 report focused on complementary policies. In the technology policy area,[75] it called for a national strategy coordinated across public and private sectors for "emerging manufacturing technologies." This would include "prioritized manufacturing technology areas," which should be used to manage a "portfolio" of federal "advanced manufacturing technology investments." To show that this strategy concept could work, the AMP2.0 group surveyed priority emerging manufacturing technology areas and developed their own pilot strategies in three areas identified by the study as priorities: advanced sensing, control, and platforms for manufacturing; visualization, informatics, and digital manufacturing; and advanced materials manufacturing.[76] The administration subsequently worked to create manufacturing institutes to cover these identified priority areas, drawing on the strategies. The federal investment was not to be solely for manufacturing institutes—establishment of R&D support for manufacturing technologies was needed, and additional institutional entities were called for. These mechanisms included manufacturing centers of excellence, technology test beds that could provide additional infrastructure backing up the institutes. The R&D and support infrastructures were to be developed cooperatively with industry; an advanced manufacturing advisory consortium was called for to provide private sector input on both the strategy and the R&D infrastructure. The report foresaw that to thrive over time, the manufacturing institutes had to be connected to a robust

R&D effort and infrastructure for ongoing advances in the technologies the institutes were supporting. In addition, a "shared National Network for Manufacturing Innovation (NNMI)" was called for to network the manufacturing institutes so ideas, technologies, and best practices could be shared across institutes. Shared processes and standards to spread implementation of new manufacturing technologies were also recommended.

In the area of workforce training and development,[77] the report recommended a national system of portable, stackable manufacturing skill certifications to be used by employers in hiring and promotion, to help production workers obtain readily transferable and recognizable skills. Development of online training and accreditation programs with federal support through job training programs was also proposed. AMP2.0 members themselves developed extensive manufacturing training toolkits and playbooks, as well as a pilot apprenticeship training program. The report proposed continuing to support these and similar efforts by industry and community colleges. Finally, the report proposed a national campaign to change the image of manufacturing around the advanced manufacturing that would be required in the future, taking advantage of the new fall "Manufacturing Day" of open plants and programs to highlight this.

The report also had a work group on "Scaleup Policy" examining the difficulty of small and midsize firms and start-ups in obtaining financing for scaling up production of new innovations. This problem had been identified in the MIT PIE study, and extensive discussions were held with venture capital firms, corporate ventures, private equity investors, and other possible sources for scale-up financing through multicity workshops on this problem. An ambitious public-private scale-up investment fund was envisioned for pilot production sites for new technologies. In addition, a better system for linking manufacturers with potential strategic partners who could aid in scale-up of production was called for. Work on this scale-up gap became one of the key contributions of the report.

The AMP2.0 project was not only about policy recommendations. The AMP industry, university, and labor participants emphasized their own hands-on efforts to develop apprenticeship programs, training toolkits, technology strategies in three promising areas, and manufacturing scale-up support concepts.

The AMP2.0 report findings were presented directly to the President on October 27, 2014, by the 18 members of the steering committee, with Dow's Andrew Liveris and MIT's Rafael Reif as lead presenters. Commerce Secretary Penny Pritzker, National Economic Council director Jeffrey Zients, and Office of Science and Technology Policy director John Holdren discussed steps for implementing the report's proposals with the president and the steering committee.[78] Simultaneously, the White House announced implementation programs, including a new apprenticeship training program and three new manufacturing institutes around advanced materials, advanced sensing and control, and digital manufacturing, tracking with report recommendations.[79] That afternoon, the National Academies hosted a forum on the report with AMP2.0 industry and university experts and involved agency and White House officials to publicly present the recommendations and findings.[80]

National Academy of Engineering Study—"Making Value for America"

Two more background elements are required to round out our story on the evolution of the advanced manufacturing policy movement, first from the National Academies and last from, of all places, Congress.

The National Academy of Engineering (NAE) report "Making Value for America" was released in March 2015.[81] The report was initiated by the late NAE president Chuck Vest, who clearly saw the significance of the manufacturing decline as it evolved and pressed for the report. It began with an interesting quotation from him: "Far too much of our nation is waiting for new ways of working to arrive. We hear lots of rhetoric about how the nature of work will change, as if it relates to some unknown distant future. The fact is that it is happening now, and we need a broader recognition of this fact and policies and education that reflect it." The NAE committee was led by Nicholas Donofrio, a former senior leader at IBM, and included officials from both major manufacturers and tech companies, and technology policy experts such as Arun Majumdar, founding director of the Department of Energy's ARPA-E and an early DOE leader on manufacturing, now at Stanford, and Theresa Kotanchek, the former technical co-lead of the AMP1.0 report.[82] It went off in a somewhat different direction than the earlier reports discussed. Rather than re-plow that ground, it looked at the implications of advanced manufacturing, operating, as Vest's quotation suggests, on the assumption that it was going to happen. It therefore represents an interesting bookend to the sequence of reports we have been discussing.

It found that technology advances and new industry business models would dramatically alter both the way products are made and distributed and also the nature of the work in creating those products.[83] It argued that the United States needed to embrace those possibilities if it was to remain a leading innovation center—one of its core strengths. It posited that firms would have to shift from making products to making value,[84] which blended services with products and endured throughout the life cycle of the product. Crucial in this process would be the value chains[85] of firms and capabilities that would serve as linked enablers. Firms had a central role in these steps, but government policies and investments in new kinds of education and training and in evolving technology advances would be required.

The report was pointing out one of the major implications of "advanced" manufacturing. The introduction of the new technologies to achieve the efficiency and productivity gains[86] required to pursue leadership in important manufacturing sectors was going to change the nature of work. Introduction of digital technologies and sensor systems throughout the production process—smart manufacturing—meant streamlining and automation, which meant altering jobs and requiring more education and ingenuity in the workforce as technology coordination became the industrial norm.[87] The training system must change to keep up with this; otherwise, the opportunity for production leadership would be lost.[88] And there may well be fewer jobs on the actual production side. The report did not quite state the offset but implied that in "making value" firms would have to create new kinds of blended jobs combining a sophisticated mix of services, distribution, and production—that is where the jobs were going to be. (And as suggested in chapter 3, looking at manufacturing as part of an hourglass of value chains means understanding that the real volume of jobs in manufacturing is not simply at the production moment but in the value chains that are dependent on it.)

The "making value" and "value chain" perspectives this report offered provided additional constructive ways of looking at advanced manufacturing—both what it could offer as a new role for production as well as new challenges it created.

Congressional Manufacturing Legislation

The final saga in this review of the major reports and efforts behind advanced manufacturing concerns congressional legislation. For government action to be enduring, it must be authorized by Congress, and a foundation of regular and relatively stable appropriations must follow. When the executive branch is committed, the policy ship can be launched, but there is no real wind in the sails unless congressional authorizations and appropriations follow; government commitments in the end follow the law and corresponding funding, not administrative fiat. If these steps do not evolve, new programs often do not survive subsequent changes in administrations.

Of course, seeking congressional approval can be highly risky, particularly in a period of deep party divisions. You can never be sure what Congress might hand you.

Particularly since 2010, Congress has been afflicted with deep ideological divisions, including within the congressional parties themselves, and a corresponding inability to move legislation. Despite this divide, Congress was able to pass significant manufacturing legislation on a highly bipartisan basis. This speaks to the political power of manufacturing, through the employment and relatively high wages it still commands, in regional American politics. Efforts by concerned companies led to support for the legislation from the National Association of Manufacturers and other business organizations, which was particularly important to building Republican support.

The first move came on the Senate side, when an unlikely bipartisan duo, Senator Sherrod Brown, a liberal Democrat from Ohio, teamed up with Senator Roy Blunt, a conservative Republican from Missouri, to introduce the Revitalize American Manufacturing and Innovation (RAMI) Act on August 1, 2013.[89] The core feature of their bill was to authorize 15 manufacturing institutes under NIST's leadership. Senators Brown and Blunt were subsequently joined by another liberal-conservative pairing, cosponsors Debbie Stabenow (D-Michigan) and Lindsey Graham (R-South Carolina); all four of their states had been affected by the manufacturing downturn. Twelve other Senate cosponsors joined over time, generally in bipartisan "Noah's Ark" pairings. The Senate bill was backed by the leading manufacturing associations as well as organized labor. Brown, for example, had 650,000 manufacturing jobs in his state of Ohio and was an early supporter of the first manufacturing institute for 3D printing, headquartered in Youngstown, Ohio.

RAMI was introduced in the House of Representatives the next day, August 2, 2013, by another bipartisan pairing, Representative Tom Reed, a conservative Republican from Upstate New York, and Representative Joe Kennedy, a liberal Democrat from Massachusetts. It eventually piled up 100 cosponsors in the House, a remarkable number, which included 51 Democrats and 49 Republicans, again lined up in Noah's Ark pairings. The power of local manufacturing jobs and firms made the politics of the bill powerful.

But this did not mean the bill would ever get to the House and Senate floors to pass. Here the role of Representative Lamar Smith, the conservative chairman of the House Science, Space and Technology Committee, became pivotal. A former reporter for the *Christian Science Monitor* in Boston for two years in the 1970s, he knew the city well and knew members of the Kennedy family. He was a fifth-generation Texan, a twenty-six-year veteran of the House, and also had a strong personal interest in space and science. Congressman Joe Kennedy was a congressional freshman, a junior member of his Science Committee, and the RAMI bill, which had been assigned to that committee because NIST was under the committee's jurisdiction, was his first major legislative project. A smart, friendly, hardworking redhead, Kennedy, a grandson of the late senator Robert Kennedy, was well versed in the importance of technology from his Stanford education and from his Boston district, which was near the area's powerful technology cluster. Kennedy appealed to Chairman Smith, and Smith decided to move the bill.

The Science Committee's Subcommittee on Research and Technology held three hearings on the bill in the summer and fall of 2013, hearing testimony from small manufacturers, the Council on Competitiveness, university technology experts, a GE scientist, a semiconductor trade association, and the bill's bipartisan lead sponsors, Congressman Kennedy and Congressman Reed.[90] Negotiations on the bill in the Science Committee ensued. The committee came back to mark up the bill in July 2014, considering an amendment in the nature of a substitute offered by both Chairman Smith and Congressman Kennedy, and six other amendments. The legislative skids had all been carefully greased—all the committee's majority and minority members were on board. The amendments were considered in a block and passed on a voice vote—the agreement between both sides meant there was no need for a contentious recorded vote. After filing a detailed report on the bill, the committee reported the bill to the House floor on September 15, 2014. Getting floor time in the House is carefully controlled by the Speaker of the House, and is limited and hard to get. Smith, however, had developed a modus operandi of bringing a number of modest noncontroversial bills that had strong bipartisan support to the House floor for consideration on the "suspension calendar," where the rules for oral debate were suspended and a bill could move to quick approval. Buttressed by the mass of bipartisan cosponsors, Smith, Reed, and Kennedy appealed to the House leadership to use this maneuver. So, on September 15, the bill was simply taken up without debate and rapidly approved by voice vote.[91] It was smooth sailing through the House, but what about the Senate?

The Senate Commerce Committee, which had Senate jurisdiction over the bill, had held a hearing in November 2013 and reported the bill out of committee in April 2014. But it was stalled.[92] The Senate rules, as usual, made things complicated. It was no accident that the Senate was named the Senate; when Thomas Jefferson, as vice president and presiding over the Senate, drafted the Senate's rules, he drew directly on the practices of the Roman Senate. The Roman Senate famously invented the filibuster; in the U.S. Senate, any determined senator can stall anything indefinitely for any reason. So when the House-passed RAMI bill came over to the Senate, Senate Commerce Committee Chairman Jay Rockefeller (D-W.Va.) and other Senate supporters of RAMI faced "holds" that blocked the bill from reaching the Senate floor for consideration. Eventually, the bill had sufficient bipartisan support in both Houses of Congress and enough dedicated backing from its sponsors and committee leaders that it was added to a monster annual omnibus appropriations bill to fund all the government agencies for the fiscal year—a "must pass" bill. As a "minibus" attached to the omnibus, it passed the House on December 11, 2014, and the Senate two days later, on December 13.

The legislation authorized the establishment of up to 15 regional manufacturing institutes across the country, each focused on a unique technology, material, or process relevant to advanced manufacturing.[93] As the Advanced Manufacturing Partnership had expounded, the institutes were to constitute a network. NIST was to be the lead agency in forming the network, but it could collaborate with other federal agencies in selecting and awarding funding institutes, which must be cost-shared by industry and state or local governments. It was required to develop and periodically update a strategic plan for the network of institutes. It also required the institutes to link to the existing Manufacturing Extension Partnership (MEP) that offered efficiency and technology advice to small manufacturers in every state, and required institutes to take on education and training roles.

Of course, in the meantime, a series of manufacturing institutes had already been launched, led by the Defense Department's Manufacturing and Industrial Base Policy office and its Mantech program, with particular military services sponsoring each institute, and by the Department of Energy through its Energy Efficiency and Renewable Energy office. The approach in the bill of giving NIST leadership for new institutes did not really match the reality of what was already evolving, but the bill amounted to an important congressional validation of the manufacturing institute model. It also called for a network of institutes for development of an ongoing strategy and gave NIST the important authority—which it did not have up to that point—to sponsor its own institutes when it could round up sufficient appropriations to do so. In the Budget Agreement of 2015, Congress provided NIST with the initial funding to launch one or more institutes, a competition that subsequently resulted in a NIST-sponsored institute.

A notoriously divided Congress had actually come together on a bipartisan basis to bless advanced manufacturing and a creative model of manufacturing innovation institutes to get there.

What can we make of all these pieces of a manufacturing puzzle that fell into place in the half decade between 2010 and 2015? It was a period of creative ferment for manufacturing. First, a series of articles and reports began to plow the ground from which new policies could grow. Next, the White House, with leadership from the president, manufacturing czar Ron Bloom, and staff on the National Economic Council and the Office of Science and Technology Policy, began to coalesce around an innovation-based strategy to try to transform American manufacturing. Innovation policy was not new to government—most understood that it had helped create the recent IT and biotech technology waves. But it was new for government to apply innovation policy to manufacturing. This was not the only fix needed, but it became central.[94]

Meanwhile, the Production in the Innovation Economy (PIE) study was evolving at MIT, informing the policy actors of its findings as they were developed. PIE's in-depth look at manufacturing created a narrative about a thinned-out ecosystem of production that was jeopardizing not simply manufacturing but also the innovation system itself, a crucial U.S. comparative advantage. It saw production as a key link in the innovation system—a weakened link. The AMP1.0 report's central contribution was to move the innovation narrative for manufacturing into policy by supporting the advanced manufacturing institute concept, which the administration jumped on and began to implement well before the report was released in 2012. The AMP2.0 report of 2014 fleshed out the innovation policy proposals, urging a public-private technology strategy around advanced manufacturing technologies and processes, linking agency R&D and the new institutes around the strategy, a network of institutes for shared learning and best practices, and new workforce training models. AMP1.0 had suggested a number of these points, but AMP2.0 fleshed out these ideas. The National Academy of Engineering's 2015 report added a larger frame—advanced manufacturing was going to be at the core of the future economy, merging services and production for new "value" models, and requiring broader education reforms to prepare the workforce both to bring it about and to work productively within it. Finally, Congress's RAMI legislation added a congressional blessing to the manufacturing institutes and, in effect, the whole project, creating a reasonable possibility that it could survive the political turmoil of the times.

The Trump administration took power in 2017, pledged to renew American manufacturing, which it made a central issue in the presidential campaign. For Fiscal Year 2017 Congress fully funded the manufacturing institutes. But FY2018 was a more complex story. The administration's March 2017 preliminary federal budget submission for FY2018, while cutting numerous federal agency science and technology programs, avoided explicit cuts to the manufacturing institutes. Because increases were planned for defense spending, when the final budget was submitted to Congress in May, the eight institutes run by DOD agencies appeared to be in good condition. But major cuts were proposed for FY 2018 for the Department of Energy's energy efficiency and renewable programs and the five institutes there were to be cut as a result. Although NIST faced cuts, its institute appeared sustainable. But the budget was only the Trump Administration's proposal; Congress then began the process of rewriting it. As a major budget battle shaped up in Congress over spending levels for FY 2018, it was still not clear as this work went to publication what the outcome for the institutes would finally be. However, a major shift in manufacturing innovation policy will likely require a higher level of administration focus in addition to maintaining institute budgets.

Meanwhile, there was a parallel development. In part stimulated by the new U.S. efforts, other nations, including Germany, Britain, Singapore, Japan, and China, began developing comparable advanced manufacturing efforts. If the United States wanted to stay in the manufacturing game, it now had few options other than pursuing and upping its game in advanced manufacturing, since its leading competitors were now pursuing similar strategies.[95]

6 The Advanced Manufacturing Innovation Institute Model

A key goal of the "manufacturing innovation institutes" was to fill a gap in the U.S. innovation system for manufacturing by creating a space where advanced manufacturing could evolve through a collaboration between industry (both small and large firms), universities, and government. According to the director of NIST's Advanced Manufacturing Office, Mike Molnar, who came from industry (Cummins Engine) to lead the NIST program, and two of his government colleagues, the aim for the new National Network for Manufacturing Innovation (NNMI) was to

> create an effective manufacturing research infrastructure for U.S. industry and academia to solve industry-relevant problems. The NNMI will consist of linked Institutes for Manufacturing Innovation (IMIs) with common goals, but unique concentrations. In an IMI, industry, academia, and government partners leverage existing resources, collaborate, and co-invest to nurture manufacturing innovation and accelerate commercialization. As sustainable manufacturing innovation hubs, IMIs will create, showcase, and deploy new capabilities, new products, and new processes that can impact commercial production. They will build workforce skills at all levels and enhance manufacturing capabilities in companies large and small. Institutes will draw together the best talents and capabilities from all the partners to build the proving grounds where innovations flourish and to help advance American domestic manufacturing.[1]

The federal award to each new institute over a five-year period was to range from $70 million to $120 million, with the consortium of firms, universities, and local government backing each new institute contributing at least a one-to-one match to leverage the federal government's investment.

Manufacturing Institutes in the Context of Innovation Policy

The manufacturing institute concept did not magically arise from nowhere, it is based on an established policy foundation. Our review of manufacturing innovation and the new manufacturing institutes falls into the context of the U.S. literature on science and technology and related innovation policy, which requires a brief explication here. The economic intellectual foundation for this field is Robert Solow's work positing technological and related innovation as the dominant causative factor in growth.[2] Paul Romer and other New Growth Theorists argued the importance of technological learning, as noted in chapter 4, as the underpinning for Solow's technological advance.[3] These two strands led to an understanding of two basic underlying innovation factors—support for R&D and follow-on technological advance, and support for Romer's concept of the human capital engaged in research that lay behind that system. Richard Nelson in turn argued the importance of understanding comparative innovation systems—of assessing the actors in an innovation system and their comparative strengths.[4] This concept we can enlarge to constitute to a third direct innovation factor, innovation organization, which can be analyzed as a connected system of innovation institutions and organizations. Against these factors, particularly the organizational factor, the U.S. innovation system took shape.

In the postwar, Vannevar Bush's highly influential "pipeline model" for the postwar organization of U.S. R&D agencies[5] was a "technology push" or "technology supply" model, with government support for initial research but with only a limited role for government in moving resulting advances (particularly radical or breakthrough innovation) toward the marketplace. Development and the later stages of innovation were left to private industry. Donald Stokes (and others) subsequently sharply critiqued the Bush pipeline model as inherently disconnected, separating system actors with few means for technology handoffs between them.[6] Lewis Branscomb and Phillip Auerswald articulated the "valley of death" critique: the disconnect in the U.S. system between research and later stage development led to system failures in commercialization of research results.[7] This theory has been the major focus of U.S. science and technology policy literature for the past twenty-five years, with resulting discussions of bridging solutions across this valley.

Of course, the pipeline model is not the only U.S. innovation system model, as noted in chapter 1. Others include "induced innovation" articulated by Vernon Ruttan as the dominant means by with industry innovates, by identifying market opportunities then innovating to fill them, typically through incremental advances.[8] Because the Defense Department (DOD) could not tolerate a disconnected model when faced with Cold War technological demands, it developed what has been termed an "extended pipeline" model.[9] Here, DOD supported not only the initial research but also development, demonstration, prototyping, testing and often initial market creation stages. DARPA, for example, represents an innovation institution organized around this much more connected system.[10] In general, U.S. innovation models in recent decades have tended to stretch their capabilities further down this innovation pipeline.[11] However, as noted in chapters 1 and 2, the U.S. innovation system has not reached the manufacturing stage.

Although there is a substantial argument that manufacturing, particularly initial production of new technologies and complex, high value products, is a significant stage of the innovation system as Suzanne Berger has articulated,[12] U.S. innovation agencies have not organized around it. The exception was Sematech which received DARPA support starting in the 1980s.[13] However, as noted above, other nations have developed what can be termed "manufacturing-led" innovation systems, which is the dominant model in Germany, Japan, Korea, and now China.[14] Emblematic of "manufacturing-led" is Japan's quality manufacturing revolution of the 1970s-80s,[15] Germany's system of industrial support through its Fraunhofer institutes and apprenticeship programs, and lately, China's rapid prototyping and scaleup capacity.[16]

The U.S. missed this model, as noted in chapters 1 and 2. Both civilian and military innovation models—pipeline and extended pipeline—focused on broader technology development, not on technologies and processes for manufacturing innovation. The U.S. therefore missed manufacturing-led innovation and paid a significant price in the decline of its manufacturing base in the early 2000s. Driven by this manufacturing decline, the U.S. is now exploring adding a "manufacturing-led" model to its other three innovation models, applying its still strong early-stage innovation system to production challenges.

This will require a very different approach from other U.S. innovation models. Its new network of manufacturing institutes is unlike anything it has tried before, each requiring a complex, cost-shared, collaboration between dozens of institutional actors, including firms, universities, community colleges, states, and federal agencies, applying aggressive technology development roadmaps, and workforce training agendas. It is modeled on Germany's Fraunhofer system, but the question remains whether this can be translated to a U.S. context. The innovation task is greatly complicated because of the reality, discussed in chapter 1, that manufacturing is a complex, established "legacy" economic sector where technological change historically meets resistance.[17] It is clearly the most significant step in U.S. innovation organization in decades and merits close evaluation.

Innovation policy theorists, as noted above, have long analyzed the gap between the "front end" of the innovation system—the research side, typically supported by government R&D through university research—and the "back end," the late-stage development through implementation phases, typically a private sector domain. To solve this structural problem, numerous bridging mechanisms have evolved, often with government support. As Philip Shapira and Jan Youtie have noted, this requires technology diffusion approaches, and a wide range of institutional intermediaries—from the Manufacturing Extension Partnership for diffusing new production technologies and processes to small manufacturers in the United States to the Fraunhofer Institutes for technology development among manufacturers in Germany—have developed.[18] The manufacturing institutes are the latest in a series of technology diffusion institutions created by various nations to cross this gap.

This approach of creating collaborative institutes between companies, small and large, universities and government agencies fits with a large literature on the role of intermediary organizations in innovation. Firms rarely innovate in isolation[19] because they must be able to acquire, absorb, and act on external knowledge to develop a competitive advantage.[20] Networks can spur the transmission of complex knowledge across firm boundaries.[21] Innovation intermediaries, which support such networks, are increasingly seen to be critical actors in national and regional innovation systems.[22] These organizations can be defined as agents linking otherwise unrelated firms and entities, to play an active role in innovation. In the innovation systems literature, intermediaries can include such institutions as university laboratories, public R&D organizations, standards institutes, and industry associations.[23] The new manufacturing institutes fit squarely within this conceptual framework.

The underlying institute aim was highly ambitious: use the institutes to create new production paradigms in a series of production areas, shared across large and small firms, their supply chains, and industry sectors. The hope was to dramatically increase production efficiency so that the United States could reenter the manufacturing sector as a strengthened competitor ready to take on lower-cost and lower-wage producers in Asia. The aim would be a restored competitive edge through more innovative products and technologies as well as corresponding efficiencies that reduced the cost disadvantage. The institutes would apply U.S. innovation advantages to the production stage, an area that, as explained earlier, had not been a focus of its innovation system. The new production paradigms would aim to be transformative, just as the technologies and processes behind mass production in the United States and quality manufacturing in Japan had previously been transformative and enabled previous eras of industrial leadership in those countries. Is this plausible? As the Advanced Manufacturing

Partnership (AMP) studies cited found, scientists and engineers are now indicating that a series of significant new production advances now appear within range.

Another way of looking at this manufacturing innovation challenge, analyst Timothy Sturgeon argues, is that China now appears to have built, as discussed, an advantage in high volume manufacturing—previously a U.S. specialty. The U.S. retains capability in two types of production, high mix manufacturing, where local market needs are met and high volume is less critical, and custom manufacturing at low volume, both of which are smaller scale.[24] If the United States moves to implement advanced manufacturing, it can raise its high mix and custom production capability, by cutting costs and raising their efficiency, to much better compete with high volume manufacturing. This could be a big equalizer for U.S. production capability. Of course, China (and Germany) now are moving rapidly on advanced manufacturing, which becomes another reason the United States must move in this direction, applying its innovation strengths before it is left behind.

What would one of these new production paradigms look like? Digital or "smart" production, sometimes called the industrial Internet of Things, provides one possible model.[25] Currently, manufacturers have fragmented and unconnected IT infrastructures and retain manual, paper-based systems that cannot provide real-time situational awareness, preventing rapid responses to problems, customers, and opportunities. Yet, removing their current systems threatens short-term disruptions and efficiency losses. Firms outsourced manufacturing, which led to further disconnects. Modern firms have begun embedding sensors in different stages of production that generate much data, but the remaining lack of connectivity prevents full use of such data in making improvements. Could an entirely new level of connectivity between IT systems, with additional sensors and data analysis capabilities, enable a new kind of smart production that is perceptive, solving problems at every step, and far more efficient? Could this dramatically affect productivity levels? Several of the new manufacturing institutes discussed here are now taking on key parts of this task. General Electric is at work on this project and Germany's Industrie 4.0 is largely organized around it. This is an example of a potential new production paradigm.

The Complex Institute and Network Model

This paradigm challenge created a complex model for the new institutes. The government's role here was not to make a single research award to a "principal investigator" to undertake a scientific research project according to a carefully delineated plan in the grant application—the usual government R&D role. Instead, the award had to relate to the needs of a large, complex mix of industrial firms that varied widely across numerous sectors and sizes, along with those of academic institutions that ranged from major research universities, to regional universities, to community colleges. And state governments were to be co-investors, along with industry and the federal government, supporting particular related projects. Furthermore, regional economic development agencies were to be involved as well. With the exception of Sematech, the federal government had not tried collaborations this complicated before. As one Defense Department official deeply involved in the advanced manufacturing effort put it, "Standing up an institute is like standing up a country."[26]

The participant mix for the institutes was complex, and so was their task list:

1. "create" new production technologies, processes and "capabilities";
2. serve as "proving grounds" to test new technologies and related processes;
3. support efforts to "deploy" new production innovations; and
4. "build workforce skills" to enhance production and processes for the emerging technologies.

The overall goal was to enable domestic manufacturing around the focused innovation area of each institute to "flourish."[27]

To enable cross-collaborations and exchanges of best practices, there was also to be a "network" of manufacturing institutes layered above the individual institutes. As advanced manufacturing took hold, a small or midsize manufacturer likely would not just have a 3D printing problem but would also have a range of future production challenges across a number of new fields, from digital production technologies to using advanced materials. Production is also anchored in regions that have tended to focus on particular production areas—cars in the Midwest, aerospace on the coasts, pharmaceuticals in the Northeast, and so on. While the institutes needed to have regional depth, they also had to translate their advances and know-how to manufacturers nationally. The institutes and their NNMI "network" had a major overarching assignment that was both regional and national.

The task for the new institutes and their network may not have been as complex as NASA's "moonshot," but it was a major one. While the Apollo moonshot was a government contract model—the government would simply pay to get there—for the manufacturing institutes to succeed, they had to be intensely collaborative across many actors, as well as jointly funded from a number of sources, with all the challenging technology advances launched in an aging, legacy industrial sector that had been in steep decline. And somehow the new institutes were to be self-sustaining within five years without further federal support. This was a very complex organizational model.

The Agencies Step Up to the Plate

The institutes did not pop up from a highly organized, well-timed governmental assembly line. They were scraped together. As set out in chapter 5, this was a period of deep ideological division politically. Rather than wait for a divided Congress to authorize and fund a new program, which could mean waiting forever, the administration cajoled the agencies to get started on setting up institutes, using existing authority with funding scavenged from other areas. As a result, the agencies were in charge and picked focus areas for manufacturing institutes that matched their missions. The AMP1.0 report had assumed that the institute focus areas would come from a bottom-up model, with industry playing the lead role in selecting focus areas. Instead, it was top-down—the agencies decided the focus areas based on their own missions, not an overall manufacturing mission. This was not all bad. Since the agencies made the selections and were in charge, they chose focus areas they cared about that would serve their agency's needs, potentially making this a more sustainable project over time, not a mandate imposed by the White House. Over time, this tended to sort itself out. The top technology areas that industry had identified as its priorities in the AMP1.0 and AMP2.0 reports turned out to mesh over time with agency missions, so the emerging institutes largely corresponded to needs highlighted in the reports. And the agency lead tended to enhance agency buy-in for the new program.

In the absence of a centrally authorized program with coordinated, fixed funding, the executive branch agencies led; legislation did not come until 2014, whereas the first institute had been created in 2012. So the cross-agency governance model immediately became complicated. Someone once defined federal cross-agency collaboration as a contradiction in terms. This made the White House's coordination role especially complex, requiring a high degree of creativity, diplomacy, and cooperativeness. Fortunately, the National Economic Council (NEC) dynamic duo of Jason Miller, a shrewd finance MBA from Chicago who had been Ron Bloom's deputy, and J. J. Raynor, a young, sharp former student leader at Duke with a consulting background, were up to the task. They had strong support from Gene Sperling, NEC's politically astute and policy-experienced leader, and then his successor, Jeff Zients, who had a record of business success, and they could also deftly apply occasional presidential intervention from a committed president at the cabinet level.

The Department of Defense (DOD) had the most money and thus launched the most institutes. It was not known for playing well with others; historically it had tended to guard its priority national security mission, and it was not prone to compromising it with other agencies. It had long had a manufacturing technology mission, embedded in its long-standing Defense Production Act[28] authority. Over the course of two world wars, it had mobilized and reorganized much of the nation's economy to meet defense needs, and many of those practices continued during the more than four decades of the Cold War. It had a rich history of "industrial policy"—that is, governmental economic interventions to assure technology and industrial outcomes—which no other agency dared politically to consider. Its "Mantech" program, based in the Office of the Secretary and with branches in each of the military services, dated back many decades but did not even rate a leader of assistant secretary level. It had not been a major defense program in decades. For example, for many years, a key Mantech mission had been to assure continued production of obsolete technologies used in overaged equipment, such as assuring availability of vacuum tubes for aging radar sets.

Suddenly Mantech had a national mission, a "presidential" in Defense parlance, directed by the president himself.[29] But it did not get a big new influx of funding, because of the congressional impasse over all new programs, so it had to rely on an existing small staff and stretch existing budgets. The initial team included Brett Lambert, a talented, experienced, highly articulate, and sharp deputy assistant secretary for manufacturing and industrial base policy, who was the first agency official to jump into the swimming pool, committing to forming the initial advanced manufacturing institute. He was aided by Neal Orringer, a politically astute former Senate Banking Committee staffer and an expert on the Defense Production Act, who creatively worked the rules and regulations to get the first institutes launched rapidly. Adele Ratcliff, a determined and bright civil servant who had been creatively nurturing a broad view of DOD's manufacturing role, and Steve Linder, a level-headed and very experienced civil servant dedicated to the defense manufacturing mission, likewise played key roles. This list has been supplemented by other committed DOD officials. More recently, Stephen Luckowski joined the cause from the Army, bringing strong expertise in materials manufacturing and becoming program manager for the fiber institute; he and others from the military services became program managers for other institutes.

Few in the top military leadership had real knowledge of or interest in DOD's manufacturing base. They fought wars; making stuff was someone else's job, and there was a big acquisition/procurement team with green eyeshades to do it. But the Mantech crew understood what a crisis DOD was facing with the decline in U.S. production strength—U.S. production capability and the ability to mobilize it had been at the heart of DOD's military superiority since the Union won the Civil War, and had proven crucial in World War II and the Cold War. Mantech's role was complicated by the reality that there were separate Mantech programs, with separate service priorities, reporting systems, and needs, in the military services, not simply in the secretary of defense's office, which also had to be brought aboard. But Mantech was increasingly worried about the decline of U.S. production depth; as Adele Ratcliff put it, "DOD needs to stop building fragile supply chains for which DOD is the only customer."[30]

One early development helped spur interest in DOD for all this. When the proposals came in for the first manufacturing institute, on 3D printing (or "Additive Manufacturing"), the match proposed by industry and states to Mantech funds was not simply one to one: the institute proponents were ready to significantly "overmatch." This was eye-opening to Mantech staff—they could get major additional leverage on their investments. This opportunity for leverage, and to work on major new technology thrusts where DOD had a stake at a larger scale, had not happened in Mantech in recent memory—suddenly they had a force multiplier.

The story at the Department of Energy (DOE) was different. Its Energy Efficiency and Renewable Energy (EERE) office worked with industry on applied energy technologies. It had long had an industrial efficiency program; industry had long been a major energy user, and there were major clean energy gains, as well as potential savings to industry, from conservation and more efficient energy technologies. The office was not a priority during the prior Republican administration, but Henry Kelly, principal deputy assistant secretary and then acting assistant secretary at EERE, from 2008 to 2012, an energy and climate expert with a PhD in physics, understood well the need to upgrade the office and its mission, and he began building it up. When it became clear by the end of 2009 that Cap and Trade legislation (to price carbon emissions and thereby incentivize low-carbon technologies) would not pass Congress, there was an additional need to drive down the price of clean energy technologies so they could compete on price with fossil fuels; otherwise they would never enter the marketplace at scale. This meant that manufacturing—the primary means to drive new technologies down the cost curve—had to be a priority along with efficiency. Kelly got this effort off the ground, helping to create the Sunshot program, for example, to drive down solar costs, before shifting to staffing the energy technology section at the White House Office of Science and Technology Policy.

Dave Danielson, the new, young assistant secretary for EERE from 2012 to 2016, made manufacturing his major new mission area. He had recently earned a PhD in materials and had committed himself to new energy technologies, first as a Boston-area venture capitalist and then as the first project director hired on the staff of the brand-new and highly innovative Advanced Research Projects Agency—Energy (ARPA-E).[31] Danielson saw the criticality of the manufacturing mission for EERE and saw that he could align with a presidential initiative to help make it happen, with backing from the Secretary of Energy Ernest Moniz. Joining him at EERE to lead a new Advanced Manufacturing Office was another project director from ARPA-E, Mark Johnson, previously a materials science and engineering professor at North Carolina State University. Both had drunk the ARPA-E "Kool-Aid" of driving hard for energy breakthroughs. EERE, a $2 billion applied R&D agency, had far less funding to spare than DOD, but still it initially pushed for two new manufacturing institutes that would match its clean energy mission. The proposed focus of DOE's first institute was something of a surprise to observers, power electronics, which meant work on wide-bandgap semiconductors. What was this? What did it have to do with advanced manufacturing? It was nowhere on the industry priority lists painstakingly assembled by the AMP1.0 and AMP2.0 studies, but on closer examination, the pick proved interesting. This emerging technology could mean major energy savings in a vast array of products and systems, including driving down costs in the production process, and it was a major new manufactured product line in itself.

The story at the Commerce Department's NIST was different, too. Its director and undersecretary, Pat Gallagher, who had made a career in NIST's nuclear reactor wing, was highly thoughtful and universally liked. He understood and gave full support to advanced manufacturing, seeing it as a continuation of NIST's mission, first set by its then secretary Herbert Hoover, to support industry-relevant technology development. Gallagher's able and highly experienced NIST associate director for innovation and industry, Phillip Singerman, led NIST's Manufacturing Extension and advanced manufacturing programs, and Mike Molnar, who liked to be introduced simply as "a manufacturing guy from industry," led NIST's new Advanced Manufacturing Program Office. The commerce secretaries, Rebecca Blank (an economist and acting secretary from 2011 to 2013) and Penny Pritzker (secretary between 2013 and 2016), were both very active in helping lead the Advanced Manufacturing Partnership (AMP), strongly backing NIST's role. Despite NIST's strong involvement in AMP, and its coordinating role among agencies, NIST was unable to shake loose congressional funding until FY2016 to establish a manufacturing institute. When it did, it avoided a "top-down" agency selection of the institute focus area, seeking "bottom-up" focus area proposals from industry and university consortia. NIST also played a supportive role in obtaining congressional approval of the 2014 advanced manufacturing legislation, which focused on NIST.

While the National Science Foundation (NSF) was the fourth major federal government actor, its basic research focus limited its ability to launch manufacturing institutes. However, Steve McKnight and Bruce Kramer in NSF's Engineering Division were very involved in the AMP reports and led NSF programs on advanced manufacturing research, including related Engineering Research Centers focused on manufacturing technologies. In addition, Susan Singer, who led NSF's higher education programs, and Celeste Carter of her division, applied NSF's Advanced Technology Education (ATE) programs to emphasize advanced manufacturing education and training in community colleges.

The Program Centerpiece: Manufacturing Institutes

The administration pledged to form 15 manufacturing institutes by the time it left office in January 2017, and these are the centerpiece of the advanced manufacturing program. The group of institutes was originally labeled the National Network for Manufacturing Innovation (NNMI) but was renamed ManufacturingUSA in 2016. The range of their technical focus is of particular note; while Germany's Industrie 4.0 advanced manufacturing initiative emphasizes the Internet of Things, that is only one of the areas featured by the U.S. institutes. The institutes' wide technical embrace suggests how far-reaching an advanced manufacturing revolution could be. This technical breadth may be what is most interesting about the U.S. approach, and it deserves enumeration, so we will now briefly describe the institutes and their technology areas.

America Makes—National Additive Manufacturing Institute[32] was the first manufacturing institute, announced in 2012. It is headquartered in Youngstown, Ohio, with a regional base in the Cleveland, Ohio, to Pittsburgh, Pennsylvania, corridor, and is focused on 3D printing technologies, also known as additive manufacturing. Additive manufacturing is a process of joining materials to make devices using three-dimensional computer model data, layer on layer, compared to subtractive manufacturing, which relies on traditional machine tools. It typically uses powdered forms of metals or polymers, and even tissue. A competitive advantage of additive manufacturing is that parts can be fabricated as soon as the three-dimensional digital description of the part is entered into the printer, potentially creating a new market for on-demand, customized manufacturing. Importantly, these processes minimize material waste and tooling requirements, as well as potentially compressing the elements and stages in the supply chain. These enable entirely new components and structures that cannot be cost-effectively produced using conventional manufacturing processes such as casting, molding, and forging. Additive manufacturing could be able to compete directly with mass production techniques if the speed of layering were significantly improved. Meanwhile, it will be employed to replace parts on-site, to reduce the need for parts inventories, and to create much more complex and intricate components beyond the reach of current processes. It could be a key enabler of mass customization—the ability to create small lots of personally designed products at the cost of mass-produced goods. This could localize production, enabling scale-down of production for the first time, despite the past history of production at ever-greater scales. It could be a breakthrough production technology for the twenty-first century.

Selected after a highly competitive process, state and industry funds from the America Makes consortium matched a $50 million federal award through the Air Force Mantech program for an approximately $100 million program. The mission of America Makes is to accelerate additive manufacturing and its widespread adoption by bridging the technology gap between research and technology development and deployment. Its roster of participants includes 53 companies, both small and large, especially in the Midwest but stretching across the nation. These include firms organized around 3D printing technologies, such as 3D Systems, major aerospace firms, such as Boeing, Lockheed Martin, United Technologies, and Northrup Grumman, where 3D printing may prove transformative, and a large number of small production firms. The 36 universities and colleges range from major research universities to community colleges. There are over 20 other organizations participating, from state agencies to industry associations.

The consortium has developed a detailed technology roadmap organized around design, materials, process, and supply chain adoption. There is also an additive materials "genome" effort to enable incremental change improvements in the time and cost required to design, develop, and qualify new materials for additive manufacturing. These use novel computational methods, such as physics-based and model-assisted material property prediction tools. The institute has worked to create an infrastructure for the sharing of additive manufacturing ideas and research on development and evaluation of additive manufacturing technologies, on engaging with educational institutions and manufacturers for training in the new field, and on linking small and midsize firms with resources to enable them to use additive manufacturing. A major emphasis of America Makes has been on R&D and technology development projects, typified by joint university-industry efforts. For example, Boeing, Honeywell, and Draper Lab in Cambridge, Massachusetts, are working to embed a suite of electronics manufacturing technologies into 3D printing processes, such as precision machining, thermoplastic extrusion, direct foil embedding, wire embedding, and wire management. There are over 30 other comparable joint university-industry development projects.

While information and IP sharing among the highly competitive larger aerospace firms proved complex, which has affected technology development, the institute has played a significant role in convening the new 3D printing community, helping participants learn which researchers and firms are working on which advances, thereby promoting connections and contracting. It also has been promoting a significantly faster and less costly process for DOD to approve new aerospace parts through simulation and modeling, which could be of significant benefit to industry.

America Makes is the most mature institute, but the pattern of activities set by America Makes is comparable to those at other manufacturing institutes, with a total of six institutes sponsored by DOD and three by DOE by fall 2016.[33] Five more were added by the beginning of 2017, for a total of 14. Table 6.1 contains a short summary of the 13 manufacturing institutes formed subsequently, emphasizing their areas of technology focus.[34]

Progress to Date

The existing institutes have already been hard at work. In 2016, the administration proffered a series of examples of what the institutes have been accomplishing:[35]

• To help anchor production of new semiconductor technologies in the U.S. and accelerate the commercialization of advanced power electronics, in March, the Power America Manufacturing Innovation Institute successfully partnered with X-FAB in Lubbock, TX, to upgrade a $100 million foundry to produce cost-competitive, next-generation wide bandgap semiconductors, enabling new business opportunities to sustain hundreds of jobs.

Table 6.1
Institute Names and Descriptions

Institute Name	Description
DMDII—Digital Manufacturing and Design Innovation Institute	DMDII was formed in 2014 with a hub located in Chicago. Digital manufacturing involves the use of integrated, computer-based systems, including simulation, three-dimensional visualization, analytics, and collaboration tools, to create simultaneous product and manufacturing process definitions. Design innovation is the ability to apply these technologies, tools, and products to reimagine the entire manufacturing process from end to end.

DMDII has 201 members, including major firms from a wide range of sectors, numerous smaller firms, and 11 universities in its first tier. Its $70 million in DOD Army Mantech funding was matched with industry and state contributions of $248 million. Its mission is digital manufacturing to lower product design costs by fostering deep connections between suppliers, to lower production costs and reduce capital requirements through better linkages from end to end of the product life cycle, to cut time to market through faster iterations, to develop and implement innovations in digital design, digital factories, and digital supply chains, and to both develop new products and improve legacy products. |
| *LIFT— Lightweight Innovations for Tomorrow (lightweight and advanced metals)* | LIFT was founded in 2014, with its hub in Detroit, Michigan, and extending regionally through the I-75 corridor, including locations in Michigan, Ohio, Indiana, Tennessee, and Kentucky. Lightweight and advanced metals offer major performance enhancements and greater energy efficiency that can improve the performance of many systems in defense, energy, transportation, and general engineered products. Lightweight metals have applications in wind turbines, medical technology, pressure vessels, and alternative energy sources.

LIFT has 78 members, from a wide range of firms, small and large, including metals and aerospace firms and automotive suppliers, and 17 universities, who matched $70 million in federal funds through the Navy's Office of Naval Research and its Mantech program. Its mission is to innovate in lightweight high-performing metals production and enable the resulting new technologies to expand into industrial base application. It is working on projects in melting, thermo-mechanical processes, powder processing, agile low-cost tooling, coatings, and joining, with widespread applications in automotive, aerospace, shipbuilding, railroads, fabrication, and other sectors. As will be subsequently discussed in chapter 8, it has been the institute leader in workforce education. |
| *Power America— Next Generation Power Electronics* | Power America was launched in 2015 to develop wide-bandgap semiconductor technology. This could enable a major increase in the energy efficiency and reliability of power electronics through |

Table 6.1
(continued)

Institute Name	Description
	semiconductor materials that are smaller, faster, and more efficient than silicon-based technologies. These are able to operate at higher temperatures, can block higher voltages, switch faster with less power loss, are potentially more reliable, and carry substantial system-level benefits. These capabilities make it possible to reduce weight, volume, and life-cycle costs in a wide range of power applications. They will have a great array of applications, including in industrial motor systems, consumer electronics, and data centers, and in the conversion of renewable energy sources (solar and wind). If widespread adoption of these technologies is accomplished in even a limited number of applications, then very significant electrical power savings, including in industrial production, could be achieved annually. The higher cost of wide-bandgap technologies is expected to decline as higher production levels are achieved.
	Power America was supported by a $70 million award from the Department of Energy's Energy Efficiency and Renewable Energy Advanced Manufacturing Office, which was matched by $70 million. It includes 17 industry partners, five universities, and three laboratories, and is based in Raleigh, North Carolina.
IACMI—Advanced Composites Manufacturing Innovation	IACMI was formed in 2015 to develop and demonstrate technologies that will make advanced fiber-reinforced polymer composites at 50% lower cost, using 75% less energy, with 95% or more reuse or recycling of the material within a decade.
	Lightweight, high-strength, and high-stiffness composite materials have been identified as a key technology that can cut across sectors, with the potential to achieve an energy-efficient transportation sector, enable efficient power generation, and increase renewable power production. The range of lightweight, high-strength composite applications is vast, from autos, to aircraft, to wind blades.
	The challenges to accomplishing this include high costs, low production speeds (long cycle times), high manufacturing energy intensity for composite materials, lack of recyclability, and a need to improve design, modeling, and inspection tools and meet regulatory requirements. Technology acceleration and manufacturing research are needed to meet production cost and performance targets, from constituent materials production to final composite structure fabrication.
	IACMI's hub is in Knoxville, Tennessee, and was supported by a $70 million award from the Department of Energy's Energy Efficiency and Renewable Energy Advanced Manufacturing Office, which was matched by $180 million. It includes 57 companies, 15 universities and laboratories, and 14 other entities.

(continued)

Table 6.1

(continued)

Institute Name	Description
AIM Photonics—American Institute for Manufacturing Integrated Photonics	AIM Photonics was formed in 2015 with hub locations in Albany and Rochester, New York. Its goal is to foster ultra-high-speed transmission of signals for communications, new high-performance computing, and sensors and imaging enabling health sector advances.
	Integrated photonics requires the integration of multiple photonic and electronic devices (for example, lasers, detectors, waveguides and passive structures, modulators, electronic controls, and optical interconnects) on a single substrate with nanoscale features. The benefits of integrating these components could be very significant: simplified system design, improved system performance, reduced component space and power consumption, and improved performance and reliability, which will enable important new capabilities and functionality with lower costs. The current photonics manufacturing sector is a collection of interrelated but largely independent businesses, organizations, and activities. It has the potential to grow into an ecosystem but lacks the organization and aggregated market strength needed to efficiently innovate manufacturing technologies for cost-effective design, fabrication, testing, assembly, and packaging of integrated photonic devices.
	Aim Photonics' focus is on building an end-to-end photonics ecosystem, including domestic foundries, integrated design tools, and automated packaging, assembly, and testing, as well as a focus on workforce development. The federal award was matched by over $200 million in state and industry support.
NextFlex—Flexible Hybrid Electronics	NextFlex was formed in 2015 with a hub in San Jose, California, within Silicon Valley. Its goal is highly tailorable devices on flexible, stretchable substrates that combine thin CMOS components with new components added through printing processes. These represent flexible and hybrid features for circuits, communications, sensing, and power sources that are unlike current silicon processors.
	Flexible hybrid electronics would preserve the full operation of traditional electronic circuits, but in novel flexible architectures and forms that allow for bending, stretching, or folding. These highly functional devices could be part of curved, irregular, and stretched objects. They could expand traditional electronic packaging to new forms, enabling new classes of commercial and defense technologies. Examples include medical devices and sensors, sensors to monitor structural or vehicle performance, sensors interoperating through the Internet or as sensor clusters to monitor physical positions, wearable performance or information devices, robotics, human-robotic interface devices, and lightweight human-portable electronic systems. This includes applications in wearable technologies, new information devices

Table 6.1
(continued)

Institute Name	Description
	and sensors, medical prosthetics and sensors, and unattended and mobile sensors.
	The DOD Mantech award was for $75 million, with an industry, state, and local government cost share of $96 million. It includes 22 member companies ranging from semiconductor firms and their suppliers, to aerospace and life sciences firms, 17 universities, and state and regional organizations.
AFFOA— Advanced Functional Fabrics of America	AFFOA was announced in April 2016 and is starting up with some 80 members by the beginning of 2017, including both small and larger firms, universities, and community colleges. It is headquartered in Cambridge, Massachusetts, and plans a series of regional nodes.
	Scientific advances have enabled fibers and textiles with extraordinary properties, including strength, flame resistance, and electrical conductivity, that could become electronic, sensor, and communications components. This new range of fibers and textiles is composed of specialty fabrics, industrial fabrics, electronic textiles, and other forms of advanced textiles. They could provide communication, lighting, cooling, health monitoring, battery storage, and many new functions never before associated with textiles. These technical textiles are built on a foundation of synthetic and natural fiber blends and multimaterial fibers that have a wide range of applications in commercial and defense sectors that go far beyond traditional wearable fabrics.
	AFFOA joins $75 million in DOD Mantech funds with some $240 million in industry and state matching support. It aims to serve as a public-private partnership to support an end-to-end innovation ecosystem in the United States for revolutionary fibers and textiles manufacturing and leverage domestic manufacturing facilities to develop and scale up manufacturing processes. It plans to provide rapid product realization opportunities, based on robust design and simulation tools, pilot production facilities, a collaborative infrastructure with suppliers, and workforce development opportunities. The institute wants to effect a revolution in fiber and textiles, incorporating IT advances and integrating intelligent devices with fibers.
Smart Manufacturing Innovation Institute	The winner of the new Smart Manufacturing Innovation Institute was announced in June 2016 by President Barack Obama and is now in its startup phase and setting its membership. It is headquartered in Los Angeles.
	Smart manufacturing can be characterized as the convergence of information and communications technologies with manufacturing processes to allow a new level of real-time control of

(continued)

Table 6.1

(continued)

Institute Name	Description
	energy, productivity, and costs across factories and companies. It was identified by the AMP2.0 report as a high-priority manufacturing technology area in need of federal investment. Tying together advanced sensors, controls, information technology processes and platforms, and advanced energy and production management systems, smart manufacturing has the potential to drive energy efficiency and manufacturing capability in a wide range of industrial sectors.
	Of the Smart Manufacturing Innovation Institute's $140 million budget, $70 million over five years is already-appropriated federal funding from the Energy Department's Advanced Manufacturing Office, and the remainder is in matching funds. The Smart Manufacturing Innovation Institute will focus on integrating information technology into the manufacturing process through devices such as smart sensors that reduce energy use. For example, the institute plans to partner with DOE's Institute for Advanced Composites Manufacturing Innovation to test advanced sensors in the production of carbon fiber. The Smart Manufacturing Innovation Institute expects to partner with more than 200 companies, universities, national labs, and nonprofits. Microsoft Corp., Alcoa Inc., Corning Inc., ExxonMobil, Google, the National Renewable Energy Laboratory, and numerous smaller firms are among the partners. The institute plans to launch five centers, focusing on technology development and transfer and workforce training, in regions around the country, headed by universities and labs in California (UCLA), Texas (Texas A&M), North Carolina (North Carolina State University) New York (Rensselaer Polytechnic Institute), and Washington (Pacific Northwest National Laboratory).
RAPID—Rapid Advancement in Process Intensification Deployment Institute	On December 9, 2016, the EERE office announced that a consortium led by the American Institute of Chemical Engineers would form the fourth institute sponsored by the Department of Energy, calling it a critical step in an administration's effort to double U.S. energy productivity by 2030. Leveraging up to $70 million in federal funding with a higher level of private cost-share commitments from over 130 partners, RAPID will focus on developing breakthrough technologies to boost domestic energy productivity and energy efficiency by 20% in five years through manufacturing processes in industries such as oil and gas, pulp and paper, and various domestic chemical manufacturers.
	Traditional chemical manufacturing relies on large-scale, energy-intensive processing. The new institute will leverage approaches to modular chemical process intensification— including combining multiple complex processes such as mixing,

Table 6.1
(continued)

Institute Name	Description
	reaction, and separation into single steps—with the goal of improving energy productivity and efficiency, cutting operating costs, and reducing waste. Process breakthroughs can dramatically shrink the footprint of equipment needed on a factory floor or eliminate waste by using the raw input materials more efficiently. For example, by simplifying and shrinking the process, this approach could enable natural gas refining directly at the well-head, saving up to half of the energy lost in the ethanol cracking process today. In the chemical industry alone, these technologies could save more than $9 billion annually in U.S. processing costs.
NIIMBL—National Institute for Innovation in Manufacturing Biopharmaceuticals	On December 16, 2016, Secretary of Commerce announced an award of $70 million to the new NIIMBL institute. This was the first institute with a focus area proposed by industry and the first funded by the Department of Commerce. The agency developed an "open topic" approach, where a new institute could cover any area not currently targeted by an existing institute. NIST had launched an "Industry-proposed Institutes Competition" as a way to provide a bottom-up topic selection process to allow industry-led consortia to propose technology areas seen as critical by regional manufacturers. NIIMBL was the result.
	NIIMBL will aim to transform the production process for biopharmaceutical products. Overall, it will seek to advance U.S. leadership in the biopharma industry, improve medical treatments, and ensure a qualified workforce by developing new training programs matched to specific biopharma skill needs. The announcement was made at the University of Delaware, which will coordinate the institute in partnership with Commerce's NIST. In addition to the federal funding, the new institute received an initial investment commitment of $129 million in matching funds from a consortium of 150 companies, educational institutions, research centers, coordinating bodies, nonprofits, and Manufacturing Extension Partnerships across the country.
ARMI—Advanced Regenerative Manufacturing Institute	On December 21, 2016, the Department of Defense announced an award to establish ARMI at a White House event celebrating the progress the National Network for Manufacturing Innovation, now ManufacturingUSA, has made. This new institute will be the seventh led by DOD.
	New Hampshire's U.S. senators and its governor joined in a parallel, in-state, bipartisan announcement of the $80 million, five-year award to establish the biomanufacturing consortium, which will be headquartered in the Manchester Millyard. The institute—led by a coalition that includes DEKA R&D Corporation, the University of New Hampshire, and the Dartmouth-Hitchcock health care system—is tasked with developing and

(continued)

Table 6.1
(continued)

Institute Name	Description
	biomanufacturing tissues and organs that can be transplanted into patients. DEKA founder Dean Kamen, a noted innovator, will direct the institute. It would pioneer next-generation manufacturing techniques for repairing and replacing cells and tissues. If successful, such technology could lead to the ability to manufacture new skin or life-saving organs for the many Americans stuck on transplant waiting lists. The institute will focus on solving the cross-cutting manufacturing challenges that stand in the way of producing new synthetic tissues and organs—such as improving the availability, reproducibility, accessibility, and standardization of manufacturing materials, technologies, and processes. Collaborations are expected across multiple disciplines, from 3D bioprinting, cell science, and process design, to automated pharmaceutical screening methods, to the supply chain expertise needed to rapidly produce and transport these live-saving materials.
REMADE— Reducing Embodied Energy and Decreasing Emissions in Materials Manufacturing	REMADE was selected by DOE on January 4, 2017, to be headquartered in Rochester, New York, and led by the Sustainable Manufacturing Innovation Alliance. REMADE will leverage up to $70 million in federal funding, subject to appropriations, and will be matched by $70 million in private cost-share commitments from over 100 partners. REMADE will focus on driving down the cost of technologies needed to reuse, recycle, and remanufacture materials such as metals, fibers, polymers, and electronic waste, and aims to achieve a 50% improvement in overall energy efficiency by 2027. These efficiency measures, DOE indicated, could save billions in energy costs and improve U.S. economic competitiveness through innovative new manufacturing techniques.
	It would aim to reduce the total lifetime energy use of manufactured materials via reuse and recycling. The institute will focus on reducing the total lifetime use of energy in manufactured materials by developing new cradle-to-cradle technologies for the reuse, recycling, and remanufacturing of man-made materials. U.S. manufacturing consumes nearly a third of the nation's total energy use annually, with much of that energy embodied in the physical products made in manufacturing. New technologies to better repurpose these materials could save U.S. manufacturers and the nation up to 1.6 quadrillion BTU of energy annually, equivalent to 280 million barrels of oil, or a month's worth of the nation's oil imports.
ARM—Advanced Robotics Manufacturing Institute	The Department of Defense proposed this new manufacturing institute to focus on building U.S. leadership in smart collaborative robotics, where advanced robots work alongside humans seamlessly, safely, and intuitively to do the heavy lifting on an assembly line or handle intricate or dangerous

Table 6.1

(continued)

Institute Name	Description

tasks with precision. It argued that people collaborating with robots, which assist them, have the potential to change a broad swath of manufacturing sectors, from defense and space to automotive and health, enabling the reliable and efficient production of high-quality, customized products.

ARM, the fourteenth ManufacturingUSA institute to be announced, was named on January 13, 2017, by the Department of Defense. It will be headquartered in Pittsburgh, and the proposal group was convened by Carnegie Mellon University. The institute will bring together a very large team, including 84 industry partners, 35 universities, and 40 other groups in 31 states. Federal funds plus industry and state cost sharing will total some $250 million; the federal commitment is for $80 million. Clemson University's Center for Workforce Development will lead the new institute's workforce training programs.

DOD described in its announcement statement the need for the new institute:

> The use of robotics is already present in manufacturing environments, but today's robots are typically expensive, singularly purposed, challenging to reprogram, and require isolation from humans for safety. Robotics are increasingly necessary to achieve the level of precision required for defense and other industrial manufacturing needs, but the capital cost and complexity of use often limits small to mid-size manufacturers from utilizing the technology. The ARM Institute's mission therefore is to create and then deploy robotic technology by integrating the diverse collection of industry practices and institutional knowledge across many disciplines— sensor technologies, end-effector development, software and artificial intelligence, materials science, human and machine behavior modeling, and quality assurance—to realize the promises of a robust manufacturing innovation ecosystem. Technologies ripe for significant evolution within the ARM Institute include, but are not limited to, collaborative robotics, robot control (learning, adaptation, and repurposing), dexterous manipulation, autonomous navigation and mobility, perception and sensing, and testing, verification, and validation.

DOD characterized the current domestic capabilities in manufacturing robotics technology as "fragmented," citing a need for better organization and collaboration to better position the United States for the global competition in this sector.

• Using next-generation metals manufacturing techniques, Lightweight Innovations for Tomorrow (LIFT), the Detroit institute focused on lightweight metals, has successfully demonstrated how to reduce the weight of core metal parts found in cars and trucks by 40 percent, potentially improving fuel efficiency and saving consumers fuel costs. In addition, LIFT has introduced curricula in 22 states to train workers on the use of lightweight metals. In the summer of 2016, 38 companies hosted students in paid manufacturing internships in partnership with LIFT.

• America Makes has attracted hundreds of millions of dollars in new manufacturing investment to its region, including helping to attract GE's new $32 million global 3D printing hub and spurring Alcoa to invest $60 million in its New Kensington, Pennsylvania facilities, both of which will benefit from proximity to America Makes and its expertise in 3D printing with metal powders.

• In addition, America Makes, with Deloitte and other partners, has created a free online course on the fundamentals of 3D printing for businesses. Over the last year, over 14,000 business leaders have taken this course to learn what 3D printing can do for their businesses.

Deloitte LLP, commissioned by DOD's Mantech, undertook an independent assessment of the institute model in 2016. Its overall findings, released in a January 2017 report, are quite positive. It found that adoption of advanced manufacturing was critical for progress in the overall domestic economy to improve productivity growth and the trade imbalance, and for job creation. In this regard, it found that the public-private partnership model of the institutes can create collaborations to improve R&D investment in manufacturing, overcome problems of collective action in the sector, reduce barriers to innovation, enable better access to intellectual property, and cut risk and cost through shared asset access.[36] Concerning technology facilitation, it found that institutes can play a significant role in making investments in manufacturing R&D less risky, particularly given the pattern of uneven investment between firms of different sizes and in different sectors. Shared advanced equipment, R&D pooling, technology roadmapping, and knowledge sharing enabled by the institutes could create significant benefits for industry participants that would be unachievable on their own.[37]

Regarding workforce training, Deloitte found that the institute model could mitigate the talent gap industrial firms now face as they move into advanced manufacturing. Institute workforce programs included assessments of workforce supply and demand, employee credentialing and certification, and technology-focused training and apprenticeship programs.[38] It also found significant progress in creating improved ecosystems for production. The portfolio of institutes, both in the range of technology focus areas and geographical reach, was a strength of the system. The institutes' high levels of membership, representing firms of different sizes and types, was a signal of the initial success of the model. The institutes were also found to be playing a role in strengthening regional economic clusters key to regional growth.[39] The Deloitte report also made a number of program recommendations, some of which, as noted, complement the list of institute challenges presented later in the chapter. However, the Deloitte review amounted to an early certification from an independent expert source that the institute model was on the right track.

Manufacturing Institute Case Studies

To get a better idea of what is evolving in the institutes at ground level, let us look at two institute case studies in more depth, one up and running and the other still scaling up.

IACMI

The Institute of Advanced Composites Manufacturing Innovation (IACMI), headquartered in Knoxville, Tennessee,[40] was selected in a competition run by and with costs shared by the Department of Energy. Its objective is to develop and demonstrate innovative technologies that will, within ten years, make advanced fiber-reinforced polymer composites at

- 50% lower cost,
- using 75% less energy, and
- reusing or recycling more than 95% of the material.

Clear and unique institute focus. Institutes including IACMI are designed to address a critical industry need with a clear and unique focus. The opportunity IACMI is attempting to meet is development of lightweight composites that offer significant benefits to energy efficiency and renewable power generation compared with current materials. This will require deployment of advanced technologies to make composites at significantly lower cost, faster, using less energy, and that can be readily recycled. Although there are numerous technical and institutional barriers, the field arguably offers significant opportunities for U.S. industry.

Consortium approach. IACMI, like the other institutes, is based on a consortium across industry, universities, and government. It includes large firms, such as Dow, Ford, GE, Dupont, and Boeing, as well as smaller firms, initially totaling 57, that reach across the chemical, automotive, wind, and aerospace industries. University participants include the University of Tennessee, Penn State, the University of Illinois, and Purdue—15 universities, labs, and colleges overall. IACMI also includes states and economic development entities. It now has some 108 participants from all sectors. The federal cost share, through the Department of Energy's Energy Efficiency and Renewable Energy office and its Advanced Manufacturing Office, is $70 million, but cost sharing from the participating states is close to that, and combined with industry, the nonfederal cost share totals some $180 million.

The core idea. The institute aims to provide access to major resources and a partnership across industry and universities to develop new low-cost, high-speed, and efficient manufacturing and recycling process technologies that will promote widespread use of advanced fiber-reinforced polymer composites. The institute seeks to link leading industrial manufacturers, material suppliers, software developers, and government and academic experts. The focus will be on dramatically lowering the overall manufacturing costs of advanced composites, cutting the energy required to form them and ensuring they are recyclable.

The industry value proposition. IACMI is working to offer four basic services that will support its industry partners:

• *Access to shared R&D resources.* Provide access to equipment, from lab level to full-scale production level, to enable demonstration, testing, and reduced risk for industry investment.
• *Applied R&D.* Leverage significant government R&D, plus cost sharing from industry, and academic investments, to create innovative solutions to challenges formed from member input.
• *A composites virtual factory.* Access to end-to-end commercial modeling and simulation software for composite designers and manufacturers through a web-based platform.
• *Workforce training.* Provide specialized training to prepare the current and future workforce for the latest manufacturing methods and technologies for advanced composites.

Addressing goals and challenges. The institute has developed five- and ten-year technical goals noted above: to reach 25% and then 50% lower carbon fiber–reinforced polymer (CFRP) cost; to reach 50% and then 75% reduction in CFRP embodied energy requirements; and to reach 80% and then 95% composite recyclability into useful products. Its impact goals, with a series of targets to be achieved over time, include enhanced energy productivity; reduced life-cycle energy consumption; increased domestic production capacity; job growth; and economic development.

Roadmap and strategic investment plans. IACMI takes a portfolio approach to projects. Its initial projects were identified in its proposal to the Department of Energy and include strengthening infrastructure capacity for materials and processing as well as modeling and simulation, and work-force development in strategic areas. The aim is national benefit, including in the automotive, wind, and compressed gas storage sectors.

A second phase involves technology roadmapping, which is driven by IACMI's chief technology officer and an industry and technology advisory board. It aims to identify key hurdles to high-impact, large-scale advanced composites manufacturing and prioritize opportunities across the materials and manufacturing supply chain.

A third area is developing a strategic investment plan, driven by IACMI's board and its technical advisory board. The aim is to change the innovation cycle to enable rapid adoption and scale-up of advanced composites manufacturing. Ongoing open project calls for technology development projects align with the strategic investment plan and technology roadmap, with an emphasis on projects with high near-term impact.

Accelerating discovery to application to production. This is a general goal and, like other institutes, IACMI will seek to

- establish a presence, at scale, in the "missing middle" of advanced manufacturing research (TRL 4–7);
- create an Industrial Commons, supporting future manufacturing hubs, with active partnering between stakeholders;
- emphasize and support longer-term investments by industry;
- combine R&D with workforce development and training.

An overarching objective will be new advanced manufacturing capabilities and industries in composites in the United States.

Shared resources. IACMI's first CEO, Craig Blue, was a veteran of Oak Ridge National Lab's Manufacturing Demonstration Facility[41] and worked to apply its success in building industry collaborations using advanced technologies and equipment at a demonstration facility. IACMI, in developing a series of shared resource facilities, believes that these must be in close proximity to industry users. It aims not to replicate what industry already has available but rather to offer new kinds of infrastructure relevant to advanced composites in industry sector ecosystems—particularly automotive, aerospace, wind, and chemicals—and is now in the process of leveraging over $100 million in investments to create such facilities. It seeks to use the regional pull of OEMs but link in supply chains to participate in them.

Shared facilities for a range of advanced composite technologies are now located in six states: in Michigan at Michigan State University, focused on vehicle technologies (Michigan is the top auto-producing state); at Ohio's University of Dayton Research Institute, for compressed gas storage; at the National Renewable Energy Lab (NREL) in Colorado, for wind turbine blades; at Tennessee's Oak Ridge National Lab and the University of Tennessee, as well as the neighboring University of Kentucky, for overall composite materials and processing technologies; and at Purdue University in Indiana (the third-largest auto-producing state), for a design, predictive modeling, and simulation facility that serves all industry sectors. These facilities serve the states with 70% of automotive production, 70% of auto R&D, the largest wind blade production area, and 60% of the manufacturers of vehicles fueled by compressed gas. IACMI is consciously focused on a national mission, developing advanced composites, but its facilities are located in regions that serve the major composites industry sectors. Taking a page from the Fraunhofer model, it is attempting to offer in-depth infrastructure, lab, and production support facilities geared to regional core industry sectors.

Applied R&D. IACMI is using its ongoing composites technology roadmapping effort, led by its technology area directors and boards, to identify key technology gaps and needs. The roadmap, in, turn, forms its technology development agenda, which falls in the Technology Readiness Level (TRL) 4–7 areas. These development projects link teams of researchers having expertise in the relevant areas with industry for collaborative efforts. This work is supported primarily from the DOE's $70 million cost share but also links to industry and state cost shares. In addition to these focused research efforts, IACMI has "open calls" for research outside its roadmap, so that the roadmap serves as an enabler, not a restriction on its R&D agenda. If companies are concerned about the need for earlier-stage science work (TRL 2–3) in particular areas, IACMI can also facilitate that R&D.

Composites virtual factory. A new design, simulation, and modeling facility has been formed at Purdue, as noted, that is accessible to industry participants for testing approaches for production of composites. It receives input from the various shared facilities working on different production sector needs to prepare modeling and simulation. In turn, it is accessible to firms working at the particular regional facilities, so there is a two-way street between the facilities' sites and the virtual site. It is the only open access composites simulation facility in the United States and one of only two in the world.

Workforce training. Overall, IACMI estimates that in 2015 there were over 380,000 job postings in composite fields in the institute's six core states, with a three-to-one difference between jobs posted and new worker supply.[42] In the institute's region, in 2014 some 128,000 certificates and degrees were awarded. IACMI's training program is tied to efforts by the major industry association for composites, the American Composites Manufacturing Association (ACMA). So far, education efforts have worked at multiple levels. At the engineering level, 15 undergraduate and graduate engineering and science interns have worked at IACMI and 100 at the shared facilities, and at the technician level, two major workforce training sessions have been held in Tennessee and Colorado, where participants numbered over 100 at each and came from many states. IACMI works with ACMA and also coordinates with another institute, LIFT, on education efforts on STEM and the area maker movement. The latter is a good example of using the institute network for help in developing particular program areas. IACMI is preparing both online and "blended" training materials to expand its reach, favoring the blended learning approach to workshops and enhancing learning-by-doing sessions with online support materials.

Overall, IACMI's leadership was particularly concerned with its speed—can it create the integration across the complex system of over 100 participants and its group of regional shared facilities that will enable fast movement of new technologies and their implementation? They tell participating firms that "we measure our success by your success"—the best success metric being successful firms. They believe that industry will only continue to respond and participate if the institute can move rapidly on technology development and implementation.

IACMI has been working to tighten its ties to two core constituencies—small manufacturers and states. It has made integration of supply chain participants into its shared facilities a priority. These include small companies, of which there are many in composites. IACMI is working to link with the area's state Manufacturing Extension Programs supported by NIST, which offer technology and support services to small manufacturers. It has a program, for example, to embed MEP staff in IACMI to collaboratively tackle workforce training efforts. Concerning states, it has state economic officials on its board, regular meetings with states, and reporting systems for the participating states. Work with the state of Indiana has been a particular success story. While the state government initially had limited interest, cost sharing at a $15 million level, it has provided major support for the new shared composites facility at Purdue and is considering another major facility investment. Its total investment may approach $115 million. Indiana has recently added an experienced technology policy expert as the "chief innovation officer" of the state's economic development corporation,[43] a signal of a new kind of approach by the state. Although IACMI is still new, sustainability is a looming issue for it as well as for the other institutes. It is working to increase its state and private sector funded projects and believes it must work to relentlessly improve its capability to move quickly in order to be in a sustainable position.

IACMI provides a good look at the structure and aims being adopted by many of the new manufacturing institutes. However, the institute model is flexible, depending on the sector to be served, and each institute can vary significantly.

AFFOA

Advanced Functional Fibers of America (AFFOA) is an institute that is still scaling up, but because its aspirational model is somewhat different, it suggests the range of approaches possible in manufacturing institutes.[44] It was announced by the secretary of defense on April 1, 2016, in Cambridge, Massachusetts, and seeks to apply a nationwide distributed prototyping model through a product development orientation. As the institute's CEO, Yoel Fink, notes, it was created in a context where textiles have not changed much—cotton dates from 5000 B.C. in Mexico and the Indus Valley, and basic industrial weaving dates from the 1780s Industrial Revolution in Britain. The following description of its hoped-for approaches spells out options that could be considered by other institutes, although, again, these are still plans, not implemented programs.

Product orientation. AFFOA is oriented toward creating new products, not simply toward manufacturing or process. This means manufacturing technology development in a product context. As AFFOA's federal program manager, Stephen Luckowski, puts it, this is "process through product."[45] Luckowski says the goal is to "prototype on production-relevant processes" so that the institute can make manufacturing technologies available and affordable within its industrial base, thus creating the supply chain of the future. AFFOA, then, puts manufacturing development and demonstration activities in this product context. It aims to create new fibers and fabrics that are smart—that are communication systems, that light up and glow, that are battery storage systems, that are health monitoring systems, or that are radiation monitors. And fibers are not only in clothing but are also in tires, composites, furniture, vehicles, and potentially many other objects— roofing and building systems, for example. The perspective of AFFOA is that manufacturing is not the end in itself. The question is, manufacturing for what? Entirely new products, not simply processes, create public engagement and understanding, and that is AFFOA's orientation—such as textiles that for the first time do significant and complex things. New processes and manufacturing approaches—for example, how to embed LEDs into a fiber—will flow from new product needs. The history of textiles has been one of continuous pressure to lower costs driving ever-lower margins; AFFOA, by introducing a wide range of advanced technologies integrated into fibers, a new step, aims to return the sector to producing high-value products, therefore generating higher margins.

Prototyping network. Although AFFOA has a central node at MIT in Cambridge, Massachusetts, in the New England region that was the nineteenth-century center for U.S. textile fabrication, the expectation is that this will be one of many nodes. It is developing a model of Fabrics Discovery Centers located near major participating universities, using diverse funding sources, from AFFOA itself to member firms.[46] The first center opened in Massachusetts in June 2017. These would colocate prototyping capabilities with advanced equipment and expertise in order to incubate and prototype new fiber technologies. Each would have an area of expertise, depending on regional firm and university expertise, focusing on low cost, rapid prototyping, and creation of new technologies and applications. They could serve start-ups as well as established firms and offer competitive prizes for students developing new fiber advances.

AFFOA's proposal included a collection of companies, from large IT firms, such as Analog Devices, Intel, and Apple, that see new IT enabling outlets through fabrics, to Nike, which does not now produce in the United States but is interested in the new fiber technologies AFFOA may enable, to advanced materials firms such as Dupont, to Inman Mills in South Carolina, which is a fifth-generation family firm still operating despite the departure of most U.S. textile manufacturing abroad, which specializes in high-quality fabrics and is likewise interested in technical fibers. The proposal also included a strong base of small and midsize firms still in fabrics and textiles; numerous universities with textile and materials technology programs, including MIT, Drexel, Clemson, North Carolina State, and Gaston College in North Carolina; and numerous states, from Massachusetts and Pennsylvania in the Northeast to the Carolinas and Georgia in the South, to the Midwest and the West. By spring 2017, AFFOA had formally signed up over 80 members.[47]

By locating and linking a wide range of fabrication technologies among its numerous member firms, including those for weaving, knitting, and assembly, AFFOA aims to enable rapid prototyping in this sector, really for the first time, which would be quickly followed by contract manufacturing capability for the newly prototyped technical fibers and fabrics. In effect, this can be a way to quickly launch new supply chains around new products.

Could this work? The first new product was attempted in June 2016, three months after AFFOA was announced, and was a complex "smart" fabric for the military. It provided a test for this new system. After a new advanced fiber, which was both functional and integrated, was developed through a noted defense lab, four AFFOA members signed up to do a rapid prototype of a full fabric. It was a unique integrated fabric, involving 40 layers of many kinds of technical fibers, each no more than a micron thick. Within two weeks of receiving the specs, Inman Mills shipped fabric back to AFFOA for DOD. It had the potential to create an entirely new, high-value product line important to military customers.

Knowledge as a resource. The institute's federal program manager, Stephen Luckowski, notes that it is engaged in efforts to build data management, modeling, and analytics throughout the textile supply chain.[48] The fibers and textiles industry generally lacks modeling, simulation, and decision tools that could facilitate predictive designs and precision manufacturing for mass customization of products. There is also a need in this sector to develop some of the basic design tools required for new electronic devices in textiles, as these do not yet exist. With its Fabrics Discovery Center capability, AFFOA potentially can build a physical and digital catalog of fibers and textiles accessible to AFFOA members, containing pedigree data that can be used by individual members or used collectively to inform standards. With its projects, AFFOA can partner with commercial companies to build design and analytical tools and work to commercialize them for broader use by industry.

IP aggregator. To enable its rapid prototyping capability, AFFOA plans to serve as a collector of intellectual property (IP) rights from its numerous university participants, again in a somewhat unique model. The universities have thousands of patents likely to be relevant to new technical fibers and materials, which, like most university patents, are largely collecting dust, unused. AFFOA will aim to represent the universities (and their faculty inventors) as their agent for this IP, seeking to collect, organize, and sort the IP into coherent groups for ease of access by companies. The universities would retain their IP rights and receive the royalties back, with AFFOA serving as the arranger to link them to industry needs through its industry members. Since numerous technical fibers will require more than one patent, AFFOA hopes to become a one-stop shop for industry and an enabler for university IP, cutting way back on patent access issues and negotiation time. When a member firm (or group of firms) builds new fiber and textile products on top of this bed of IP, they retain proprietary rights for their own products. But a requirement of the IP access through AFFOA is that follow-on production be in the United States—this is how AFFOA assures that manufacturing gains from the federal institute investment flow to the nation.

Efficient decision making. Since a goal of AFFOA is to create a large and varied network, it has a simple and straightforward membership agreement for its participants of only a few pages. This is in contrast to the lengthy agreement of dozens of pages often required when IP is involved, which necessitates a lengthy legal review and follow-on negotiations. It should be of particular benefit to participating small and midsize firms. It has enabled a relatively rapid member sign-up rate.

While many institutes have boards that attempt to represent all of their stakeholders, these can be unwieldy, with 40 or more members. AFFOA has created a small board of ten for more rapid decision making (with a mix of large and small firms, two universities, and an advanced technology firm) but also has a way to link in its government overseers from DOD's Mantech program so they can be partners and collaborators. There are relatively small councils for efficient technology development (with topical technical work groups), workforce development, and economic impact (to include the states), and topical councils on particular issues enable other participants to be involved. A stakeholder council brings in the full membership group.[49]

Enabling start-ups. Few manufacturing institutes so far have contemplated a role for start-ups, but AFFOA is a bit different. It expects that its rapid prototype capability, accessible to small manufacturers, and its IP enabler role, will actually help enable production start-ups in the fiber area—something that has not often occurred in the United States in recent decades. If a start-up has an idea, it can license compatible IP through AFFOA, then take advantage of the rapid prototyping to derisk the technology—to prove it can be produced, to test and retest it, and to understand its exact production cost—and then be in a far better position to seek financing, whether from a venture firm or corporate collaborator. The start-up would have the produced "thing," not just an idea of the "thing," to take to its potential financers. It could also use the AFFOA distributed network as its contract manufacturer. This rapid prototyping capability might conceivably start to resemble the prototyping capability that China has been able to achieve in areas like Shenzhen. Its Fabrics Discovery Centers will aim to serve start-ups as well as established firms and to nurture new technologies.

In addition, the fashion and design programs at participants like Drexel are also part of AFFOA, as are leading technical schools like MIT, Virginia Tech, and NC State. Fabric and fiber start-ups tying new technology to design could actually link together through the AFFOA network—perhaps curing a deep system disconnect. The state of Pennsylvania, working with Drexel, is planning its own new start-up incubator to enable this new set of possibilities, and other incubators, or links to established incubators, could follow.

Still unfolding are AFFOA's education and training programs. The textile sector has experienced massive employment cuts in recent years, which has discouraged talent from entering the sector. Wages also remain low because of intense international competition, which has wiped out much of the sector. Existing firms complain they are not attracting talented employees, and remedying this will be critical if the sector is to adopt dramatic new technology advances. If a new line of fiber and fabric technologies can evolve to enable and create new, highly functional technologies, higher margins could enable wage advances and create workforce interest. However, the systems for training and education, including online and blended approaches that link university expertise, community colleges, and industry, still need to develop through AFFOA to help the sector get around this dilemma. In general, education has not been a top initial institute priority; this will be needed to serve member needs. The education programs are enablers, as we will discuss in chapter 8; they can create change agents that can lead industries to shift their manufacturing models.

To summarize, the following interesting ideas are being developed at AFFOA:

• AFFOA's *product orientation* as opposed to process orientation appeals to firms that in the end need to develop products. The process advances that, with this new advanced technology, must accompany product evolution are built into the model. New products also supply clearer pictures to the public and policymakers of what the new institute might yield than complex process descriptions can provide.

• AFFOA will attempt to build a strong and varied network of firms with a wide range of expertise to *enable rapid prototyping* in a sector that has had few new products in the recent past. The linkages between firms of varying expertise not only could enable prototyping but could rapidly shift to *contract manufacturing*. AFFOA talks about how it wants to bring Moore's Law for semiconductors to fiber and fabric by creating a system and accompanying network for rapid prototyping, rapid product development, and rapid production that could enable rapid implementation of major advances.

• It will build the prototyping on a base of IP rights where it will act as an *intellectual property aggregator* for universities that through their research hold IP relevant in this area. By serving as an agent for the universities and creating a one-stop shop for industry product developers, it hopes to speed product development. Universities are always touchy about their Bayh-Dole Act IP rights derived from federally funded R&D, but AFFOA will aim not to displace their rights but instead better enable industry access to them, with royalties flowing back to the universities.

• Its *small, streamlined board* and *short member agreement* may help encourage efficient decision making and expand participation.

• Its network for prototyping and potential for contract manufacturing allows AFFOA to serve as a *supply chain creator for small and midsize firms*. This has been an issue for many institutes, which are organized around technology innovation that small firms, which do not conduct R&D, can only play a limited role in. This capability to create a supply chain through its prototype network may be a better way to bring small manufacturing firms into the manufacturing institutes. It is also a mechanism for encouraging *start-ups*, which could obtain a rapid prototyping capability that enables rapid product development and thereby help them obtain follow-on financing.

Challenges Faced by the Manufacturing Institutes

The manufacturing institute program was launched very rapidly by the administration, in response to a policy crisis—a sharp decline in a major U.S. economic sector, manufacturing, in the aftermath of the 2008–2009 recession. Because of a congressional ideological deadlock, the administration was unable to start with a clean slate to design and launch a completely new program. Instead, for funding and organization it had to turn to existing agencies with their existing programs and funding, grafting new programs onto established organizations. So, the large foot of a very innovative new program for manufacturing innovation had to be squeezed into a series of existing agency program shoes. Needless to say, it could not be a perfect fit. All said, launching such a major new, innovative program in such a short time was a remarkable political accomplishment, requiring dedication from many talented people from both the public and the private sectors.

Like any new program, some of the experimental pilots will fail and some will succeed. Only a few of the new institutes have been around long enough to even start to evaluate their progress against their mission statements; the others are still infants. Transforming a massive economic sector like manufacturing through innovation is not a short-term project. Clearly, there has been major progress in getting some important R&D and technology strategies off the ground in a range of important new technology areas that could dramatically affect the future of manufacturing. This is a significant accomplishment. In light of this progress in getting the institutes up and running, it is now an appropriate time to think hard about the overall model and a new stage of features and improvements that can now be considered. We can now see a new set of challenges that have come up as the institutes have evolved and consider how to meet them. A number of institutes are already addressing them, so many represent, in effect, best practices that are now evolving, highlighted here as lessons relevant to the full group. So the list that follows, developed from discussions with institute leaders, federal agency officials, and participating university experts, represents a number of early lessons learned that may have more general application, as well as enhancements that can be considered for the network overall.

Orientation toward technology missions versus production needs. Manufacturing institutes created to date are working in topic areas selected by the federal R&D agencies to meet their missions, not necessarily to also fit the needs of the manufacturing sector. They have tended to be more oriented toward technology development rather than other tasks. This is not a surprise. As noted, the institutes were created by and through established mission R&D agencies, and their focus therefore had to be on topics that fit the missions and needs of the agency (DOD and DOE) under available authorizations and appropriation laws. And the agencies understand and focus primarily on mission R&D, which has carried through to the institutes. These agency missions did not include the future of U.S. manufacturing—at DOD, the core mission is national security, and at DOE it is energy technology; the funding from these agencies has to fit and serve those missions. In only one case—the Commerce Department/NIST 2016 "open topic" competition—did industry itself propose the topics, although the other agencies have now invited comments from industry in the selection of focus topics. It must be added that after the initial rounds of institutes, the agencies have attempted more industry and university outreach on topic selection through Requests for Information (RFIs) and workshops, but the topic must still meet priority agency needs. So, in effect, the advanced manufacturing effort to date has been to launch interesting and significant new technology areas tied to agency missions, not solely to manufacturing innovation breakthroughs needed by manufacturing sectors. Fortunately, however, these two pathways have largely converged.

The AMP2.0 report identified core criteria for selecting focus areas for advanced manufacturing institutes ("manufacturing technology areas"—MTAs), which, although not formally applied by the agencies, remain illuminating and relevant:

1. *Industry or market pull*. Does there exist a current "pull" or demand for this MTA by industry? If industry is not yet adopting this MTA, is there a strong perceived pull by the market or consumers?

2. *Cross-cutting*. Does this MTA cut across many sectors (automotive, aerospace, biotech, infrastructure) and across multiple sizes of manufacturers in the supply chain network?

3. *National or economic security*. Does failure to have U.S. competence or dominance in this MTA pose a threat to national security or to economic security? Does a lack of U.S. competence severely disadvantage the U.S. competitiveness position of the supply network?

4. *Leveraging U.S. strengths*. Does this MTA leverage an already available workforce and education system, unique infrastructure, or policies?[50]

The application of this logical set of selection criteria by the AMP2.0 work group resulted in prioritization of three top technology areas for future institutes: advanced sensing, control, and platforms for manufacturing; visualization, informatics, and digital manufacturing; and advanced materials manufacturing. In fact, agency-selected institute topics did result in the formation of institutes embracing these general technology areas— the Smart Manufacturing Institute, the Digital Manufacturing and Design Innovation Institute, the Advanced Composites Manufacturing Innovation Institute, and the Lightweight and Modern Metals Institute. The detailed technology strategy that the AMP2.0 work group prepared for each topic proved particularly useful as guidance for the Digital Manufacturing and Design Innovation Institute as it started up. So there has been an effort to apply the results of the AMP2.0 criteria in some of the topic selections. But, generally speaking, the areas for institute focus must still be more oriented toward new technologies the agencies must seek to meet their authorized missions than toward overall manufacturing sector needs. Fortunately, as noted, there has been significant overlap; NIST's director of the Advanced Manufacturing Program Office, Michael Molnar, estimates that 9 of the 11 technology areas recommended in the AMP1.0 report are receiving focus at the existing and planned institutes.[51] But a more systematic approach for other technology areas to be selected could create more new production opportunities.[52] If additional institutes are created in the future, agencies could be encouraged to more formally weigh the AMP2.0 criteria listed here in their topic selection process.

Halt in federal support after five years. Starting with the announcement of the first manufacturing institute, America Makes, there has been a requirement that the institutes be self-sustaining without federal funding support after five years. The Revitalize American Manufacturing Act, passed in 2014, likewise adopts a five-year term for federal support to manufacturing institutes created by NIST.

This approach follows the Sematech model, where DARPA's funding for Sematech, the semiconductor industry consortium, ended after five years. This was a politically appealing idea—the feds could pull out after five years, manufacturing would be fixed, and somehow the institutes would continue. In contrast, as will be discussed, Germany's Fraunhofer Institutes face no such cutoff of their federal government support after a relatively short, fixed term. The assumption that the institutes can go independent in five years is problematic. Reinvigorating manufacturing innovation is going to be a long-term project, not a short-term one, and requires technology realism, not technology magic.

For Sematech, a five-year transition worked because, compared with a manufacturing institute, Sematech received massive funding ($100 million a year from DARPA, which was matched by industry), the improvements needed in semiconductor manufacturing processes were studied and understood quickly and could be implemented in a relatively short period, and the industry itself began to expand rapidly with advances in new integrated circuits and thus had new resources to manage the improvements. The Sematech effort, which focused on the manufacturing process for semiconductor equipment and technologies, was relatively straightforward compared with the complex and longer-term tasks faced by the manufacturing institutes.

The federal government historically has funded R&D because of what economists term a "market failure." As critical as R&D is for innovation, in a highly competitive, globalized world, firms are increasingly unable to take on the risk of research because the chances for returns from it are inherently speculative. In industry after industry, major firms in recent decades have sharply curtailed or closed down their R&D labs—the demise of the famous Bell Labs is not an isolated example. The surviving industrial labs are increasingly focused on late-stage development work directly tied to incremental product improvements. This trend among major firms likely is more apparent in the manufacturing sector than in any other; small and midsize manufacturers rarely undertook significant research to begin with. So the technology innovation role of the institutes fills a significant gap in the manufacturing sector for firms small and large. While some of the technologies being pursued by the manufacturing institutes may be sufficiently advanced after five years of development that industry will be prepared to take the risk of further implementation, many will not. A major aim of the advanced manufacturing effort was to bring innovation into close reach of small and midsize manufacturers in particular; picking up advanced technology R&D even after five years is simply not going to be an option for small and midsize firms, and will be a problem for major firms facing steep competition, even if the collaborative, shared research model at an institute, which could cut development costs and risks for participants, continues after the end of federal support. In other words, significant areas of economic market failure are enduring; they do not get fixed in five years but instead continue.

Most of the technologies that new institutes are being organized around will require a longer-term evolution than the five-year term currently fixed for federal support before they are ready for implementation at scale. Technology development and implementation likely will still be incomplete after five years in areas such as lightweight and composite materials, the range of digital and additive manufacturing technologies, wide-bandgap semiconductors, photonics, flexible electronics, smart fibers, and regenerative tissue engineering. We will not be close to technology maturity in any of these new areas even if there is significant progress through the institutes over the next five years. Significant breakthroughs are still required in many of these areas as well as extensive follow-on development.

How could this five-year federal termination clause be managed?[53] This deadline is now creeping up on the first institutes. Given the collaborative, shared-risk R&D model for the institutes, they first need to work hard to *encourage firms to stay engaged and cost share*. Second, interest and support from state and regional governments should also continue—their manufacturing sectors will likely remain important to their regional economic development, so their interest should remain. The *institutes need to work to continue the state and regional government cost sharing. This continued industry and state support could be a prerequisite for an extension of federal support.*

How could that occur? The most straightforward mechanism could take the form of *an evaluation process as the initial five years comes to a close, with an opportunity for an institute to obtain a renewed term of funding* if performance has been successful. Alternatively, the institutes should be eligible to *apply for federal R&D funding from mission agencies*. Although in the past these agencies have not had portfolios directly in manufacturing R&D, they have had related research in particular technology areas. AMP2.0 recommended that R&D strategies[54] be developed through the agencies for advanced manufacturing areas, with collaboration from industry and universities. That can still be undertaken and can help guide further federal R&D investments in research undertaken at manufacturing institutes. A third approach could acknowledge that the institutes are an interesting new delivery mechanism for a range of initiatives and projects aside from R&D. *The agencies could elect to define (working with the institutes) a range of program enhancements and provide another term of federal support for these enhancements* through a follow-on cooperative agreement. Whichever approach is chosen, given the evolving longer-term development and needs of the institutes, some mechanism for treating the initial federal award as seed funding, with a continued level of federal cost sharing thereafter, will likely be required for a significant additional period beyond the initial five years. The executive branch needs to work on follow-on funding support mechanisms.

To summarize, there is an underlying problem for the institutes because of their relatively short five-year federal time horizon in that the institutes have a longer-term project model and too short a time frame within which to meet it. Reframing of the time horizon is necessary. Given the societal and economic costs of manufacturing decline to the United States, a cross-agency federal price tag for 14 institutes totaling approximately $225 million a year is insignificant. The policy approaches discussed present reasonable alternatives to what was an initial time horizon not fully thought through. But this problem presents an early crisis for the institute model and must be acted on.

The research governance model. The manufacturing institutes were formed by federal mission agencies, and these carried over their regulatory and organizational perspectives as they began this effort. Agencies have tended to treat and manage their institutes like the animals they are familiar with—as research recipients. So, the agency governance model is an R&D supervisory model (through cooperative agreements), and agencies have tended to see their role as that of research supervisors. Agency leaders see this issue, of course, but their legal frameworks tend to require it. Yet the role of the institutes is much broader—building lasting collaborations with support systems across a wide range of firms in varying sectors, not only for research but for testing, technology demonstration and feedback, product development, and workforce education and training.

This is a very complex and ambitious model, and requires a different governance and support model than much more straightforward research projects that involve small teams of scientists and single "principal investigators," not massive collaborations involving from 50 to over 100 actors. Despite the extensive cost sharing from industry and states, with frequent overmatching of federal funds, the federal agencies tend to apply their research oversight rules to govern their cost-shared funding as well as their federal funding. This approach may not help move the institutes toward the still possible requirement that they be independent operations within five years. To summarize, the governance system for federal research in many cases may not foster the kind of collaboration required for the nonresearch aspects of the institutes' tasks and may not prepare the institutes to be self-sustaining and enduring. Thought needs to be given to how the governance model is working, including administrative delays in launching new institutes. For example, should the cost-shared funding from industry and states be controlled by the agency, or should the institutes set these parameters with the contributing stakeholders? Do the agencies need to shift from traditional research contract supervision and oversight to encourage a more collaborative model with states and local governments, and especially industry? If so, how could this be undertaken?

Support from the network. The AMP2.0 report recommended that the growing group of manufacturing institutes be joined together into a supporting network. The report proposed "a governance structure that maintains autonomy for individual institute operations while creating a public-private network governing council that oversees the broader performance of the network and the sustainability of the individual institutes."[55] NIST has been working to implement this recommendation. The network, labeled ManufacturingUSA as of 2016, can serve a range of needs, as NIST understands well. As each new institute is launched, it should not have to "reinvent the wheel." There have been many lessons learned about how to constitute governing boards and legal structures, how to manage intellectual property,[56] how to set up tiers of participants, how to organize regional outreach efforts, how workforce education programs can be assembled, and so forth. A strong network organization could help ensure that common problems are shared by the institutes and tackled in common, and that best practices and lessons learned by individual institutes are studied and shared across the network.[57] Launching new institutes has often been taking up to a year; that is too long, and the complexity of the process and participation requirements has sometimes been discouraging smaller firms, in particular, from participating. Considering the complexity of the model, a launch period is not unreasonable, but could the network help significantly speed up that process by standardizing and packaging possible solutions for common issues such as governance, website security, education programs, and IP arrangements? Again, NIST's Advanced Manufacturing National Program Office, acting with the other agencies, is starting to take on this task.

There is another important task for the network. The factory of the future will not be built around just a single manufacturing technology strand—3D printing, for example. Instead a series of advanced technologies will need to be pulled together—digital production, advanced materials, photonics, bio and nanofabrication, power electronics, and robotics will need to be joined with 3D printing on the new factory floor.[58] Yet the institutes, for good technology development reasons, are focused on particular strands. However, we won't get to the factory of the future without pulling all these strands together. This need for cross technology experimentation is another critical role for the network.

At an August 6, 2016, meeting of the directors of the existing institutes hosted by NIST, the issue of creating the network as its own governance entity began to come to the forefront.[59] Most institute directors had been understandably preoccupied with the massive task of getting their own institutes up and operating. But at the August meeting many started to reconsider this, seeing the potential value of the network to serve the group with shared services and by tackling common problems. A leader of the network was selected from among the directors to start to take on these tasks. A self-governing institute network could provide a powerful boost to an efficient, sustainable, sharing system of institutes.

Emphasis on technology development versus implementation. The manufacturing institutes' primary role so far has been as R&D shops—which is not surprising given the goal of developing new manufacturing technologies and the R&D missions of the agencies that created them. Considering the shortage of manufacturing research in the U.S. innovation system, this fills an important gap and is an early and critical mission. The institutes thus tend to look like mini-NSFs, focused on technology development, and to date most have been less organized around the technology implementation side of their mission. For example, one of the strengths of China's manufacturing sector is its ability to rapidly scale up new production prototypes through such rapid prototyping centers as Shenzhen, which abounds in small prototyping shops. The primacy of the technology development role is logical for institutes—they will need technologies to implement—but most realize that implementation also needs to be a priority.

The AMP1.0 report envisioned institutes organized at Technology Readiness Levels 4 through 7 ("Technology Development," to "Technology Demonstration," to "System and Subsystem Development"),[60] as discussed in chapter 5. Instead, a reasonable amount of the institutes' research to date appears to be more oriented toward somewhat earlier stages of this range (nearer "Research to Prove Feasibility," to "Technology Development").

Since the agencies have tended to organize institutes around new technologies still some distance from industry implementation, a number therefore require additional development to move into range of industry users. This may be inevitable given the gap in U.S. R&D directly on manufacturing research, although over time this will create an implementation gap in the role of the institutes. But without more process technologies, demonstration, testing, and feedback systems, the institutes may limit their ability to bring in small and midsize manufacturing firms because sought-after technologies are not ready for these stages, where the smaller firms could pick them up. As the Deloitte report found, too heavy a focus on technology development could "create a gap in the institutes' ability to deliver on technology commercialization."[61] Most institute leaders understand this well, and many are pressing ahead with demonstration and testing capabilities, but the issue continues to need focus.

In summary, technology development is clearly important and central, but the institutes need to be sure to build in the additional tasks required for TRLs 5–7 further down the innovation pipeline so the evolving technologies can be implemented, especially by smaller and midsize firms. Chapter 8 on workforce education further delineates some of these issues.

Supply chain involvement. As noted, institutes often had to focus initially on project calls for technology development R&D that typically involve university and major firm researchers; smaller firms are usually not included, because they have limited R&D capability. Yet, as most institute leaders understand, the new technologies will not be adopted unless smaller firms understand and use them. For this to occur, the institutes must also embrace a full supply chain approach, with supply chains as integrated groups engaged in technology demonstration, testing, and training. Institute directors understand that they need to keep this task high on their agendas. Backing from the smaller manufacturers that are part of these supply chains also will be key to getting political support at the state level for ongoing efforts to support advanced manufacturing. So, for the sustainability of the institutes, it will be important for small firms to be involved, and engaging them through their participation in supply chains may be the best mechanism. Since, as we will discuss, manufacturing ecosystems tend to be regional, a supply chain approach will also be important in establishing a regional as well as national base for the institutes.

Workforce training. There is a similar potential problem for the role of the manufacturing institutes in workforce training and engineering education. Without engineering teams and a workforce fluent and skilled in the new technologies in small as well as large firms, the evolving advanced manufacturing technologies simply cannot be implemented. States have long played an education and training role, particularly through their community colleges, and this is a good way to involve them in the institutes. While a few institutes, led by LIFT, have seen that workforce training can be an early "win" for the institutes in serving their industrial sectors and building their networks of contacts with firms, states, and community colleges, others are playing catch-up. Agency contract and program officers for the institutes tend to be technology oriented, not education experts, so most focus on the R&D side of the institute role. And the institute directors themselves come from the engineering and industry sides, generally with limited background in workforce education.

However, institutes should not be "either/or"—they need to master both sets of tasks to fully serve their industry sectors. The agencies should ensure a workforce education focus across the institutes and work to get best practices to all. A few institutes, led by LIFT (discussed in chapter 8), are well ahead in forming new education approaches, and these could benefit and serve other institutes. Institutes could also play roles connecting industry participants with existing federal workforce programs[62] and bringing these programs together, taking advantage of the institutes as a new training delivery mechanism. Online and blended learning approaches and platforms, in particular, could serve the whole system. The evolving NNMI network should play a constructive role in bringing best education practices across the institutes, and this was indeed a topic at the institute directors meeting in August 2016.

The role of the states. From the outset, participants in the AMP1.0 and 2.0 process, including government, industry, and university participants, saw a critical balance challenge for the institutes. In the end, all manufacturing is local, embedded in production and innovation ecosystems that are very regional. So, the manufacturing institutes must keep one leg in regional manufacturing economies; that is where their industry and university constituencies are. Yet the technologies the institutes are developing are also going to be needed nationally and will not just evolve in one region—they must translate into the national economy. 3D printing will be needed not just in northeast Ohio but also nationally, in many regional economies and in many industrial sectors. Keeping one leg in regional economies and the other leg in the national economy creates a complicated, bifurcated model for the institutes.

One issue some of the institutes are facing is that, with an emphasis on R&D projects as their initial focus, they may become too tilted toward a national approach and need more balance. If the federal role ends after a five-year term, the regional and local roles the institutes can play become vital—support from a core group of states could be key to an institute's survival. If the institutes are not closely tied to regional economies early on, the support from states simply will not develop to the depth necessary. For example, if the America Makes 3D printing institute is not actively helping the economy of Youngstown, its headquarters, then support from the state of Ohio likely will not materialize. A national focus must also translate into a local focus and local gains.

The state governors were not at the table when the AMP reports and plans were being developed—they were not participants.[63] Part of that was because of the ideological divide that has grown in the last decade between the historical political parties, even at the state level; it became harder for the administration to invite governors from both sides to the table, although it considered doing so. And advanced manufacturing technology development to support a regional manufacturing ecosystem was a new idea—it was never a part of the economic development toolset applied by the states, which all too often is a zero-sum game where one state provides large tax subsidies to entice major firms to leave another state and move to theirs.

Could this traditional approach change? NIST (working through its Manufacturing Extension Partnership and Commerce's Economic Development Administration), worked with the National Governors Association (NGA) to creatively support an NGA "Policy Academy" for states, offering workshops and competitive planning grants to interested states to enable them to develop state manufacturing strategies to strengthen their manufacturing base.[64] This 2011 program proved to be a very good tool for helping states to understand their production sectors and consider technology and workforce roles. Of the seven states that developed state manufacturing strategies,[65] all became participants in manufacturing institutes, and four became institute headquarters. State policymakers care deeply about their manufacturing sectors because they are often central to their state economies and job creation. Programs like NIST's Policy Academy can play a key role in nurturing sophisticated state manufacturing programs and strong regional manufacturing institutes. The Economic Development Administration in the Commerce Department has had a program called Investing in Manufacturing Communities Partnership (IMCP) that has continued aspects of this approach, although at a regional rather than state level.[66]

In summary, building state support by tying an institute to regional economies will be a key pillar for the institute's success and, indeed, survival. One of the reasons NIST's Manufacturing Extension Partnership (MEP) has endured is because it is anchored in the states—every state has one. The program is popular with small manufacturers because it delivers important manufacturing know-how that makes them more competitive. This is also an important constituency for governors, and running a sound MEP program has proved a good way for governors to connect politically with this constituency. MEP therefore provides an example for the institutes. For new governmental programs to survive and thrive, they not only need a strong substantive policy design but also must have a sound political support design that will sustain them. The political design is not easy—it must not distort the substantive policy design to serve political ends, and it must support the substantive policy design and keep it strong but still build support to sustain it.[67] The institutes need to find the right mix of political design with substantive design; developing a strong regional economic focus is important not only for the substantive model of a strong institute but also for a political design that will assure future support. Of course, a number of institutes aware of this need for balance are working to solidify state support—IACMI, for example, has a series of state satellite technology centers in its core participating states, and LIFT has fully engaged its core states in developing state-based workforce training programs.

While the state role in the U.S. system is not R&D, states do play a significant role with small businesses and in workforce training and education. Engaging small manufacturers that are part of regional industrial supply chains in the manufacturing institutes is also a key way to engage state support. Secondly, the workforce training role of the institutes, which is inherently regional, provides another means to engage the states. Institutes need to build these programs.

Measuring progress. As the institutes and their supporting federal agencies understand, if they are to be sustainable, they will need to demonstrate the progress they are making on technology development and workforce education. Developing performance metrics, then, is a key step. Working with the institutes, NIST's Advanced Manufacturing National Program Office, which supports the network, has issued initial guidance for this process,[68] agreed to by the institute directors. It calls for institutes to collect data on institute participants, including the number of small and midsize manufacturers actively involved, on active R&D projects and their progress on meeting key technical stages, on levels of cost-sharing support by source, on the number of students reached in workforce training efforts, and on workforce trainers trained. This is a constructive step.

Further work is needed on tracking progress against the technology roadmaps institutes are developing. Deloitte has recommended looking at the stages of evolution the institutes must go through, from start-up, to

R&D execution, to longer-term outcomes, and developing benchmarks for progress at each stage.[69] It will also be important to ensure that the institutes and network are on track to meet longer-term goals, such as progress on trade balances in advanced technology goods, new technologies developed and implemented, and advanced manufacturing workforce supply— new measurements will be needed. Finally, it will be vital to keep track of competing nations to judge whether the level of U.S. institute investment is adequate to meet the challenge of leading in advanced manufacturing deployment.[70] The institutes will continue to need to justify their support as well as to plan their future progress, and common but manageable measurement systems will be key.

An underlying problem: federal R&D for advanced manufacturing technologies and the need for technology strategies. A significant issue that affects the ability to meet a number of the challenges discussed earlier is the past lack of focus by the federal R&D agencies on research on manufacturing. As discussed earlier, the United States in the postwar period assumed it would be a leader in manufacturing and did not feel the need to make it an R&D focus. That is part of the reason that a number of the manufacturing institutes tend to have a somewhat earlier-stage Technology Readiness Level focus than proposed in the Advanced Manufacturing Partnership report—foundational research work in manufacturing technologies still needs work. If ongoing federal mission agency R&D can focus more on enabling manufacturing technologies, that could be an important complement to the manufacturing institutes, helping create new manufacturing paradigms. To be clear, many of the discoveries needed for this shift are well under way; ongoing federal research has supported major advances in areas such as digital and sensor technology, advanced materials, photonics, robotics, flexible electronics, and composites. The potential manufacturing paradigms are in sight, which is a major part of what makes them so interesting, but future research needs to be more systematically applied to production. Unless the R&D side is better linked to institutes, which focus on applied work, they could become stranded, over time losing their ability to bring on new manufacturing technology advances.

A working example of this functional connectivity between research and technology development and implementation, often cited by MIT's Rafael Reif, cochair of the AMP2.0 effort, is provided by the semiconductor industry. The Sematech effort, discussed earlier, that organized this sector around a systematic technology roadmap that kept it following Moore's Law for over three decades, is well known and was a model for institutes. Less well known is that Sematech has been accompanied by a Focus Center Research

Program, with joint DARPA and industry support, for earlier-stage break-through research at a series of universities. In addition, the Semiconductor Research Corporation (SRC) supplements this for industry and university applied research. Sematech itself has assembled these elements, emphasizing industry technology implementation and roadmapping. It has been a system with extensive connections between research, application, and implementation, with links and handoffs at each stage. While it appears that Moore's Law is coming to an end for silicon-based technologies, this system stands as an organizational model. All three stages will be needed in advanced manufacturing. The institutes are somewhat like Sematech, but we also need focused research flowing into them for them to thrive. We now have the institutes and, in parallel, federal government R&D agencies that fund much research on areas relevant to manufacturing, such as advanced materials, digital technologies, wide-bandgap semiconductors, and photonics. But this R&D support from federal agencies is not linked to the institutes.

The administration took an initial step down this pathway of translating research toward the institutes. In April 2016, the Subcommittee on Advanced Manufacturing (SAM) of the National Science and Technology Council (an arm of OSTP used for interagency collaborations) released a report, "Advanced Manufacturing: A Snapshot of Priority Technology Areas across the Federal Government."[71] It attempted a prerequisite for this, identifying and communicating work in R&D areas that were priorities to more than one agency, many of which were related to the work and needs at the institutes. It cataloged ongoing federal R&D efforts in emerging technologies that can also be manufacturing priorities: advanced materials manufacturing; biomanufacturing to support bioengineering, regenerative medicine, and other advanced bioproducts; and continuous manufacturing of pharmaceuticals. It also looked at research directly relevant to the technologies focused on by the initial manufacturing institutes.

Many of these agency efforts are significant. One highlighted example concerned the Energy Materials Network, a $40 million Department of Energy project, which included integration of computational capabilities into experimental materials research, development of new multiscale computation, informatics, and data management tools, and new technologies for modeling and validating new materials manufacturing processes, for a new "materials genome" for optimal advanced materials. These and other research assets, if linked to institute needs, could be significant. The report lays the groundwork for the next logical step—developing technology strategies around the emerging manufacturing paradigms, bringing together R&D agencies and their leading researchers with the institute experts and researchers from industry and universities. The strategies could be the linkage mechanism, helping guide work by both groups. As previously noted, technology strategies, including R&D, were a specific recommendation in the AMP2.0 report.

These collaborative technology strategies, jointly developed by industry, university, and government experts, would be periodically updated to guide both agency research and the institute's efforts, and could become more like technology roadmaps over time. Such technology strategies, organized around the institutes' technology focus areas, will be critical in linking research advances and the institutes' agendas for technology evaluation, testing, and implementation. Without them, the system will be flying blind.

Federal procurement for advanced manufacturing technologies. There is an additional dimension to the federal role as well. Federal agencies, particularly its largest procurement agency, DOD, could play a significant role in creating initial markets for new manufacturing technologies. 3D printing is not only a potentially very important new manufacturing process. It also enables production of a series of new technologies and components, some of which, particularly in the aerospace and tissue fabrication areas, may be of major interest to DOD. Using procurement to advance the technologies it needs is a traditional role for DOD. For example, after integrated circuits were developed in 1959 by Robert Noyce and Jack Kilby, the initial market for some four years belonged solely to DOD and NASA. As the technology was perfected for military and space markets, civilian markets gradually opened up and, of course, became dominant.

The Defense Department could play a comparable and critical initial market-creation role for new products from new generations of manufacturing technologies, but its procurement system has to become aligned with the results being developed by the institutes and their participating firms. This should be achievable. For example, the General Accountability Office (GAO) has studied the potential of 3D printing technologies emerging from America Makes and has identified an extensive series of military needs to which these could be matched.[72] It recommended that the Office of the Secretary of Defense develop and implement an approach "for systematically tracking department-wide activities and resources, and results of these [3D Printing] activities; and for disseminating these results to facilitate adoption of the technology across the department." Just as the federal R&D system needs to be tied to the manufacturing institutes around technology strategies to optimize ideas and research inputs to assist the institutes, government procurement needs, particularly at DOD, could be aligned with the results—the output—coming from the institutes to help create initial markets to disseminate their advances.

Lessons from the Fraunhofer Institutes

The federal government's manufacturing innovation institutes were purposely developed from the German Fraunhofer Institute model, so an examination of this model can help illuminate lessons for the U.S. institutes. In particular, the Fraunhofer model can provide insights on optimal organizational and governance approaches for the U.S. manufacturing institutes, which are still evolving.

One key difference between the two approaches must be noted up front. Germany cofunds the Fraunhofer Institutes as a permanent program, so the Fraunhofers are not intended to be self-sustainable after initial government-level support. In contrast, as noted, the U.S. institutes' approach assumes federal government support will halt after five years. Therefore, there is a key difference between the two approaches. Unlike the Fraunhofers, the U.S. institutes require a structure that will help enable their longer-term continuation following the halt of federal support, unless the U.S. government finds ways to continue its assistance at some level. However, similar to the Fraunhofer model, the institutes could also draw long-term regional, state, and local government-level support.

It should also be noted that there are many differences between German and U.S. industrial and innovation systems. Germany's innovation system, as noted, is "manufacturing-led," in contrast to that of the United States. Germany's industrial ecosystem avoided the thinning-out that has afflicted the U.S. system. Germany maintains a strong financing system for supporting scale-up of its industrial firms. While the U.S. has developed a strong entrepreneurship and start-up system (issues in this system are discussed later), Germany instead focuses on bringing innovation into and through its existing small and midsize firms, in significant part using the Fraunhofer system. German federal and regional governments offer stronger export supports than the U.S. system. The German workforce model has highly centralized training and is much more heavily unionized than in the United States. Despite these many differences, there are still important lessons to be learned, especially from the Fraunhofer system.

Overall Fraunhofer organization. The Fraunhofer Gesellschaft refers to the organization supporting application-driven research (in U.S. terms,

Technology Readiness Levels 4–6) in Germany. There are approximately 80 research units, including 60 institutes, within the Fraunhofer organization, which share common governance systems and operate under an umbrella organization at the national level.[73] The institutes support applied research through a collaboration of industry-, university-, and government-supported researchers at each institute.

The institutes have some 17,000 employees and operate with an annual budget of around €1.6 billion. The budget is comprised of approximately 35% core government/state funding, 23% public funding won from competitive bids, 34% private sector funding, and 7% from licensing.

A British evaluation concluded that, "The Fraunhofer model has a strong governance structure, which ensures a clear strategy in support of national priorities, but also recognizes the importance of individual centres [Institutes] having institutional autonomy."[74] A Work Foundation study found that, "The Fraunhofer Institutes are managed on a 'federal' model, which provides stability and national profile as well as local flexibility. A single independent board agrees on major elements of strategy, and shapes the seven key research themes which stretch across the 60 individual institutions. However, individual institutions have wide powers to negotiate individual research project contracts, and to establish inter-institutional links for themselves."[75]

The Franuhofer Institutes typically have a minimum of 100 staff and have a minimum annual budget of around €10 million, although some are much larger. There are approximately a dozen research topics around which the various institutes are organized, as well as more cutting-edge themes they explore to help shape future priorities. The 60 institutes are spread across the country, but strong regional metropolitan clusters, such as in Berlin or Dresden, have groups of institutes.

The central Fraunhofer organization provides a governance structure at a national level for the network of Fraunhofer Institutes, which can be viewed as somewhat comparable to the proposed ManufacturingUSA network now being implemented by NIST in the United States. This central organization supports application research and creates a Fraunhofer national network, identity, and brand. A British study emphasized that "within this federal structure, individual Fraunhofer Institutes do have a high degree of autonomy to set their own research priorities and pursue commercial opportunities, and to compete with each other to win funding from business or the public sector."[76]

The structure created by the Fraunhofer statute.[77] This organizing and governance document (as revised in 2010) describes the system structure equivalent to the ManufacturingUSA network. The overall Fraunhofer Gesellschaft (the organization for the institute network) has a government structure of qualified members, with a senate and general assembly that includes selected members, including representatives of the 60 institutes. These play roles in general governance and in selecting central organization leadership. This leadership is through an executive board composed of the organization's president and four members, who must include two scientists/engineers, a business leader, and a senior civil service representative. The executive board works on research policy and generally supervises the individual institutes and the organization's working and technical support groups.

The individual institutes are charged with "carrying out the Organization's research work."[78] "Each Institute shall be managed by one or more Institute Director[s]," with the executive committee entitled to nominate one member of the institute's management with general management responsibilities, in agreement with the institute's management.[79] Each institute

- plans the Institute's "scientific work";
- is "free to organize its own scientific projects and is not subject to any restrictions concerning the choice, order and manner of execution of the Institute's scientific projects";
- manages the business activities of the Institute bearing full responsibility for correct administration and utilization of funds to the Organization, and must meet planned budgets;
- is charged "to endeavor to acquire contract research work";
- draws up budgets for the Institute;
- develops reports for the Organization's Executive Board and technical groups.[80]

In summary, the Fraunhofer Statute allows individual institutes substantial autonomy for their scientific agendas and work, working under overall guidance and support from the central organization.

Outside evaluations of the Fraunhofer model. The British parliament evaluated and interpreted the Fraunhofer model as it worked to adopt a variation on it. A 2011 parliamentary report on a new program of Technology and Innovation Centres (TICs) in the United Kingdom supported organizing their funding along a Fraunhofer model with approximately one-third long-term core central government funding, one-third competitive government-supported research funding, and one-third private sector contracts.[81]

The parliamentary report on the TICs found that the Fraunhofer Institutes utilize "simple" corporate governance principles with "a high level of autonomy for the individual Fraunhofer Institutes." For its own TICs, the committee recommended a similar arrangement, proposing each center have a "Management Board," an "autonomous" board that "will oversee the program of work." An overall "Oversight Committee" would oversee the network of TICs, supported by a "Technology Strategy Board" to support overall technology strategy efforts. The committee favorably noted testimony that the TICs "need to operate at arm's length from the government" to be effective, although an "element of coordination" was needed to assure the TICs did not duplicate each other's work.[82] This is an instructive summary of how the Fraunhofer Institutes operate as well.

To summarize, the Fraunhofer organization operates each institute relatively autonomously, but it is within a strong, supportive network governance model. The institutes receive core federal government support on a continuing basis but also raise funds from regional governments and industry. A given institute within this system can bring in new partners, compete for research, and work with other institutes, as well as control its budgeting and research. It differs in that the sponsor of each institute is the overall Fraunhofer organization, unlike in the U.S. model, where a specific federal government-level agency sponsors each of its manufacturing institutes. In the Fraunhofer system, institute sponsorship and federal government core funding continue in the long term, while in the United States it is currently limited to five years. Full self-sustainability of each institute is simply not a goal in the Fraunhofer system, unlike the current U.S. manufacturing institute approach, although the Fraunhofers do seek research support from industry for approximately one-third of their funding and rely on local government support for another third. The U.K. model of Technology and Innovation Centres is still evolving,[83] but government reports recommended continuing governmental long-term support but an arm's length relationship between an institute and the central government, along Fraunhofer lines. The first major lesson is the need for continuing nonlimited-term federal government support for the institutes, as discussed in the previous section. Realistically, the U.S. system needs to move in that direction.

The Franuhofer system has been highly successful in making German manufacturing a world leader, and there appear to be important lessons from it for U.S. manufacturing institutes. First, the central Fraunhofer organization is very important in supporting the individual institutes and in providing best practices and contributing research advances across the system. While individual institutes have significant autonomy, allowing creativity to operate bottom-up, the central organization—in U.S. terms, the network—is the governance system. As noted, in the United States, particular federal R&D agencies supervise each institute, supplemented by industry and university boards. Building up the network system in the United States appears critical to strengthening the overall system through sharing advances and practices. It can also develop into more of a governance system as the group of institutes takes on more self-government mechanisms for a true public-private collaboration model. With the development of the institute network ManufacturingUSA in 2016, NIST began to pursue this task, asking the institute directors to take leadership, which could enable sharing of practices and collaborative programs across institutes. A second major lesson, then, is the need for progress on self-governance from the U.S. institute network.

In addition, a significant strength of the Fraunhofer system is the way it brings academic engineers and scientists into research work on production-related technologies and processes. In the United States, university scientists and engineers are just not directly involved in the technology challenges around the production system; this has not been an area of particular federal R&D interest which funds them.[84] The Fraunhofers created a community within academic science and engineering closely attuned to industry technology issues; putting a strong base of university talent on this task could also be a role for the new U.S. manufacturing institutes. Finally, the technology validation approach the Fraunhofer labs provide[85] for new "hard" technologies being developed by German firms also bears investigating. By helping firms understand how to improve the technologies they are nurturing and design them for efficient production, this validation process helps move ideas toward markets. A variant of this approach, discussed in chapter 7, is being implemented at the Boston Fruanhofer's TechBridge project. This might be a capability the institute network in the United States may want to consider, perhaps in cooperation with NIST. A third major lesson, then, is ensuring enduring links between university researchers and industry through the institutes, including through the technology validation approach used by Fraunhofer labs.

In addition to a working network, the institutes need a continuous learning capability to stay ahead of issues, a role that the Fraunhofer system has performed, lately in coordination with larger government study projects on "Industrie 4.0" advanced manufacturing. NIST and NSF have therefore also created a "think and do tank," *MForesight*—the Alliance for Manufacturing Foresight—to continuously evaluate technical and policy issues the institutes as a group face. MForesight seeks to provide "ideas and insights to business and government decision-makers on emerging technology trends and opportunities for public-private investments in advanced manufacturing."[86] Its portfolio of study projects also aims to promote technology innovation that can bridge the gap between research and manufacturers. This is a fourth Fraunhofer lesson: the need for specialized continuing studies of manufacturing systems and technologies. MForesight is an initial attempt to tackle this.

There is a fifth challenge remaining for the United States that is raised by the Fraunhofer system. To some extent, the United States is trying to do advanced manufacturing on the cheap.[87] The 14 institutes the United States has formed will cost it approximately $225 million a year. The German Fraunhofer system's cost is far higher—some $2 billion a year.[88] America Makes, charged with enabling 3D printing, is spending $50 million in federal funds over five years; the country of Singapore is planning a $500 million expenditure on this and related technologies.[89] The Manufacturing Extension Partnership (MEP) in the United States, with outreach efforts to small manufacturers in each state, is budgeted at some $130 million in federal funds each year; Canada, with a much smaller industrial economy, spends more on a similar program.[90] Germany's Industrie 4.0 plans to spend billions on digital production in the coming years;[91] the two U.S. manufacturing institutes working in this area will spend a small fraction of this. China is planning much higher levels of investment in advanced manufacturing than the United States.[92] Can the modest investments the United States is contemplating achieve the scale needed for an industrial transformation? This is a fifth Fraunhofer lesson: technology and process leadership in manufacturing is not cheap and requires a significant government role in technology development.

Of course, there could be an additional perspective on the U.S. numbers. The industry and state cost sharing in the institutes bolsters the total somewhat. But if the R&D being undertaken by the various mission research agencies in fields directly relevant to advanced manufacturing is included, the number starts to approach the scale that may be required. For example, there is a rich mix of research programs on advanced materials at NSF, DARPA, NASA, NIST, and DOE's EERE, already cataloged and identified as relevant to manufacturing advance by an OSTP-led interagency working group.[93] But, as noted, those programs are still disconnected from the manufacturing institutes, and there is no feed-in system yet on the table. Serendipity is not a substitute for connection.

Summary

The advanced manufacturing institute effort had a promising start in the United States, addressing what has become a critical gap in the U.S. system for manufacturing innovation. This has been accomplished through dedicated work by a group of federal officials working across agency lines, with administration leadership, as well as a unique industry-university working group, the Advanced Manufacturing Partnership, which developed two major action-oriented reports.

The preceding discussion included a series of key findings:

• To be successful, the institute model needs to continue to find technology areas with applications across many industries and in industries with long supply chains that may be slow to take up technology advances.

• The advanced manufacturing institutes need both regional buy-in and national engagement to survive.

• Federal funding for institutes is uncertain after five years, and states alone may not be willing to take up the mantle for a program that has national as well as local focus. Funding fatigue from firms, especially larger ones, can be an issue, too. So, the federal convening role remains critical, and mechanisms for continued federal funding are very important.

• While the United States originated the advanced manufacturing approach, it is facing intense competition in this area as numerous other nations pick up the model; it needs these manufacturing institutes to avoid falling behind its industrial competitors.

• A serious gap remains between federal R&D programs and the institutes; this gap needs to be filled for the institutes to fill a core mission of bridging technology advances between universities and industries.

Now that the basic framework is in place with a group of 14 institutes, this is a good opportunity to consider enhancements to the model. The institutes face a series of challenges, including those just listed, that will need to be met by new policies:

• improving the current research agency governance model;

• continued federal government support after the initial five-year commitment;

• creating a strong network of institutes where administrative, IP, other best practices, and research advances can be shared;

• an emphasis within the institutes on technology implementation as well as technology development, which means engaging supply chains and smaller firms;

• ensuring institute emphasis on workforce training and education; and

• ensuring linkages between institutes and regional economies in addition to serving manufacturing technology development at the national level.

Specific policy recommendations in this regard are set out in the detailed discussions of these topics.

In addition, federal R&D in advanced manufacturing technologies at mission agencies should be better connected and contribute to the institutes. This would help the institutes bolster their agendas with more technology advances for implementation efforts with participating firms. Technology strategies developed by institutes and their industry, university, and government experts will be critical in linking research efforts to the institutes. In addition, federal procurement, another traditional tool for technology advancement, could be applied to create initial markets for new technologies emerging from the institutes.

Finally, there are important lessons from Germany's Fraunhofer organization and institutes, which served as the model for the U.S. institutes. Although the Fraunhofer Institutes have significant autonomy, the overall organization allows participatory governance, as well as sharing of practices and research. The U.S. institutes could benefit from a strong institute network, providing both access to best practices and a shared governance model. The role of the Fraunhofers in bringing university science and engineering to bear on complex industry technology challenges is also worthy of emulation. The role of the Fraunhofer Academy in workforce training and their lab-based technology validation process for new technologies (discussed in chapters 7 and 8) should also be reviewed. The continuing central government support of Fraunhofer Institutes, which is not term restricted, unlike the current situation in the United States, has been critical for their sustainability and strength, and the United States should consider this. The Fraunhofers' role as a policy think tank for manufacturing, which the MForesight organization, supported by NSF and NIST, is now developing, also deserves emulation. Finally, the United States needs to move to the level of ongoing support suggested by the Fraunhofer system.

With 14 institutes and a new administration in place in 2017, this is a good time to hit a pause button and assess the opportunities and challenges. Institute directors have been noting that there is a certain amount of "donor fatigue." Major companies that share the cost of the institutes are often participating in a number of them and are reluctant to spread themselves too thin. There are also limits to how much more cost-share funding they are prepared to commit. States are starting to have the same problem—there are practical limits to the number of institutes that even a strong manufacturing state can effectively contribute to and participate in. Given the reality that the sustainability of the institute model is still an open question, now may be a good time to look hard at both missions the institutes may want and need to address based on lessons learned to date and ways to make the institute model sustainable over a more extended time frame.

Fourteen institutes are not enough, as Fraunhofer's 60 institutes suggest. There are still numerous promising technology areas identified in the AMP reports and elsewhere that require new institutes in order for them to scale up. So, the model needs to continue to evolve over time. But a critical priority that needs to be addressed now with the first 14 is to make sure the initial lessons they are learning, detailed here, are implemented across the board. Indeed, additional support should first go to meet this priority.

Is this worth the effort? Can the potential economic impact of the institutes justify the challenge of launching this new model for technology diffusion? In 2016, NIST-supported independent economic studies of four advanced manufacturing technologies being pursued by the institutes—additive manufacturing, advanced robotics, roll-to-roll production technologies, and smart manufacturing technologies—found annual cost savings through increased production efficiencies from these four areas alone would equal over $100 billion for U.S. manufacturers. The percentage reductions in production costs for manufacturers from these four (in the varying ranges of applicable manufacturing sectors where they would operate) were 18.3% ($4.1 billion efficiency saving) for additive manufacturing, 5.3% ($40.1 billion) for robotics, 14.7% ($400 million) for roll-to-roll technologies, and 3.2% ($57.4 billion) for smart manufacturing. The four sector studies looked only at benefits directly attributable to closing identified technical gaps in each area. If larger-scale outcomes are achieved, such as through new and improved products, improved production quality, job creation, a more productive skilled workforce, and long-term industry growth and competitiveness, the effects are potentially far higher.[94] The data suggests the potential power of the new institute model.

7 Start-up Scale-up: Addressing the Manufacturing Challenge for Start-ups

Jonathan Huebner, a physicist at the Naval Air Warfare Center at China Lake, California, 370 miles from Silicon Valley, had many years' experience designing advanced weapons systems using software, materials, and energy systems. He began to tire of what he felt were increasingly mediocre innovation ideas coming to him. In 2005, he wrote a paper titled "A Possible Declining Trend in Worldwide Innovation,"[1] which launched a contrarian vision into what everyone had been assuming was a breathtaking era of exponentially expanding innovation. Huebner defined an innovation rate—"the number of important technological developments per year divided by the world population"—and argued that the rate was in decline and was also limited by economic limits on financing increasingly complex innovation, with the entry of new innovation shaped like a bell curve.[2] Using information he compiled on significant science and technology advances plotted against world population data, he found that world technology advancement had peaked in the mid- to late nineteenth century. Using U.S. patent filings as a proxy for technology advances and comparing it against U.S. population, he found a U.S. technology rate peak in 1915, despite advancing education levels and GDP since then.[3] Could this be true—with developments such as nanotechnology, quantum effects, and now gravitational waves coming into view, and dark matter and dark energy still only working suppositions? There seems to be plenty of new physics alone to play with, apart from advances in other fields.

Obviously, Huebner's finding was highly debatable, and was promptly taken on by other analysts,[4] but it struck a chord with some in Silicon Valley, which at the time was still feeling the results of the dot-com bust. More recently, as discussed later in this chapter and in chapters 4 and 9, economist Robert Gordon has echoed this theme.[5] Peter Thiel, ironically a founder of Internet-based PayPal, and who made the first outside investment in social media site Facebook, picked up Huebner's theory and famously commented in 2011, "We wanted flying cars, instead we got 140 characters."[6] Thiel decried the Valley's shift from its initial hardware focus developing semiconductors and computers to low-cost, copycat software apps when society needed big, complex, hard-technology "things" in energy, transport, health, and aerospace. Whether there were less or more technological advances available to the world, Thiel's statement was an indictment of what was coming out of Silicon Valley. Maybe there was an innovation system problem, not an innovation availability problem?

The Innovation Gap for Technology Development

Lewis Branscomb and Phillip Auerswald thought so. In 2002, they wrote a classic in innovation literature, "Between Invention and Innovation,"[7] putting flesh on what was then a skeletal idea of a "Valley of Death"[8] at the early stage of technology development, lying between the proof of concept/invention and product development stages. As is well understood, they noted that technological innovation was critical for long-term economic growth; although established firms typically undertake incremental advances, radical technological advancement with truly new products and services was required for new industries and markets and corresponding major steps in growth.[9] Branscomb and Auerswald cited economist Martin Weitzman's statement that "the ultimate limits to growth may lie not as much in our ability to generate new ideas, so much as our ability to process an abundance of potentially new seed ideas into usable forms,"[10] arguing that a gap in support for early-stage technology development was thwarting that transition.

Their study found that although there was major federal support for research, little funding extended to early-stage technology development. They found that venture capital (VC) funding was available for potentially high-growth ventures, but only when they were close to production after the firm had worked through its technology development. While angel investors were more active at this early stage, their total funding was modest; little corporate funding was available for anything other than incremental advances that complemented their existing technologies.[11] Thus, Branscomb and Auerswald found, markets supporting early-stage technology development were highly inefficient, resulting in a significant gap in the U.S. innovation system.

An Innovation Gap Where High-Potential Start-ups Stagnate

Could this technology development gap be yielding a start-up decline? As economist Robert Litan noted in the wake of the 2008 recession, "America's great challenge is to . . . bring about a substantial increase in the numbers of highly successful new companies. . . . Nothing less than the future welfare of America and its citizens is at stake."[12] So the nurturing of start-ups has policy significance. The Kauffman Foundation has long compiled an entrepreneurship index to indicate the growth or decline in the number of U.S. start-up companies. That index showed a steep decline in total start-ups from 2009 to 2013, hitting a twenty-year low in 2012 before an uptick began in 2014 that by 2016 neared pre-2008 recession levels if not prior historical levels.[13] A number of economists, including Litan, noting that start-ups had become key to the U.S. innovation-based growth model, looked beyond the 2009–2013 decline. Noting that firm exits were exceeding firm entries, they expressed concern about a long-term decline in net firm formation from 1978 to 2011. This led to concern about the declining pace of job creation, which they linked to this business dynamism decline.[14] If the United States depended on new firm creation for its growth rate and jobs, it was not a pretty longer-term picture.

But treating all entrepreneurs alike can lead to the anomalous grouping of new "Mom and Pop" corner stores with biotech start-ups. Within the last few years, this has started to change, as academics have begun creating new indices to focus more explicitly on innovative, technology-based firms, which have much greater potential to scale up and grow than, say, a neighborhood dry cleaner. In 2016, the Kauffman Foundation started adding "growth entrepreneurship" to its annual index. This new Kauffman index incorporates the rate of start-up growth, the share of scale-ups in the start-up mix (that is, the percentage of firms that have grown to employ more than fifty people in the first ten years), and high-growth company density, to better measure trends in *growth* entrepreneurship in the United States.

This new growth entrepreneurship index shows a deep decline from 2009 to 2013, clearly affected by the Great Recession, but it has now returned toward the level before the financial crisis.[15] However, the individual components of the index present a less positive picture. The rate of start-up growth hit a twenty-year low in 2012 before ticking slightly upward, which is similar to the trend for the share of scale-up start-ups.[16] But of these high-growth firms, over 47% fall into five industries: software, health, IT services, advertising and marketing, and business products and services.[17] The positive rise in the index of growth entrepreneurs, while a welcome improvement, seems somewhat confined to relatively few sectors of the economy.

Economists Jorge Guzman and Scott Stern worked on another way to dive into the overall data and look at the kinds of firms that were particularly important for growth—firms that were based on science and technology innovations.[18] These firms—sometimes called gazelles—have a much higher potential growth rate because such innovation can scale better and faster than more commonplace firms such as restaurants. Such firms appear particularly critical to growth. How was the United States doing in creating these technology-based innovative firms? Looking at firms in 15 states that contributed more than half of U.S. GDP, they developed characteristics they could track for such high-potential firms, such as intellectual property held, name, legal structure, and other factors.[19] These characteristics were in turn tested against signals of higher-growth outcomes (using data on firms obtaining IPOs or entering high-value acquisitions). They found that these kinds of high-potential firms went into decline after the dot-com bubble in the early 2000s but that in 2010 a rise began, and by 2014 the United States had reached the third-highest level of entrepreneurship growth in a quarter century for such quality firms.[20]

Although the number of high-potential start-ups appears to be back on the rise and returning to sound levels, the study found that the ability of these start-ups to scale up may still be stagnating. Using a new methodology, these researchers found that a high-potential start-up begun in 1996 was four times as likely to experience a growth event—that is, an IPO or high-value merger—within six years than a start-up begun in 2005 and measured for a growth event through 2011.[21] Of course, the 1996 start-up experienced the dot-com bubble, and the 2005 start-up followed the dot-com bust, but even so, the size of the differential suggests a problem in scaling up start-ups. There are also significant regional variations in scale-up—where you start matters. While there has been some overall recovery in scale-up rates for start-ups that began in 2009–2011, the recovery is still quite weak. As a companion study concluded, "While the supply of new high-potential-growth startups appears to be growing, the ability of U.S. high-growth-potential startups to commercialize and scale seems to be facing continuing stagnation. Policy interventions to enhance the process of scale-up may be more impactful than those that simply aim to increase shots on goal."[22]

The Innovation Gap for Manufacturing Start-up Scale-up

So far, we have reviewed an innovation gap in support for technology development and another for high-potential start-ups overall in achieving scale-up. There is an additional and compounding innovation gap problem affecting start-ups that need to manufacture their products. While the advanced manufacturing institute model detailed in chapter 6 addresses innovation at large, midsize, and small manufacturing firms, to date it has largely focused on existing firms and has not encompassed new entrepreneurial start-ups. These start-up firms face not only an early-stage technology development gap, as Branscomb and Auerswald have described, but also a production scale-up gap. Start-up scale-up is a problem in general, and particularly for manufacturing start-ups.

This third category of firms, then, comprises the start-up and entrepreneurial firms that manufacture products based on their own new innovative technologies, typically emerging from university research centers. As summarized in chapter 5, Elizabeth Reynolds, Hiram Semel, and Joyce Lawrence of the MIT Production in the Innovation Economy (PIE) project studied a group of such highly innovative start-up firms in the Boston area and found that these face an additional problem in scaling up production.[23] While the innovations from this group were often able to command initial venture capital funding, their venture firms lacked the financing capacity to launch significant production. They found that venture firms are typically organized around a timetable that is well suited to the IT—and increasingly software—firms that have historically led the venture sector, in which the technology becomes a marketable product within five to seven years. But the firms in the study group aimed to produce manufactured goods in sectors that had a development cycle that could last a decade or more. The MIT study found that many of the venture firms did not abandon their start-up firms after more than five to seven years, but if their technology remained promising, they instead put them into what could be termed "income maintenance." This means that the firm would be sustained at a basic funding level but when such firms were well along the path of product design and they asked their venture firm for financing for scale-up to actual production, they were usually told no, that the venture firm lacked the depth and resources to finance the capital required for investment in local production, and the start-ups were typically referred to contract manufacturers in Asia.

This has important implications. The initial stage of production of a new technology involves significant engineering advances and original design, and frequently requires reworking the underlying science and the innovation itself. It is a highly creative stage and part of the innovation process, not divorced from it, as previously discussed. The U.S. firm's innovation team, if relying on a contract manufacturer, often spent significant time abroad with that manufacturer; much of the innovation is transferred in that process, and the capability for follow-on incremental advances tends to shift overseas. So while the start-up may have its technology produced and enter into markets, important aspects of its "know-how" move offshore. This means that when production capability shifts offshore, significant aspects of innovation capability shift with it. These advanced technology start-up firms represent the next generation of U.S. technology and manufacturing firms; this gap in scale-up financing means that important in-depth innovation features may be transferred abroad and may become the basis for future major innovations in both processes and products there.

The Venture Capital Availability Problem and Financing Alternatives

Data on venture capital availability further substantiates this story. Ben Gaddy, Virun Sivaram, and their colleagues have studied venture capital funding in the clean energy sector.[24] They found that venture capital investments in new energy technologies between 2006 and 2014 reached a high point in 2008 and have been in substantial decline since then. Although VC investment in new energy technologies increased between 2004 and 2008 from $1 billion to nearly $5 billion, an annual growth rate of close to 50%, after 2008 this level (A-round deals, the first substantial round of venture capital financing) fell back to the 2004 level.[25] Less than half the $25 billion invested in clean energy was returned to investors in the 2006–2011 period. Over 90% (on average) of clean energy investments failed to return their invested capital in 2008–2011, and in 2008, 2009, and 2011, no clean energy investments returned twice their invested capital.[26] The failure rate of software firms in these periods was considerably lower. Following the financial crisis in 2008, the major decline in the price of oil, the failure of Congress to pass carbon-pricing climate legislation, and the collapse of a number of solar companies because of solar panel overproduction in China, VC clean energy investment dipped substantially.

In addition, investments in energy technology firms require large capital commitments to scale up. For venture firms, large investments in cleantech tend to be both higher risk and yield lower returns than either software or biotech. Gaddy and colleagues note that between 2006 and 2011 even clairvoyant VCs investing in cleantech would have made 20% less than if they had invested in software and biotech.[27] Another reason venture funding is pulling out of clean energy is that the energy technology timetable does not fit the timetable VCs seek to apply. Typically, VCs will make five years of progressive investments and over the next five years expect to see returning profits. However, the time frame for clean energy firms to mature can be twice that especially when companies are attempting to introduce new technologies, materials and processes into the market. A third issue concerns exit strategy, where established firms will acquire the start-up. The exit rate for software firms was 11.9%, while only 3.8% of clean energy firms were acquired in the same 2006–2011 period.[28] Venture firms have limited interest in funding firms, such as in the energy technology space, that have little chance of being acquired, because this affects the ability of their investors to obtain a prompt return.

Because of its lower risk, lower capital requirements, shorter-term timetable, and stronger exit strategy, software is a much better bet for VCs than longer-term, capital-intensive sectors like energy technology. A snapshot of a representative period, the first quarter of 2016, for early-stage and seed venture funding in all economic sectors nationwide bears this out.[29] In that period, there were a total of 1,011 venture deals. Of these, there were 467 deals in software and IT services; biotechnology placed second, with 124 deals. These three categories combined captured $7.8 billion of the total deal volume of $12.7 billion. No other sector was close. Biotech is very different from software—with much larger capital requirements and a longer-term technology development timetable. Why do VCs support that sector, too? The answer is that biotechnology firms, although requiring a far longer commitment than for software or IT services firms, continue to attract venture funding support (1) because patents tend to be more powerful in the life sciences sector than in physical science sectors in assuring longer-term monopoly rents, (2) because the Food and Drug Administration's three clinical trial stages allow firms to evaluate and better manage investment risks at each phase, and (3) because FDA's final safety certification for a new drug virtually guarantees a significant market for drugs that serve sizable disease markets. The combination, then, of FDA's three approval stages, which allow benchmarking of investor risk, and its final certification, which virtually guarantees a market and is protected for the rest of a product's patent term, helps VCs manage investor risk; no other economic sector has such a system for risk management.

In contrast, the entire industrial/energy category had only 50 deals, worth $620 million, and medical devices, another capital-intensive industry, had 58 deals, worth $521 million, in the first quarter of 2016. Looking at A-round investments from 2004 to 2014 in "hard" technologies—new materials, chemicals, processes, and hardware integration firms—VC investors lost nearly $1.25 billion, while software returned 3.7 times what was invested.[30]

The pie chart in figure 7.1 bears all this out, illustrating how U.S. industrial and service sectors shared total venture capital investment in 2015, based on National Venture Capital Association data.[31] The pie slices show the dominance of software, which amounted to 40% of the 2015 venture total ($23.7 billion). Biotechnology accounted for 13% of the total ($7.67

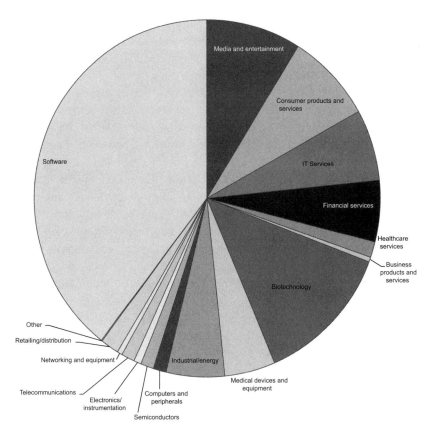

Figure 7.1
Distribution of VC Investments in 2015.
Source: Peter L. Singer, based on NVCA and PwC data, July 2016.

billion). Various service sectors (including "Media and Entertainment") had a 30% share of venture capital investment in 2015. The entire category of "Industrial and Energy" funding is small in comparison, with a 5% share ($3.24 billion in 2015).

In other words, although starting in the 1980s VCs were the great engine for scaling up the IT revolution and then the biotech revolution, they are not providing significant support to many of the other sectors of the economy that tend to create more jobs and be more capital intensive. If VCs are not going to play a role in scaling up technology firms that plan to manufacture, where could substitute financing come from?

Are there other means to scale up start-ups that plan to manufacture? *Initial public offerings (IPOs)*, once a frequent means of raising scale-up capital, have been in sharp decline. Between 1995 and 2015, U.S. IPOs decreased from 578 to 183 per year, although for firms backed by venture capital this decline was only from 183 to 77.[32] The sector that saw the largest increase in number of IPOs was biotechnology, which increased from 16 in 1995 to 41 in 2015, making up 53.2% of all VC-backed firms to go public in 2015.[33]

Mergers and acquisitions (M&As) can be another scale-up device, potentially enabling innovative start-ups to partner with larger firms with deeper pockets for scale-up. Unlike IPOs, M&As have not been in decline.[34] It is hard to break out from overall merger totals those between innovative start-ups and larger firms aiming to further the technology, but M&As are a standard exit route for VCs, and such data is available. As with the underlying venture funding, two sectors dominate. The software sector makes up the greatest share of annual M&As for VC-backed firms, with just over 50% in 2015. However, even though there were over seven times as many venture-backed acquisitions of software firms as biotech companies in 2015, the average biotech deal was nearly twice as large as the average software deal.[35] As biotech companies move their products closer to market, their value increases rapidly, which is indicative of the more monopolistic markets (based on the power of patents in the health sector) that biotech firms operate in compared with the markets for many software companies.

Crowdfunding, a new source of financing where large numbers of investors can contribute small sums online, was authorized by the JOBS Act of 2012.[36] By 2013, $5.1 billion was being raised for new firms through crowdfunding. However, crowdfunding to date has tended to favor services or products that can be readily understood by consumers and promptly brought to market, not the production of complex technologies that require long-term development. The JOBS Act also authorized *mini-IPOs*. Because of delays in Securities and Exchange Commission regulations and issues with state auditors, only a small number of firms have been able to use this mechanism to date.[37] *Traditional bank lending* has always been hard for start-ups to obtain because they lack an income stream and collateral. In economist Hyman Minsky's panoply of debt, they fall into the riskiest category, where there is no cash flow and the firm is betting its underlying asset (its new technology) will appreciate enough to cover its liabilities.

A number of new approaches to help start-ups have been tried in recent years other than by making more capital available. These can include elements such as the creation of a community and familiarity with local opportunities, or family offices where well-to-do families are sometimes prepared to undertake higher risk, perhaps if societal benefits are involved. These could potentially reduce some uncertainty and help firms outside of software and biotech. However, the data shows that VC funding (which is in turn tied to follow-on IPO or M&A exit strategies) remains by far the largest pool of funding for innovation-based start-ups—close to $60 billion in 2015—and that it is dominated by software and biotech start-ups, as well as service-oriented firms.

The second Advanced Manufacturing Partnership (AMP2.0) project picked up on a growing awareness of VC financing problems for start-ups and the findings from the PIE report noted here. It identified the gap in financing for production scale-up, which limited the ability of non-IT products to be designed, produced, and to enter markets, as a major problem in the U.S. manufacturing system, and it studied possible solutions.[38] The AMP2.0 work group on "Scale-up Policy" held a series of multicity workshops looking at financing mechanisms that could make investment in the scale-up to production more attractive to capital markets. The workshops included experts from a wide array of banking, venture capital, private equity, and corporate venture firms and evaluated ways to move capital-intensive technologies into commercial production. It also looked at available federal financing options.[39] To increase this capital access, which the work group found affected small and midsize manufacturers with innovative ideas as well as entrepreneurial start-ups, the AMP2.0 report recommended the following:

> *Launch a public-private scale-up investment fund for first at-scale production facilities.* By offering low-cost loans to private-sector investors in "first-of-a-kind" production facilities, a public-private Scale-Up Fund could incentivize additional investment in [such new] production facilities, ensuring that technologies invented in the United States can be made in the United States. The fund would award loans to investment funds or investor consortia in an equivalent amount to half the cost of the project being financed, and support investments of at least $40 million, to address investments at the scale where access to finance becomes truly challenging. This mechanism can be used, for example, to incentivize a U.S. equipment supply base for nascent manufacturing technologies such as additive manufacturing. Given the need to maintain a diverse portfolio of investments and the scale of manufacturing projects (easily $40 million to more than $150 million), the public-private investment fund would need to be able to provide $5 to 10 billion in capital over time, split across private funding and public loan guarantees (where generally $1 of public funds can create the equivalent of $10 of guarantees).[40]

In addition, it recommended modifying the current New Markets Tax Credit program to include features that would enable tax credits for new and expanded production facilities for smaller manufacturers and start-ups, and federal support for a web-based platform that would enable potential corporate strategic partners to obtain information on technologies and related production plans of smaller manufacturers and start-ups.[41] These were clearly ambitious proposals. Although the White House was supportive, Congress, in a period of scarce resources, was simply unwilling to consider the new financial tools recommended.

None of the various emerging financing mechanisms discussed, then, is either positioned or at the scale needed to offset the inability of venture capital firms to undertake the higher risk of scaling up complex, science-based, innovative technologies that require manufacturing. Venture capital firms, by far the largest source of support for start-ups, for very understandable market return and risk management reasons, have focused on two sectors, software and biotechnology. These are important sectors and certainly deserve support. However, the data shows that there is indeed a gap in the innovation system for scaling up innovative start-ups outside of the software, biotech, and service sectors.

Societal Implications

If technological and related innovation is the dominant causative factor behind historical U.S. economic growth, expanding the scope of the economic sectors that innovative start-ups can reach into could be important to broader economic growth. The reason to support entrepreneurship and start-ups is to increase societal levels of innovation to improve growth; if we wall off the access of entrepreneurship largely to two sectors and leave much innovation to die on the vine, the consequences for the economy and society will be serious.

There may be an underlying rule here: we get the innovation we pay for. If we invest in certain kinds of innovation, that is the kind of innovation we will get. If, for societal as well as economic reasons, we want to broaden the kinds of innovation entering the economy and society—for example, new energy technologies, or technologies that must be manufactured—we will need to find ways to broaden our innovation support mechanisms.

There is another reason to attempt to fill this innovation system gap. Manufacturing is well known for its ability to serve as the economy's largest job multiplier.[42] Complex, capital-intensive, science-based technology goods require manufacturing. As noted in chapter 3, manufacturing tends to create value chains of firms and accompanying jobs that reach, on the input side, from resources, to R&D, to suppliers and component makers, then to the production stage itself, and then, on the postproduction output side, from distribution, to retail, to repair, and to product life cycle.[43] The employment at the production stage itself is only a part of the employment that stems from the larger system. Software does not require manufacturing, and biotechnologies generally require less. Software especially does not require, and therefore does not create, comparable value chains and corresponding employment. If we are curtailing start-ups that make hard technologies, we are therefore affecting job creation and our employment rate. Both software and biotechnology are vital, for different reasons, but they are not enough.

Since in recent years the United States has been facing the consequences of what has been called a "jobless recovery" (a very slow job-recovery rate) following the Great Recession, of growing income disparity, and, as noted, of a significant decline in median income between 1990 and 2013 for men without college degrees, this issue of creating quality jobs is a significant societal challenge.[44] As will be explored in chapter 9, leading economists are arguing that the economy has fallen into a state of "secular stagnation" with insufficient demand and resulting slow growth, low inflation, and low interest rates.[45] Per capita GDP growth in the United States averaged 2.4% for the forty years starting in 1961, but for the past fifteen years it has averaged only 0.9%.[46] A McKinsey study showed that 81% of the U.S. population was in income brackets with flat or declining income over the past decade.[47] While in 2016 the unemployment rate fell to 4.9%, this counts only those actively looking for work; there are some five million fewer workers in the workforce than was projected in 2005, about half the decline resulting from an aging population but the other half not fully accounted for.[48] While the steep declines of the Great Recession affected these numbers, the subsequent recovery has not been robust—for example, per capita GDP growth since 2010 has been well below 2%. There is also a growing anxiety about what has been termed "jobless innovation"[49]—a growing host of innovations that enter economic sectors that create fewer jobs or that replace jobs.[50] If such problems are to be overcome, part of the answer may be by expanding the access of innovative start-ups to a broader spectrum of the economy, including in sectors that create more jobs that require manufacturing.

In 2000, economist Robert Gordon authored a paper asking, "Does the New Economy Measure Up to the Great Inventions of the Past?"[51]—a question he continues to write about. He argued that the Internet would not have the same transformative impact on productivity (economic output per hour of work) as earlier innovation waves such as electricity and air transport. The concept was controversial at the time; it came out in a period of rapid productivity increases predating the dot-com bust. But his underlying point is interesting: some innovation areas may have more economic impact than others.

Germany's continuing major focus on "manufacturing-led" innovation,[52] including through its Fraunhofer Institutes and workforce training programs, presents a contrasting approach. As noted in chapter 3, 20% of its workforce is employed in manufacturing, compared with 8% in the United States. Its manufacturing wages are over 60% higher than in the United States, yet it runs a major trade surplus in manufactured goods. Germany does not have strong start-ups or VCs. It instead has strong "mittelstand" firms buttressed with support systems that help them keep renewing their production innovation capability. Unlike the United States, its innovation system is oriented around manufacturing, a strong job-creating sector, and its innovation system is therefore more oriented toward job creation. Again, we get the innovation we invest in: software is not a strong job-creating sector—in some cases, it may be the reverse—and biotech serves a health sector that is not strong in adding to economic productivity gains. If we want job-creating innovation as opposed to "jobless innovation," we may have to tune up our innovation system to do it. Software and biotech offer important advances, but they may not be the only kinds of innovation we want to bring to market.

An alternative example is offered by Elon Musk, who left Silicon Valley for the Los Angeles area after selling his share of start-up Pay Pal.[53] As part of that location shift, he went from software to taking on a series of dramatic hard-technology challenges, using his PayPal gains to provide initial financing for his hard-tech start-ups. Dedicated to space exploration and to solving the energy challenge, he founded SpaceX, grew Tesla, and supported Solar Cities, all of which are now well along in the scale-up process as highly innovative, major companies and significant employers. Musk is a unique exception to the current software start-up model Silicon Valley seems locked into, but he shows that breakthrough innovation is achievable in hard, job-creating technologies.

An important part of the answer, then, may be to look at the organization of the innovation system itself. Despite problems that neoclassical economists have in tracking the complex innovation system and viewing it as exogenous, not endogenous, to the economy,[54] it is widely acknowledged by economists to be at the heart of economic growth. This system is not locked in on some kind of "invisible hand" economic autopilot. It is a flexible, dynamic system that responds to a range of inputs and organizational approaches. If the United States limits investment in innovation to the fruits of software, biotech, and certain service sectors because of the financing challenges discussed, then it will get innovation in those sectors, not others. Inputs affect outputs. If the United States wants to address challenges of "jobless recovery" and "jobless innovation," one step would be to adjust the innovation system to expand the entry of innovation into a wider range of economic sectors.

"Innovation Orchards": Substituting Space for Capital

In a May 2015 *Washington Post* op-ed titled "A Better Way to Deliver Innovation to the World," MIT president Rafael Reif proposed an alternative.[55] He argued that the current U.S. innovation system, based on venture capital support for start-ups, was not suited "to support complex, slower-growing concepts that could end up being hugely significant." This included disruptive new technologies emerging from basic scientific advances in non-"digital" areas that were not "market-ready." He wrote that if new technologies have "a good shot of producing returns within five years, they are magnets for talent and venture capital—and eventually for big companies that often buy startups whole. But this system leaves a category of innovation stranded: new ideas based on new science. . . . [These] may take 10 years, which is longer than most venture capitalists can wait. The result? As a nation, we leave a lot of innovation ketchup in the bottle."

Reif proposed an interesting potential solution to close this gap and accelerate the process from "idea to investment": create spaces for start-ups that would be rich in technology, advanced equipment, and know-how to enable the start-up to undertake advanced prototyping, demonstration, testing, and pilot production. In effect, he proposed substituting space for capital. This technology-rich space could bridge the missing venture funding support for what Reif called "tangibles"—complex, more capital-intensive, longer-term, hard technologies, which could also be "tangible-digital hybrids"—since those steps in the product design and development process would be what venture capital, if it was available, would have funded. He proposed establishing coalitions of "funders from the public, for-profit, and not-for-profit sectors" to support these new spaces and the start-ups that would populate them. He believed that regional firms would increasingly need to follow emerging innovations and that some could also be persuaded to support this new model, which he called "innovation orchards." These new support communities would support innovators with the resources, facilities, and mentorship, as well as bridge funding, they need to successfully derisk and commercialize their technology. If the emerging start-up technology was derisked, demonstrated, and proven, it could potentially move within range of more traditional financing, such as partnerships with existing firms and corporate venture and venture capital funding.

Reif also proposed that there may be "ways to shorten the full span from idea to impact, reducing it from, say, 10 years to five." He suggested it "may be possible to reproduce the process of rapid, relatively low-cost refinement and interaction that is so powerful in advancing purely digital concepts." The "innovation orchards" model may be able to help with that step as well, such as by creating parallel development paths for both ongoing research and production design and testing.

Models Relevant to "Innovation Orchards": Cyclotron Road, TechBridge, and The Engine

The proposed "orchards" would be anchored in existing innovation clusters, taking advantage of the mix of firms, small and large, and capabilities typically present in them. It would add a new institutional element building on "cluster theory."[56] The orchards could also build on existing mechanisms to help start-ups: the growing number of regional technology incubators that generally serve start-ups in their early stages, the SBIR (Small Business Innovation and Research) program, the Bayh-Dole Act system of licensing new technologies from university research, NSF's new Innovation Corps program to train university researchers in how to initiate start-ups, and various state and university programs for technology commercialization.[57] But the "orchards" model would fill an important gap in the existing mechanisms around start-up scale-up.

There are some working models that are comparable to the "innovation orchard" concept Rafael Reif has proposed; two are discussed here at length, and each offers different insights on how this approach might work.[58] A third has recently been formed at MIT.

Cyclotron Road
Lawrence Berkeley National Laboratory, a Department of Energy lab managed by the University of California, formed Cyclotron Road (CR) in July 2014 as an early-stage clean energy technology incubator. The project was supported by the Advanced Manufacturing Office in DOE's Energy Efficiency and Renewable Energy office and was founded by Ilan Gur,

previously a program director at DOE's ARPA-E, where he worked on energy storage, solar, and advanced materials. Cyclotron Road describes itself as "a home for top entrepreneurial researchers to advance technologies until they can succeed beyond the research lab."[59]

Lawrence Berkeley Lab is an energy lab with an $820 million annual budget and has 4200 employees and six major national user facilities adjacent to the UC Berkeley campus.[60] Cyclotron Road aims to link the lab—with its technology, equipment, and knowledge base—at the early, prefirm stage, with a group of competitively selected energy technologists who want to form start-ups. There are 16 such start-up groups located in a facility next to the lab with access to it and its resources. The start-up teams receive DOE seed funding and salaries for two years to pursue technologies tied to DOE's mission of nurturing new energy technologies. As DOE's Johanna Wolfson explains,

> The idea was that, within the CR program, innovators would continue to do the hardcore scientific and technical research needed in order to prove out the "hard" technology product they envision, while they are concurrently learning to wrap a business model around the would-be product. This distinction matters when you start trying to think about where else they could do that. Not at a university, or as a staff scientist at a national lab—there is no business mindset nor particular incentive to take the entrepreneurial leap. Not at an incubator—the equipment and expertise for the hard research isn't there, and you'd be expected to have brought in angel or venture funding already and be paying for yourself. Not at a corporate research lab (anymore), as those labs aren't supporting the disruptive breakthrough developments. Really nowhere—the practical result of which no one was taking the really hard innovations and trying to develop them into a business, because there's no place or mechanism by which to do it. That's why CR was born.[61]

Cyclotron Road, with the lab, provides supporting mentorship and expertise and help in pursuing technical feasibility for the start-ups' technologies. The start-ups are not "home alone"—in addition to access to advanced equipment and technologies to perfect their technologies, they get access to strong supporting networks in the lab and at UC Berkeley, and, through connections and advisory groups, to nearby Silicon Valley and to potential industry partners. An aim is to validate business and technology models to enable the technology to scale.

Cyclotron Road follows a five-element approach to find and develop promising energy technologies.[62] This is not a linear set of steps; they can proceed in parallel and in different sequences.

1. *Recruit outstanding innovators.* Cyclotron Road states that, "Top-notch innovation can't occur without top-notch people. We look for outstanding

talent willing to go 'all-in' to drive their energy technology from lab to market." They aim at innovators who want to develop start-ups starting at the prefinancing stage, and now have their third cohort in place, totaling some 16 teams selected from pools of more than one hundred applicants each. So CR is talent oriented, looking for capable entrepreneurs with sound and exciting technology ideas, capturing these ideas at an early stage.

2. *Select projects focused on commercial and scalable technical solutions to maximize energy market impact.* Cyclotron Road is focused on commercial energy breakthroughs that have realistic potential for impact at scale. It attempts to assist innovators in identifying product markets to demonstrate potential customer reach and technical feasibility as early as possible. The process of evaluating technical and economic feasibility and making potential technologies manufacturable at competitive cost are important parts of this process.

3. *Leverage existing R&D assets through the partnership with Lawrence Berkeley Lab.* For start-ups working in hard technologies, the cost and time needed to set up a research lab, procure advanced equipment, obtain equipment training, and set up safety protocols are significant barriers. But having this setup is key to developing and testing advanced prototypes. Cyclotron Road resolves this through its partnership with Lawrence Berkeley Lab. Start-up leaders work directly with Berkeley Lab experts using cutting-edge equipment almost from the time they join the program. This immediate access to R&D facilities dramatically reduces the start-up costs for hard-technology projects while providing innovators the opportunity to fail and pivot efficiently based on early results—substantially derisking technologies while continuing to revise their business model. This rich access to technology is a key distinction between CR and most technology incubators.

4. *Support innovators with seed funding, mentors, and networks.* Cyclotron Road, through DOE and Lawrence Berkeley Lab, provides salaries and seed funding for two years, using DOE's entrepreneurial and technology education role to enable its innovators to focus full-time on their projects, and also helps enable federal R&D funding by meeting any cost-sharing requirements. It links its hard-tech entrepreneurs, R&D executives, investors, and government researchers as mentors for its start-ups, helping them with the technical and business advice necessary to take their projects to the next level. Networking with other entrepreneurs and industry, and at technology events, is also built into the model.

5. *Connect innovators with commercial partners.* Cyclotron Road argues that, "There is no one-size-fits-all business model for hard tech. Our goal is to

maintain the viability of multiple pathways technologies to scale." It aims to help its start-ups find the optimal commercialization path and funding sources, considering a range of partners, including:

- Other government sources—CR and DOE can help move its entrepreneurs toward commercialization with additional grants, for instance from EERE, ARPA-E, DARPA, and various SBIR programs, as well as state funding, for instance from the California Energy Commission (CEC).
- Corporations—Firms can partner with entrepreneurs in joint development projects, minority equity investment, or outright acquisition.
- Venture Firms—Venture financing is limited for early-stage hard technologies, but as the technology is derisked, it may be available for some firms at later stages. Venture capital can also provide leverage on top of nondilutive grants and help innovators scale when the technology is proven and the market opportunity is sufficiently clear.
- Family Offices—Family offices are becoming increasingly interested and creative in their ability to extend equity and debt financing to cleantech entrepreneurs.
- Nonprofits—Some innovations can be effectively brought to scale through nonprofit or open-source development models.

The first cohort of start-ups at CR, which has now "graduated," included the following start-up groups, which suggest the kinds of work CR will support:

- Mosaic Materials, which is working on new metal-organic adsorbents to reduce the cost and emissions impact of chemical separations that are required in the production of a wide range of commodity chemicals;
- Visolis, which focuses on the bio-based production of carbon-negative, high-performance polymers, which could be much more efficient and less expensive than petroleum-based processes and cut greenhouse gas emissions;
- Spark Thermionics, which is working on directly converting heat to electricity by using compact, microfabricated thermionic energy converters, which could replace conventional heat engines;
- CalWave, which aims to convert ocean waves into electricity for baseload power and for fresh water through desalination;
- PolySpectra, which works to print functional materials with tailored forms and functions in a single step—called "functional lithography"—for example, for paintable photonic crystals for energy-efficient windows; and
- OPUS 12, which aims to recycle carbon dioxide into chemicals and fuels by using an electrochemical process.

This first cohort had a strong pattern of early success:[63] 100% of teams built a first prototype or secured funding to do so; 30 high-tech manufacturing innovation jobs are already supported by new companies founded by Cyclotron Road innovators; Cohort 1 raised over $15 million of foundational research funding and initial private investments; and all teams are funded for their next stage of development beyond the program. The cost to support the cohort at Lawrence Berkeley Lab was less than $4 million; of the $15 million the cohort raised so far in the public and private sectors, approximately $10 million was for follow-on research and $5 million was from initial private investments.

Cyclotron Road excels at providing innovators with help on research, initial demonstration, and production design. However, national labs are not as adept at industry-grade demonstration requirements or manufacturing design; it is not their mission, and CR is using strong advisory committees and mentors to optimize those inputs.

Interestingly, CR may represent a new approach to tech transition for the DOE. The department has been working for decades to improve the transition of technologies from its labs into commercial products. However, well-paid lab scientists with assured employment and interesting scientific work have only a limited incentive to leave their labs and create new, high-risk companies around their technologies. While established companies can license technologies from the labs, their interest in technology licensing tends to be limited to incremental advances that fit their existing technologies and business plans. But locating energy technology start-ups just outside DOE lab gates with access to lab technologies and know-how may be a more effective new way to transition technologies. The DOE is definitely interested in the CR model—Argonne National Lab, near Chicago, has now created a similar model, called Chain Reaction Innovations, to "help entrepreneurs bridge the commercialization valley of death,"[64] Oak Ridge National Lab is creating "Innovation Crossroads," and others may evolve to take advantage of lab facilities and expertise.[65]

TechBridge

This energy technology program was started in 2013 through the Boston Fraunhofer Center, a nonprofit R&D center and branch of the German Fraunhofer network.[66] It was founded by Johanna Wolfson, a physical chemist with a PhD from MIT who subsequently shifted to work on comparable models at DOE, and is currently led by Jacqueline Ashmore, who has an applied math PhD and experience in scientific analysis and innovation partnerships. Although TechBridge had initial DOE funding,[67] it follows a different approach than Cyclotron Road by identifying potential industry partners for start-ups based on technologies the larger firm is interested in, linking the two, and then performing a detailed technology evaluation and validation of the start-up's technology to help set the pathway for its scale-up. Whereas CR is about innovators, TechBridge is about industry needs and tech validation linked to the innovators. The essence of TechBridge is to lend credence to advanced technologies through industry-driven validation and demonstration projects that Fraunhofer assists on; it is less about the innovators themselves doing the work, as in the case of CR. As a respected and trusted third party, Fraunhofer's work matters to the established industry players that want to innovate but are risk averse about new technologies. It is about using the lab as an independent way to do validation, demonstration, and building of an industry-ready product, and then, with that lab validation mechanism, it is a way of derisking start-up technologies for industry and corporate partners.[68] It is the other side of the coin from CR, which operates the other way around.

TechBridge has developed its own four-step "method" that defines its role and how it attempts to pave the way for innovative new energy firms to attract partners, funding, and customers:[69]

1. *Define.* TechBridge works with program sponsors—typically larger companies—to determine the scope and goals of each project, typically focusing on innovation in a particular topic of strategic interest to the sponsor or in a specific region (and often collaborating with a government sponsor). This is key for the TechBridge approach—working on a concrete innovation of strong interest to the sponsor and then tying this interest to a developing technology.

2. *Identify.* With a sponsor, need, and technology pinned down, TechBridge then executes a comprehensive search and selection process for a start-up that can meet the technology need. The start-up must integrate strong technical and business expertise.

3. *Design.* Fraunhofer, as an independent third party, uses its domain experts to design a customized technology validation or demonstration project that integrates the goals of the sponsor with those of the selected start-up. Fraunhofer is noted for its skill and expertise in the tech validation process—will the start-up's emerging technology work, can it be efficiently produced and how, and is it financially able to solve the challenge? Here, TechBridge tries to design a practical implementation process that fits the best development of the technology given the sponsor's timetable and financial limits. Above all, the project must bring the technology to a relevant "go/no-go" decision point for the industry sponsor.

4. Execute. The technical projects are executed at Fraunhofer research facilities[70] and in real-world demonstration settings. Projects include optimizing and testing prototypes; conducting field demonstrations in real-world conditions; performing system integration work; and evaluating manufacturability. Practical problems such as maintenance and ease of technology operation and installation are considered. Fraunhofer plays the role of third-party independent evaluator for both sponsor and start-up, preparing the start-up for the partnership and the scale-up of its technology in practical settings. Its process typically takes about four months, providing independent, trusted information on the innovation.

The technology validation process noted in step 4, through the highly respected Fraunhofer labs—an independent third party—is unique and particularly valuable for both the start-up and the supporting company. The start-up is aided by a thorough evaluation of its technology and detailed recommendations for production design and process solutions. This can demonstrate that the proposed technology can work and can be produced. The larger firm in turn can be reassured by the validation step that it is getting a sound and manufacturable solution to its challenge to the start-up. It lowers risk for both sides.

As Nathalie Bockelt has noted, "While CR tends to work bottom-up, focusing on entrepreneurial researchers with ideas, providing them access to technology, then linking them to possible funding support, TechBridge tends to work . . . top-down. It finds significant supporters (typically larger firms) in need of innovations, then seeks to link them to startups with the capability to pursue these innovation challenges, while providing technical support and validation."[71]

TechBridge has been able to test out and refine its business concept and demonstrate that the model could provide real value. Specifically, it has developed data showing that companies of similar development stage and quality were nearly twice as likely to receive follow-on funding from the private sector within two years if they had received Fraunhofer validation services compared with those that had not.[72]

Both Cyclotron Road and TechBridge provide instructional models for means to scale up start-ups in preparation for the production process.[73] But could the model scale? Could universities adopt it?

The Engine
On October 26, 2016, MIT's president, Rafael Reif, led an effort to create another variation of the "innovation orchard" model, called The Engine, located adjacent to MIT's campus in Kendall Square. He argued,

From listening to entrepreneurs across the region, we are concerned that many new-science innovations with great potential for addressing humanity's most serious challenges are being stymied on the long trek to the marketplace. Why? Because turning a brand-new piece of science into a world-changing technology that is optimized, tested and ready for manufacture at scale can take more than a decade, longer than venture capitalists (VCs) can reasonably wait. The result is that our society's current system for funding and commercializing new ideas—so effective with relatively quick-to-market digital products—leaves many "tough technology" solutions permanently stranded.[74]

MIT created a 26,000 square foot space in the heart of the innovation hothouse of Kendall Square to serve up to 60 start-ups, with access to outstanding technology, equipment, and know-how. While it will help some early-stage start-ups get off the ground (particularly from MIT), there are already numerous start-up incubators in the area for such firms. So The Engine can serve primarily as a kind of graduate school for area start-ups, assisting them when they have developed business plans and prototypes and are moving into product design with the advanced proto-type, demonstration, testing, and perhaps pilot production phases. The start-ups could be both resident and nonresident, using the equipment and knowledge assets. They would enter for one-year terms, which could be extended. A series of advisory committees have been set up with MIT faculty, as well as outside experts, to assist in different technology and other support areas.

The Engine will also serve as a staging area so that as its start-up firms move toward production, it can link them to a series of secondary nodes, which will include strong area companies interested in linking to start-ups in a range of technology areas, from medical devices to energy. Lincoln Lab, a noted defense research and engineering lab administered by MIT, also plans to be a node, offering access to its highly respected rapid prototyping capabil-ity. Although The Engine is clearly following Reif's concept of substitut-ing space for capital, it would also offer bridge funding (raised outside the university's academic budget and endowment) to help its start-ups scale. Launched with $25 million raised by MIT, The Engine has worked with a group of area investors, more interested in strengthening the region's inno-vation than in gain, to pool resources at a larger scale and have built the bridge fund to $150 million.[75] These investors are public-spirited, recogniz-ing the high risk of science-based startups and not expecting VC-type mar-gins. So there is a high-risk but for-profit investment feature.

All these tools could accelerate the time for the technology scale-up and help derisk participating start-ups so they can attract financing from VCs and corporate venture funds and form alliances with existing firms. The Engine will be independent of MIT and plans to help both start-ups coming out of MIT and those from other regional sources.

MIT clearly hopes The Engine it is creating to help fill a growing gap in the regional innovation ecosystem for "hard"-technology start-ups would also become a model for other universities and regions to consider. As President Reif put it:

> When it comes to the most important problems humanity needs to solve— climate change; clean energy; fresh water and food for the world; cancer, autism, Alzheimer's, infectious disease—*there is no app for that.* We believe The Engine will help deliver important answers for addressing such intractable problems— answers that might otherwise never leave the lab. Because many of these solutions depend on tangible technologies, we have high hopes that they will ultimately produce not only new companies, but new industries, new forms of manufacturing and new jobs. And if we can truly make The Engine hum, we hope it might become a model that would be useful to other ecosystems, as well.[76]

Linking Start-ups to Small Manufacturers: Greentown Lab and MassMEP

Most technology-based, innovative start-ups now come from university research benches through researchers, postdocs, and grad students. These start-ups know their research but not manufacturing. The Greentown Lab-MassMEP partnership[77] between start-ups and small manufacturers has attempted to get the start-ups past this innovation gap; it offers an additional feature to the "innovation orchards" approach.

Greentown Labs is an energy technology start-up incubator located in Somerville, adjacent to Cambridge, Massachusetts, and MassMEP is the Massachusetts branch of the NIST-sponsored Manufacturing Extension Partnership. The MEP program dates from the 1980s manufacturing competition with Japan and works in every state to bring the leading manufacturing technologies and processes to small American manufacturers. The 250,000 small manufacturers employing less than 500 workers produce a major portion of U.S. goods; they are the suppliers and component makers for the OEMs (original equipment manufacturers)—the larger manufacturers. But MEP has been a program for existing small manufacturers; helping start-ups manufacture has not been part of the MEP equation.

In November 2014, Greentown and MassMEP partnered on a one-year pilot program called the Greentown Labs-MassMEP Manufacturing Initiative, to link start-ups to local manufacturers to help them get their new technologies production-ready. The program was created and run by Micaelah

Morrill, a program director at Greentown Labs, and Peter Russo, the growth and innovation program director at MassMEP.

Morrill saw that even start-ups with initial funding and an initial prototype still had trouble moving to the production stage. During their one-year pilot, Morrill and Russo identified the barriers that prevent start-ups and established small and midsize manufacturers from working together, and they developed a system to address them. Their initiative developed a way for start-ups moving toward production to connect to manufacturer partners and move their prototype to production-ready design.

Barriers between the two sides. An initial Greentown survey found not only that start-ups and manufacturers did not know each other or how to find each other but that there were cultural and communication barriers between them. They were speaking in different languages from different worlds.

Start-ups often thought they had to manufacture in Asia; if they were fortunate enough to have venture capital support, their VC firm often told them to do this.[78] They were often unaware how much manufacturing capacity remained nearby—after all, the United States is still the second-largest manufacturing nation by output. They also had little sense of the advantages of working in close proximity to collaboratively resolve ongoing design problems. While the start-ups did thorough research, they generally had little to no experience with production processes. The small manufacturers were the other side of the coin—they conducted no R&D but knew production processes and technologies intimately. While start-ups typically made connections online, small manufacturers interested in teaming with start-ups made connections by word of mouth, by telephone, and through face-to-face relationships.

When it came to design for manufacturing, start-ups were often out of their depth: they were uncertain of their own production needs and of what questions to ask. The two sides simply had different communication styles, time frames, and incentives. Finally, the start-ups did not understand the levels of overhead and costs for developing an advanced, manufacturable prototype, and how this required most small manufacturers to be assured of a longer production run to recoup costs and make a profit. Small-lot production often will not work for most innovative, complex products.

Yet the two sides needed each other. The start-ups had to understand and succeed at production and needed expert allies to get there. The small manufacturers did not undertake R&D but were interested in the possibility of growing past their current supplier networks by producing innovative goods to scale their production. A number also wanted to help their communities by helping the start-ups and to inspire their employees by working with start-ups.

The pilot program. To get across these barriers, Greentown Labs and MassMEP developed a multipart program to educate and organize start-ups on production issues and enable connections with area manufacturers. Because of the barriers between the two sides, the program had to be intensely face-to-face—an online computer matching service was not going to work. The program included surveys, a series of "office hours" meetings and workshops, and face-to-face sessions in which start-ups received one-on-one advice and guidance for effective communication with manufacturers along with general design-for-manufacturing information.

1. *Survey.* Two required surveys, one to start-ups and one to interested manufacturers, helped each to focus and develop expectations for the other.

2. *"Office hours."* Office hours were available to Greentown Labs start-ups, along with other hard-tech start-ups in the area, hosted by Peter Russo from MassMEP, an experienced manufacturer, along with other manufacturing experts and Greentown Labs staff. The process helped start-ups determine the types of manufacturing capabilities they needed, understand production processes, and consider their production design. When the start-ups thought they were nearly ready to begin manufacturing, Russo would review their plans and help with the design, in a thirty to forty minute session. After incorporating Russo's feedback, the start-ups would come back for a second, shorter meeting. Once their design was closer to readiness, Russo and Morrill would help connect them to a manufacturer.

3. *Workshops.* To educate start-ups about manufacturing processes, Greentown Labs hosted workshops and "lunch and learns" for groups of Greentown and other start-ups. These brought manufacturers to Greentown for half-day informational panels, after which start-ups could meet one-on-one with the manufacturing representatives and start to build relationships. Workshops focused, for example, on production processes, such as extrusion and injection molding, or on types of materials.

Greentown's involvement formally ended after the first connection was made; the process of negotiating and signing a contract was left to the manufacturer and the start-up. No subsidies were provided—the start-up had to find its own funding for the deal, which gave both sides a major stake in the outcome. But Morrill and Russo continued to provide mentorship and advice to both start-ups and manufacturers as they progressed in their relationships.

Results. In the one-year pilot, 32 start-ups were interested in participating in the program and 83 manufacturers were interested in working with start-ups. The program facilitated some 140 connections between start-ups and manufacturers and resulted in 19 signed contracts. Proximity mattered, as suggested in chapter 4. Working with local manufacturers meant an intimate and prompt collaborative process for production design that solved many design problems and challenges. Both Greentown and MassMEP have continued to follow up on their pilot, fostering connections. Learning from the Greentown-MassMEP model, DOE has now begun an entrepreneur education effort in manufacturing, Build4Scale.[79]

The Greentown Labs-MassMEP initiative to link start-ups and small manufacturers is a complementary feature for the "innovation orchards" model. One is pursuing the full scope of the innovation process through technology scale-up, and the other enables start-ups to link to the initial production stage of the innovation process. But this initial production stage is clearly part of the innovation process; missing it amounts to an innovation system gap. The combination of approaches can integrate the manufacturing process into the start-up innovations, helping to ensure that their prototypes can become commercially viable.

Complementary Models—Lessons from Cyclotron Road, TechBridge, The Engine, and Greentown-MassMEP

Each of the models explored provides a different menu for an "innovation orchard" approach, and each provides potential complementarity.[80] Although The Engine, Cyclotron Road, TechBridge, and Greentown Lab/ MassMEP were formed only recently, each offers lessons.

Cyclotron Road creates a home for early-stage innovators forming start-ups, a space rich in technology, equipment, and know-how. It draws on a top DOE lab, putting start-ups led by talented teams of scientists and engineers, picked through a highly competitive selection process, into an outstanding R&D facility, where they also receive business mentorship. In economic terms, CR represents the efficient deployment of an existing asset—a strong energy lab. Despite the discouragement new start-ups have faced from the sharp decline in VC support for clean tech, CR gives them a great home, pays their salaries for two years, and removes many of the barriers to product design. An important measure for CR's success is that, regardless of what happens to the start-up itself, CR is keeping strong talent in clean tech. It shows that top-notch innovators will flock to an intense, "all-in" setting that offers significant support and that linking lab scientists to start-ups to share expertise can work. It demonstrates that modest funding and an existing technology asset—the lab—can potentially leverage additional outside funding. The major challenge for CR is having its start-ups show tangible relevance to potential industry partners or investors who can assist in implementing the technology as they emerge from their term at CR. Because its energy lab partner lacks expertise in commercial manufacturing design and scale-up, it must also bridge this space. In summary, CR shows that a space rich in technology, equipment, and know-how can be key to transitioning start-ups; although CR is only in its third cohort of start-ups, it looks quite promising.

TechBridge brings a different set of lessons to the table. The challenge that TechBridge is trying to solve is that without deep industry-applied knowledge and support, start-ups have great difficulty showing the industrial viability of their new technologies to investors, customers, and, particularly, potential industry partners. TechBridge works in a different way than CR. It goes to established industrial firms and asks them to consider innovations they need and will fund, and then it shops these requests to qualified start-ups that can offer to undertake the innovation. TechBridge is an independent expert, quality matchmaker between the two sides and helps protect each of them—particularly helping the start-up on managing its intellectual property. TechBridge's Fraunhofer lab system then validates the start-up's technology innovation, certifying how the technology can best be optimized and produced—a key third-party validation role that helps both sides move toward a working partnership. TechBridge leads both parties to field demonstration projects that can derisk the new technology for follow-on implementation. The key features that TechBridge offers are industry partners, technology validation, demonstration, refining the prototype, and developing manufacturing feasibility. It is a different role than CR's, but potentially highly complementary—you could attach this step to a CR-like space. Interestingly, of 17 start-up companies that have come through TechBridge's process as of 2016, 95% have survived, and have obtained $94 million in follow-on funding and 13 new industry partnerships.

The Greentown Lab-MassMEP program for linking start-ups to capable small manufacturers offers a third complementary element. The problem it addresses is that innovative start-ups emerging from university labs know their research but generally lack manufacturing knowledge. The program helped equip start-ups with basic manufacturing knowledge, alerted them to gaps and issues in their manufacturing designs, and then facilitated a highly personal, face-to-face system for linking and building trust between small regional manufacturers and start-ups at area incubators for production scale-up—creating advanced prototypes and pilot production of initial products. This, too—linking start-ups to strong local manufacturers to scale up to production—is a complementary piece that can snap into an "innovation orchard" model to help it work.

The Engine, although still at the early start-up phase, is positioned to absorb lessons from the other models. Its bridge fund raised from area investors to help start-ups with scale-up, and its idea of linking its start-ups to secondary nodes (strong area firms or labs) with the specialized expertise many start-ups need, are new and complementary features. In particular, it represents a way universities could engage in this start-up challenge. Since university research has become a cornerstone for technology advancement, universities are increasingly playing a regional economic role in addition to their historical education and research roles. While many universities have technology transfer programs that help start-ups emerging from campus research, and have links to incubators that support start-ups at early stages of development, few have focused on the scale-up stage. The Engine, then, could be one model for how interested universities could operate at this stage.

Summary

Start-ups represent the next generation of technology. If start-ups move their production offshore, this affects the strength of the overall innovation system, because production, particularly initial production of new technologies, is part of the innovation system. Ultimately, it means that an important innovation capability has shifted with the shift of production. So enabling innovative start-ups that require manufacturing fills a gap in the innovation system.

However, these kinds of innovative, hard-technology start-ups are running into increasing difficulty in scaling up to the manufacturing stage. Venture capital financing has been key to the entrepreneurial start-up system pioneered by the United States since it supported the computing, semiconductor, and then biotechnology advances in the 1980s. However, venture capital is increasingly focused on the software, biotech, and service sectors, where risks can be reduced, and away from longer-term, higher-risk, hard technologies. While there may be other start-up financing options, these are not at a scale or positioned to provide significant help to hard-technology start-ups.

Despite the importance of innovation to economic growth, the United States is narrowing its innovation to several sectors, thereby affecting its potential growth rate. We will get the innovation we pay for, and if we are unable to invest in a broad range of technologies, we simply will not get them. In addition, the United States is not supporting innovation in significant job-creating sectors. Start-ups that manufacture and are unable to do so are particularly worth noting because of the role of manufacturing as the sector with the highest job-multiplier effects. So problems of "jobless recovery," "secular stagnation," and "jobless innovation" are in part tied to this increasing gap in the innovation system.

Are there ways to get hard-tech start-ups that manufacture out of this box and on the road to scaling up? The concept of "innovation orchards," proposed by MIT president Rafael Reif, offers a promising approach, where partnerships between universities, industry, and government can offer spaces rich in technology, equipment, and know-how for promising start-ups to scale up, in effect substituting space for capital. Initial models for this approach include Cyclotron Road, based at DOE's Lawrence Berkeley Lab, and TechBridge, housed in the Boston Fraunhofer Center. Although new, The Engine at MIT offers another model. A complementary feature for this "orchard" model has been developed by Greentown Lab and MassMEP in the Boston area, where start-ups ready to undertake advanced prototypes, product design, and pilot production can be linked to small manufacturers who can help them scale.

Reversing our problems with "jobless innovation" may require us to adjust the innovation system to expand the entry of innovation into a wider range of economic sectors other than software and biotech. The "innovation orchard" experiments reviewed here may provide models.

8   Workforce Education and Advanced Manufacturing

First, some facts. There are currently 12.3 million manufacturing workers in the United States, 8.1% of the total employed in the U.S. workforce. According to the National Association of Manufacturers,[1] the average manufacturing worker earned $79,553 in compensation in 2014, compared with $64,204 for the average worker over all industries, a 20% difference; 92% of manufacturing workers were eligible for employer-provided health benefits, compared with 79% of workers over all firms, a 13% difference; 46% of manufacturing workers work at firms employing less than 500. There were 251,857 firms in the manufacturing sector in 2013; all but 3702 had less than 500 employees, and three-quarters had less than 20 employees. Despite its huge trade deficit in manufactured goods, goods produced in the United States are increasingly being traded in international markets; U.S. manufacturers exported $1.4 trillion in goods in 2014, almost double the amount exported in 2000. These exports—increasingly of complex, high-value-added goods—support higher-paying jobs; production employees in the top tier of the "most trade-intensive industries" in 2014 earned an average compensation of almost $94,000, 56% higher than employees of producers of goods that were less trade-intensive. But manufacturing jobs, as previously noted, because they link together so much economic activity all across the economy, continue to have the highest multiplier effect of any sector: a dollar's worth of final demand for manufacturers generates $1.48 in other services and operations.[2] In contrast, for example, retail and wholesale trade sectors have much lower multipliers, generating 54 cents and 58 cents, respectively.

What does this tell us about the manufacturing workforce? Manufacturing remains a massive economic sector, with a better-paid workforce, with better benefits, compared with other sectors, particularly in high-value export sectors. Much of this workforce is employed at small firms, which complicates training delivery. The sector is also becoming increasingly subject to intense global competition.

Manufacturing Workforce Supply

Public views of manufacturing will affect supply; how does the public assess manufacturing work? A 2014 public opinion survey from The Manufacturing Institute and Deloitte[3] found overwhelming support for this sector: 90% believe manufacturing is very important or important to American economic prosperity, 89% believe the same regarding America's standard of living, and 72% said it was very important or important to national security. A massive 82% believe the United States should invest more heavily in manufacturing, but 75% of the survey respondents believe manufacturing jobs are the first to be moved offshore to other nations, and only 37% say they would encourage their children to have a career in manufacturing. Given the history of production moving offshore and the loss of manufacturing jobs in the first decade of this century, this should not be surprising, despite the wage differentials noted. Of the respondents in the Deloitte survey, 84% ranked job security and stability as important job-selection criteria, but only 41% agreed that manufacturing jobs were stable and provide more job security relative to other industries. These public concerns in turn have translated into concerns by industry leaders about workforce shortages.

In 2015, Deloitte undertook a survey of senior industry executives to gain their perspectives on future manufacturing workforce needs.[4] There were strong concerns from this group about existing shortages of skilled workers in production-related jobs, and even stronger concerns about meeting future needs. Projecting from their survey, the Deloitte report states that there is an expectation at the executive level that an additional 600,000 jobs will be added to the manufacturing sector, with 3 million more to be generated by 2020 to replace retiring workers. A significant majority of these will be for skilled positions, requiring technical degrees and training. Of these jobs, over a million are expected to go vacant, affecting production capacity.

If there are existing and future problems supplying skilled workers, what does this mean for advanced manufacturing? A foundational problem that advanced manufacturing faces is that if it is to materialize, it requires a workforce well trained in these new advanced production technology and process areas. If the existing production system faces shortages of skilled workers, how will advances be squeezed in?

The Deloitte report is tempered somewhat by a 2014 study by Weaver and Osterman.[5] Surveying at the plant manager level, not the higher-level executives, they asked specifically about how much time was needed to fill job openings, not about shortages. In effect, they were seeking the supply data behind assertions of shortages. They found no current emergency—some 75% of open manufacturing jobs were filled within a month. They also found that manufacturing sector wages, while generally higher compared with other sectors, had not increased as significantly as would have been expected if there had been a labor shortage. Weaver and Osterman's findings contrast with Deloitte's survey of senior management and suggest the complexity of the manufacturing labor market.

There is a complicated range of employment within manufacturing. There is, overall, a pay premium for manufacturing workers,[6] as noted. This is because the production process is capital intensive, where manufacturers require skilled employees to develop advanced processes and operate complex and sophisticated equipment.[7] Within manufacturing, there is a wide range of wage bases between employers, even within particular sectors. As economist Susan Helper puts it:

> Manufacturers compete with each other using very different "production recipes." Even within narrow industries, the top 25 percent of firms measured by compensation level pay more than twice as much per worker as the bottom 25 percent. The high-wage firms often can remain profitable because they adopt practices that yield high productivity—but only with a skilled and motivated workforce. These practices include increasing automation while having all workers participate in design and problem-solving. For decades, unions helped ensure both a supply of skilled workers and a fair distribution of the value they helped create; the decline of unions is an important factor facilitating the adoption of low-wage strategies by some employers.[8]

As part of this range, at the lowest end for the lowest skills, there are low wages; one study estimates that a surprisingly high number of production workers receive public assistance, predominantly in the South.[9] Some of the manufacturers' complaints, embodied in the Deloitte survey, might be about trying to attract skilled employees for lower wages—in effect, some may be complaining that there is a major shortage of new Cadillacs for sale at $10,000. Generally, manufacturing wages have been slow to rebound since the recession;[10] labor shortages, of course, are generally signaled by wage rises, which has not been the case. Although a reported 5.2% rise in median income for 2015 across the economy may signal some change,[11] this 2015 median income was still 1.6% below the 2007 median and 2.4% below the 1999 median.[12] The Weaver and Osterman findings underscore that the manufacturing labor market is clearly complex, regional, and covers a wide range of employers and job areas.

However, Osterman and Weaver did find that between 18% and 25% of firms they surveyed were having difficulty filling production positions.

These tended to include firms requiring more advanced skills, including higher-tech smaller firms. They found that 12% of firms had to reduce production levels because of an inability to find workers.[13] This signals that there is still good reason for concern.

Data from the Bureau of Labor Statistics helps us understand the elements within the term "manufacturing workers."[14] We can consider essentially three categories for U.S. manufacturing workers: production-level workers (low skilled), machinists, technicians, welders, and other skilled workers (highly skilled), and engineers, researchers, and scientists (very highly skilled).[15] These categories are changing: the first category of employees—assemblers and basic production workers—was once more dominant. But the second category of skill level—highly skilled, often called "middle skilled"[16]—is now the growing category, with twenty years of significant growth. Production work—blue-collar jobs—now only make up some 40% of manufacturing jobs.[17] This can be seen in manufacturing workforce trends: overall, production occupations had average hourly wage increases in the recession recovery period from 2008 to 2011 of 5.5%, while more highly skilled machinist manufacturing jobs, for example, had a 7.4% wage increase in the same period.[18] This helps us understand that there are different perspectives to skill shortages in manufacturing; the workforce supply situation appears more acute in the highly skilled category and less acute for those with lower skills.

An Organization for Economic Cooperation and Development (OECD) study comparing workforce skills across developed countries found weakness in skills in the U.S. workforce. Analyses of this "PIAAC" study results for millennials—young adults between the ages of 16 and 34—showed that U.S. millennials performed well below the OECD average in all skill domains studied.[19] This could be an additional factor in why employers are seeking higher skills.

This is part of a general trend in U.S. labor markets—required skills are moving steadily upscale. If middle-skill jobs are defined to include some college education, BLS found that these jobs now include 37.7 million workers, rising from 28.7% of the workforce population in 2006 to 33.4% in 2012; in the same period, low-skill workers declined 7.5% and very high-skill workers increased 2.7%.[20] A study by Alicia Modestino that identified 272 middle-skill occupations in which more than a third of employees in each had some college or an associate's degree found that between 2006 and 2012 labor demand decreased for low-skill jobs by 5.4%, increased for very high-skill jobs by 6.6%, and the middle-skill category was stable at close to one-third of jobs.[21] Harry Holzer has found that most of these occupation categories have been shifting from high-volume, low-tech jobs to low-volume, high-tech jobs.[22]

One study found that for new job openings and replacement of retiring employees from the beginning to the end of the decade ending in 2018, 78% of these positions will require high or middle skills and only 22% low skills; these new high- or middle-skill jobs will require education beyond high school.[23] Another way of looking at this is that most of the new jobs this century will require skills held by only a minority of the current workforce. A recent study by Georgetown's Center on Education and the Workforce shows that in the period from 2007 to 2016—the Great Recession and its recovery—8.6 million jobs were filled by persons with a bachelor's degree or higher, 1.3 million jobs by those with an associate's degree or some college, and there was a decline of 5.5 million jobs for those with high school diplomas or below.[24] Nearly all the new jobs postrecession—11.5 million out of 11.6 million—went to those with at least some postsecondary education.[25] A Federal Reserve study found that the U.S. labor force overall is going through a "job polarization," with lower-skill cognitive and routine manual jobs in decline and jobs that require higher-skill cognitive and nonroutine manual skills growing.[26] This upscale skills trend is moving through the manufacturing sector as well: between 1985 and 2014, employment of workers with a bachelor's degree in the production sector has increased by 70%.[27] Manufacturing workers—new and existing—must upgrade their skills over time, and upgraded skills appear to be a prerequisite for advanced manufacturing.

Underlying Problems in the Skills-Training System in Manufacturing

Why has the workforce training system in the United States been failing to meet this challenge? Labor economist Richard Freeman sets out some basics: "The United States has an exceptional labor market. With less institutional regulation than is found in any other major advanced country, it relies on decentralized wage setting to determine pay and provides workers with lower safety nets to deal with unemployment, disability and health problems. It gives managers great rewards and power. . . . Some see the U.S. market as the nearest thing to the 'invisible hand' market of economic theory."[28] He has also worried, as recited in chapter 1, that, "Inequality is now at Third World levels" and that real wages have continued to stagnate.

Economist Gary Becker, in his noted work on human capital, argued that U.S. labor markets generally supply suboptimal levels of skills training.[29] This is because labor market competition between firms tends to create an underinvestment in skills training because the gains from such training cannot be adequately appropriated by the firm providing the training. In other words, companies are not willing to invest in worker skills because competitor companies frequently acquire these trained employees, avoiding their own workforce training investment and preventing the first company from recapturing its training investment. So employers, to the extent that they provide training, build their programs around skills needed only by that firm and that are more valuable for their firm than for others—"specific"[30] skills. This practice avoids promoting worker transferability. For more "general" skills, firms tend to require that they be acquired by the worker before joining the firm. The employee, then, has to bear the burden of obtaining the general skills training, which is, in turn, the prerequisite for acquiring the firm-specific skills. Many potential employees are simply not in a position to invest in acquiring general skills, which limits the skilled worker base, thereby damaging all the participants in the labor market.

This situation has been exacerbated by a "thinning out" of the U.S. manufacturing ecosystem, as identified in MIT's Production in the Innovation Economy (PIE) study.[31] It found that pressure from financial markets to maximize short-term returns led larger firms to divest their vertical assets and focus on "core competency." Firms correspondingly avoided investments in areas of less direct gains, including investments in worker training. Thus, larger firms were under pressure to reduce support for the ecosystems that also helped their smaller-firm supplier bases. Smaller firms, in turn, faced comparable financial pressure from the decline in their traditional financial support source, "local banking." The regional bank, with traditional personal, face-to-face customer relations with its area manufacturers, has been displaced by national and indeed international banking return models, placing "local banking" in decline. Both large and small firms, then, increasingly were pressed to avoid investments in what could be called the "manufacturing commons," where benefits reached across firms in the sector, including investments in worker training. A training decline, then, is one consequence of the "thinning out" of the manufacturing ecosystem. It has been exacerbated because federal funding for employment training has fallen by half as a share of GDP from the mid-1980s to the present.[32]

Lessons from the German Model

As previously noted, Germany, unlike the United States, has an innovation system that is "manufacturing-led." Its manufacturing firms pay their manufacturing workforce wages that are over 60% higher than those for

U.S. manufacturing workers and it runs a major trade surplus in goods led by areas like cars, machinery and capital goods; its trade surplus is currently the largest in the world. The public assumption in the United States has been that with high wages and high costs, the United States necessarily will lose the manufacturing sector to lower-cost, lower-wage competitors; Germany shows that to be an incorrect assumption. One critical way it sustains its system is through a highly skilled workforce. As observers have noted, when a need for production innovation reaches a German factory, the entire workforce becomes engaged on the factory floor; from technicians to design engineers, the whole workforce team tends to work on the problem collectively. This has not been the past history of major manufacturers in U.S. factories, where, starting in the late nineteenth century, engineers, seeking to elevate their professional status, tended to separate themselves from the factory floor workers in an "upstairs/downstairs" arrangement. Since innovation increasingly tends to require collective engagement with diverse inputs, that hierarchical arrangement can be fatal. When Japan's quality revolution forced the United States to rethink the production process, some of this was fixed, but the collective engagement on German factory floors is not often replicated on U.S. factory floors.

The Mittelstand firms. Germany has major firms with worldwide brands, but the mainstays of its manufacturing sector are its small and midsize firms, the "Mittelstand," which produce over half of its economic output.[33] Although these firms (defined as having less than 500 employees and annual revenue of less than €50 million) are often family owned and many decades old, they have found ways to keep innovating and updating themselves on a continuing basis. While the United States tends to rely on startups and entrepreneurs to introduce innovation, Germany has systems in place—including in workforce training—so that legacy firms keep renewing their capabilities. The Mittelstand are very export oriented, buttressed by a strong export financing system. These firms are 96.6% of all German companies, employ almost 60% of all workers, produce 56.5% of value-added output, and, in particular, house 82.2% of German trainees.[34] Although workforce training is expensive for smaller firms in Germany and elsewhere, Germany's Mittelstand still provide training for over four out of five of the country's apprentices, in an apprenticeship-based training system. The Mittelstand, as Germany's Ministry of Economic Affairs and Energy puts it, "train the nation."[35] Unlike smaller firms in the United States, they conduct R&D: companies with fewer than 250 staff invest more than twice as much in total R&D as companies with between 250 and 499 employees. More than 70% of companies with fewer than 20 employees engage in research with several partners.[36] They tend to retain their employees long-term. The firms invest in training, and they provide additional compensation for these increased skills, which encourages retention. This enables a growing skill base within the firm, which further enables and is enhanced by R&D. This increases its innovation capacity and therefore its competitiveness. It is a virtuous cycle. How does it work?

Dual education system. The German work/education system[37] has evolved as a major alternative to university education; the United States has nothing like it. Only about a quarter of German students emerge from its education system without either a university degree or a technical certificate, which assures highly marketable skills. The apprenticeship system is the major alternative to college. It is called "dual education" because it requires substantial cost sharing by companies, regional governments, and the trainees themselves. Regional governments fund a system of vocational schools, which focus on foundational education and skills training; apprentices attend these one to two days a week or for block periods, and the government pays for their full tuition. Companies pay for training onsite, at their plants and facilities. These offer quite sophisticated "hands-on" training programs. The apprentices work for low wages to get the combination of vocational school and onsite training—they typically receive a fifth of a laborer's wage. The training system largely reduces the need for German firms to rely on an external labor market.

The involved firms, small and large, have close ties to the vocational schools, and a significant role in shaping their curriculum, which is regularly reviewed to update techniques and skills taught. So the training system is very job-relevant, but the training certification is marketable across firms. While training at Mittelstand firms will typically be on the factory floor, large companies also, in effect, run onsite schools in dedicated training facilities. Firms share training and facilities to offset costs and share expertise, and smaller firms receive training subsidies. The apprentices, by their willingness to accept low wages for multiyear training, help to make the costs workable for the firms, but the reward of strong, certified, and therefore marketable skills turns out to be well worth the sacrifice. Before they can complete their apprenticeship, students must take tests that evaluate their knowledge from both the vocational school education and the onsite firm's more "hands-on" training. The certifications are recognized across German regions and firms.

Interestingly, the training institutions are not state-controlled but instead private (although subsidized), with correspondingly more flexibility than a state institution and with which firms appear more willing to cooperate, although they can sanction underperforming and noncomplying training institutions. Unions dominate manufacturing employment in Germany, and their support for the apprenticeship system and their participation in collective bargaining wage arrangements across sectors stabilizes wage levels and thereby reduces the ability of a firm to pay to hire away another firm's trained apprentices. In summary, Germany has constructed a system that gets around the economic disincentives highlighted by Becker that create structural problems for training in the United States.[38] The system produces over 200,000 skilled production workers each year.[39]

The Fraunhofer Academy. Another key element in the German system comes from the Fraunhofer organization. The Fraunhofer Academy[40] is tied to the Fraunhofer Institutes—some 60 of them across the country—which specialize in particular technology areas. While apprentices can continue to receive onsite training from the companies they work for, the academy can substitute for the vocational school role, offering education one or two days a week or for a block period. It is particularly useful in providing education in high-tech fields in emerging complex industry sectors—advanced energy technologies, big data, or composite fibers, for example. This brings advanced manufacturing into the training system. The Fraunhofer Academy increasingly offers online courses and content though iAcademie. Apprentices who go through these academy programs can bring the new skills back to their workplaces—it is an effective new skill dissemination tool. Technology ideas and skills transfer best on two feet, through people, not technical plans, because, unlike plans, people bring all the tacit know-how with them. So Fraunhofer Institutes play a key education and training role in advanced production-related technologies through their Fraunhofer Academy, and this is a key way to disseminate technology advances. There is a potential model here for the new U.S. advanced manufacturing institutes: their education and training programs should not be a sideline but rather a key part of the technology development and dissemination effort.

AMP2.0 Report Proposes a U.S. Apprenticeship Model and Other Options

The United States is not Germany: it has far less unionization and far more decentralized labor markets. Germany's two-tiered workforce—apprentice and permanent workers—is present only to a small degree in the United States. Could there still be ways the German apprenticeship model might work in the United States?

The Advanced Manufacturing Partnership 2.0 report in October 2014 made a series of recommendations for building the skilled production workforce needed for advanced manufacturing, including a new apprenticeship approach. Apprenticeships are not entirely new to the United States. The report noted that, according to Labor Department estimates, in 2014 there were 398,000 registered apprentices in a range of fields, including manufacturing, in the United States, through programs run by labor unions or individual companies.[41] However, this was a sharp decline from the 490,000 apprentices early this century, and far below the 1.5 million apprentices across all sectors in Germany, including manufacturing.

To revive the apprenticeship model, AMP2.0 proposed a new model through a coalition of companies partnered with community colleges and labor market intermediaries. AMP participants developed a pilot project led by three major production companies and two community colleges to develop a workable, validated, and replicable model that could be implemented on a more widespread basis. It required completion of an associate's degree at a connected community college and parallel completion of a Department of Labor skill certification—a two-year project. Accompanying the pilot was a "playbook"—a detailed "how to" instruction manual for employers and colleges on how to implement and develop this approach.[42] AMP also promoted a "Live, Work, Earn" model developed by a statewide consortium of Minnesota community colleges, employment centers, and more than 25 manufacturers to match training with available jobs. The model includes "employer-driven competency-based apprenticeships, curricula alignment with national [skills] credentialing systems and bridging modules for veterans and other underrepresented populations."[43]

Ideas always have informative histories. This consortia approach built on a framework developed by a prior NSF-supported effort, AMTEC.[44] This was formed in 2005 because of concerns from community colleges in states with major auto manufacturing plants about a need to improve training to keep up with production advances in that sector. AMTEC now includes 12 community colleges and 18 auto companies and suppliers working across five states. Annette Parker, founding director of AMTEC, moved to the presidency of South Central Community College in Minnesota and was a key contributor to these workforce efforts at AMP2.0. AMP found that the comparable "Live, Work, Earn" project was a model that could be developed nationwide; it incorporated critical concepts and proposals that AMP2.0 proposed for public-private apprenticeship and training concepts. It could also build on and coordinate with existing union apprenticeship programs.

Apprenticeship, as AMP2.0 clearly understood, was an ambitious approach in the United States, but it argued that the skills required for advanced manufacturing would encourage employers increasingly to turn to it, so it worked to develop model approaches, shared between community colleges (with public investments) and employers. Could the 250,000 small manufacturing firms participate—do they have the financial resources? A lesson from Germany was that apprenticeships worked there in significant part because, in effect, all employers jumped into the apprenticeship swimming pool together. Few were left outside the pool to game the system. Unlike Germany's heavily unionized workforce, unionization is in decline in the United States, so union-sanctioned apprenticeship training has been declining as well. Instead, U.S. implementation of apprenticeships at a larger scale would require regional supply chains of small and large firms, including competitors, to engage together, along with publicly supported community colleges, to avoid the labor market disincentives for training that Becker identified. It would initially be particularly difficult because many small employers are not prepared to manage the additional costs of training.

There could be a state role in encouraging and enabling the apprenticeship model. South Carolina, which happens to be home to a number of German firms with major production facilities there that understood the model, took a comprehensive approach to apprenticeships. By offering employers a modest $1000 tax credit per apprentice and forming a state office to market apprenticeships and assist employers in implementing them through the state community and technical college system, the state as of 2014 had over 5000 apprentices in training.[45] The programs can be tailored to particular company needs regionally within the state.

In addition to the apprenticeship model, AMP2.0 advanced other workforce proposals. It called for investment and implementation of *nationally recognized, portable, and stackable skill certifications* that employers can use in hiring and promotion decisions.[46] Such a system could be very useful in enabling employee mobility by providing transferable credentials. This could also encourage training programs, because recognized credentials would more clearly signal training's value, and therefore help employers and employees alike in meeting skill needs. They could raise wages for skills, reduce hiring costs, enable a more flexible labor market through increased worker mobility, and encourage a better-trained and higher-quality workforce. Currently, many skill areas lack a credentialing system, and such systems can vary regionally and in quality in assuring skills. Where they exist, many employers do not adequately understand or recognize them.

The National Association of Manufacturers' Manufacturing Institute and other organizations have been working on new credentialing programs for manufacturing, including identifying key work-based learning elements within different skills. Identifying these elements could help enable skills that could be acquired in learning modules, which would guide the construction of education and training programs to support them. The AMP2.0 report found that successful credentialing approaches should assure easy entry, exit, and reentry throughout a manufacturing career, assure certificate training that is organized in modules that can be acquired over time and stacked to help working adults keep building their skills, and assure that credentials are aligned with community college for-credit education programs and correspondingly with education grant programs (such as Pell and Workforce Investment Act programs).[47] AMP called for systematic efforts to increase awareness among employers and in education institutions of credentialing systems, demonstrate successful credentialing programs based on supporting evidence and data, and provide funding to support credentialing programs to get over roadblocks in the ability of statewide systems to adopt them.[48]

The report also called for "*career pathways.*" This is a workforce development approach that tries to transition workers from education programs, such as secondary schools, community colleges, or college programs, into the workforce. This approach offers services that tie academic competency and credentials to technical skills, particularly those in increasing demand. They require partnerships between community colleges, secondary schools, workforce and economic development agencies, employers, and labor organizations. There are already programs working on this. Florida's FLATE program, discussed below, has a particularly noted program that forms these partnerships.[49] And the Florida Department of Education has a strong precollege through college framework for manufacturing education.[50] Linking community colleges to teaching skills needed by regional employers appears particularly important, although coordination is needed at all education levels. The report noted that there is a particular opportunity to create online programs to help in these career pathways. This would include making these programs eligible to receive federal support through federal job-training programs.

While skilled production employees are one requirement for advanced manufacturing, skilled engineers are another. New *advanced manufacturing engineering education* appears to be a prerequisite. Unless the engineering groups at production facilities understand advanced manufacturing—exactly what it entails, how to put it in place, and the opportunities it creates—it simply will not be implemented. This affects both the education that new engineers receive at engineering schools and reeducating the existing workforce. A similar issue exists for other technologists working in manufacturing who were trained at four-year or community colleges. Here, online education, which has proven particularly relevant to lifelong learning, may be a key tool. Engineers are already well trained, but they need to update and add to their skills by building on what they already know. The AMP report called for efforts to develop curricula and new courses in advanced manufacturing technologies, and development of "online training and accreditation programs."[51]

NSF's Advanced Technology Education (ATE) Program

The National Science Foundation's conceptual beginnings lie in Vannevar Bush's famed 1945 advocacy paper for postwar science organization, *Science, the Endless Frontier*.[52] Bush argued that science education was one of the four critical pillars for the federal support for science he envisioned and that subsequently came about. NSF had long emphasized university-level science education, but in 1992 Congress passed legislation[53] creating a new NSF program focused on community colleges and technical education, the Advanced Technological Education (ATE) program, bringing a new element to both NSF and education.

Community colleges are arguably the vital focus of both current and future U.S. workforce education—they are the indispensable institutions in this space. The Advanced Technological Education program at NSF connects two-year community colleges with industry to confront skills gaps at the technician level.[54] It supports some 38 centers across the country, providing training for technician careers in seven technology areas, as well as supporting educational materials, professional development, student recruiting and retention, and program improvement. It is NSF's largest community college effort. Some 40% of the program's approximately $60 million budget goes to its centers, and the rest funds the support elements and systems for the centers. One of the seven technology focus areas is advanced manufacturing, and some seven centers (of the total of 38) support high-end skills in areas such as mechatronics, robotics, control systems, IT-driven logistics, biomanufacturing, micro- and nanomanufacturing, optical devices, medical devices, advanced welding, additive manufacturing, chemical processing, and ship and auto manufacturing. ATE centers typically involve regional consortia of community colleges with industry participation; often they include a strong research university that can help the consortia develop the skill curriculum. Industry is a critical partner, and the program is structured to reach into small manufacturing firms.

What do these centers do? They reach far beyond the classrooms of the particular community colleges into the collaboration space. For example,[55] the Northeast Biomanufacturing Center in Pennsylvania (not officially classified as one of the advanced manufacturing centers, but its role overlaps heavily with manufacturing) developed training courses used in over two-thirds of the nation's biotechnology degree programs (both two-year and four-year institutions). Its workshops in six states trained over 100 high school teachers one year, who in turn taught thousands of high school students. Its online labs, online education, industry-developed textbook, widely used lab manual, and the center's outreach-oriented website itself were all part of its efforts. It supported cell culture, purification, and quality control microbiology skills; the industries served included biopharmaceutical firms, and now also includes biofuels, bioplastics, industrial enzymes, and replacement tissues and organs.

Florida's ATE ("FLATE") has received particular recognition as a model for integrating national skill standards into technician two-year degrees across the state. It created an industry-defined and endorsed Engineering Technology two-year degree, which was integrated into the Florida system, and developed 18 frameworks for 15 different community college certificates, and for eight specializations for such degrees. It was a critical collaborator across the state, developing this program with 12 partner colleges, 44 Florida manufacturing companies, the Florida Department of Education, Workforce Florida, the Manufacturers Skill Standards Council, the Manufacturers Association of Florida, and regional manufacturing associations, with 14 community college Engineering Technology degree programs implemented by 2013.[56] At that time, enrollment in that multifaceted degree program at community colleges reached over 1100. It also worked on articulation agreements coordinating high school curricula with such community college programs, supported Florida career academy legislation, backed a new state center for manufacturing workforce training initiatives, and its industry and community college partners leveraged over $75 million in state and local workforce funding for its programs. It has a large outreach program to change manufacturing's image, with some 4400 students and nearly 500 teachers and parents participating in the 209 "Made in Florida" Industry Tours it backed in 2014 with its partners; its Manufacturing Day Partnership reached 67 Florida schools in 23 counties.[57] ATE programs like FLATE have served as implementers for the kinds of recommendations the AMP2.0 report advanced.[58]

ATE's advanced manufacturing programs are also interesting because they connect with the large number of small manufacturing firms that do not have the capacity to support a true apprenticeship program. As noted, although a major portion of U.S. production is through small firms, these firms often do not have the funding to support apprentices. ATE offers a kind of hybrid approach—a joint industry, community college, and research university mechanism short of a full apprenticeship but somewhat comparable for worker outcomes. This creates some tension with actual apprenticeship programs, but the space the ATE programs create for the integration of internships into all ATE projects and centers, which lead to direct employment, rounds out the suite of strategies needed to prepare a skilled workforce.

ATE also provides leverage to other programs. It has built ties with the advanced manufacturing institutes, working through Memoranda of Understanding between NSF and the DOD and DOE to support integrated efforts for technician training and tying ATE centers to the institutes' workforce efforts. It also has links to NIST's Manufacturing Extension Partnership, which offers advisory services to small manufacturers throughout the country, to NIST's Industry and University Cooperative Research Program awardees, and to the Department of Labor's Trade Adjustment Assistance Community College and Career Training (TAACCCT) program and its awardees noted later in this chapter. Five of the ATE national centers, for example, provided technical support and sharing of best practices to assist TAACCCT awardees.[59]

Employment and Training Administration Programs

Of course, ATE is not the only federal program. The Department of Labor's Employment and Training Administration runs much larger and more expansive efforts, but they tend to be focused on different needs. It offers broad programs for adult, youth, and dislocated workers.[60] Its adult and dislocated worker program under the Workforce Investment Act of 1998,[61] as amended in 2014,[62] offers services through One-Stop Career Centers. These offer core services around job search and placement assistance and labor market information. More intensive services include comprehensive assessment and help with individual employment plans and with counseling and career planning. Training services link workers to job opportunities and to basic skills and occupational training services. Workforce investment boards operate at the state and local levels with required business participation to provide regional guidance, assessment, and collaborations with employers for these programs. The workforce investment network (WIN) is an online network to link workers with opportunities to upgrade skills.[63] Much of this is focused on unemployed workers or workers who have lost jobs through trade dislocation. Priority is given to those with low incomes and those on public assistance.

While these can be important services serving many, most do not match up with the development of new training and education regimes for advanced manufacturing. In the economic stimulus legislation of 2009, Congress set up the TAACCCT program with $2 billion in funding for community colleges to deliver career training programs.[64] While often tied to advanced skills training, funding for this program lasted for three years. Its short-term nature limited the evolution of enduring new training delivery models. The last administration recognized the remaining skills training need, and in 2014 the Vice President led a project to promote "job-driven" training efforts.[65] The new administration backs new apprenticeship programs.

This brings us to the advanced manufacturing institutes. Is there a gap they can fill to promote advanced manufacturing skills? Could this be a new delivery model?

The LIFT Workforce Education Model—A Case Study for the Manufacturing Institute Role

Lightweight Innovations for Tomorrow (LIFT) has been a leader on the education and training side among the manufacturing institutes.[66] It was the first to allocate a significant portion of its federal cost share—10%, or $7 million—to workforce education. And it was the first and still probably the only institute to recognize the centrality of education in creating the change agent community that could lead to major production shifts at major industry sectors in advanced manufacturing. It benefited from the leadership of its education and training programs by Emily DeRocco, a former assistant secretary of labor for employment and training and head of the Manufacturing Institute, who helped pioneer nationally portable, industry-recognized manufacturing skill certifications.

LIFT saw that there would be no new metals technology paradigm unless there was a workforce—at both the technician and engineering levels—ready to implement it. It saw that while the technology development mission of the institutes would take an extended period to evolve, education and training were immediate needs the institutes could help deliver that would create immediate "wins" for the institute, building strong ties with states, area governments, and industry. While the skills to accompany the new technologies would have to await the technology development, there were critical skills that would make workforces "technology ready" that needed immediate attention.

LIFT, which is still just over two years old, developed a strategy for its education programs that embodied four basic steps that could be both replicable and scalable at other institutes. The first step entailed looking at the labor market for skilled employees in sectors related to the LIFT task of developing lightweight metals relevant to the transportation, defense, and other commercial sectors. It developed an in-depth picture of, first, demand for such employees, then supply, and then skill gaps that required filling in its core region (Michigan, Ohio, Indiana, Kentucky, and Tennessee). While most institutes have tended to focus at the engineer level, LIFT looked at 142 occupational categories, from design through production, including such technician categories as metalworking and welding but also looking at the engineer level as well as support jobs in areas such as marketing and sales. It first assessed workforce demand and then the actual workforce supply for these categories, including the availability of programs in its region for industry certification and degrees. Comparing job demand and supply data enabled a close look at skill needs. All of this was aimed at the understanding needed for workforce readiness for LIFT's potential new production technologies. The identified skills gaps enabled the creation of initial training and education delivery programs on which new skill sets needed as part of LIFT's mission could also be built. In the meantime, they served immediate needs for LIFT's participating firms.

The workforce data went to LIFT's workforce teams, which were the second step. LIFT convened major groups of industry and company leaders, and representatives from the participating states, local governments, universities, community colleges, K-12 education, economic development and workforce investment programs, and community-based organizations. There are some 120 officials on these state LIFT teams—in Michigan, Ohio, Tennessee, Indiana, and Kentucky,[67] that then set to work to define the skills gaps and develop partnership initiatives to fill them. LIFT provides the seed capital to support these projects, which are all replicable, scalable, and sustainable beyond the use of LIFT funds. In LIFT's first eighteen months, $3.6 million of its federal share was matched by additional state, local, and industry cost sharing, for a total program of $11.3 million. With modest resources and an ability to act, these state teams got "smart fast" on the skills challenges and became, according to its education leaders, empowered groups.

The third step, education and training delivery mechanisms, largely uses programs already in the states that can handle additional roles. There are STEM programs in secondary schools oriented toward basic STEM skill needs. There are foundational programs to help employees acquire the basic skills so more advanced skills can be added to them. There are programs that can be enhanced in community colleges and technical colleges. The workforce development programs can be supplemented with "work and learn" opportunities, combining theory and work-based applied learning. And there are engineering programs at the university level as well, including internships with learning outcomes for engineering students as well as journeymen. LIFT's test beds use these programs. There is virtual—online—education, for example, in coordination with the Battelle-endorsed Learning Blade program, now providing mission contexts in a gaming environment in schools in 32 states. LIFT's state teams are also collaborating with the Manufacturing Extension Partnership programs in those states for new "work and learn" coordination at the workplace level of smaller firms. They are also coordinating with both NSF's Advanced Technology Education (ATE) program at eight of its centers for bringing strong technical skill education to community colleges and with Department of Education programs.

LIFT has undertaken 23 delivery programs and two repeat programs as of the fall of 2016, ranging from STEM education at the high school level, to technician training, to engineering:[68]

• With Learning Blade, created an online education program on lightweight aircraft on an interactive platform that has reached 100,000 STEM students in 32 states.
• Supported an electric vehicle GrandPrix with teams from six high schools competing at Indianapolis Speedway.
• With ASM, expanded and enhanced the Materials Science Camps for training 1000 teachers in advanced materials who in turn teach over 10,000 students.
• Supported 100 student interns at 38 companies with the Indiana Conexus "work and learn" program.
• Delivered "Right Skills" accelerated training for 70 returning military veterans with NIMS in Indiana.
• With area companies, including Ford and GE, and the UAW, helped develop a Kentucky high school program for 100 students annually in a "Manufacturing Technology Technician Pathway" with a series of skills certifications; in the program's first rollout, 40 students have received jobs or follow-on training.
• Supported "Work and Learn" partnerships in Ohio to train 80 interns in hands-on lightweight metals skills at industry sites.
• Developed, in partnership with Tennessee Tech, an interactive Automotive Assembly-line Virtual Reality experience, placing students on a virtual factory floor with lightweight components, and offered the activity to students across the Detroit area.

• Other region-wide initiatives include a "Makerminded" web portal to link potentially thousands of area high school students with world-class STEM and advanced manufacturing activities, instructor training to close skill gaps in industrial technology maintenance, and a robotic blacksmithing competition to spur innovation in metalworking.

Ahead are a LIFT learning lab at its headquarters in Detroit and a Military Manufacturing Training Center model for service members to earn civilian manufacturing credentials during their transition period from the military, preparing them for the most in-demand manufacturing jobs immediately upon separation. LIFT is still relatively new, so its menu of pilots and programs is still starting up, with much experimentation. It views all of its education and workforce initiatives as replicable and scalable throughout its region and nationally. There is a trainee systems view here: engagement and introductory programs for manufacturing careers, to self-assessment programs, to community college and university programs, to self-paced training and simulated hands-on learning, to actual hands-on applications and skills assessment, to industry credentials.[69]

All of this is being received well by LIFT's federal overseers, including at the Office of Naval Research and DOD Mantech, which are both supportive. And there has been support from NIST, MEP, NSF's ATE, and the Department of Education. Representatives from these federal programs are advisers to LIFT on its Education and Workforce Committee, along with area industry officials.[70] The one agency with major training assets not yet significantly involved is the Department of Labor; its participation should be encouraged by federal officials.[71]

So LIFT offers a regional workforce supply, demand, and skills examination process; state teams from industry, government, and the full continuum of education programs to assess regional needs; and links to a mix of delivery mechanisms. What is next? The technologies that LIFT is starting to develop are now entering the pipeline. It is now possible to start to see what new skill sets will be required, which would be step four. LIFT has created a 2016 Roadmap Master Plan, seeking to align educational programming with technology development.[72] It has begun to engage its university partners, led by engineering deans, to work on defining the new skill requirements and translating them into curriculum components. LIFT is also initiating a partnership with the Association for Public and Land Grant Universities (APLU), whose members include 28 universities within LIFT's immediate five-state footprint, to develop Expert Educator Teams, supported by the National Center for Manufacturing Sciences, to help systematically define new skills and recommend education and workforce development alignment initiatives. LIFT is facing a five-year limit for federal support; it expects that the institute's education and training program and impact can be an important component of its sustainability plan.

LIFT's workforce education system is starting to operate at the kind of workforce scale that will be needed to support transition and commercialization of new technologies, processes, and materials developed and deployed by the institute. This means implementation of its new technologies will be possible because the workforce will be technology-ready, not technology-deficient. So LIFT is developing training and education programs tied to new skills that can be implemented in parallel with technology advances. At LIFT, the workforce is not an afterthought that five years into the institute's projects will suddenly become a massive barrier. Instead, the workforce will be an enabler and an asset for industry growth and regional economic development. Too many other institutes have treated workforce education as secondary, focusing their initial resources on technology development, which may leave them behind where their institute must be, given the need to have the workforce ready when the technology is ready. The workforce education effort needs to be understood by the institutes as a core technology dissemination system. LIFT provides replicable models for how they can catch up.

LIFT is not the only interesting model emerging from the institutes. While LIFT is working with an existing sector, metals, where new materials and technologies could be transformative, AIM Photonics is working to create an emerging sector that does not really exist yet. While LIFT can productively work on upgrades for an existing workforce, networking with state and other programs, AIM Photonics effectively needs to create a new workforce. This requires a somewhat different strategy. The AIM Academy is preparing new online and blended education programs, coordinating between its members and regional community colleges. In particular, it has developed a very interesting mechanism where the technical group developing its photonics technology roadmap works closely with the workforce education group, which is developing a parallel workforce roadmap. This combination aims to ensure that a trained workforce, from engineers to technicians, is ready to implement each stage of the technology roadmap within the relevant time frame. Since a number of institutes will be creating new territory, this is a particularly relevant model for them. But the approach of tying the technology roadmap to a parallel workforce roadmap provides a lesson to all the institutes.

Create an Institute Workforce Demand-Side Focus in Addition
to a Supply-Side Focus

Thomas Kochan, who studies employment and workforce issues at MIT's Sloan School of Management, has examined the manufacturing institute workforce education program and made a series of recommendations for further optimizing it.[73] He proposes the following:

1. *Including the workforce in the application process.* In the review process for selecting institute teams, there should be an explicit review of workforce approaches and a specific weight accorded to that part of the application. Factors in this review should include "not just a focus on the anticipated skills workers will need but on how the design of the technology is integrated with workforce capabilities and skills. This would embody an integrated socio-technical development process so that the workforce issues are not an afterthought."

2. *Ongoing workforce evaluation.* The institutes, as they are launched, should review, on an ongoing basis, whether the creation of quality jobs is being built into the institute designs and plans, and those of their participants. Because participating firms will always face the temptation to outsource the advanced manufacturing developments they are participating in to a contractor or to an offshore supplier, "predictions about both number and quality (including anticipated wage and benefit levels and skills required) of the jobs need to be considered" and the results should be reviewed.

3. *Expert evaluation.* The institutes, as part of their ongoing evaluations, need to engage experts knowledgeable about high-performance production in the institute's sectors. These experts can build models for how new advanced manufacturing work systems can drive high-performance manufacturing with corresponding skilled jobs; most industries have somewhat comparable models for undertaking this. "Each Institute should be expected to be developing a model to achieve high productivity / performance by incorporating the evidence on high performance work systems into their planning and decision making."

Kochan notes that this kind of evaluation would take the institute workforce role out of only the "supply side" of training adequate numbers and put it into the "demand side" as well—"how work is incorporated into the technical development process and the organizational strategic planning and implementation." Of course, metrics and coherent plans will be needed on the supply side as well, tracking institute training programs, their performance, results, and employment. Overall, the institutes will be judged in significant part on the jobs—particularly quality jobs—they help create and encourage, and they need to be encouraged to adopt sophisticated and workable training approaches.

As noted in chapter 6, most manufacturing institutes have focused on their technology development role with education as a secondary issue; education needs more focus at many. At the April 2017 meeting of institute directors, some thirty institute education leaders also gathered for a day of planning and exchanges on institute workforce training. This was a positive sign but Kochan's "demand side" perspectives deserve institute consideration.

Summary

Data indicates a growing need to upgrade the manufacturing workforce to higher levels of skills, which appears to be a prerequisite for advanced manufacturing. A close look at Germany's systematic workforce training system—likely the best in class worldwide—suggests the advantages of an apprenticeship program. But adoption of apprenticeships in the United States is complicated by a structural problem in the incentives to employers for offering training, a lower rate of unionization, the thinning-out of the U.S. manufacturing ecosystem in the last two decades, and the pervasiveness in U.S. production of small manufacturers that may not be able to afford such a program. There is, however, a possibility that states may be able to take on apprenticeship approaches, using employer incentives and tying them to state-supported community colleges. Another lesson from Germany is that its Fraunhofer Institutes, which support systemwide collaboration between firms and engineering institutions for innovation in production, can support advanced training programs.

The Advanced Manufacturing Partnership (AMP) reports placed much stress on workforce training and education, at both the skilled worker and engineering levels. They recommended apprenticeships, and created pilot programs for them, but also nationwide skills credentialing systems with supporting training curricula, career pathways for step-by-step training of skilled technicians, and new advanced manufacturing engineering efforts.

Community colleges appear to be critical institutions in the U.S. system. NSF's Advanced Technological Education (ATE) program has engaged consortia of these colleges, sometimes with technical support from a regional research university, to develop new high-skill training regimes in coordination with industry. A number of its centers also build career pathways by linking programs at middle and secondary schools with community colleges, four-year college programs, and industry. The ATE programs appear to be closely tied to the training recommendations from the AMP reports.

The manufacturing institutes appear to be positioned to help fill the gap in U.S. labor markets for high-skill training. The LIFT institute in particular appears to be developing models for workforce training, systematically engaging state governments and firms in its core states in new training program elements, with programs linked to secondary schools, community colleges, participating employers, and area universities. Like the Fraunhofer Academy in Germany, LIFT sees that workforce training programs are critical for advanced manufacturing technology dissemination, not only training for the sake of training. It is a key way the institutes can scale their new technology developments.

Thomas Kochan has argued that as they design their workforce programs, manufacturing institutes also need to consider the "demand side" in addition to the supply role. In other words, well-designed workforce programs are a way to achieve high-performance production in new advanced manufacturing technologies and processes. They need to be built into the new production design process, not treated simply as a less direct input. If skilled workforce training plans are closely integrated into technology development, they become a critical enabler of new production, not simply a contributor.

There is also a new training toolset now becoming available. In parallel to the AMP reports, new online higher education programs began to be offered at significant scale, and this resource appears to be particularly relevant in the context of lifelong learning.[74] As the AMP reports suggested, online programs could be a new tool in skills training. How might this be implemented?

One approach, first recommended in 2011 by Martin Schmidt, technical co-lead for the AMP1.0 report, could be what he called "ManufacturingX." It would encourage the universities participating in a particular manufacturing institute with its particular technology focus to develop such online training courses in the advanced technology for both engineers and skilled technologists already in the workforce. They could work with the participating employers as well as community colleges in developing the curriculum. The online course, offered through a community college or state university, could convey critical information, but "hands-on" learning in the new technologies would be required as well. Participants could take the basic course online at their own pace, but like the Army Reserve, every couple of weekends they might attend an intensive "hands-on" learning session, perhaps at an institute employer's factory. This kind of setup would help make the course manageable for those already working 9 to 5. Community colleges operate on a financial basis of filling a 30-person classroom before they can offer a course in person. Since advanced manufacturing skills would only be of limited interest initially, online courses offer a way for groups of colleges to cooperate on a common offering and still make the financial equation work. The manufacturing institutes and their participating employers should be able to collaborate to provide sites for hands-on training in the technologies to improve the learning process. Over time, a nationwide advanced manufacturing curriculum could be built up and made available through the new online platforms and joined with blending learning—a potential role for the manufacturing institute network.

Comparable work is already under way. As noted, a number of manufacturing institutes, including LIFT, are working on online training courses. MForesight, a think tank for advanced manufacturing supported by NIST and NSF, has now created "Manufacturing 101—An Education and Training Curriculum for Cleantech Hardware Entrepreneurs," with modules such as materials selection, production processes, design for manufacturing, supply chains, standards, and manufacturing partnerships.[75] At the end of 2016, as part of the annual National Defense Authorization Act, Congress passed legislation creating a "manufacturing universities" program to encourage universities and nonprofits, working with industry, to develop new programs in advanced manufacturing; online and blended learning approaches could qualify for funding.[76] MIT has developed a new online course, available on its MITx and edX platforms, on "Fundamentals of Manufacturing Process," covering manufacturing processes such as thermoforming and 3D printing; principles of rate, quality, cost, and sustainability; application of production design principles; and emerging technologies such as robotics and connected machines.[77] Since the connective tissue of supply chains will be critical in a thinned-out manufacturing system, a supply chain focus will also be critical. MIT has also created a new "micro masters" in supply chain management with a ten-month series of online courses and the opportunity for blended learning as well, which is proving popular.[78] NSF's ATE program sponsors a National Center for Supply Chain Technology, with education programs that include a new etextbook with extensive training videos.[79] The Department of Energy's Energy Efficiency and Renewable Energy office has created Build4Scale, an online education effort that will focus on teaching entrepreneurs basics of manufacturing processes, core design-for-manufacturing principles, and materials selection trade-offs.[80] Other programs are moving in on this space as well. These kinds of online tools also allow a "blended learning" approach and could help advanced manufacturing training reach the scale that will be needed. Coupled with, for example, ACT's WorkKey programs with employers for critical thinking and academic skills, the Manufacturing Skill Standards Council's program for credentials for a wide range of technical skills, and Amatrol's new lower-cost, multi-skill training technologies, progress is possible.

Creative new workforce training programs and technologies have opened the door for new innovative solutions to the increasing demand for skilled manufacturing laborers. Recent developments have shown that an advanced manufacturing sector cannot thrive based solely on technological innovation but requires engagement of the whole ecosystem, from firms and suppliers of all sizes to their employees, to thrive. New manufacturing technology know-how cannot be confined to the university lab bench; it must get onto the factory floor. Workforce education equals technology dissemination.

9 Manufacturing and the Future of Work

Throughout the book, we have touched on issues of employment, inequality, innovation, and technology. Going forward, will these trends continue, and, if so, what does that mean for workers? In the last few years, a wide range of authors have joined in the discussion, raising a range of questions. Will technology displace large numbers of workers? Will manufacturing jobs still exist? What industries, if any, will see employment increases? Will inequality be exacerbated? These questions are not new, but once again we have to ask whether technological advances will reach a point where the past is no longer a guide for the future. For over two hundred years, technological advances have stoked concerns among workers that automation will leave them jobless. While we can all be confident that the economy of the future will not look like today's, we can also be confident that while automation will displace workers over time, new jobs will also be created. The manufacturing sector has been and will continue to be at the center of this emerging debate.

Automation and Job Destruction

On Monday, November 18, 1811, the *Times* of London reported,

> For some time past the wholesale hosiers, who have stocking-weaving establishments in the county of Nottingham, have been obliged to curtail their hands; this produced considerable discontent among the workmen. Their riotous spirit was, however, increased by the trade having brought into use a certain wide frame for the manufacture of stockings and gaiters, which was a considerable saving in manual labour, tending still farther to the decrease of the hands employed. On Sunday se'nnight last this being generally known, a number of weavers assembled at different places in the vicinity of Nottingham, and commenced their career of outrage by forcibly entering the houses of such persons as used particular frames.[1]

The riots spread throughout the Midlands with English textile workers targeting and destroying new, more efficient looms. The situation in Great Britain was exacerbated by the economic burden of the Napoleonic Wars, which contributed to falling wages and rising food costs.[2] The movement was purported to have been led by Ned Ludd, though it is likely that this was a pseudonym used by various leaders. The Luddites, of differing occupational groups, continued to sporadically break machines until the movement faded away by 1817.[3] By 1833, around four-fifths of the textile industry workers were children and women, which helped dampen labor disruptions.[4]

Roger Luckhurst notes that throughout the eighteenth century, there was rising anxiety about automation as a result of mechanical devices that began entering the public consciousness, such as Wolfgang von Kempelen's The Turk, a chess-playing automaton that later proved to be a hoax, and Jacques de Vaucanson's duck, made of four hundred parts. While looms were sporadically destroyed in the eighteenth century by frustrated workers, the nineteenth-century Luddites, in comparison, were a movement organized in response to increasing technological unemployment.[5] Luddism is an example of the complex interconnection between employment and class politics. Paul Lindholdt suggests that it also should be viewed as a form of rebellion in the context of the American and French Revolutions. This may explain why in May 1812, in the midst of the Napoleonic Wars and rising tensions with the United States, 14,400 British troops were sent to quell the uprising.[6] The Luddites, just one example from that time period, highlight the complex nature of technological change and the difficulty of abstracting it away from contemporaneous social and political changes.

The complete history of anxiety about technology is far too extensive to address here. However, it is worth noting that as early as 1765, William Mildmay was writing about the possibility that machinery might eliminate the need for labor in the future. He argued stopping progress was not an option, to assure that Britain was not outcompeted by other countries.[7] Historically, technology has both created new jobs and eliminated others, yet there have always been more net new jobs created than destroyed.[8] Over the centuries entire job categories have been replaced by technological progress. Refrigerators have eliminated the need for ice cutters and milkmen, radios obviated the need for lectors to provide news and entertainment to workers, and electricity eliminated the need for lamplighters.[9] Of course, the number of people working in those jobs was modest, but it highlights the extent of change in work patterns over the last 160 years. The single largest displacement of workers in the United States occurred between 1810 and 1960, when the percentage of the population employed in the agricultural sector dropped from 80.9% to 8.1%.[10] Technological displacement is not new.

The concerns about wide-scale unemployment as a result of technological change were largely considered irrelevant in economics by the end of the nineteenth century, because of the historical record of job creation.[11] Famously, John Maynard Keynes, in his essay "Economic Possibilities for Our Grandchildren," presented a view where major productivity gains would reduce the need to work. Looking back over economic history, Keynes posited, "Thus we have been expressly evolved by nature—with all our impulses and deepest instincts—for the purpose of solving the economic problem. If the economic problem is solved, making will be deprived of its traditional purpose."[12] Is there an absolute level of economic prosperity that satisfies people's wants and limits the need to work? There may be, but we have not yet reached that point. According to Gallup, in 2014 the typical full-time employee in the United States worked an average of forty-seven hours per week.[13] So what is different this time?

The Current Debate over Technological Displacement

The answer given by Brynjolfsson, McAfee, and Ford is that the IT revolution is fundamentally different from all other technology revolutions up to this point. In 1965, Gordon Moore observed that roughly every year and a half (later revised to every two years), computing power doubled. The power of computers was in essence growing at an exponential rate. Brynjolfsson and McAfee state that this is unique to IT: no similarly high rate of growth can be seen in the fuel efficiency of cars or how much weight a train can carry.[14] Historically, limitations imposed by the laws of physics were overcome by engineers through work-arounds and tinkering.[15] These trends of exponential improvement in speed have applied throughout IT, not just for microchips.[16] This progress can be seen in the rapid improvement of smartphones. In the early part of this century, BlackBerry devices allowed people to use email, make calls, text, and even browse the Internet. A little over a decade later, popular phones from Samsung and Apple still perform these functions. But to Brynjolfsson and McAfee's point, not only are the phones exponentially faster and more powerful, but other IT infrastructure has improved in tandem. The capability to stream high-definition video on one's cell phone is now possible across the country.

In addition to the unique exponential growth in IT, the other distinctive factors frequently cited are that software has a near zero marginal cost (additional copies can be produced at no additional cost) and is nonrival (use by one consumer does not limit use by other consumers). Most popular cell phone apps illustrate this. After the program is completed, the cost to create each new copy is negligible. Essentially, the difference in cost between a copy of software being downloaded by one hundred people as opposed to ten thousand people is minimal, especially in comparison to nearly every other product.[17] An example of this cheap replicability of digital goods combined with network effects is Facebook, where the value for each consumer increases as more people join. This leads to what Martin Ford calls a winner-take-all distribution.[18] This distribution means that, in the marketplace, digital goods tend toward monopoly, suggesting that Schumpeter's analysis of monopolies may be particularly relevant for this sector. Microsoft appeared overly aggressive to many in trying to take advantage of the network effect for its software products. As a result, Microsoft fought antitrust charges from the U.S. and E.U. governments for twenty-one years.[19] Software is similar to utilities in its natural tendency toward monopoly, but, aside from a few exceptions, low barriers to entry have kept the sector competitive.

Authors like Brynjolfsson, McAfee, Ford, and Cowen tend to point to the same set of examples of emerging or groundbreaking technologies in their arguments about how the economy will develop. The defeat of Garry Kasparov by IBM's Deep Blue computer in 1997 signaled that in a game of defined rules, the capabilities of brute force computing could surpass the best human mind. By 2005, the era of competitive human-computer chess matches all but drew to an end when a top-ranked player lost all but one match, which ended in a draw.[20] IBM's Watson marked another step forward when it won on the game show *Jeopardy!*, beating two former champions. In this case, Watson has to break down the question in order to know what to search for in its database. The possible answers it finds are then ranked before it buzzes in, if the top answer meets a high enough degree of certainty.[21] This was a substantial step forward over a fourteen-year period. These advancements, according to Ford, leave white-collar jobs in finance and other areas vulnerable to displacement.[22]

There are already certain jobs that have started seeing the effects of IT-based automation. Automated securities trading or algorithmic trading now accounts for 75% of total market volume.[23] Despite this, employment in the financial sector still increased from around 7.8 million to 8.2 million between 2000 and 2016.[24] However, financial automation carries its own risks. In October 2014, ten-year Treasury bonds saw a sudden drop of 33 basis points only to increase 27 basis points, all within fifteen minutes. This was seven standard deviations from the daily average, or an event that over 1.6 billion years is only expected to occur once. Two years later, the U.S. Treasury released its report on the incident without finding a clear cause but suggesting it was likely the result of algorithmic trading.[25] Another occupation, not likely to trigger a market panic, where employment has been chipped away by software is journalism. Aside from the impact the Internet has had on newspaper revenues, certain kinds of stories can now be written by software. Automated Insights and Narrative Science provide software to news agencies like the Associated Press, Fox, and Yahoo to create certain financial reports and provide sports coverage.[26] The speed of development and breadth of applicability of algorithms along these lines remains to be seen.

The crux of the argument about large-scale job-displacing technology centers on machine learning. Ford argues, "If there is one myth regarding computer technology that ought to be swept into the dustbin it is the pervasive believe [sic] that computers can do only what they are specifically programmed to do."[27] There have been a number of demonstrations of deep learning, an advance in machine learning, ranging from handwriting, face, general object, and speech recognition to natural language processing, object recognition, and robotics.[28] Brynjolfsson and McAfee point to a range of technologies, such as Rethink's Baxter, a trainable robot, Boston Dynamics' BigDog, a quadruped robot capable of traversing rough territory, and the Kiva robot used in Amazon warehouses, to argue that we are at an inflection point.[29] Their point, like Ford's, is that these technologies are now capable of performing nonroutine tasks.

For Brynjolfsson and McAfee, Ford, and Cowen, the outcome of the expanded capabilities of machines will be a higher rate of economic inequality. The middle class will continue to thin out, with jobs replaced by new technologies, but demand for low-wage, low-skill work and high-skill, high-wage work will still predominate.[30] This is predicated on the idea that labor market polarization, posited by David Autor and others (discussed in earlier chapters), will continue into the foreseeable future. Cowen views the United States as likely to be divided into two distinct classes; however, there is likely to be a cheap education system, because of advances in online education, ensuring that society is meritocratic. Since property values in most cities would be too expensive, separate low-income communities would be set up. He states, "In essence, we would be recreating a Mexico-like or Brazil-like environment in part of the United States, although with some technological add-ons and most likely with greater safety."[31] Economist Peter Temin argues that a dual economy, based on race and class inequality, already exists in the United States.[32] For Cowen, health care costs will rise, creating a worsening budget deficit, but higher levels of taxation will be out of the question because of tax shelters and the rising political power of the rich.[33] Perhaps neofeudalism lies in our future? A less fatalistic view is offered by Brynjolfsson and McAfee; they view rising inequality as far more manageable. In the short term, the use of Pigouvian taxes,[34] a carbon tax, and taxes on economic rents, on land or superstars, could ameliorate the problem. Over the long run, they advocate for a negative income tax as the best way to guarantee a basic income while maintaining an incentive for work.[35] In these scenarios, new jobs, mostly low skilled, replace the middle-skill jobs that are displaced by technology; however, there is still some space for policy decisions to influence this outcome.

Martin Ford presents the most extreme example of the three overviewed here. Both Cowen and Ford use examples about chess to present the advancements in machine learning. In the wake of Kasparov's defeat by Deep Blue, a new form of chess gained prominence. Player and computer work together to take on an opponent in what is called Freestyle chess. The human/computer team consistently outperforms a computer alone. Surprisingly, the best Freestyle chess players are not among the elite of traditional chess.[36] Technology of this type is complementary to human labor. For Ford, the concern is that, even though there will be instances of complementary technology, these will not be sufficient to stave off rising technological unemployment. Ford suggests that unemployment will increase, further exacerbating competition and driving down wages. Over time, inequality grows to such an extent that a consumption-based economy begins to falter. Insufficient consumer demand, over time, will slow economic growth.[37] Diminishing returns on education mean, for Ford, that a guaranteed basic income is the only real solution.[38] The future of capitalist markets appears in doubt to Ford.

The Response to the Technological Displacement Theorists

Economist David Autor presents a different view. He argues, in an article titled "Why Are There Still So Many Jobs?," that most commentators tend to overestimate the amount of automation that will substitute for labor as opposed to complementing it.[39] His view is that automation, overall, can complement work, increasing the opportunity to create quality employment.[40] He notes that people's desire for new products and services appears insatiable, so we will not run out of job opportunities. However, there is an economic inequality issue: a "barbell" is growing with an upper middle class on one end, with sharply rising incomes, and a growing number of lower-end, lower-paying service jobs on the other. In the middle is a decline in middle-skill jobs—such as in manufacturing. While part of the barbell story is automation and computerization, which have knocked some of the rungs out of traditional ladders to success, overall, increasing productivity creates more societal income and higher skills opportunities. The largest problem U.S. society is now facing is low productivity growth, because this affects the income available to address social well-being. Low productivity, however, signals limited adoption of automation. Michael Handel picks up this story. He suggests that while artificial intelligence, advanced robotics, and expert systems could have a job effect over time, the progress of these technologies to date has been limited. Incremental advances in e-commerce, Internet services, and online and mobile delivery have been ongoing; they tend to require new skills but have not been creating large-scale job disruption.[41]

Technology historian David Mindell supports this perspective. He takes an in-depth look at human-robot interaction in four major areas of robotics advances: undersea operations, space exploration, drones, and driverless cars.[42] In each, he finds deep complementarity between robots and people—each has skill sets that enhance the other's. This is in line with the famous 1960 work on computing by J. C. R. Licklider (the theorist behind the Internet and personal computing). Licklider saw computing on a human-computer continuum, a "man-machine symbiosis" where both sides together optimize a greatly improved combined performance,[43] which indeed has been the overall history in this sector to date. Even Rethink Robotics' Baxter, a voice-commanded robot that slightly resembles C-3PO of Star Wars fame and could be viewed as perhaps the most radical step in person displacement, is not close to a human replacement. Baxter aims at assisting manufacturing workers, undertaking mundane and repetitive tasks so the person can do more—it can support humans under their direct control and direction but cannot replace them. It is human-machine interaction again, a new tool, a "cobot."[44]

The types of jobs that are susceptible to automation remain up for debate. Manufacturing is the typical focus. As we have seen in earlier chapters, it has had high rates of productivity gains and shrinking employment. Machine learning or deep learning will likely affect manufacturing at the production level, but it also holds the potential to eliminate a number of white-collar jobs. Frey and Osborne looked at 702 occupations to estimate the probability that they would be automated. They found that 47% of jobs in the United States have a high risk of being automated.[45]

Atkinson points out issues with Frey and Osborne's study. First, the occupations they predict to lose the most jobs are the very jobs that have seen limited productivity growth recently. A second point is that over twenty years, their estimates would mean labor productivity would increase 3% a year,[46] whereas the current rate is in the 1% range. The time frame in which these advances take place is vital. The nineteenth and twentieth centuries saw tremendous growth, much faster than seen in the last decade. Historically, faster technology growth invariably has been associated with lower levels of unemployment. If technology advances at an accelerating rate over the next few decades, we would expect to see a vast increase in wealth, which is unlikely to be extracted from the economy but instead reinvested in some manner. This is another reason to discount at least the near-term effects of technological displacement.

Another economic proposition that has been used to critique technological unemployment is the lump of labor fallacy. As Atkinson notes, the fallacy is that there is a fixed amount of work to do, with no new work appearing when it is done.[47] For example, early concerns about the entry of computing foresaw effects on some existing job categories but not the growth in a wide range of IT professionals now required to operate, maintain, improve, and expand these systems. It is important to remember that the lump of labor fallacy has been politically polarizing in the past. As Tom Walker notes, the lump of labor fallacy first came into popular use at the end of the nineteenth century in arguments against the transition to the eight-hour working day.[48] Luigi Pasinetti makes an interesting point about technological progress: unemployment can be offset by the introduction of new goods or more goods into the market, by shorter working days, or by a combination of the two that is decided by society.[49] Essentially a society has the choice of what to do with its productivity gains. These can lead to economic growth and rising standards of living, or the standard of living could be maintained but people would have significantly more leisure time. It is safe to say that in the United States, growth has been accorded more importance than leisure over the last century.

An OECD study found that in analyzing the number of jobs at risk of automation, the better approach was to analyze the task content of individual jobs instead of average task content in each occupation.[50] This is because there is great variability of tasks within particular occupations.[51] This more targeted approach found much lower numbers for the share of jobs potentially at risk of automation within an extended period. Using the OECD's Survey of Adult Skills (PIACC), which included workers' reports of actual tasks involved in their work, the study estimated that just 9% of jobs across 22 surveyed nations, including the United States, were at high risk of being automated over time. The levels ranged from 6% to 12% across these developed nations; the United States was at 10%. The high-risk jobs were defined as those for which at least 70% of tasks were automatable.

A larger share of jobs (25%) were found to be partially (50%) automatable, but the more likely course would be that the jobs themselves would be restructured and carried out differently. Generally, workers with lower education appeared to be at highest risk of displacement.[52]

Evidence for Significant Technological Displacement Today?

Predictions of wide-scale unemployment in the near future should lead us to ask, what is the impact of technology on employment today? One study looking at OECD countries between the 1970s and the first decade of the twenty-first century found that the countries with high rates of technological adoption saw unemployment rates increase only slightly, while those countries that fell behind technologically saw employment conditions deteriorate significantly more.[53] A narrower study looked at the introduction of mainframe computers, personal computers, and the Internet between the 1970s and 1990s, finding in each instance that unemployed workers in affected sectors had more difficulty finding jobs.[54] James Bessen found that while there is no evidence that automation has had a significant impact on employment in the United States, there is evidence of automation driving inequality.[55] This is consistent with the findings of economists Goldin, Katz, and Autor, discussed in earlier chapters, on the ever-increasing requirements for technical knowledge in an industrial economy, the need for growing education to stay ahead of this curve, and adverse economic effects and growth in inequality for those that cannot keep up with these technical skill and education curves.

There does not seem to be anything approaching a consensus that net technology-based employment displacement is a significant factor in the economy right now or will be in the immediate future. For example, the ever-increasing number of robots used in manufacturing is no secret. But it appears that the speed at which robots are being installed in production has slowed significantly, even though the largest decrease in manufacturing employment seems to correspond with this slowdown (see figure 9.1). A study by Graetz and Michaels examines the impact of robots in 17 developed countries between 1993 and 2007. They find that over this period of time growing use of robots increased labor productivity and GDP growth annually by 2% and 3.14%, respectively, which is comparable to estimates of the impact of the initial introduction of steam power in nineteenth-century Britain. Additionally, they find some evidence, though it is not quite statistically significant, that low- and middle-skilled workers' hours may have decreased. Highly skilled workers appeared not to have been affected. Graetz and Michaels also found some evidence of "congestion

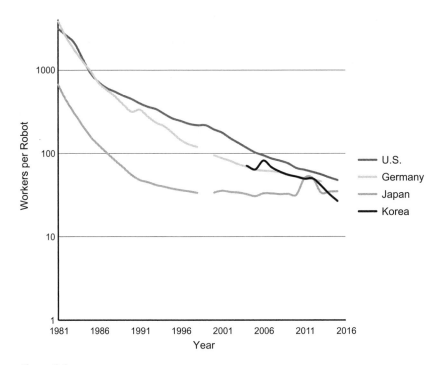

Figure 9.1

Number of Manufacturing Employees for Each Industrial Robot.

Source: Compiled by P. L. Singer, September 2016, from Federal Reserve Economic Data, Employment by Economic Activity, https://fred.stlouisfed.org; D. Comin and B. Hohij, Cross-Country Technological Adoption: Making the Theories Face the Facts, *Journal of Monetary Economics*, January 2004; International Federation of Robotics and United Nations Economic Commission for Europe, World Robotics: 2015, 2014, 2013, 2010, 2009, 2005, 2004, https://ifr.org/worldrobotics.

effects" from robot installation, with diminishing marginal gains.[56] The automotive industry uses robots more extensively than any other manufacturing sector, an estimated 39% of all industrial robots;[57] it is possible that congestion effects in the automotive industry may help explain the slowdown in the rate of robot installation in manufacturing overall.

Recent work by Acemoglu and Restrepo, largely using the same data as Graetz and Michaels, examines the impact of increased exposure to robots on 19 industries in U.S. commuting zones (local economic areas developed by the USDA Economic Research Service in the 1980s) between 1990 and 2007. They find a decrease in the employment to population ratio nationally of around 0.34%, for every additional robot per thousand workers, as well as a decline in wages by around 0.5%. There are currently some 1.5

to 1.75 industrial robots per thousand U.S. workers. Employment losses are partially offset in other commuting zones as a result of price decreases and new employment in other industries. Interestingly, when their analysis is limited to the industries most exposed to robot adoption they find a decrease in the employment to population ratio, and to wages, of only 0.18% and 0.25%, respectively, noting that losses in other industries must be the result of other factors like negative demand spillover.[58] Acemoglu and Restrepo acknowledge that the limited increase in offsetting employment is somewhat surprising. However, employment increases could only occur in their model if there were significant cost savings, over 50%, from the introduction of new robots.[59] Acemoglu and Restrepo note this analysis is only a first step in part due to methodological limitations, but they do find that robots have a negative effect on wages and employment. They project that somewhere in the range of 360,000 and 670,000 jobs have been lost to robots in the United States over the seventeen years studied, a relatively modest number,[60] so it remains to be seen whether current trends continue or the rapid expansion of robots envisioned by Brynjolfsson, McAfee, and Ford comes to pass.

There is a rich mix of new information technologies headed toward the workplace. It includes advanced robotics, the internet of things, embedded sensors, big data and analytics, cloud infrastructure, artificial intelligence, and machine learning. If the manufacturing institutes are successful, a series of new technologies could create the factory of the future. These will have to be brought together into a system, but one can envision a factory that features a mix of digital production, assistive robotics, 3D printing, advanced materials, nanofabrication, photonics, power electronics, and other new production technologies. It is a powerful snapshot, but will this new factory have many employees? A look at one of today's most advanced manufacturers can be illustrative.

An advanced semiconductor wafer fab is the most automated contemporary factory—it is close to a "lights out" factory, and can feel devoid of people. It is an example of what advanced manufacturing may look like. But there are still jobs there. In 2013, GlobalFoundries built an advanced wafer fab for 300mm wafer production in upstate New York.[61] The multibillion dollar facility is the size of six American football fields, and capable of operating 24 hours a day. GlobalFoundries employs a range of skilled workers, including wafer fab operators, technicians (combined these are a significant majority of employees), engineers, and managers. At the end of 2013, there were 2,200 people employed in these positions. Many more people were indirectly employed through the economic activity the factory created. The ratio of support or indirect jobs to the direct, on-site jobs, was estimated at roughly 5 to 1—the indirect jobs GlobalFoundries counted totaled approximately 11,000. Despite all the automation a fab presents, employment is still significant—there are a lot of employee cars in the fab's very large parking lot.

The introduction of productivity-enhancing technology in the U.S. economy seems to be slowing at this time rather than increasing, given the capital investment and productivity decline data cited in chapter 3. Does this suggest that weak consumption demand because of technology, as Martin Ford proposed, is now occurring? Or is what economists term "secular stagnation" the result of other forms of economic malaise? There do not seem to be many signals yet of the massive wave of technology-based job displacement the theorists cited here are predicting. It could still come, but at most it has been gradual in some sectors and it is not yet at hand in the larger economy.

Since there has not been a surge in automation investment, we are unlikely to see this kind of technological disruption tomorrow, although future disruption is likely inevitable. The factory of the future envisioned above is a good distance away because the component technologies the manufacturing institutes are focusing on are on five- to ten-year development cycles. Then they will have to be collected, experimented with and put into a system. Even then, there will still be on-site, complementary, and indirect jobs, as the advanced semiconductor fab example suggests. The leaders of Toyota's autonomous car initiative, noted roboticists Gil Pratt and John Leonard, offer another instructive example: they believe that the complexity of urbanized area driving, such as the infamous left turn problem, means that going entirely driverless may be a decade away.[62] They are now focused on just making cars safer. So displacement appears to be a problem that will be unfolding over two decades, not immediately, allowing us time to consider the necessary adjustments. Workforce training, for example, already is a priority for upgrading skills so fewer will be left behind, as discussed in chapter 8.

Instead, the economy, and its manufacturing sector, appear caught in more of a low-growth, low-productivity phase than a technological boom, that requires attention now. As Nauna Hejlund, vice president of the Danish Confederation of Trade Unions, put it, "New technology is not the enemy of the workers, old technology is."[63]

Secular Stagnation

In the wake of the Great Recession, as in nearly all recessions since the Great Depression, the idea of secular stagnation resurfaced. The idea was first proposed by Alvin Hansen in his 1938 presidential address to the American Economic Association. According to Hansen, secular stagnation can be summarized as "sick recoveries which die in their infancy and depressions which feed on themselves and leave a hard and seemingly immovable core of unemployment."[64] At its most basic level, the economy ends up stuck with low growth and high unemployment because of a shortfall of investment. There are three outlets for investment, in Hansen's view: technological progress, population growth, and new land or resources. Compared to the nineteenth century, it appeared that over the first decades of the twentieth century, population growth was slowing significantly and foreign investment opportunities and the amount of territory to be settled were diminishing. Technological innovation was the best outlet for investment in order to return the economy to full employment, but Hansen simultaneously acknowledged that technological unemployment might also occur.[65] The only way out of a depression was through large new investments, but the investments needed to be made in new industries or techniques.[66] However, if there was insufficient technological progress, policies that increased consumption would be necessary.[67] In the United States, public investment during World War II provided the stimulus Hansen was talking about, ending the decade-long stagnation.

The concept of secular stagnation has frequently reemerged since Hansen first introduced the idea in 1938. Writing in 1950, Benjamin Higgins sought to lay out a formalized model of secular stagnation. As Higgins notes, by 1950 the United States had seen seven consecutive years of full employment. Even so, the trauma of the 1930s still weighed heavily on economists and influenced research at the National Bureau of Economic Research (NBER) to determine whether stagnation was still a threat lurking under the surface.[68] In the postwar period, there were critiques questioning whether secular stagnation was theoretically sound or even if there were historical examples of stagnation. By the 1960s, secular stagnation had almost entirely disappeared from the economic discourse.[69] The economic policies of the 1960s and the Vietnam War helped kick off over a decade of high inflation and, by the mid-1970s, correspondingly high unemployment rates. Not surprisingly, with another economic crisis at hand, secular stagnation resurfaced. At the end of the 1970s, Anthony Scaperlanda suggested that the U.S. economy was entering a secular phase of increasing underemployment. Scaperlanda was working with the model developed by Higgins, who had defined the concept of stagnation as exactly that, no growth at all, not low growth.[70] For Keynesian economists, secular stagnation has been a useful path of analysis during economic recessions.

Following the economic crash in 2008 and the slow recovery that followed, it may have been just a matter of time before the secular stagnation thesis reemerged. If secular stagnation is now upon us, what are its causes, and what are the proposals to counter it? In particular, does manufacturing, with its historical function of driving productivity gains, have a role to play?

The Summers Formulation

It was Lawrence Summers, starting in 2013, who made Hansen's theory an important part of the current U.S. policy discussion. Summers's demand-side secular stagnation largely revolves around the concept of the zero lower bound (ZLB) on nominal interest rates. It is worth noting that central banks can implement negative nominal interest rates; Switzerland, Sweden, Denmark, and Japan have done this. The Bank for International Settlements has raised concerns about the uncertainty surrounding negative rates, especially if retail deposit rates go negative.[71] Negative real interest rates are much more likely to occur when the excess of savings over investment drives down the interest rate in an attempt to restore equilibrium by shifting some savings into investment (see figure 9.2). Summers's argument is that with interest rates around zero, a country's output is insufficient to support full employment.[72] Summers lists a number of factors hampering investment

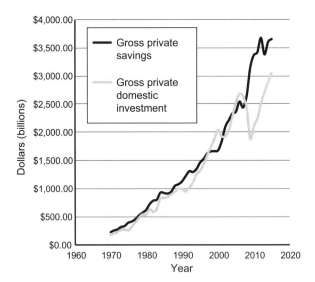

Figure 9.2
Savings and Investment.
Source: Federal Reserve Bank of St. Louis. US Bureau of Economic Analysis (BEA), Gross Private Saving [GPSAVE]. https://fred.stlouisfed.org/series/GPSAVE; US Bureau of Economic Analysis (BEA), Gross Private Domestic Investment [GPDI]. https://fred .stlouisfed.org/series/GPDI.

demand: decreasing population growth, a relative decrease in the cost of capital goods, and excess money not being used by large corporations. On the savings side, Summers cites excessive reserve holdings among developing countries, postcrisis financial regulations, inequality, and increasing intermediation costs.[73] This excess of savings over investment slows growth and increases unemployment. An interesting way Summers highlights the problem is that it is a case of Say's Law that has been inverted: instead of supply creating its own demand, demand is unable to create sufficient supply.[74] The secular stagnation argument suggests that the problem of low growth will persist unless there is a fiscal stimulus. Monetary policy alone is insufficient because of the zero lower bound.

Alternative Causes for Secular Stagnation

Not all agree with Summers's formulation. Former chair of the Federal Reserve Ben Bernanke was skeptical about this formulation of secular stagnation because in his view the low real interest rates associated with it are unlikely to stay negative for a sustained period of time and because of its failure to evaluate the international dimensions of these developments.[75]

Robert Gordon offered a different prognosis. He posited that the current low-growth environment and secular stagnation are the result not of insufficient demand but that supply-side issues are the real drag on the economy. As has been noted throughout this book, there has been declining overall total factor productivity (TFP) growth in the United States (with periodic exceptions) since the 1970s. Gordon notes that from 1972 to 1996 and 2004 to 2014, TFP growth was 0.52% and 0.54%, respectively. During the IT revolution, TFP increased to 1.43%, but that was still below the pre-1970 levels.[76] So the question is whether the IT revolution is fading and we can temporarily expect to see low or no gains, or, as Gordon suggests, is there a permanent decline in technological advancement? Gordon believes there are only minimal gains to be had from IT and the retail sector has largely finished its transition from small scale to large scale, with the corresponding advances in supply chains, distribution, and inventory management.[77] For Gordon, addressing a number of "headwinds" presents the best option for improving growth. These are educational attainment, income inequality, changing demographics, government debt, and a social breakdown in the United States.[78] Gordon's view that we have already picked the low-hanging fruit of technological development and that there are only limited advances ahead is highly disputed and is hard to subscribe to. A recent IMF report suggests that there has not been a slowdown in technological progress but rather efficiency problems in the use of technology.[79] However, the techno-optimists covered at the beginning of the chapter likely swing too far in the opposite direction.

Another theory that explains the current low-interest-rate, low-growth economy has to do with a shortage of safe assets. Essentially, in the wake of the Great Recession, investors from countries around the world sought to purchase assets with much lower risks. This flood of money progressively pushed interest rates lower and lower until they reached the zero lower bound, at which point output decreases to return to equilibrium. The countries with the safest assets bear the brunt of having large capital inflows, which leads to the appreciation of their currencies. This has been the position of the United States. In scenarios such as these, monetary policy is ineffective. According to Caballero, Farhi, and Gourinchas, the most effective policy in these circumstances is fiscal expansion that is debt financed, meaning that the government increases the stock of safe assets.[80] As was noted earlier, in fact, most of the interest rates in advanced countries remained near, and in some instances less than, zero through 2016. The increasing demand for U.S. Treasuries (where price and yield move inversely) as well as the appreciation of the dollar in the years after the recession lends credence to the safe assets scarcity argument. This is a strong indicator that there is sufficient demand for government securities that a debt-financed fiscal expansion could still be implemented at a fairly low interest rate.

Alternative Policies for Secular Stagnation

Just as there are a variety of explanations for the slow economic recovery since the recession, the policy recommendations vary as well. The debt financing approach was applied at the height of the crisis in 2008 and 2009 as countries throughout the world resorted to massive monetary and fiscal stimuli. The initial response was coordinated to prevent the collapse of the international financial system. The Federal Reserve opened currency swap lines with 12 countries between September 18 and October 29, 2008.[81] Between 2007 and 2009, there was a short-lived revival of Keynesian economics.[82] In the process, the bailouts essentially moved private debts onto the public balance sheet; in the United States, debt was around 63% of GDP at the end of 2007 but had ballooned to 101% at the end of 2012.[83]

However, as in the 1930s, austerity subsequently became the preferred policy because sovereign debt was viewed as a destabilizing force.[84] A number of economists, including Carmen Reinhart and Kenneth Rogoff in their book *This Time Is Different: Eight Centuries of Financial Folly*,[85] provided austerity with academic credibility. More recently, austerity has largely been discredited, not for the first time, as a preferred policy during difficult economic situations, given the evidence that it slowed the recovery and exacerbated the recession.[86] The austerity imposed on Greece became an example of austerity's counterproductive effects, with its devastating effects on the country's economy.[87]

Fiscal Stimulus and Its Multiplier

If the track record for fiscal consolidation is so poor, is there evidence that fiscal stimulus actually increases growth? There is a general consensus that, during recessions, fiscal policy becomes a more important policy tool, especially when monetary policy begins to reach its limits.[88] There has been a debate for decades on the effectiveness of fiscal policy, which revolves around the concept of a fiscal multiplier. A fiscal multiplier is the change to GDP from either a 1% increase or decrease of public expenditure. Olivier Blanchard and Daniel Leigh released an IMF working paper in 2013 suggesting that the fiscal multiplier had been underestimated. Blanchard and Leigh noted that there had previously been work estimating multipliers in situations where the zero lower bound applied, but the available data was largely limited to the 1930s.[89] They found that it was likely that the multipliers being used in calculations at the start of the crisis were around 0.5, less than half of the actual multiplier.[90] The implications of this are large: if there are reductions in public spending of 1% of GDP, this means the economy shrank by more than 1%. Estimates of multipliers vary extensively based on the model applied, which can range from New Keynesian, neoclassical, and old Keynesian models that do not assume that markets clear. Auerbach and Gorodnichenko reviewed a number of these models and found that fiscal stimulus is probably effective and that potential adverse consequences of crowding out private investment or stoking inflation are unlikely to occur during a recession.[91] Ultimately, there is no universal multiplier, but rather it is very likely that there is a different multiplier for different countries and situations.

An Infrastructure Stimulus

One of the most common policy proposals for a stimulus is a large-scale infrastructure investment. This investment falls into the category of what economics considers "public goods" (traditionally roads, bridges, sewers, and similar projects) and is what Summers calls for to boost demand and get the country out of a period of secular stagnation. There are a number of reasons why increasing infrastructure spending has appeal. First and foremost is the deteriorating condition of the country's infrastructure. The American Society of Civil Engineers (ASCE) most recently gave U.S. infrastructure a D+, suggesting that $3.6 trillion needed to be invested by 2020.[92] While this is far from an impartial analysis, it is suggestive of the condition of roads and bridges. The World Economic Forum has ranked U.S. infrastructure behind places like Hong Kong, Singapore, and the United Arab Emirates.[93] The other big appeal of infrastructure is the demographics of the potential workers. In September 2016, the unemployment rates for individuals with less than a high school diploma or a high school diploma were 8.5% and 5.2%, respectively. People with a college degree or higher had an unemployment rate of 2.5%.[94] Additionally, from 1994 to 2014, the labor force participation rate for men aged 24 to 54 declined from 91.7% to 88.2%. The decline for women over that time period was half as much.[95] There is a fairly strong case that infrastructure projects would create jobs for a demographic segment that has struggled over the last decade and a half.

What would this infrastructure spending look like in practice? Summers suggests an increase of 1% of GDP over ten years for infrastructure, about $2.2 trillion, raised through debt financing. If real interest rates remained low, Summers notes, the returns—economic growth and a larger tax base— would be greater than the cost of borrowing.[96] There are a number of questions raised by a decade-long debt-financed project. Public spending on infrastructure has been slowly declining over the last half century. In 1959, 3.0% of GDP was spent on infrastructure, but that had fallen to 2.4% in 2014.[97] Between 2003 and 2014, federal spending on infrastructure fell 19%.[98] Part of the problem is that the Highway Trust Fund has been funded largely by a national gas tax, which Congress, because of its inability to agree on any kind of tax increase, has kept frozen at 18.4 cents since 1993, even as fuel efficiency and construction costs have risen.[99] If the tax had been inflation indexed, it would have been around 45 cents by 2016. A major transportation infrastructure investment without a corresponding effort to address its long-term financing and maintenance would, over time, be problematic from a transportation perspective,[100] ultimately affecting its benefits. There are thus concerns about debt financing for infrastructure, especially if user fees are not even discussed.

In the same vein as the fiscal multiplier, the economic gains from infrastructure investment are subject to debate. In 2014, the IMF came out in support of increasing public infrastructure, noting that efficiently managed projects could be debt financed without increasing debt-to-GDP ratios.[101] Not surprisingly, other recent work came to different conclusions. For example, Yanushevsky and Yanushevsky found that an infrastructure stimulus cannot decrease debt-to-GDP ratios.[102] Work by Chandra and Thompson on the effect of new interstate highways in rural areas found that the counties where new roads pass through see economic growth but that is essentially offset by economic declines in adjacent counties.[103] Studies by Duranton and Turner focusing on urban areas as well as Fraumeni's analysis at the national level find only small gains from highway construction[104] aside from short-term employment. None of this undercuts the need to invest in infrastructure, which is vital to a well-functioning economy, but a debt-financed stimulus is probably the wrong type of funding.

The American Recovery and Reinvestment Act (ARRA), passed in 2009 at the height of the crisis, provides a small case study of an infrastructure stimulus. The complete ARRA package exceeded $800 billion. Between April 2009 and March 2011, $25.2 billion, or 9.6% of the spending between those dates, was spent by the Department of Transportation on infrastructure.[105] Estimates of the number of jobs saved or created by 2011 fall between 1.2 million and 3.6 million.[106] The ARRA was successful in halting the downward spiral the economy was on. However, it did show that there were limits to how much additional money could be spent on infrastructure in a fairly short period. While $25.2 billion was spent, an additional $17.5 billion had been obligated over those two years.[107] This suggests that a $2.2 trillion package spent over ten years is most likely going to be heavily backloaded. It is likely that $220 billion a year will not find its way into the economy for an extended period, and the ARRA shows that the number of "shovel-ready" projects is probably much lower than expected. Additionally, with an unemployment rate of 5% in fall 2016, there is much less slack in the economy and much less need to boost short-term employment. We would expect the fiscal multiplier for infrastructure to be much lower than it was a few years ago, and by the time the bulk of the stimulus is spent, it will likely be even lower, assuming the economy continues to improve slowly over time.

One common model that explains the life span of major new innovations is based on Kondratiev waves. There is often a period of decades while the technology goes through R&D, demonstration, and pilot phases, attempting to reach readiness for economic adoption. This is followed by roughly a decade of rapid growth, with widespread adoption and corresponding productivity gains from the technology. This levels off to a more moderate level of growth based more on incremental advances, which can endure for decades until eventually full technology maturity is reached.[108] Robert Gordon notes that big advancements happen only once; for instance, the improvement in the performance of automobile engines between 1906 and 1940 has not been repeated since then.[109] The development of the interstate highway system followed a similar course. Before World War II, there had been a slow expansion of highways in the United States, but the large expansion began under Eisenhower, coinciding with the maturing of the internal combustion engine, and continued until the 1970s. It appears that the productivity gains from interstate construction declined significantly in the 1960s and 1970s.[110]

A critical point is that significant productivity gains from public works projects seem to be linked to either facilitating or expanding access to major new technologies. For the internal combustion engine, these were road building programs. The Rural Electrification Administration loans during the 1930s helped raise the productivity of farming.[111] There can be little doubt that investing in the country's dams, bridges, drinking water, ports, and roads is constructive. Investments in these kinds of projects, however, are not now tied to the introduction of a major new technology wave—the waves behind this kind of infrastructure have already been largely implemented. Therefore, the resulting long-run productivity gains and corresponding growth resulting from traditional infrastructure, while important, are likely to be fairly minimal.

As has been discussed here and in earlier chapters, there appears to be a trend of ongoing low productivity growth. An infrastructure stimulus is not the answer to this problem. Returning to Gordon's and Summers's theories about secular stagnation, it is fair to suggest that the United States is facing problems on both the demand and supply sides. The problem of quality jobs for the non–college-educated working class over the past fifteen years has been previously highlighted and is exacerbated by continuing secular stagnation.

There is an additional problem that has yet to be adequately addressed. There is a well-known oncoming demographic shift as more baby boomers retire, which will present additional challenges. However, as of 2015, the dependency ratio in the United States is nearly identical to what it was in 1982.[112] And right now the problem appears to be exactly the opposite. Fewer Americans in their prime working years have jobs, while more Americans older than fifty-five are working than before. The decline of manufacturing jobs has contributed to this problem, and this trend began before the recession. As Charles, Hurst, and Notowidigdo have argued, before the recession, declining employment in manufacturing was offset and partially masked by an increase in construction jobs as a result of the housing bubble.[113] This should raise further questions about whether an infrastructure stimulus will do much more to help solve the underlying structural problems than the construction boom during the housing bubble did.

To summarize, the problem driving secular stagnation is not short-term employment as it was in the Great Recession; we are past that phase. Instead, the economy faces low productivity and low growth, and a corresponding inability to tackle its problems of income inequality and the creation of quality jobs, as well as a skewed age demographic for employment. These are deeper structural problems and will not be resolved by a stimulus program focused on short-term employment and stimulus investments that yield limited productivity gains.[114]

A Role for Advanced Manufacturing in Addressing Secular Stagnation?

The decline of manufacturing has been widely recognized and discussed. Within the economic mainstream, as discussed in chapter 4, this is explained away as the natural course for an advanced economy. It is the next structural transition, this time from a manufacturing economy to a service economy. Like agriculture, manufacturing has high productivity levels, so output can continue to increase even as employment falls. Historically, manufacturing has maintained high productivity gains; according to the Bureau of Economic Analysis, between 1997 and 2015, the real value added of manufacturing increased by about 40%.[115] Although there were measurement problems with this estimate,[116] it suggests the productivity scaling factor that manufacturing can provide for an economy.

This is not to say it is possible for the country to return to the 1979 level of 19.5 million manufacturing employees, but the incredible drop in employment in this sector during the decade starting in 2000 is also not necessarily indicative of the future of manufacturing. As discussed in chapter 3, however, the real employment gains from advanced manufacturing lie not at the production moment in the factory itself—the narrow center of the hourglass—but in the much larger top and bottom of the hourglass, in the inputs and outputs to that production moment. Thus, the significant gains are in the value chains of firms spread through the hourglass that provide inputs (from resources, to components, to R&D) and outputs (from distribution, to retail, to product life-cycle support). As discussed, measuring manufacturing employment at the factory level misses its connective role in the economy; the real gains of advanced manufacturing are in the hourglass. And since future firms, as discussed in chapter 3, are likely to blend produced goods with services, this process of making the attached services more tradable also brings productivity gains to the service side.

A substantial investment in advanced manufacturing offers an opportunity to directly address the underlying trend driving working-class unemployment, wage problems, and prime-age worker unemployment. This will not work as a short-term stimulus—there is significant time required for implementation. However, the current economic problems are structural, not cyclical, and this approach does address some of the most critical issues. In addition, unlike the traditional infrastructure approach discussed earlier, which is not tied to a technology-driven new innovation wave, advanced manufacturing is by design tied to a major set of technology advances, as detailed in chapters 5 and 6. Although aimed at what is an established, legacy sector—manufacturing—advanced manufacturing aims to follow the pattern of technology-driven innovation waves such as mass production and quality manufacturing. By tying support for the infrastructure around advanced manufacturing to what could be technology advances of significant impact, the potential productivity gains would far exceed "pothole filling."

Support for advanced manufacturing does not fit into a traditional infrastructure "public good" approach. Manufacturing infrastructure (except in wartime or in an economic crisis, such as when the federal government took over much of the auto sector during the Great Recession) has traditionally been privately held. Economists have long cautioned against "industrial policy" as an inefficient governmental intervention into the marketplace.[117] However, the design of advanced manufacturing programs is that they will be led by industry, not by government, with government contributing traditional "public goods" in its advanced manufacturing efforts through its historical R&D and education roles, both long recognized in economics as necessary because of market failures.

Bringing together two- and four-year colleges and universities with consortia of large and small manufacturers, as well as government R&D agencies, can provide a concrete path for manufacturing technology advances as well as for workers to return to the value chains of firms that manufacturing enables. This is an opportunity for the government to restructure its workforce training and put in place a more effective system than Trade Adjustment Assistance programs, as discussed in chapter 4. Another reason this is an important investment is because manufacturing, particularly production of new technologies, holds a vital place in the U.S. innovation system. Although mainstream economics has had difficulty distinguishing between the productivity attributes of different economic sectors, as reviewed in previous chapters, manufacturing indeed matters.[118] A manufacturing-based stimulus may be weaker in the short term than investing in traditional infrastructure, but because of the inclusion of supply-side factors, long-term growth is of more importance. Will we confront a world like the ones described by Ford, Cowen, Brynjolfsson, and McAfee? It is not likely to happen soon, unless current investment and productivity trends are reversed. As with computing, a symbiosis between people and machines may evolve; the trend may move towards cobotics. However, in the meantime, the relationship between production and jobs has not been suspended. It is still worthwhile to begin finding ways, such as through manufacturing's high job multipliers, to address the already significant inequality problem. Investing in advanced manufacturing may be a key step toward adapting to the twenty-first century.

10   Conclusion: Manufacturing Matters More Than Ever

The first decade of the twenty-first century was a painful one for American manufacturing. Production jobs fell by one-third, manufacturing output, investment, and productivity rates declined, and the trade deficit in manufactured goods reached ever more worrisome levels. A series of market failure problems became visible. On the demand side, too many production companies, especially small and medium-sized firms, lacked information, resources, and knowledge to implement new methods and new technologies to keep up with low-cost competitors abroad. On the supply side, larger firms, driven by an "asset light" financial model, failed to support the smaller firms in their supply chains. The smaller firms were increasingly "home alone"[1] as the production ecosystem thinned out. Some 60,000 factories closed during the period. Part of the resulting fallout was social disruption, hitting the American working class hard. The story since then has been better, but this sector is by no means healthy, still facing deep structural problems. Improvement is needed if society is to address challenges such as economic inequality and creating quality jobs. High on that improvement list is the need to bring strong innovation into the manufacturing sector. This could help reverse stagnant productivity levels and hasten the efficiency gains needed to make the sector competitive with lower-wage and lower-cost producers abroad.

The central idea in this book is that there could be new production paradigms that could transform the sector. These paradigms have occurred before: the development of mass production in the United States and creation of quality manufacturing in Japan are two prime examples. These stemmed from technology advances that were translated into new production process and business models. Could the United States develop new production paradigms to drive up production efficiency and drive down costs so it could better compete with low-cost producers, particularly in Asia? Technologists now tell us that there are a series of major production-related technologies emerging that could allow us to create new production paradigms that could dramatically shift the way complex, high-value goods are made. This is the core concept of advanced manufacturing. These technology advances must also be accompanied by the new process and business models to implement them. The advanced manufacturing institutes have been created both to form new paradigms and to scale them.

But there are many more building-block ideas we must consider.

Lessons from U.S. Manufacturing History

A close examination of key events in U.S. manufacturing history (in chapter 2) called out a series of lessons about production. Early Industrial Revolution history tells of the importance of "mind and hand"—of how much of innovation is achieved not simply through learning but learning by doing. The practical development and application achieved by producing and implementing a technology makes the innovation real—it is a critical part of innovation. There are also lessons here about the innovation process itself: the breakthrough moment comes only after years of "expert performance"—years of study and testing that enable the breakthrough—but R&D alone is not enough. Innovation only scales if it goes through relentless engineering and reengineering, testing, and demonstration in the scale-up to manufacturing. Mass production itself teaches a further lesson. It showed the importance of not simply the production technology advance but also of accompanying it with production process and business model advances. Innovation was needed in all three areas.

The long effort in the United States in the first half of the nineteenth century to develop interchangeable machine-made parts, a critical step in achieving mass production, taught us lessons about a government's role. Only the government's long-term, patient capital over decades enabled its armories to develop the early machine tools for producing interchangeable parts; the risks of such long-term development were simply too steep for the private sector to overcome. This patient capital problem remains in our economy; because of the risk, industry remains focused on shorter-term incremental advances, not radical advances. The major technology advances of the second half of the twentieth century—aviation, space, electronics, nuclear power, computing, and the Internet—were all radical technology advances, and all stemmed from the Defense Department's "connected" innovation system, which undertook research, development, demonstration, testing, and often initial market creation. The governmental role in the U.S. innovation system, then, has been important in radical innovation and corresponding innovation waves in the economy. Sematech, a 1980s–1990s effort to restore U.S. semiconductor manufacturing to technology leadership, was initially cost-shared by the Defense Department's DARPA in a collaborative model including industry, government, and universities. It was an early model for a collaborative government role in advanced manufacturing. All of these efforts stemmed from a "challenge" model—setting a technology challenge for major advances and organizing a project around meeting it. This provides lessons for organizing current advanced manufacturing efforts.

One additional lesson from examining this series of manufacturing events is that the U.S. innovation system, as it evolved in the postwar period, was organized around technology challenges outside of manufacturing. U.S. manufacturing leadership was a given at the end of the war; it dominated world production, so manufacturing was not the problem. The problem at that time was creating a strong "front end" R&D system, continuing what had been started during the war. So the U.S. innovation system, largely erected during and following the war, never focused on innovation in production, instead focusing on a series of other technology challenges. As discussed, other nations do not operate this way—Germany, Japan, Taiwan, Korea, and now China have organized their innovation systems around manufacturing. The United States has paid a price for failing to better organize innovation for production.

The Attempt to Build Advanced Manufacturing

In the period of aftershocks from the Great Recession (detailed in chapter 3) between 2010 and 2015, creative new manufacturing policies began to evolve. Initially, a series of articles began to advocate new policies. It was new for the U.S. government to apply innovation policy to manufacturing, but the administration, with leadership from the president, assembled an innovation-based strategy, formed by an industry-university collaboration, to try to transform American manufacturing.

It was guided by a series of major reports, reviewed in chapter 5. The Production in the Innovation Economy (PIE) study from MIT pictured a thinned-out ecosystem of production that was jeopardizing not simply manufacturing but the innovation system itself, a crucial U.S. comparative advantage. The administration named a task force of industry CEOs and university presidents, the Advanced Manufacturing Partnership (AMP), which supported forming advanced manufacturing institutes, based in part on Germany's Fraunhofer Institutes, to develop a series of advanced manufacturing technology paradigms. The administration began to implement this program well before the AMP1.0 report was released in 2012. In 2014, a second report, AMP2.0, fleshed out the manufacturing innovation policy proposals, advocating a public-private technology strategy around advanced manufacturing technologies and processes, linking agency R&D and the new institutes around the strategy, creating a network for the institutes for shared learning and best practices, and new workforce training models. An innovation approach was certainly not the only policy necessary for manufacturing recovery but was both a central one and the big new idea.

A 2015 report by the National Academy of Engineering added a broader perspective: advanced manufacturing would be at the core of the future economy, merging services and production for new economic "value" models. Finally, Congress passed bipartisan manufacturing legislation, effectively approving the manufacturing institutes and the advanced manufacturing project. In parallel, a series of competitor nations began their own advanced manufacturing initiatives, leaving the United States with little choice but to continue its new advanced manufacturing focus.

The governmental collaborative role proposed in these reports was needed as a catalyst to help overcome a series of structural barriers.[2] There were adverse factor conditions, including problems in access to capital for investment and access to workforce skills, particularly for the smaller firms that made up the great majority of U.S. manufacturing firms. There was imperfect information: smaller firms that were thinly capitalized and unable to undertake R&D therefore lacked knowledge about new technologies, processes, and business models that could have made them more competitive. There was technology lock-in, as firms of all types developed path dependency on routines, systems, and embedded production technologies that they were reluctant to change, leading to suboptimal operations. The capacity of firms to absorb new technologies and knowledge that could improve their competitive posture, especially the smaller firms, had become limited. While many production firms failed in this Darwinian period, many of the evolutionary survivors still lacked the financing and know-how to undertake the innovations they needed for production leadership.

Economics and Manufacturing

The new manufacturing innovation policies were also needed in part because economics, which has historically dominated U.S. domestic policymaking, had incorrectly read so many aspects of manufacturing. As recounted in chapter 3, a series of established economic views reassured us that manufacturing decline would be offset by other economic gains. The nation was losing manufacturing jobs because of major productivity gains, not because the sector was falling behind; an economy centered on manufacturing would in the natural order of economics be replaced by a service economy; low-wage, low-cost producers abroad must inevitably displace domestic higher-cost ones. Forget about the loss of commodity production; the nation's innovation advantage would always enable it to retain a lead in making high-value, advanced technologies. The benefits of free trade would always outweigh any short-term adverse trade effects, which would be manageable, and innovation is distinct from production, so innovation capacity remains even if the production is distributed worldwide. Unfortunately, none of these arguments proved correct.

Chapter 4 looked in depth at how economics has handled manufacturing, including the developments in mainstream economics that helped bring us down this path. While early economics developed in parallel with the Industrial Revolution, and Adam Smith clearly saw its economic significance, this story somehow got increasingly lost in recent decades. While growth economics gives us an understanding of the significance of technology-based innovation (and the related advances around it) as the leading cause of economic growth, metrics-based neoclassical economics has had great difficulty in treating the complex systems around technology innovation in economic terms—it is critical but "exogenous." "New Growth Theory" economists have tried to put innovation back into an "endogenous" economic box, but this project is incomplete, which means that economists have so far been unable to model the innovation system, much less the manufacturing stages that are a part of it. Productivity thinking has helped; evidence emerged that low-productivity sectors, especially in the service sector, could drag down economy-wide growth—Baumol's cost disease. The way to lessen this drag on the economy is to have a strong innovation system to boost productivity. Without a healthy manufacturing sector, arguably, the innovation system breaks down. The early IT revolution is just one example of innovation interdependence, where the productivity gains have been in both the manufacturing and service sectors; "hard" technologies were the enablers for services.

While economists, starting with David Ricardo, long assumed the universal gains of free trade, more recent New Trade Theory has also been focusing on productivity as a core competitive factor in trade. Economists, led by Paul Samuelson, noted potential long-term adverse consequences of trade for trade losers, and David Autor and his colleagues tracked those enduring consequences in U.S. manufacturing communities. New Trade Theory has been moving away from a national perspective to a more focused sector-level perspective, taking into account heterogeneous firms (firms differing in size). What this has revealed is that with increasing competition, innovative firms, which are disproportionately larger firms, tend to thrive, while smaller, less productive firms that cannot afford to invest in research and development decline. Policies such as advanced manufacturing innovation, organized to improve production efficiency across firms of different sizes, could be read as consistent with addressing this problem. However, mainstream neoclassical economics seems a step behind these developments, not fully incorporating New Growth Theory, productivity perspectives, and New Trade Theory and their possible implications for a new economic look at manufacturing. Instead, much of mainstream economics still seems unready to look beyond current concepts and thus is unable to more realistically examine the importance of particular economic sectors such as manufacturing.

New Models: The Manufacturing Institutes

In contrast, since economies do not stand still waiting for economic concepts to catch up, the emerging field of innovation policy has been stepping into this gap, trying to understand the implications of and formulate responses to the U.S. manufacturing decline. Based on recommendations from the industry and university-led Advanced Manufacturing Partnership, as noted, the administration (as discussed in chapter 6) embarked on an ambitious innovation effort: use new manufacturing institutes to create new production paradigms in a series of production areas, shared across supply chains of large and small firms and across industry sectors. The goal was to increase production efficiency so that the United States could manufacture high-value goods in competition with lower-cost and lower-wage producers in Asia. The institutes would apply U.S. innovation advantages to the production stage, an approach that, as explained earlier, had not been a focus of its innovation system. The new production paradigms would aim to be transformative, just as the technologies and processes behind mass production and quality manufacturing had previously been transformative and had created manufacturing leadership. The AMP studies cited found it could be done: scientists and engineers are indicating that a series of significant new production advances now appear within range.

The manufacturing institutes aimed to overcome a series of deep sectoral problems, identified in chapter 3. Because smaller manufacturers had increasingly been left "home alone," with previous networks of supporting firms eroding around them, the institutes aimed to restore the production ecosystem, with collaborative opportunities across supply chains to adopt advanced production technologies and processes. Taking a lesson from the problems created by the severing of production-innovation links enabled by distributed production, the institutes sought to reconnect the two, embedding innovation into the production system. Because a declining manufacturing sector had been failing its workforce, the institutes were designed to implement new education programs to build the workforce skills required for advanced manufacturing and corresponding opportunities for employees to advance.

All but a few of the 14 manufacturing institutes are still in their early stages, so now is a good time to assess lessons some institutes have been developing, and possible corresponding enhancements to the model across the system. The following examples, as identified in chapter 3, are now being learned:

• It now appears, for example, that *federal cost-sharing must continue beyond the initial five years* first contemplated for the institutes. Such a clear structural problem in the U.S. innovation system is simply not going to be repaired in so short a period, and the timetable for ambitious institute technology results to be developed and scale into the massive production system is going to be longer than a five-year project. Agencies should consider an extended term for successful institutes.

• There needs to be a parallel *emphasis within the institutes on technology implementation as well as technology development*, which means strong engagement with supply chains and smaller firms.

• A strong *network across and between the institutes* is clearly needed for sharing best administrative and organizational practices and for scaling up the technologies and processes starting to emerge.

• If the institutes are to be enduring, their *technologies need to translate not only at the national level but into regional economies*, since strong, continuing support from states and smaller firms will be needed to sustain the institutes and make implementation successful.

• Optimal *institute and network governance* approaches need evaluation; the best emerging approaches to achieve this need to be compared and developed.

• Perhaps most significant of all, *federal R&D at mission agencies needs to be much better linked to the institutes*, because institute technology development—focused on later stages—will require a continuous flow of new technology ideas and advances. Without this, their institute technology efforts cannot stay robust.

While there are more technology sectors of real promise that new institutes beyond the initial 14 could address, the priority for the immediate future should be on translating these lessons learned across the institutes, building an institute network, and linking the R&D programs to the institutes.

The Trump administration, since taking office in 2017, has not developed an explicit position on the future of the manufacturing institutes. Congress fully funded the fourteen institutes for Fiscal Year 2017. The Administration has continued vocal support for strong American manufacturing and new apprenticeships, but its support for the manufacturing institutes has been inconsistent. Its Fiscal Year 2018 budget continued the institute program supported by the Defense Department, but proposed to cut the institutes supported by the Department of Energy as part of major budget reductions there. If a production innovation program is to have continuing impact, this requires both consistent support for the institutes and stronger engagement. An agenda for implementing the lessons learned by the institutes should be a priority.

Workforce Education as a Dissemination Model

Without a trained workforce ready to implement them, advanced manufacturing technologies and processes coming out of the institutes simply will not happen. This is true at both the engineering and skilled-worker levels. Because the United States (as discussed in chapter 8) probably has the most decentralized labor market among developed nations, this is an especially hard task. One of the jobs of the manufacturing institutes is to foster the workforce education and training needed for the technologies they are developing. This would be a new training delivery system in the United States, requiring links to universities for curriculum development, community colleges for curriculum delivery, online and blended learning approaches, and links to existing industry, state, and federal training programs for additional support. While too many institutes are lagging in this area, being focused on their major technology-development tasks, some are creating innovative new systems. These institute leaders grasp (as Germany's Fraunhofer Academy demonstrates) that workforce and engineering training is a critical advanced manufacturing dissemination model—it is a key way that advanced manufacturing is implemented and scales. Advanced manufacturing knowledge will be in significant part tacit knowledge, and tacit knowledge walks on two feet. Training is therefore technology dissemination. This is a critical task that advanced manufacturing initiatives must embrace.

Scaling up Manufacturing Start-ups

Another core idea in the book (the subject of chapter 7) concerns the next generation of production. Increasingly, the United States has turned to its entrepreneurship system of creating start-up firms backed by venture capital to launch its new technologies. The system came into its own to support the information technology innovation wave of the 1980s and 1990s, built around supporting "hard" technologies in the computing and semiconductor fields. In recent years, however, it has shifted significantly to software, which requires little capital or infrastructure and no production, and succeeds or fails quickly. Along with biotechnology and services like media and entertainment, software now dominates venture funding. The system simply is not supporting technologies that require manufacturing, because they require longer-term and higher-risk investments that do not match the VC timetable and risk profile. As discussed, that means that the next generation of innovative manufactured technologies and goods may not be produced in the United States. This has major implications for the longer-term future of U.S. innovation as well as production. A further implication is that the United States will get (over time) the innovations it invests in—if it is investing in sectors, such as software and biotech, with low levels of job creation, it will be significantly limiting its job creation potential. This emerging "jobless innovation" system risks further social disruption.

Are there alternatives to venture support to boost start-up scale-up for nonsoftware "hard" technologies? Although alternative financing systems do not appear readily at hand, Rafael Reif of MIT has proposed a very different fix, arguing that space could be substituted for capital. That is, create spaces very rich in technology, equipment, and know-how, which he terms "innovation orchards," for start-ups entering product design, to get them through the advanced prototype, demonstration, testing, and pilot production stages. This is what VCs would be funding anyway. Of course, some bridge funding will still be needed, but these technology-rich spaces would move much further down the pathway to actual scale-up and innovation implementation than current start-up incubators, which tend to be earlier stage. Models for this are evolving. MIT is creating one such orchard, which it calls "The Engine." The Department of Energy cannot rely on fossil fuel firms for technology innovation; it must have creative start-ups to nurture the new energy technologies needed. But with VC support of energy technology falling by 80% between 2008 and 2016, it must find another approach. So it has created three such orchards for energy start-ups, drawing on the technology resources of three major energy labs. This innovation orchard approach may prove key for getting to the next generation of technology-based innovative start-ups that must manufacture complex, high-value goods.

The Future of Work and Secular Stagnation

Roughly every quarter century or so, an alarm goes up that automation will be systematically eliminating jobs on a massive scale. As discussed in chapter 9, a number of writers are now projecting that the IT revolution, and continuing advances in artificial intelligence and robotics, has made widespread technological displacement of jobs inevitable. In the past, whenever productivity-increasing automation has occurred, there has always been net job creation. Is this historical reality over? Is now going to be different? To date, however, there does not seem to be major evidence of this technological displacement. Low productivity levels and low levels of capital plant and equipment investment suggest that it will not occur soon. Even in robotics, the direction appears to be more toward the kind of "man-machine symbiosis" that J. C. R. Licklider envisioned for computing early on. "Cobotics," where assistive robots aid and are directed by human workers, appears to be the current trend, not robots eliminating the workforce. These automation developments may be more gradual than some have been predicting; the sky doesn't seem to be falling quite yet.

The problem for the future of work right now seems to be more tied to what economists are calling "secular stagnation"—a period of low GDP and low productivity growth that affects the creation of the quality jobs needed to improve economic inequality. While mainstream economists are arguing for a major stimulus package to fund traditional infrastructure like roads and bridges to reverse the stagnation, a close examination suggests that while these are important, they may not yield the productivity gains they did in the past. Advanced manufacturing, a new kind of infrastructure, which is tied to the economic gains of technological innovation, may provide a higher productivity pathway.

Overcoming the Legacy Sector Barriers

Chapter 1 posited that manufacturing was a complex, established "legacy" sector, laced with a series of classic legacy sector barriers that limit the sector's ability to adopt innovation. The preceding chapters of this work discussed ways out of that box. They identified a series of launch pathways for the entry of new production technologies, and the supporting policies needed to enable their entry. The technologies that the new advanced manufacturing institutes are attempting—from 3D printing, to digital production, to advanced composites, to photonics—represent technology pathways that could create new production paradigms if tied to corresponding processes and business models for implementation.

Also needed, as chapter 6 delineated, is an effort by mission R&D agencies to link their research relevant to the various institutes' technologies to the later-stage work being undertaken by the institutes. Without this new input, the technologies sought by institutes could become stranded over time. Collaborative technology strategies jointly developed by industry, university, and government experts would also be needed. These would be periodically updated to guide both research and the institutes, and could become more like technology roadmaps over time. Since workforce training is a key technology dissemination and implementation approach, as reviewed in chapter 8, the institutes, working in concert with other education actors, also need to pursue this direction. Overall, change agents will be needed to move technology advances into production at scale; perhaps the companies involved in the institutes can collaboratively take on this role.

There are also gaps in the manufacturing innovation system that need filling. The manufacturing institutes themselves represent an attempt to fill a gap in that system, helping to bring small and midsize firms along with larger ones into a new collaborative production ecosystem for innovation. The "innovation orchards" model discussed in chapter 7 also fills a gap, helping to enable start-ups focused on "hard" technologies and making things to overcome a gap in financing, particularly from venture capital sources, for production scale-up.

Manufacturing Still Matters

In conclusion, the larger issue facing the United States is that the social disruption will not just fade away. As discussed in earlier chapters, between 2000 and 2010, U.S. manufacturing employment fell by 5.8 million jobs, from 17.3 million to 11.5 million, and five years later it had only recovered to 12.3 million.[3] An economic study by David Autor and his colleagues titled "The China Shock" tells us that from 1999 to 2011, growth in imports from China alone cost some 2.4 million jobs.[4] In that study of 700 urbanized areas, adult workers in the top quarter of areas affected by competition from Chinese goods experienced a loss of annual income of $549 per capita, offset by federal assistance of only $58. Another study found a "lost decade" of depressed employment and earnings following the Great Recession, the effects of which may extend into the 2020s;[5] manufacturing was the hardest-hit sector.

As recited in earlier chapters, manufacturing was in the past an important pathway to the middle class for those with a high school education—particularly white males. Yet earnings per person for white male high school graduates fell by 9% between 1996 and 2014, while earnings for white male college graduates rose over 22% over the same period.[6] In 2014, average income for white male high school graduates was only $36,787, compared to $94,601 for college graduates. Manufacturing jobs also had been key to the emergence of an African American middle class in Midwest and Northeast urban centers, and through sectors such as textiles and furniture in the South; the manufacturing decline hit this community especially hard, erasing a route to the middle class. These were all clear signals of a loss to middle-income ranks and of growing social inequality. A working class was being left behind. Diving deeper, full-year employment of men with high school diplomas but not college degrees went from 76% in 1990 to 68% in 2013.[7] The share of these men who did not work at all went from 11% in 1990 to 18% in 2013. Importantly, the median income of men without high school degrees fell by 20% between 1990 and 2013; for men with high school diplomas or some college medium income fell 13% in the period. It is not an accident that restoring manufacturing was a frequently cited subject in the highly divisive 2016 presidential election. The American Dream had assumed growing economic well-being for all. The decline of manufacturing was a wild card factor that spelled growing social disappointment and corresponding social disruption. The outcome of the 2016 presidential election brought this reality home to all—it was in significant part a postindustrial backlash.

The United States can ignore manufacturing and allow it to continue to erode, but the consequences to U.S. innovation capability and therefore to economic growth appear to be problematic. It also now appears that there are consequences for the nation's social fabric and democratic values as well. In 1987, as the manufacturing competition between the United States and Japan was at its height, Stephen Cohen and John Zysman wrote a book[8] titled *Manufacturing Matters*—it matters even more now. A new strategy of innovation-driven advanced manufacturing offers one pathway out of America's economic problems.

Notes

1. Introduction: Social Disruption, Legacy Barriers, and Innovation Challenges in U.S. Manufacturing

1. William B. Bonvillian, Donald Trump's Voters and the Decline of American Manufacturing, *Issues in Science and Technology* 32, no. 4 (Summer 2016), http://issues.org/32-4/donald-trumps-voters-and-the-decline-of-american-manufacturing/.

2. Melissa S. Kearney, Brad Hershbein, and Elisa Jacome, Profiles of Change: Employment, Earnings and Occupations from 1990–*2013* (Washington, DC: Brookings Institution, 2015).

3. Kearney et al., Profiles of Change.

4. Doug Short, Household Incomes: The Decline of the Middle Class, *Advisor Perspectives*, September 16, 2016 (Chart: Real Household Incomes: Cumulative Growth, based on Census Bureau and Bureau of Labor Statistics data; income stated chained in 2015 dollar values), https://www.advisorperspectives.com/dshort/updates/2016/09/19/household-incomes-the-decline-of-the-middle-class.

5. Ibid. (Chart: Real Household Incomes: The Growing Gap between Median and Mean).

6. Richard B. Freeman, *America Works: The Exceptional U.S. Labor Market* (New York: Russell Sage Foundation, 2007).

7. Claudia Goldin and Lawrence F. Katz, *The Race between Education and Technology* (Cambridge, MA: Harvard University Press, 2008).

8. David H. Autor, David Dorn, and Gordon H. Hanson, The China Shock: Learning from Labor Market Adjustment to Large Changes in Trade, NBER Working Paper 21906, National Bureau of Economic Research, Cambridge, MA, January 2016, http://www.nber.org/papers/w21906.

9. A. Michael Spence, The Impact of Globalization on Income and Employment: The Downside of Integrating Markets, *Foreign Affairs* 90, no. 4 (July–August 2011), 28, 41.

10. The legacy sector points discussed in this section are explored in depth in William B. Bonvillian and Charles Weiss, *Technological Innovation in Legacy Sectors* (New York: Oxford University Press, 2015).

11. Bureau of Economic Analysis (BEA), Value Added by Industry Group by Percentage of GDP (Table 5a) (Washington, DC: BEA 2013 data).

12. Bureau of Economic Analysis (BEA), News Release BEA 17-02,—Value Added by Industry Group as a Percentage of GDP (Table 5a), January 19, 2017, https://www.bea.gov/newsreleases/industry/gdpindustry/2017/pdf/gdpind316.pdf.

13. These sectors are explored in Bonvillian and Weiss, *Technological Innovation in Legacy Sectors*, 67–87, 112–117, 170–176.

14. These characteristics are detailed in ibid., 55–66.

15. See the discussion of this point in ibid., 6–7.

16. The Defense Department developed system-of-systems engineering to integrate new and old engineering systems to meet significant new program requirements. See, for example, Mo Jamshidi, ed., *System of Systems Engineering* (Hoboken, NJ: John Wiley and Sons, 2009).

17. These models are discussed at length in Bonvillian and Weiss, *Technological Innovation in Legacy Sectors*, 23–30, 181–196.

18. Vannevar Bush, *Science, the Endless Frontier: A Report to the President on a Program for Postwar Scientific Research* (Washington, DC: U.S. Government Printing Office, July 1945).

19. Vernon Ruttan, *Technology Growth and Development: An Induced Innovation Perspective* (New York: Oxford University Press, 2001).

20. Although he did not use the term "extended pipeline," Vernon Ruttan wrote about the Defense Department's role in evolving these technologies. See Vernon Ruttan, *Is War Necessary for Economic Growth? Military Procurement and Technology Development* (New York: Oxford University Press, 2006).

21. National Science Board (NSB), *Science and Engineering Indicators 2016*, International Comparisons of Gross Domestic Expenditures on R&D and R&D Share of Gross Domestic Product, 2013 or Most Recent Year, Table 4.4 (Washington, DC: National Science Board, January 2016).

22. Ibid.

23. International Trade Commission, Antidumping and Countervailing Duty Investigations, as of March 30, 2017, https://www.usitc.gov/trade_remedy/731_ad_701_cvd/investigations.htm.

24. Jared Walczak, Location Matters: Effective Tax Rates on Manufacturers by State, Tax Foundation, Sept. 1, 2015, https://taxfoundation.org/location-matters-effective-tax-rates-manufacturers-state/.

25. Organization for Economic Co-operation and Development (OECD), Revenue Statistics—OECD countries: Comparative tables, *OECD.Stat,* as of April 10, 2017, https://stats.oecd.org/Index.aspx?DataSetCode=REV.

26. See, Paul Krugman, Border Tax Two-Step (Wonkish), *The New York Times,* Jan. 27, 2017, https://krugman.blogs.nytimes.com/2017/01/27/border-tax-two-step-wonkish /?_r=0; Greg Mankiw, Is a VAT good for exports?, *Greg Mankiw's Blog: Random Observations for Students of Economics,* May 18, 2010, http://gregmankiw.blogspot.com/2010 /05/is-vat-good-for-exports.html.

27. Bureau of Labor Statistics (BLS), Labor Force Statistics from the Current Population Survey, Unemployment Rate 2006–16, October 2016, http://data.bls.gov /timeseries/LNS14000000. (This dataset does not account for problems of longer-term unemployment and workers who have left the workforce.)

28. Robert Atkinson, *Think Like an Enterprise: Why Nations Need Comprehensive Productivity Strategies* (Washington, DC: Information Technology and Innovation Foundation [ITIF], May 2016, e-book), 31, http://www2.itif.org/2016-think-like-an -enterprise.pdf?_ga=1.141453106.1482316035.1476207219.

29. Robert Atkinson, Restoring Investment in America's Economy, report (Washington, DC: Information Technology and Innovation Foundation [ITIF], June 13, 2016), 3, http://www2.itif.org/2016-restoring-investment.pdf?_ga=1.113675271.1482316035 .1476207219.

30. Bureau of Economic Analysis (BEA), Shares of Gross Domestic Product: Gross Private Domestic Investment [A006RE1Q156NBEA]; Bureau of Economic Analysis (BEA), Shares of Gross Domestic Product: Personal Consumption Expenditures [DPCERE1A156NBEA]; Bureau of Economic Analysis (BEA), Personal Saving Rate [PSAVERT].

31. Robert Gordon, *The Rise and Fall of American Growth* (Princeton, NJ: Princeton University Press, 2015).

2. The Backdrop: Manufacturing's Economic History

1. The account that follows is drawn from Robin McKie, James Watt and the Sabbath Stroll That Created the Industrial Revolution, *The Guardian,* May 29, 2015, http:// www.theguardian.com/technology/2015/may/29/james-watt-sabbath-day-fossil-fuel -revolution-condenser; William Rosen, *The Most Powerful Idea in the World* (New York: Random House, 2010), 115–134.

2. Rosen, *The Most Powerful Idea in the World,* 36.

3. Ibid., 116–117.

4. Merritt Roe Smith, *Harpers Ferry Armory and the New Technology* (Ithaca, NY: Cornell University Press, 1977), 28.

5. Letter, Eli Whitney, to Treasury Secretary Oliver Wolcott, Jr., May 1, 1798, Eli Whitney Collection, Yale University Archives, https://www.eliwhitney.org/7/museum/eli-whitney/arms-production.

6. Merritt Roe Smith, *Military Enterprise and Technology Change* (Cambridge, MA: MIT Press, 1985), 47.

7. Merritt Roe Smith, Eli Whitney and the American System of Manufacturing, in *Technology in America: A History of Individuals and Ideas*, 2nd ed., ed. Carroll W. Pursell, Jr. (Cambridge, MA: MIT Press, 1990), 47.

8. Letter of Eli Whitney, III, March 20, 1890, from New Haven, CT, reprinted in Edward Craig Bates, The Story of the Cotton Gin, *New England Magazine*, May 1890, republished by Westborough, Massachusetts Historical Society, 1899, 19, https://ia902308.us.archive.org/17/items/storyofcottongin00bate/storyofcottongin00bate.pdf.

9. Smith, Eli Whitney and the American System of Manufacturing, 48.

10. Eli Whitney, The Manufacture of Firearms, 1812 memoir, Eli Whitney Collection, Yale University Archives, https://www.eliwhitney.org/7/museum/eli-whitney/arms-production.

11. Eli Whitney Museum and Workshop, Arms Production at the Whitney Armory, Mechanization in the Early Period, The Factory, https://www.eliwhitney.org/7/museum/eli-whitney/arms-production, and https://www.eliwhitney.org/7/museum/about-eli-whitney/factory.

12. Eli Whitney Museum and Workshop, Arms Production at the Whitney Armory, Mechanization in the Early Period, https://www.eliwhitney.org/7/museum/eli-whitney/arms-production.

13. Smith, *Harpers Ferry Armory*, 201–202.

14. Merritt Roe Smith, John H. Hall, Simeon North and the Milling Machine: The Nature of Innovation among Antebellum Arms Makers, *Technology and Culture* 14, no. 4 (October 1973): 573–591.

15. Smith, *Harpers Ferry Armory*, 199.

16. Smith, John H. Hall, Simeon North and the Milling Machine, 578.

17. Ibid., 582.

18. Smith, *Harpers Ferry Armory*, 200–208.

19. See the discussion of the role of defense technology investment at Harpers Ferry and in twentieth-century sectors in Vernon Ruttan, *Is War Necessary for Economic Growth? Military Procurement and Technology Development* (New York: Oxford University Press, 2006).

20. Ibid., 25–27.

21. Nathan Rosenberg, ed., *The American System of Manufactures* (Edinburgh: University of Edinburgh, 1969).

22. An exception was the Brunel-Bentham factory in Portsmouth, which made wooden ship's blocks. It was operating by 1805 and involved 45 machines. See Charles R. Morris, *The Dawn of Innovation* (New York: Public Affairs, 2012), 70–74.

23. Ibid., x.

24. Ibid., x–xi.

25. Alexis de Tocqueville, *Democracy in America*, trans. Gerald Bevan, introduction by Isaac Kramnick (London: Penguin, 2003, originally published 1835 and 1840), pt. I, chaps. 2–3; Morris, *The Dawn of Innovation*, 284–286. Slavery created a tragic exception to the American middle class for African Americans.

26. Morris, *The Dawn of Innovation*, 189, 274.

27. Ibid., 280.

28. Ron Chernow, *Titan* (New York: Vintage, 1997).

29. This discussion of Ford's production system draws on Ruttan, *Is War Necessary for Economic Growth?*, 29–30.

30. Ibid., 33.

31. G. Pascal Zachary, *The Endless Frontier: Vannevar Bush, Engineer of the American Century* (Cambridge, MA: MIT Press, 1999), 85–86, 96–97, 98–101, 103, 106.

32. William F. Trimble, *William A. Moffett, Architect of Naval Aviation* (Annapolis, MD: U.S. Naval Institute Press / Bluejacket Books, 2007), 166–199.

33. David Zimmerman, *Top Secret Exchange: The Tizard Mission and the Scientific War* (Montreal: McGill-Queen's University Press, 1996), 119–120, 192. (Frank Whittle's turbojet engine designs were transferred to the U.S. Army Air Corps initially in 1940 through the Tizard Mission and through subsequent 1941 discussions.)

34. William B. Bonvillian and Charles Weiss, *Technological Innovation in Legacy Sectors* (New York: Oxford University Press, 2015), 9–11, 181–186, 244–246.

35. Robert D. Atkinson, *The Past and Future of America's Economy: Long Waves of Innovation That Power Cycles of Growth* (Cheltenham: Edward Elgar, 2004); Carlota Perez, *Technological Revolutions and Financial Capital: The Dynamics of Bubbles and Golden Ages* (Cheltenham: Edward Elgar, 2002).

36. Regarding models of innovation dynamics, see Bonvillian and Weiss, *Technological Innovation in Legacy Sectors*, 181–196.

37. The discussion of VLSI draws on M. Mitchell Waldrop, *The Dream Machine*, Sloan Technology Series (New York: Viking, 2001), 418–419.

38. Larry D. Browning and Judy C. Shetler, *Sematech: Saving the U.S. Semiconductor Industry* (College Station: Texas A&M Press, 2000); Leslie Berlin, *The Man behind the Microchip: Robert Noyce and the Invention of Silicon Valley* (New York: Oxford University Press, 2005), 281–305.

39. The discussion of supercomputing draws on Ruttan, *Is War Necessary for Economic Growth?*, 105–106.

40. President Barack Obama, Executive Order—Creating a National Strategic Computer Initiative, July 29, 2015, https://obamawhitehouse.archives.gov/the-press-office /2015/07/29/executive-order-creating-national-strategic-computing-initiative. See also Thomas Kalil and Jason Miller, Advancing U.S. Leadership in High Performance Computing, White House Blog, July 29, 2015, https://obamawhitehouse.archives .gov/blog/2015/07/29/advancing-us-leadership-high-performance-computing.

41. The discussion of software draws on Ruttan, *Is War Necessary for Economic Growth?*, 197–209.

42. David C. Mowrey, The Computer Software Industry, in *Sources of Industrial Leadership: Studies of Seven Industries*, ed. D. C. Mowrey and R. R. Nelson (Cambridge: Cambridge University Press, 1999), 145.

43. R. N. Langlois and David C. Mowrey, The Federal Government's Role in the Development of the U.S. Software Industry, in *The International Computer Software Industry*, ed. David C. Mowrey (New York: Oxford University Press, 1996), 71.

44. Waldrop, *The Dream Machine*, 175–187; J. C. R. Licklider, Man-Computer Symbiosis, *IRE Transactions on Human Factors in Electronics* 1 (March 1960): 4–11, http:// groups.csail.mit.edu/medg/people/psz/Licklider.html.

45. Waldrop, *The Dream Machine*, 198–203.

46. Ibid., 4–5.

47. Warren Bennis and Patricia Ward Biederman, *Organizing Genius* (New York: Basic Books, 1997), 196–218.

48. William B. Bonvillian, The Connected Science Model for Innovation: The DARPA Model, in *21st Century Innovation Systems for the U.S. and Japan*, eds. Sadao Nagaoka, Masayuki Kondo, Kenneth Flamm, and Charles Wessner (Washington, DC: National Academies Press, 2009), 206–237.

49. Waldrop, *The Dream Machine*, 5.

50. Bennis and Biederman, *Organizing Genius*, 63–86.

51. Michael A. Hiltzik, *Dealers of Lightning: Xerox PARC and the Dawn of the Computer Age* (New York: HarperCollins, 1999); Douglas K. Smith and Robert C. Alexander, *Fumbling the Future: How Xerox Invented, Then Ignored, the First Personal Computer* (New York: William Morrow, 1988); Waldrop, *The Dream Machine*, 331–394, 407–410.

52. Waldrop, *The Dream Machine*, 5–6.

53. Ibid., 375–380.

54. Ibid., 462–465.

55. Ibid., 465.

56. William B. Bonvillian, The New Model Innovation Agencies: An Overview, *Science and Public Policy* 41, no. 4 (2014): 425–437.

57. Dan Breznitz and Peter Cowhey, America's Two Systems of Innovation: Recommendations for Policy Changes to Support Innovation, Production and Job Creation, report (San Diego, CA: Connect Innovation Institute, February 2012).

58. For a general discussion, see Peter L. Singer, Federally Supported Innovations: 22 Examples of Major Technology Innovations that Stem from Federal Research Support (Washington, DC: Information Technology and Innovation Foundation [ITIF], February 2014), http://www2.itif.org/2014-federally-supported-innovations.pdf?_ga =1.194445550.2108411368.1483563653.

59. Both systems are delineated in Bonvillian and Weiss, *Technological Innovation in Legacy Sectors*, 206–217. See also Charles Weiss and William B. Bonvillian, *Structuring an Energy Technology Revolution* (Cambridge, MA: MIT Press, 2009), 13–26.

3. International Competition and the Decline of U.S. Manufacturing

1. Rafael Aguayo, *Dr. Deming: The American Who Taught the Japanese about Quality* (New York: Simon and Schuster Fireside, 1991).

2. Kaoru Ishikawa, *What Is Total Quality Control? The Japanese Way* (Englewood Cliffs, NJ: Prentice–Hall, 1985).

3. Two books in particular played a role in helping U.S. industry and policymakers understand what Japan had undertaken: James P. Womack, Daniel T. Jones, and Daniel Roos, *The Machine That Changed the World* (New York: Free Press, 1990); Michael L. Dertouzos, Richard K. Lester, Robert Solow, and the MIT Commission on Industrial Productivity, *Made in America: Regaining the Productive Edge* (Cambridge, MA: MIT Press, 1989).

4. John F. Krafcik, Triumph of the Lean Production System, *Sloan Management Review* 30, no. 1 (1998): 41–52.

5. The story of the U.S. response to Japan's quality manufacturing paradigm is detailed in Kent Hughes, *Building the Next American Century—The Past and Future of American Economic Competitiveness* (Washington, DC: Woodrow Wilson Center Press, 2005), drawn on here.

6. Ibid., 60–61.

7. Ibid., 45–49.

8. Ibid., 50–51, 74–77, 85.

9. Robert M. Solow, *Growth Theory: An Exposition*, 2nd ed. (New York: Oxford University Press, 2000), ix–xxvi; Robert M. Solow, Nobel Prize Lecture, December 8, 1987, http://nobelprize.org/nobel_prizes/economics/laureates/1987/solow-lecture.html/.

10. Hughes, *Building the Next American Century*, 153–168.

11. Omnibus Foreign Trade and Competitiveness Act of 1988, Pub. L. No. 100-418, 19 U.S.C. § 2901 et seq. (1988).

12. Hughes, *Building the Next American Century*, 137–141.

13. Ibid., 290. Gore led passage of the High Performance Computing Act of 1991, Pub. L. No. 102-194, 105 Stat. 1594 (1991), 15 U.S.C. § 5501 (1991), to support the emerging "information superhighway."

14. See Hughes, *Building the Next American Century*, 170–198. Technology legislation of the period is summarized in William B. Bonvillian, The New Model Innovation Agencies: An Overview, *Science and Public Policy* 41, no. 4 (2014): 429–433.

15. Larry D. Browning and Judy C. Shetler, *Sematech: Saving the U.S. Semiconductor Industry* (College Station: Texas A&M Press, 2000).

16. The developments reviewed in this subsection, and sources discussing them, are detailed in Bonvillian, The New Model Innovation Agencies, 429–430.

17. This "industrial policy" concern remains embedded in partisan U.S. politics, but although the manufacturing institutes created in the 2012–2016 period, as discussed later, could be branded in this way, the fact that the institutes were industry-led and cost-shared, as well as the crisis in manufacturing employment and plant closings, tended to overcome such concerns, and bipartisan legislation supporting the institute model passed, as noted later, in 2014.

18. This is not to suggest that research and work on manufacturing was eliminated. For example, NIST continued its collaborative research with industry on production technologies, NIST's MEP programs to bring "lean" production techniques to small firms continued, the Mantech programs at the Defense Department and the industrial efficiency programs at the Energy Department continued, and DARPA conducted a series of research projects on production technologies and efficiencies. See, for example, Defense Advanced Research Projects Agency (DARPA), Adaptive Vehicle Make (AVM) program website, http://www.darpa.mil/program/adaptive-vehicle-make. A central organizing focus was missing from these efforts, however, and they were not of large scale.

19. Dale Jorgenson, U.S. Economic Growth in the Information Age, *Issues in Science and Technology* 18, no. 1 (Fall 2001), http://www.issues.org/18.1/jorgenson.html.

20. Data derived from World Bank, Historical GDP—GDP (current U.S.$) (U.S. and Japan totals for 1990 and 2005), http://data.worldbank.org/indicator/NY.GDP .MKTP.CD?locations=US; http://data.worldbank.org/indicator/NY.GDP.MKTP.CD ?locations=JP.

21. The dimensions of U.S. "industrial policy" are discussed in in Glenn R. Fong, Breaking New Ground or Breaking the Rules—Strategic Reorientation in US Industrial Policy, *International Security* 25, no. 2 (Fall 2000): 152–162; Glenn R. Fong, ARPA Does Windows: The Defense Underpinning of the PC Revolution, *Business and Politics* 3, no. 3 (2001): 213–237.

22. Glenn R. Fong, Follower at the Frontier: International Competition and Japanese Industrial Policy, *International Studies Quarterly* 42, no. 2 (1998): 339–366.

23. China Passes U.S. as Largest Manufacturer, *Wall Street Journal*, March 14, 2011, http://247wallst.com/2011/03/14/china-passes-the-us-as-largest-manufacturer/ (citing *IHS Global Insight* report).

24. This section is drawn from William B. Bonvillian, Reinventing American Manufacturing, *Innovations* 7, no. 3 (2012): 101–104.

25. Barry C. Lynn, *End of the Line* (New York: Doubleday, 2005), 1–18.

26. Robert D. Atkinson, Enough Is Enough: Confronting Chinese Innovation Mercantilism, report (Washington, DC: Information Technology and Innovation Foundation [ITIF], February 2012), http://www2.itif.org/2012-enough-enough-chinese -mercantilism.pdf; Adams Nager, Calling Out Chinese Mercantilism, *International Economy*, Spring 2016, 62–64, http://www.international-economy.com/TIE_Sp16 _Nager.pdf. Techniques include currency manipulation, tariffs, forced technology transfer, industrial subsidies, forced joint venture requirements, controls on foreign purchases, discriminatory standards, weak patenting, and intellectual property (IP) theft. See also on IP theft, Michael Riley and Ashlee Vance, It's Not Paranoia if They're Stealing Your Secrets, *Bloomberg Business Week*, March 19, 2012, 76–84. Compare Edward S. Steinfeld, *Playing Our Game: Why China's Rise Doesn't Threaten the West* (Oxford: Oxford University Press, 2010), 230–234, with Carl J. Dahlman, *The World under Pressure: How China and India Are Influencing the Global Economy and Environment* (Stanford, CA.: Stanford University Press, 2012), 182–205.

27. Dahlman, *The World under Pressure*.

28. Paul A. Samuelson, Where Ricardo and Mill Rebut and Confirm Arguments of Mainstream Economists Supporting Globalization, *Journal of Economic Perspectives* 18, no. 3 (Summer 2004): 135–137, 144–145. http://www.nd.edu/~druccio/Samuelson .pdf. As will be explored in chapter 4, this work builds on his earlier Stolper-Samuelson theorem, where there are two goods and two factors of production—capital and labor—and specialization remains incomplete. One of the two factors—the one that is more scarce—must end up worse off as a result of opening up to international trade

in absolute terms. The theorem anticipates the effect of globalization on developed nations' wages and income distribution. See Wolfgang Stolper and Paul A. Samuelson, Protection and Real Wages, *Review of Economic Studies* 9 (1941): 58–73.

29. David Autor, David Dorn, and Gordon Hanson, The China Syndrome: Local Labor Market Effects of Import Competition in the United States (MIT Economics paper, August 2011), http://economics.mit.edu/files/6613.

30. David Autor, David Dorn, and Gordon Hanson, The China Shock: Learning from Labor Market Adjustment to Large Changes in Trade, NBER Working Paper 21906, National Bureau of Economic Research, Cambridge, MA, January 2016, http://www .nber.org/papers/w21906.

31. Andrew Foote, Michel Grosz, and Ann Huff Stevens, Locate Your Nearest Exit: Mass Layoffs and Local Labor Market Response, NBER Working Paper 21618, National Bureau of Economic Research, Cambridge, MA, October 2015, http://www.nber.org /papers/w21618.

32. Danny Yagan, The Enduring Employment Impact of Your Great Recession Location, working paper, University of California—Berkeley, April 2016, https://sites .google.com/site/dannyyagan/greatdivergence.

33. A. Michael Spence, The Impact of Globalization on Income and Employment: The Downside of Integrating Markets, *Foreign Affairs* 90, no. 4 (July–August 2011): 28–41, http://www.viet-studies.info/kinhte/MichaelSpence_Globalization_Unemployment .pdf.

34. Dan Meckstroth, , China Has a Dominant Share of World Manufacturing, MAPI paper, Manufacturers Association for Productivity and Investment (MAPI) Foundation, Washington, DC, January 2014, https://www.mapi.net/blog/2014/01/china-has -dominant-share-world-manufacturing.

35. Ibid., citing estimates in the United Nations National Accounts Main Aggregates Database, based on the international classification of manufacturing (ISIC D), http:// unstats.un.org/unsd/snaama/resQuery.asp.

36. Ernie Preeg, Farewell Report on U.S. Trade in Manufactures (Washington, DC: Manufacturers Association for Productivity and Investment [MAPI] Foundation, August 15, 2016), https://www.mapi.net/forecasts-data/my-farewell-report-us-trade -manufactures.

37. Jonas Nahm and Edward Steinfeld, Scale-Up Nation: Chinese Specialization in Innovative Manufacturing (MIT working paper, March 12, 2012), 4–5, later published in Jonas Nahm and Edward S. Steinfeld, Scale-Up Nation: China's Specialization in Innovative Manufacturing, *World Development* 54 (2013): 288–300, http://dx .doi.org/10.1016/j.worlddev.2013.09.003; Daniel Breznitz and Michael Murphree, *Run of the Red Queen: Government, Innovation, Globalization and Economic Growth in China* (New Haven, CT: Yale University Press, 2011).

38. Nahm and Steinfeld, Scale-Up Nation, *World Development*, 289–300.

39. Nahm and Steinfeld, Scale-Up Nation, MIT paper, 10–19.

40. Catherine L. Mann, Globalization of IT Services and White Collar Jobs, International Economics Policy Briefs PB03-11 (Institute for International Economics, December 2003), http://www.iie.com/publications/pb/pb03-11.pdf.

41. Gary Pisano and Willy Shih, Restoring American Competitiveness, *Harvard Business Review*, July–August 2009, 114–125, http://hbr.org/hbr-main/resources/pdfs /comm/fmglobal/restoring-american-competitiveness.pdf.

42. Census Bureau, Foreign Trade Statistics, Trade in Goods with Advanced Technology Products, 2015, https://www.census.gov/foreign-trade/balance/c0007.html#2015.

43. Clayton Christensen, *The Innovator's Dilemma* (Cambridge, MA: Harvard Business School Press, 1997).

44. Nahm and Steinfeld, Scale-Up Nation, MIT paper, 4–5.

45. The authors gratefully acknowledge that concepts and material first published in Bonvillian, Reinventing American Manufacturing, is drawn on in the following sections.

46. Bureau of Labor Statistics (BLS), Current Labor Statistics (CES) (Manufacturing Employment), http://data.bls.ces. See the detailed review of manufacturing job loss in Robert D. Atkinson, Luke A. Stewart, Scott M. Andes, and Stephen Ezell, Worse than the Great Depression: What the Experts Are Missing about American Manufacturing Decline (Washington, DC: Information Technology and Innovation Foundation, March 2012), 4–19, http://www2.itif.org/2012-american-manufacturing -decline.pdf.

47. Robert E. Scott, Manufacturing Job Loss: Trade Not Productivity Is the Culprit, report, Economic Policy Institute, August 11, 2015, http://www.epi.org/publication /manufacturing-job-loss-trade-not-productivity-is-the-culprit/ (citing BLS data).

48. BLS, CES (Manufacturing Employment).

49. Atkinson et al., Worse than the Great Depression, 47; Bureau of Economic Analysis (BEA), Fixed Assets Accounts Tables, Investment in Private Fixed Assets by Industry, Table 3.7ESI, revised Sept. 7, 2016, https://www.bea.gov/iTable/iTable.cfm?ReqID =10&step=1#reqid=10&step=3&isuri=1&1003=138&1004=2000&1005=2010&1006 =a&1011=0&1010=x.

50. Ibid. See analysis in Atkinson et al., Worse than the Great Depression, 47–58.

51. Luke A. Stewart and Robert D. Atkinson, Restoring America's Lagging Investment in Capital Goods (Washington, DC: Information Technology and Innovation Foundation [ITIF], October 2013), 1, http://www2.itif.org/2013-restoring-americas -lagging-investment.pdf.

52. Bureau of Labor Statistics (BLS), Databases, Tables & Calculators, Quarterly Census, Manufacturing Establishments 2001–2015, http://data.bls.gov/pdq/SurveyOutputServlet.

53. China Passes U.S. as Largest Manufacturer, *Wall St. Journal*, March 14, 2011.

54. Scott, Manufacturing Job Loss.

55. Ibid.

56. Atkinson et al., Worse than the Great Depression, 30–42.

57. Susan Houseman, Christopher Kurz, Paul Lengermann, and Benjamin Mandel, Offshoring Bias in U.S. Manufacturing, *Journal of Economic Perspectives* 25, no. 2 (2011): 111–132, http://pubs.aeaweb.org/doi/pdfplus/10.1257/jep.25.2.111; Susan Helper, Timothy Krueger, and Howard Wial, Why Does Manufacturing Matter? Which Manufacturing Matters? (paper, Metropolitan Policy Program, Brookings Institution, Washington, DC, February 2012), 7, http://www.brookings.edu/~/media/Files/rc/papers/2012/0222_manufacturing_helper_krueger_wial/0222_manufacturing_helper_krueger_wial.pdf; Michael Mandel, How Much of the Productivity Surge of 2007–2009 Was Real, *Mandel on Innovation and Growth* (blog), March 28, 2011, http://innovationandgrowth.wordpress.com/2011/03/28/how-much-of-the-productivity-surge-of-2007-2009-was-real/.

58. Atkinson et al., Worse than the Great Depression, Table 26 at 29, citing BEA data; BEA, Economic Industry Accounts, Percent Changes in Chain-Type Quantity for Value Added by Industry 2008–13, Table E.1, July 2014 (and prior year tables), https://www.bea.gov/scb/pdf/2014/07%20July/Dpages/0714dpg_e.pdf.

59. Suzanne Berger and the MIT Task Force on Production and Innovation, *Making in America* (Cambridge, MA: MIT Press, 2013), 28–33.

60. BLS, Labor Productivity and Costs, Productivity Change in the Manufacturing Sector, http://www.bls.gov/lpc/prodybar.htm; Scott, Manufacturing Job Loss. See also Atkinson et al., Worse Than the Great Depression, 39.

61. Atkinson et al., Worse than the Great Depression, 42 (adjusted from BLS data).

62. Scott, Manufacturing Job Loss; Atkinson et al., Worse than the Great Depression, 39; A. Stettner, J. Yudken, and M. McCormack, Why Manufacturing Jobs Are Worth Saving, Century Foundation, June 2017, 1–2.

63. Helper, Krueger, and Wial, Why Does Manufacturing Matter?, 9–10. Compare Erik Brynjolfsson and Andrew McAfee, *Race against the Machine* (Lexington, MA: Digital Frontier, 2011).

64. Adams B. Nager and Robert D. Atkinson, ITIF, The Myth of America's Manufacturing Renaissance: The Real State of U.S. Manufacturing (Washington, DC: Information Technology and Innovation Foundation [ITIF], January 2015), 2–3, http://www2.itif.org/2015-myth-american-manufacturing-renaissance.pdf.

65. DG Trade Statistics, World Trade in Goods, Services, FDI, January 2016, http:// trade.ec.europa.eu/doclib/docs/2013/may/tradoc_151348.pdf.

66. BEA, Foreign Trade, Exports, Imports and Balance of Goods by Selected NAICS-Based Product Code, Exhibit 1 in FT-900 Supplement for 12/15, February 5, 2016, https://www.census.gov/foreign-trade/Press-Release/2015pr/12/ft900.pdf.

67. BEA, Trade in Goods with Advanced Technology Products, 2015, Exhibit 16, https://www.census.gov/foreign-trade/balance/c0007.html.

68. BEA, U.S. International Trade in Goods and Services, Exhibit 1, February 5, 2016, https://www.census.gov/foreign-trade/Press-Release/2015pr/12/ft900.pdf.

69. Global Macro Monitor, chart, U.S. Employment in Manufacturing, using BLS data, https://www.creditwritedowns.com/2012/05/chart-of-the-day-us-manufacturing -unemployment-1960-2012.html. Nonfarm payrolls in manufacturing peaked in 1979 at 22%, stabilized around the 17% level in the 1980s and 1990s, and then sharply declined in the following decade to 9% in 2012.

70. Federal Reserve Bank of St. Louis, Economic Research, Trade Weighted U.S. Dollar Index: Major Currencies, updated May 9, 2016, https://research.stlouisfed.org/fred2 /series/DTWEXM.

71. Compare Willem Butler and Ebrahim Rahbari, The "Strong Dollar" Policy of the U.S.: Alice in Wonderland Semantics vs. Economic Reality, *Vox*, *CEPR Economic Policy Portal*, July 28, 2011, http://voxeu.org/article/strong-dollar-policy-us.

72. World Bank, data, Household Final Consumption Expenditure (% of GDP), table, http://data.worldbank.org/indicator/NE.CON.PETC.ZS.

73. Michael Hennigan, Germany's Record Trade Surplus in 2015, *finfacts*, February 10, 2016 (citing Statistisches Bundesamt, Wiesbaden, 2015), http://www.finfacts.ie/Irish _finance_news/articleDetail.php?Germany-s-record-trade-surplus-in-2015-US-UK -France-in-deficit-520. See also, Statistisches Bundesamt (Destatis), Foreign Trade, Ranking of Germany's trading partners in foreign trade—2016, Wiesbaden, April 12, 2016, https://www.destatis.de/EN/FactsFigures/NationalEconomyEnvironment/ForeignTrade /Tables/OrderRankGermanyTradingPartners.pdf?__blob=publicationFile;

74. Robert D. Atkinson, *The Past and Future of America's Economy—Long Waves of Innovation That Power Cycles of Growth* (Cheltenham: Edward Elgar, 2004), 3–40. For a general discussion, see Carlota Perez, *Technological Revolutions and Financial Capital: The Dynamics of Bubbles and Golden Ages* (Cheltenham: Edward Elgar, 2002), 3–46. The quality manufacturing wave, discussed later, was led in the 1970s to 1980s by Japan.

75. Vernon W. Ruttan, *Is War Necessary for Economic Growth? Military Procurement and Technology Development* (New York: Oxford University Press, 2006).

76. Suzanne Berger, *How We Compete: What Companies around the World Are Doing to Make It in Today's Global Economy* (New York: Doubleday Currency, 2006), 251–277.

77. Jessica R. Nicholson and Ryan Noonan, What Is Made in America? (Washington, DC: Department of Commerce, Economics and Statistics Administration (ESA), 2014), http://www.esa.doc.gov/sites/default/files/whatismadeinamerica_0.pdf.

78. Ibid.

79. Susan Helper and Timothy Kruger, Supply Chains and Equitable Growth, report (Washington, DC: Washington Center for Equitable Growth, September 2016), 12–14, http://cdn.equitablegrowth.org/wp-content/uploads/2016/09/30134051/092816 -supply-chains.pdf.

80. National Science Board (NSB), *Science and Technology Indicators 2016* (Washington, DC: National Science Foundation, January 2016), chap. 4, R&D: National Trends And International Comparisons, Highlights, https://www.nsf.gov/statistics/2016 /nsb20161/#/report/chapter-4/highlights.

81. Ibid., chap. 4, Highlights. According to this report, the largest global science and technology (S&T) major gains occurred in the "Asia-10"—China, India, Indonesia, Japan, Malaysia, Philippines, Singapore, South Korea, Taiwan, and Thailand—as those countries integrated S&T into economic growth. Between 2003 and 2013, the U.S. share of global research and development (R&D) dropped from 35% to 27%, whereas it grew from 27% to 40% in the Asian (East, Southeast, and South Asia) region during the same time.

82. Gregory Tassey, Rationales and Mechanisms for Revitalizing US Manufacturing R&D Strategies, *Journal of Technology Transfer* 35, no. 3 (June 2010): 297, http://hbr .org/hbr-main/resources/pdfs/comm/fmglobal/restoring-american-competitiveness .pdf.

83. National Science Foundation/National Science Board, *Science and Technology Indicators 2016*, Figure 4.3, http://www.nsf.gov/statistics/2016/nsb20161/#/downloads /chapter-4.

84. National Science Board (NSB), *Science and Engineering Indicators 2016*, Table 4-7, Funds spend for business R&D performed in the U.S.: 2008–13 (Washington, DC: National Science Board Jan. 2016), https://www.nsf.gov/statistics/2016/nsb20161/# /report/chapter-4/u-s-business-r-d.

85. Tassey, Rationales and Mechanisms for Revitalizing U.S. Manufacturing.

86. William B. Bonvillian and Charles Weiss, *Technological Innovation in Legacy Sectors* (New York: Oxford University Press, 2015), 206–217. See also Dan Breznitz, Why Germany Dominates the U.S. in Innovation, *Harvard Business Review*, May 27, 2014, https://hbr.org/2014/05/why-germany-dominates-the-u-s-in-innovation/; Dan Breznitz and Peter Cowhey, America's Two Systems of Innovation: Recommendations for Policy Changes to Support Innovation, Production and Job Creation, report (San Diego, CA: Connect Innovation Institute, February 2012).

87. BLS, CES (Manufacturing Employment); President's Council of Advisors on Science and Technology (PCAST), Advanced Manufacturing Partnership, Capturing Domestic Competitive Advantage in Manufacturing, AMP report (Washington, DC: White House, May 2012), 26; Small Business Administration (SBA), Frequently Asked Questions About Small Business, Small Businesses Comprise What Share of the U.S. Economy (SBA Sept. 2012). https://www.sba.gov/sites/default/files/FAQ_Sept_2012 .pdf; International Trade Administration (ITA), Trading Companies, One third of goods trade (by value) came from SMEs, http://www.trade.gov/mas/ian/build/groups /public/@tg_ian/documents/webcontent/tg_ian_005369.pdf.

88. Federal Reserve Bank of St. Louis, Economic Research, Manufacturing as a Percentage of GDP, Q3 2015, citing BEA data, https://research.stlouisfed.org/fred2/series /VAPGDPMA.

89. BEA, Value Added by Industry, Manufacturing Sector (2014 data), http://www .bea.gov/iTable/iTable.cfm?ReqID=51&step=1#reqid=51&step=51&isuri=1&5114 =a&5102=1.

90. BLS, Industries at a Glance, Manufacturing, NACIS 31-33, Workforce Statistics, March 2016, http://www.bls.gov/iag/tgs/iag31-33.htm#workforce.

91. Helper, Krueger, and Wial, Why Does Manufacturing Matter?, 4–5.

92. Solow, *Growth Theory*; Solow, Nobel Prize Lecture.

93. Tassey, Rationales and Mechanisms for Revitalizing US Manufacturing R&D Strategies, 290.

94. Mark Muro, Sid Kulkarni, Jacob Whiton, and David Hart, America's Advanced Industries: New Trends (Washington, DC: Brookings Institution, September 2016), 4.

95. Ibid., 5–6.

96. Ibid., 4, 7.

97. Dan Meckstroth, The Manufacturing Value Chain Is Bigger Than You Think, report (Washington, DC: MAPI Foundation, February 16, 2016), 1–2, https://www .mapi.net/forecasts-data/manufacturing-value-chain-much-bigger-you-think.

98. The Bureau of Economic Analysis defines "value added of an industry, also referred to as gross domestic product (GDP)-by-industry," as "the contribution of a private industry . . . to overall GDP. The components of value added consist of compensation of employees, taxes on production and imports less subsidies, and gross operating surplus. Value added equals the difference between an industry's gross output (consisting of sales or receipts and other operating income, commodity taxes, and inventory change) and the cost of its intermediate inputs (including energy, raw materials, semi-finished goods, and services that are purchased from all sources)."

BEA, Frequently Asked Questions, What Is Industry Value Added, March 2006, https://www.bea.gov/faq/index.cfm?.faq_id=184.

99. Meckstroth, The Value Added Chain Is Bigger Than You Think, 11, 13.

100. Insights shared by Susan Helper, Carleton Professor of Economics, Case Western Reserve University, communication of April 15, 2016.

101. The authors gratefully acknowledge that concepts and material first published in William B. Bonvillian, Donald Trump's Voters and the Decline of American Manufacturing, *Issues in Science and Technology* 32, no. 4 (Summer 2016): 31, is drawn from here.

102. Jon Coder and Gordon Green, Comparing Earnings of White Males by Education, for Selected Age Cohorts, High School vs College Graduates (Annapolis, MD: Sentier Research, October 2016), 1, charts 1 and 2 at 7. http://www.sentierresearch.com/StatBriefs/Sentier_Income_Trends_WorkingClassWages_1996to2014_Brief_10_05_16.pdf (based on Census Bureau data).

103. Ibid., 1.

104. Nelson D. Schwartz, Small Factories Emerge as a Weapon in the Fight against Poverty, *New York Times*, October 28, 2016.

105. Stettner et al., Why Manufacturing Jobs, 2. Michael Handel notes that the first decade of the twenty-first century was not the first time a U.S. manufacturing decline resulted in working-class inequality effects; the rise in Japan's manufacturing sector and the recession of the 1980s had similar effects. See Michael J. Handel, Northeastern University, Presentation on Skills, Job Creation and Labour Market, Conference on Smart Industry: Enabling the Next Production Revolution, OECD and Sweden Ministry of Enterprise and Innovation, Stockholm, September 18, 2016.

106. A. Michael Spence, The Impact of Globalization on Income and Employment: The Downside of Integrating Markets, *Foreign Affairs* 90, no. 4 (July–August 2011): 40.

107. Bradford Jensen, Dennis Quinn, and Stephen Weymouth, Winners and Losers in International Trade: The Effects on U.S. Presidential Voting (paper, Georgetown University, Washington, DC, June 10, 2016) (portions of the analysis conducted for the Census Bureau), http://cmepr.gmu.edu/wp-content/uploads/2016/10/jqw_trade_voting.pdf; David Autor, David Dorn, Gordon Hanson, and Kaveh Majlesi, Importing Political Polarization? The Electoral Consequences of Rising Trade Exposure, NBER Working Paper 22637, National Bureau of Economic Research, Cambridge, MA, September 2016, http://www.nber.org/papers/w22637.

4. Economic Perspectives on Manufacturing

1. The Maddison-Project, http://www.ggdc.net/maddison/maddison-project/home.htm, 2013 version.

2. For a concise overview of Physiocracy, see Agnar Sandmo, *Economics Evolving: A History of Economic Thought* (Princeton, NJ: Princeton University Press, 2011), 24–27.

3. Adam Smith, *An Inquiry into the Nature and Causes of the Wealth of Nations*, ed. Edwin Cannan, 1904 (Library of Economics and Liberty), I.10.82, http://www.econlib.org/library/Smith/smWN.html.

4. Ibid., V.1.777.

5. Sandmo, *Economics Evolving*, 57.

6. Smith, *The Wealth of Nations*, I.1.3.

7. Ibid., I.1.8.

8. Ibid., I.1.8.

9. Ibid., II.3.1.

10. Ibid., IV.2.15.

11. David Ricardo, *On the Principles of Political Economy and Taxation*, 1821 (Library of Economics and Liberty), 7.15–7.16, http://www.econlib.org/library/Ricardo/ricP2a.html.

12. Dani Rodrik, *Economics Rules: The Rights and Wrongs of the Dismal Science* (New York: Norton, 2015), 17.

13. See, for example, Vaclav Smil, *Made in the USA: The Rise and Retreat of American Manufacturing* (Cambridge, MA: MIT Press, 2015), 180–184.

14. Harald Hagemann, Solow's 1956 Contribution in the Context of the Harrod-Domar Model, annual supplement, *History of Political Economy* 41 (2009).

15. Robert M. Solow, A Contribution to the Theory of Economic Growth, *Quarterly Journal of Economics* 70, no. 1 (February 1956): 65–66.

16. Hagemann, Solow's 1956 Contribution, 76–77.

17. Ibid., 79.

18. Robert M. Solow, Technical Change and the Aggregate Production Function, *Review of Economics and Statistics* 39, no. 3 (August 1957): 312.

19. Ibid., 320.

20. N. Gregory Mankiw, David Romer, and David N. Weil, A Contribution to the Empirics of Economic Growth, *Quarterly Journal of Economics* 107, no. 2 (May 1992).

21. Robert J. Gordon, *Productivity Growth, Inflation, and Unemployment: The Collected Essays of Robert J. Gordon* (Cambridge: Cambridge University Press, 2004), 15–17.

22. Ibid., 13.

23. Kenneth J. Arrow, The Economic Implications of Learning by Doing, *Review of Economic Studies* 29, no. 3 (June 1962): 155.

24. Matthieu Ballandonne, Creating Increasing Returns: The Genesis of Arrow's "Learning by Doing" Article, *History of Political Economy* 47, no. 3 (2015): 452.

25. Ibid., 457.

26. Ibid., 472.

27. Peter Thompson, How Much Did the Liberty Shipbuilders Learn? New Evidence for an Old Case Study, *Journal of Political Economy* 109, no. 1 (2001): 106.

28. L. A. Sawyer and W. H. Mitchell, *The Liberty Ships: The History of the "Emergency" Type Cargo Ships Constructed in the United States during the Second World War*, 2nd ed. (London: Lloyd's of London Press, 1985), 8, 9, 122, 140, 145.

29. Thompson, How Much Did the Liberty Shipbuilders Learn?, 103–104.

30. Paul M. Romer, Increasing Returns and Long-Run Growth, *Journal of Political Economy* 94, no. 5 (1986): 1003.

31. Ibid., 1004.

32. Robert E. Lucas, Jr., On the Mechanics of Economic Development, *Journal of Monetary Economics* 22 (1988): 31.

33. Larry E. Jones and Rodolfo E. Manuelli, Neoclassical Models of Endogenous Growth: The Effects of Fiscal Policy, Innovation and Fluctuations, in *Handbook of Economic Growth*, vol. 1A, ed. Philippe Aghion and Steven N. Durlauf (Amsterdam: Elsevier, 2005).

34. Paul M. Romer, Endogenous Technological Change, *Journal of Political Economy* 98, no. 5 (1990): 77–78, http://pages.stern.nyu.edu/~promer/Endogenous.pdf.

35. Ibid., 77.

36. Ibid., 99.

37. Philippe Aghion, Ufuk Akcigit, and Peter Howitt, What Do We Learn from Schumpeterian Growth Theory?, NBER Working Paper 18824, National Bureau of Economic Research, Cambridge, MA, February 2013, 2.

38. Elhanan Helpman, *The Mystery of Economic Growth* (Cambridge, MA: Belknap, 2004), 45–46.

39. Aghion, Akcigit, and Howitt, What Do We Learn from Schumpeterian Growth Theory?, 14.

40. Robert J. Gordon, U.S. Productivity Growth: The Slowdown Has Returned after a Temporary Revival, *International Productivity Monitor* 23 (Spring 2013): 14.

41. Berhold Herrendorf, Richard Rogerson, and Akos Valentinyi, Growth and Structural Transformation, in *Handbook of Economic Growth*, vol. 2B, ed. Philippe Aghion and Steven N. Durlauf, (Amsterdam: Elsevier, 2014), 861.

42. Daron Acemoglu and Veronica Guerrieri, Capital Deepening and Nonbalanced Economic Growth, *Journal of Political Economy* 116, no. 3 (2008): 468–469.

43. Herrendorf, Rogerson, and Valentinyi, Growth and Structural Transformation, 899. The concept originated in William Baumol and William Bowen, *Performing Arts, the Economic Dilemma: A Study of Problems Common to Theater, Opera, Music, and Dance* (New York: Twentieth Century Fund, 1966).

44. William D. Nordhaus, Baumol's Diseases: A Macroeconomic Perspective, *B.E. Journal of Macroeconomics* 8, no. 1 (2009): 2.

45. Ibid., 20–21.

46. Ibid., 16.

47. See Jochen Hartwig, Has "Baumol's Disease" Really Been Cured? Working Paper 155, Swiss Institute for Business Cycle Research, Zurich, Switzerland, November 2006; Jack E. Triplett and Barry P. Bosworth, "Baumol's Disease" Has Been Cured: IT and Multifactor Productivity in U.S. Services Industries, Paper presented at 3rd ZEW Conference on The Economics of Information and Communications Technologies, July 4–5, 2003.

48. Gordon, U.S. Productivity Growth,14.

49. Based on a comparison of total nonfarm payrolls and manufacturing employment from the Bureau of Labor Statistics (BLS), All Employees: Total Nonfarm Payrolls [PAYEMS], FRED, Federal Reserve Bank of St. Louis, https://fred.stlouisfed.org /series/PAYEMS, and Bureau of Labor Statistics (BLS), All Employees: Manufacturing [MANEMP], FRED, Federal Reserve Bank of St. Louis, https://fred.stlouisfed.org/series /MANEMP.

50. Carolyn Dimitri, Anne Effland, and Neilson Conklin, The 20th Century Transformation of U.S. Agriculture and Farm Policy, USDA Economic Research Service, Economic Information Bulletin, no. 3, June 2005, 2.

51. Herrendorf, Rogerson, and Valentinyi, Growth and Structural Transformation, 890.

52. U.S. Department of Agriculture, Food Availability (Per Capita) Data System, USDA Economic Research Service, August 2016, http://www.ers.usda.gov/data-products /food-availability-(per-capita)-data-system/summary-findings.aspx.

53. Bureau of Economic Analysis (BEA), Real Personal Consumption Expenditures: Durable Goods [PCEDGC96], FRED, Federal Reserve Bank of St. Louis, https://fred .stlouisfed.org/series/PCEDGC96; Bureau of Economic Analysis, Real Personal Consumption Expenditures: Nondurable Goods [PCNDGC96], FRED, Federal Reserve Bank of St. Louis, https://fred.stlouisfed.org/series/PCNDGC96.

54. See the discussion in Suzanne Berger and the MIT Task Force on Production in the Innovation Economy, *Making in America* (Cambridge, MA: MIT Press, 2013), 28–33.

55. Stephen Parente, The Failure of Endogenous Growth, *Knowledge, Technology, and Policy* 13, no. 4 (Winter 2001).

56. Kenneth I. Carlaw and Richard G. Lipsey, Does History Matter? Empirical Analysis of Evolutionary versus Stationary Equilibrium Views of the Economy, *Journal of Evolutionary Economics* 22 (2012).

57. Richard R. Nelson and Sidney G. Winter, *An Evolutionary Theory of Economic Change* (Cambridge, MA: Harvard University Press, 1982).

58. Richard R. Nelson, *National Systems of Innovation* (New York: Oxford University Press, 1993), 3–21, 505–523. See also, Freeman, Formal Scientific and Technical Institutions (1992).

59. Innovation organization models, including those for production, are discussed at length in William B. Bonvillian and Charles Weiss, *Technological Innovation in Legacy Sectors* (New York: Oxford University Press, 2015), 181–239.

60. University of Pennsylvania, Openness at Constant Prices for United States [OPENRPUSA156NUPN], FRED, Federal Reserve Bank of St. Louis, https://fred.stlouisfed.org /series/OPENRPUSA156NUPN.

61. Census Bureau, U.S. Trade in Goods and Services—Balance of Payments (BOP) Basis, February 7, 2017.

62. Bureau of Economic Analysis (BEA), Value Added by Private Industries: Manufacturing as a Percentage of GDP [VAPGDPMA], FRED, Federal Reserve Bank of St. Louis, https://fred.stlouisfed.org/series/VAPGDPMA.

63. Gregory Mankiw, News Flash: Economists Agree, *Greg Mankiw's Blog*, February 14, 2009, http://gregmankiw.blogspot.com/2009/02/news-flash-economists -agree.html.

64. Elhanan Helpman, *Understanding Global Trade* (Cambridge, MA: Harvard University Press, 2011), 28.

65. Ibid., 29–30.

66. Office of the United States Trade Representative, Indonesia, https://ustr.gov /countries-regions/southeast-asia-pacific/indonesia.

67. Kenneth Rogoff, Paul Samuelson's Contributions to International Economics (May 2005), 4, http://scholar.harvard.edu/files/rogoff/files/samuelson.pdf.

68. Donald R. Davis and Prachi Mishra, Stolper-Samuelson Is Dead and Other Crimes of Both Theory and Data, in *Globalization and Poverty*, ed. Ann Harrison (Chicago: University of Chicago Press, 2007).

69. Helpman, *Understanding Global Trade*, 56–62.

70. John McCallum, National Borders Matter: Canada-U.S. Regional Trade Patterns, *American Economic Review* 85, no. 3 (June 1995).

71. Mitchell Morey, Preferences and the Home Bias in Trade, *Journal of Development Economics* 121 (2016): 24.

72. Donald R. Davis, David E. Weinstein, Scott C. Bradford, and Kazushige Shimpo, Using International and Japanese Regional Data to Determine When the Factor Abundance Theory of Trade Works, *American Economic Review* 87, no. 3 (June 1997): 421.

73. Farhad Rassekh and Henry Thompson, Factor Price Equalization: Theory and Evidence, *Journal of Economic Integration* 8, no. 1 (Spring 1993): 15–18.

74. Alexander Simoes, U.S.-Kenya Bilateral Trade, The Observatory of Economic Complexity, http://atlas.media.mit.edu/en/.

75. Alexander Simoes, What Does the United States Export to Germany? (2014), The Observatory of Economic Complexity, http://atlas.media.mit.edu/en/visualize /tree_map/hs92/export/usa/deu/show/2014/; Alexander Simoes, What Does Germany Export to the United States? (2014), The Observatory of Economic Complexity, http:// atlas.media.mit.edu/en/visualize/tree_map/hs92/export/deu/usa/show/2014/.

76. Paul Krugman, The Increasing Returns Revolution in Trade and Geography, Nobel Prize Lecture, December 8, 2008, 337–338.

77. Elhanan Helpman, Increasing Returns, Imperfect Markets, and Trade Theory, in *Handbook of International Economics*, vol. 1, ed. R. W. Jones and P. B. Kenen (Amsterdam: Elsevier, 1984), 335.

78. Helpman, *Understanding Global Trade*, 85.

79. Krugman, The Increasing Returns Revolution in Trade and Geography, 338–339.

80. Helpman, *Understanding Global Trade*, 89.

81. Ibid., 107.

82. World Bank, Foreign Direct Investment, Net Inflows (BoP, current US$), http:// data.worldbank.org/indicator/BX.KLT.DINV.CD.WD.

83. Jonathan Cummings, James Manyika, Lenny Mendonca, Ezra Greenberg, Steven Aronowitz, Rohit Chopra, Katy Elkin, Sreenivas Ramaswamy, Jimmy Soni, and

Allison Watson, Growth and Competitiveness in the United States: The Role of Its Multinational Companies, McKinsey Global Institute, June 2010.

84. Helpman, *Understanding Global Trade*, 135–137.

85. Ibid., 152–154.

86. Alexander Simoes, United States Data, The Observatory of Economic Complexity, http://atlas.media.mit.edu/en/.

87. R. Colin Johnson, Samsung Breaks Ground on $14 Billion Fab, *EE Times*, May 8, 2015.

88. Boeing, Everett Production Facility: Overview, http://www.boeing.com/company /about-bca/everett-production-facility.page.

89. Census Bureau, Industry Snapshot: Manufacturing, http://thedataweb.rm.census .gov/TheDataWeb_HotReport2/econsnapshot/2012/snapshot.hrml?NAICS=31-33.

90. Philippe Aghion and Rachel Griffith, *Competition and Growth: Reconciling Theory and Evidence* (Cambridge, MA: MIT Press, 2005), 83.

91. David Autor, David Dorn, Gordon H. Hanson, Gary Pisano and Pian Shu, Foreign Competition and Domestic Innovation: Evidence from U.S. Patents, NBER Working Paper 22879, National Bureau of Economic Research, Cambridge, MA, December 2016, 37.

92. Joseph A. Schumpeter, *Capitalism, Socialism, and Democracy* (New York: Harper Perennial Modern Thought, 2008), 83. First published 1942.

93. Bureau of Labor Statistics (BLS), All Employees: Manufacturing [MANEMP].

94. Paul Krugman, Domestic Distortions and the Deindustrialization Hypothesis, NBER Working Paper 5472, National Bureau of Economic Research, Cambridge, MA, March 1996.

95. Ibid., 23.

96. Census Bureau, U.S. Trade in Goods and Services—Balance of Payments (BOP) Basis, February 7, 2017.

97. Ibid.

98. Smith, *The Wealth of Nations*, II.3.1.

99. For a concise discussion of neoclassical economics' difficulty modeling production see Jonathan Schlefer, Entering the Realm of Production, in *The Assumptions Economists Make* (Cambridge, MA: Belknap Harvard, 2012), 99–120.

100. Jagdish Bhagwati, The Computer Chip vs. Potato Chip Debate, *Moscow Times*, September 2, 2010, https://themoscowtimes.com/articles/the-computer-chip-vs -potato-chip-debate-1075.

101. Jagdish Bhagwati, The Manufacturing Fallacy, *Project Syndicate*, August 27, 2010.

102. Christina Romer, Do Manufacturers Need Special Treatment?, *New York Times*, February 4, 2012, http://www.nytimes.com/2012/02/05/business/do-manufacturers -need-special-treatment-economic-view.html?_r=0.

103. Bureau of Labor Statistics (BLS), Civilian Unemployment Rate [UNRATE], FRED, Federal Reserve Bank of St. Louis, https://fred.stlouisfed.org/series/UNRATE.

104. Gregory Tassey, Rationales and Mechanisms for Revitalizing US Manufacturing R&D Strategies, *Journal of Technology Transfer* 35, no. 3 (June 2010): 283. http:// www.scienceofsciencepolicy.net/sites/default/files/attachments/Tassey%20on%20 Manuf%20JTT%20June%202010.pdf.

105. Susan Helper and Howard Wial, Strengthening American Manufacturing: A New Federal Approach (paper, Metropolitan Policy Program, Brookings Institution, Washington, DC, September 2010).

106. W. David McCausland and Ioannis Theodossiou, Is Manufacturing Still the Engine of Growth? *Journal of Post Keynesian Economics* 35, no. 35 (Fall 2012).

107. Robert Heilbroner, The Embarrassment of Economics, *Challenge*, November– December, 1996, 49.

108. Fred Block and Margaret R. Somers, The Power of Market Fundamentalism: Karl Polanyi's Critique (Cambridge, MA: Harvard University Press, 2016), 34.

109. Robert Heilbroner, The Embarrassment of Economics, 47.

110. An accessible overview of the development of behavioral economics is Richard H. Thaler, *Misbehaving: The Making of Behavioral Economics* (New York: Norton, 2015).

111. Paul Romer, The Trouble with Macroeconomics, *American Economist* (forthcoming; initially delivered as the Commons Memorial Lecture of the Omicron Delta Epsilon Society, January 5, 2016), 21, https://www.law.yale.edu/system/files/area /workshop/leo/leo16_romer.pdf.

112. Hugo Sonnenschein, Do Walras' Identity and Continuity Characterize the Class of Community Excess Demand Functions?, *Journal of Economic Theory* 6, no. 4 (1973).

113. Paul Krugman, How Did Economics Get It So Wrong? *New York Times*, September 2, 2009, http://www.nytimes.com/2009/09/06/magazine/06Economic-t.html.

114. Judith Banister, China's Manufacturing Employment and Hourly Labor Compensation, 2002–2009, Bureau of Labor Statistics (BLS), June 7, 2003, 3.

115. Bureau of Labor Statistics (BLS), All Employees: Manufacturing [MANEMP].

116. David H. Autor, David Dorn, and Gordon H. Hanson, The China Shock: Learning from Labor Market Adjustment to Large Changes in Trade, NBER Working Paper 21906, National Bureau of Economic Research, Cambridge, MA, January 2016, 2.

117. Ibid., 37–38.

118. David H. Autor and David Dorn, The Growth of Low-Skill Service Jobs and the Polarization of the US Labor Market, *American Economic Review* 103, no. 5 (2013).

119. David Spector, Is It Possible to Redistribute the Gains from Trade Using Income Taxation?, *Journal of International Economics* 55, no. 2 (December 2001).

120. J. David Richardson, Trade Adjustment Assistance under the United States Trade Act of 1974: An Analytical Examination and Worker Survey, in *Import Competition and Response*, ed. Jagdish Bhagwati (Chicago: University of Chicago Press, 1982), 325.

121. Ibid., 328.

122. Katherine Baicker and M. Marit Rehavi, Policy Watch: Trade Adjustment Assistance, *Journal of Economic Perspectives* 18, no. 2 (Spring 2004): 240–241.

123. Kara M. Reynolds and John S. Palatucci, Does Trade Adjustment Assistance Make a Difference?, *Contemporary Economic Policy* 30, no. 1 (January 2012): 43, 46.

124. Bureau of Labor Statistics (BLS), All Employees: Manufacturing [MANEMP].

125. Nick Timiraos, Aid for Workers Untouched by Debate over Trade Deal, *Wall Street Journal*, May 10, 2015.

126. Reynolds and Palatucci, Does Trade Adjustment Assistance Make a Difference?, 58.

127. Census Bureau, Real Median Family Income in the United States [MEFAINUSA672N], FRED, Federal Reserve Bank of St. Louis, https://fred.stlouisfed.org/series /MEFAINUSA672N.

128. Facundo Alvaredo, Anthony B. Atkinson, Thomas Piketty, Emmanuel Saez, and Gabriel Zucman, The World Wealth and Income Database, http://www.wid.world/.

129. President Barack Obama, The Way Ahead, *The Economist*, October 8, 2016, 23 (citing Census Bureau and Council of Economic Advisors data). Compare Kirby G. Posey, Household Income 2015. American Community Survey Brief ACSBR/15-02 (Washington, DC: Census Bureau, September 2016), 2–3, https://www.census.gov /content/dam/Census/library/publications/2016/demo/acsbr15-02.pdf (2015 U.S. median household income increased 3.8%), and Census Bureau, New American Community Survey Statistics for Income, Poverty and Health Insurance, CB16-159, September 16, 2016, http://www.census.gov/newsroom/press-releases/2016/cb16 -159.html, with Census Bureau, Income, Poverty and Health Insurance Coverage in the United States 2015, CB16-158, September 13, 2016, http://www.census.gov /newsroom/press-releases/2016/cb16-158.html (2015 median U.S. household income increases 5.2%). See Trudi Renwick, How the Census Bureau Measures Income and Poverty, Census Bureau, September 8, 2016, http://blogs.census.gov/2016/09/08 /how-the-census-bureau-measures-income-and-poverty-4/.

130. Jared Bernstein, Meilissa Boteach, Rebecca Vallas, Olivia Golden, Kali Grant, Indivar Dutta-Gupta, Erica Williams, and Valerie Wilson, 10 Solutions to Fight Economic Inequality, Talkpoverty.org, June 10, 2015, https://talkpoverty.org/2015/06/10/solutions-economic-inequality/.

131. Claudia Goldin and Lawrence F. Katz, The Race between Education and Technology: The Evolution of U.S. Educational Wage Differentials, 1890 to 2005, NBER Working Paper 12984, National Bureau of Economic Research, Cambridge, MA, March 2007.

132. Daron Acemoglu and David Autor, Skills, Tasks and Technologies: Implications for Employment and Earnings, *Handbook of Labor Economics*, vol. 4b, ed. David Card and Orley Ashenfelter (Amsterdam: Elsevier, 2011), 1070.

133. National Center for Education Statistics, Fast Facts: Educational Attainment, https://nces.ed.gov/fastfacts/display.asp?id=27.

134. National Science and Technology Council (NSTC), Committee on STEM Education, Federal Science, Technology, Engineering, and Mathematics (STEM) Education: 5-Year Strategic Plan (Washington, DC: White House Office of Science and Technology Policy, May 2013), https://www.whitehouse.gov/sites/default/files/microsites/ostp/stem_stratplan_2013.pdf.

135. Gene M. Grossman and Elhanan Helpman, Growth, Trade, and Inequality, working paper, Princeton University, Princeton, NJ, June 30, 2016, https://www.princeton.edu/~grossman/Growth_Trade_and_Inequality_063016.pdfgr.

136. Randal E. Bryant, Kwang-Ting Cheng, Andrew B. Kahng, Kurt Keutzer, Wojciech Maly, Richard Newton, Lawrence Pileggi, Jan M. Rabaey, and Alberto Sangiovanni-Vincentelli, Limitations and Challenges of Computer-Aided Design Technology for CMOS VLSI, *Proceedings of the IEEE* 89, no. 3 (March 2001).

137. Michael Polanyi, *The Tacit Dimension* (Garden City, NY: Doubleday, 1966), 4.

138. Maria Majewska and Urszula Szulczynska, Methods and Practices of Tacit Knowledge Sharing within an Enterprise: An Empirical Investigation, *Oeconomia Copernicana* 2 (2014).

139. James E. Driskell, Paul H. Radtke, and Eduardo Salas, Virutal Teams: Effects of Technological Mediation on Team Performance, *Group Dynamics: Theory, Research and Practice* 7, no. 4 (December 2003): 317.

140. Nile W. Hatch and David C. Mowery, Process Innovation and Learning by Doing in Semiconductor Manufacturing, *Management Science* 44, no. 11, pt. 1 of 2 (November 1998).

141. These innovation models are explored in Bonvillian and Weiss, *Technological Innovation in Legacy Sectors*, 6–11, 181–196.

142. Gerald Carlino and William R. Kerr, Agglomeration and Innovation, NBER Working Paper 20367, National Bureau of Economic Research, Cambridge, MA, August 2014, 17–20.

143. Stuart S. Rosenthal and William C. Strange, Small Establishments/Big Effects, in *Agglomeration, Organization and Entrepreneurship, Agglomeration Economics*, ed. Edward L. Glaeser (Chicago: University of Chicago Press, 2007), 300.

144. Edward L. Glaeser, Introduction, in Glaeser, *Agglomeration, Organization and Entrepreneurship, Agglomeration Economics*, 7.

145. National Science Board, *Science and Engineering Indicators 2016*, U.S. R&D Expenditures, by Performing Sector and Source of Funds: 2008–2013 (Washington, DC: National Science Board, January 2016).

146. National Science Board, *Science and Engineering Indicators 2016*, Funds Spent for Business R&D Performed in the United States, by Size of Company: 2008–2013 (Washington, DC: National Science Board, January 2016).

147. National Science Board, *Science and Engineering Indicators 2016*, Funds Spent for Business R&D Performed in the United States, by Source of Funds and Selected Industry: 2013 (Washington, DC: National Science Board, January 2016).

148. National Science Board, *Science and Engineering Indicators 2008*, Company and Other Nonfederal Funds for Industrial R&D Performance in the United States, by Industry and Company Size: 2001–05 (Washington, DC: National Science Board, January 2008).

149. Semiconductor Industry Association, *Factbook 2014* (Washington, DC: Semiconductor Industry Association, 2014).

150. John Markoff, Moore's Law Running Out of Room, Tech Looks for a Successor, *New York Times*, May 4, 2016.

151. Tim Cross, After Moore's Law, *The Economist* (Technology Quarterly), March 12, 2016, http://www.economist.com/technology-quarterly/2016-03-12/after-moores-law.

152. Ibid.

153. Dale W. Jorgenson, U.S. Economic Growth in the Information Age, *Issues in Science and Technology* 18, no. 1 (Fall 2001), http://issues.org/18-1/jorgenson/.

154. Nicholas R. Lardy, Manufacturing Employment in China, *PIE Realtime Economic Issues Watch*, December 21, 2015.

155. National Science Board, *Science and Engineering Indicators 2008*, R&D Performed Abroad by Majority-Owned Foreign Affiliates of U.S. Parent Companies, by Selected Industry of Affiliate and Host Region/Country/Economy: 2002–04 (Washington, DC: National Science Board, January 2008); National Science Board, *Science and*

Engineering Indicators 2012, R&D Performed Abroad by Majority-Owned Foreign Affiliates of U.S. Parent Companies, by Selected Industry of Affiliate and Host Region/Country/Economy: 2012 (Washington, DC: National Science Board, January 2012).

156. KPMG, Innovated in China: New Frontier for Global R&D, *China 360*, August 2013.

157. Alex Webb, Apple's Cook Announces New China R&D Center on Beijing Trip, *Bloomberg*, August 16, 2016, and Arjun Kharpal, Apple Plans Two More R&D Centers in China as its Challenges in the Country Continue, *CNBC*, March 17, 2017.

158. Census Bureau, 2014 Statistics of U.S. Businesses Annual Data Tables by Establishment, U.S., NAICS sectors, larger employment sizes up to 10,000+, September 29, 2016, https://www.census.gov/data/tables/2014/econ/susb/2014-susb-annual.html.

159. Jae Song, David J. Price, Fatih Guvenen, Nicholas Bloom, and Till von Wachter, Firming Up Inequality, NBER Working Paper 21199, National Bureau of Economic Research, Cambridge, MA, May 2016.

160. Al Gini, Work, Identity and Self: How We Are Formed by the Work We Do, *Journal of Business Ethics* 17 (1998).

161. Schumpeter, *Capitalism, Socialism, and Democracy*, 106.

5. Advanced Manufacturing Emerges at the Federal Level

1. Bureau of Labor Statistics (BLS), Spotlight on Statistics, The Recession of 2007–2009 (Washington, DC: Bureau of Labor Statistics, February 2012), 2, http://www.bls.gov/spotlight/2012/recession/pdf/recession_bls_spotlight.pdf.

2. Bureau of Labor Statistics (BLS), *The Economics Daily*, December 8, 2009, http://www.bls.gov/opub/ted/2009/ted_20091208.htm.

3. The authors gratefully acknowledge that material for this chapter and chapters 6 and 7 initially appeared in William B. Bonvillian, Advanced Manufacturing: A New Policy Challenge, *Annals in Science and Technology* 1, no. 1 (2017).

4. Gregory Tassey, Beyond the Business Cycle: The Need for a Technology-Based Growth Strategy (paper, NIST Economic Analysis Office, Washington, DC, February 2012), 2, http://www.nist.gov/director/planning/upload/beyond-business-cycle.pdf.

5. In this period, there were a number of significant articles on the U.S. manufacturing predicament that provided a foundation for the studies reviewed here, although the MIT study discussed was in many ways the most extensive and far-reaching. Such articles included the following: Gregory Tassey, Rationales and Mechanisms for Revitalizing U.S. Manufacturing R&D Strategies, *Journal of Technology Transfer* 35, no. 3 (June 2010); Erica Fuchs and Randolph Kirchain, Design for Location? The Impact

of Manufacturing Offshore on Technology Competitiveness in the Optoelectronics Industry, *Management Science* 56, no. 12 (December 2010): 2323–2349; Susan Houseman, Christopher Kurz, Paul Lengermann, and Benjamin Mandel, Offshoring Bias in U.S. Manufacturing, *Journal of Economic Perspectives* 25, no. 2 (2011); Dan Breznitz and Peter Cowhey, America's Two Systems of Innovation: Recommendations for Policy Changes to Support Innovation Production and Job Creation, report (San Diego, CA: Connect Innovation Institute, February 2012); Robert D. Atkinson, Luke A. Stewart, Scott M. Andes, and Stephen Ezell, Worse than the Great Depression: What the Experts Are Missing about American Manufacturing Decline (Washington, DC: Information Technology and Innovation Foundation, March 2012); Susan Helper, Timothy Kruger, and Howard Wial, Why Does Manufacturing Matter? Which Manufacturing Matters? (paper, Metropolitan Policy Program, Brookings Institution, Washington, DC, February 2016), https://www.brookings.edu/wp-content/uploads/2016/06/0222 _manufacturing_helper_krueger_wial.pdf.; Stephanie Shipp, N. Gupta, B. Lal, J. Scott, C. Weber, M. Finin, M. Blake, S. Newsome, and S. Thomas, Emerging Global Trends in Advanced Manufacturing, Report P-4603 (Arlington, VA: Institute for Defense Analysis, March 2012), https://www.wilsoncenter.org/sites/default/files/Emerging _Global_Trends_in_Advanced_Manufacturing.pdf; William B. Bonvillian, Reinventing American Manufacturing: The Role of Innovation, *Innovations* 7, no. 3 (2012); Gary P. Pisano and Willy C. Shih, *Producing Prosperity* (Cambridge, MA: Harvard Business School Publishing, 2012). Numerous reports on manufacturing in this period are listed and summarized in Yiliu Zhang, Daniel Kuhner, Kathryn Hewitt, and Queenie Chan, Future of U.S. Manufacturing—A Literature Review, pts. I–III, MIT Washington Office, Washington, DC, August 2011, January 2012, July 2012, http://dc.mit.edu /resources/policy-resources.

6. For disclosure, author Bonvillian, as director of MIT's Washington Office, served as an adviser on these efforts to President Hockfield and to MIT's subsequent Production in the Innovation Economy (PIE) studies, http://web.mit.edu/pie/.

7. MIT Roundtable on Developing National Innovation Policies, Summary, March 1, 2010, http://dc.mit.edu/sites/default/files/MIT%20Innovation%20Roundtable.pdf.

8. MIT Washington Office, MIT Reports to the President, 2009–10, MIT Efforts on Policy Innovation Challenges, (Cambridge, MA.: Massachusetts Institute of Technology 2010), 1-32-1-33, http://dc.mit.edu/sites/default/files/pdf/2010%20MIT%20 DC%20Annual%20Report.pdf [and search: dc.mit.edu under "Policy Resources/ Manufacturing"]

9. Ibid., 1-33-1-34; MIT Roundtable on The Future of Manufacturing Innovation— Advanced Technologies, Summary, March 29, 2010, http://dc.mit.edu/sites/default/ files/pdf/Roundtable%20The%20Future%20of%20Manufacturing%20Innovation. pdf [search: dc.mit.edu under "Policy Resources/Manufacturing"]; Peter Dizikes, A Manufacturing Renaissance for America? At an MIT Forum Experts Examine New Ways to Pursue a Good Old Idea: Making Things, MIT News Office, March 31, 2009, http://news.mit.edu/2010/future-manufacture-0331.

10. Michael Dertouzos, Robert Solow, Richard Lester, and the MIT Commission on Industrial Production, *Made in America: Regaining the Productive Edge* (Cambridge, MA: MIT Press, 1989); James Womack, Daniel T. Jones, and Daniel Roos, *The Machine That Changed the World: The Story of Lean Production* (New York: Free Press, 1990).

11. MIT Roundtable, The Future of Manufacturing Innovation—Advanced Technologies, March 29, 2010, 3.

12. Suzanne Berger and the MIT Industrial Performance Center, *How We Compete: What Companies around the World Are Doing to Make It in Today's Global Economy* (New York: Doubleday Currency, 2006).

13. MIT Roundtable, The Future of Manufacturing Innovation—Advanced Technologies, March 29, 2010, 5.

14. Ibid., 5–8.

15. Suzanne Berger and the MIT Task Force on Production and Innovation, *Making in America* (Cambridge, MA: MIT Press, 2013), vi–vii.

16. Christina Romer, Do Manufacturers Need Special Treatment?, *New York Times*, February 4, 2012, http://www.nytimes.com/2012/02/05/business/do-manufacturers -need-special-treatment-economic-view.html?_r=0.

17. Stephen Ezell, Our Manufacturers Need a U.S. Competitiveness Strategy, Not Special Treatment, The Innovation Files, Information Technology and Innovation Foundation (ITIF), February 9, 2016, http://www.innovationfiles.org/our-manufacturers -need-a-u-s-competitiveness-strategy-not-special-treatment/.

18. President's Council of Advisors on Science and Technology (PCAST), Report to the President on Ensuring American Leadership in Advanced Manufacturing (Washington, DC: PCAST, June 24, 2011), https://obamawhitehouse.archives.gov/sites /default/files/microsites/ostp/pcast-advanced-manufacturing-june2011.pdf.

19. Ibid., PCAST Chairs' introductory letter, i.

20. Senator Barack Obama, 2004 Democratic National Convention Keynote Address (speech, Democratic National Convention, Boston, July 27, 2004).

21. PCAST, Ensuring American Leadership in Advanced Manufacturing, ii.

22. Ibid., v.

23. Ibid., iii.

24. Ibid., iii–v, 33.

25. Ibid., iv.

26. White House, Office of the Press Secretary, President Obama Launches Advanced Manufacturing Partnership, June 24, 2011, https://obamawhitehouse.archives.gov

/the-press-office/2011/06/24/president-obama-launches-advanced-manufacturing
-partnership.

27. Andrew Liveris, *Make It in America: The Case for Reinventing the Economy* (Hoboken, NJ: John Wiley and Sons, 2011).

28. Names of AMP1.0 Steering Committee members from companies and universities can be found in President's Council of Advisors on Science and Technology (PCAST), Advanced Manufacturing Partnership Steering Committee, Report to the President on Capturing Domestic Competitive Advantage in Advanced Manufacturing (Washington, DC: PCAST, July 2012), vii, https://obamawhitehouse.archives.gov /sites/default/files/microsites/ostp/pcast_amp_steering_committee_report_final_july _17_2012.pdf; White House, Office of the Press Secretary, Report to President Outlines Approaches to Spur Domestic Manufacturing Investment and Innovation, press release, July 12, 2012, https://obamawhitehouse.archives.gov/the-press-office/2012 /07/17/report-president-outlines-approaches-spur-domestic-manufacturing-investm

29. White House, Office of the Press Secretary, President Obama Launches Advanced Manufacturing Partnership, statement at Carnegie Mellon University, June 24, 2011.

30. MIT News Office, Hockfield to Co-chair U.S. Manufacturing Partnership, June 24, 2011, http://news.mit.edu/2011/hockfield-obama-manufacturing-0624.

31. Overseen by the AMP Steering Committee (which consisted of the industry CEOs and university presidents), the effort was led by staff from the firms, universities, and agencies listed (mixed in with outside experts consulted) in Appendix B, 47–50 and vi, in PCAST, Advanced Manufacturing Partnership Steering Committee, Report to the President on Capturing Domestic Competitive Advantage in Advanced Manufacturing, https://obamawhitehouse.archives.gov/sites/default/files/microsites/ostp/pcast_amp _steering_committee_report_final_july_17_2012.pdf. For disclosure, author Bonvillian worked on the AMP1.0 and AMP2.0 reports as a member of the assigned MIT support group.

32. Jessica Chu, American Made? MIT Forum Examines the Role of Manufacturing in Rebuilding the Economy, MIT News Office, September 16, 2011, http://news.mit .edu/2011/manufacturing-event-pie-0916.

33. Ibid.

34. Appendix B lists names of both outside experts and AMP participants from its member universities and companies; names from the participant organizations identify those who participated in the work groups and in development of the report proposals. See PCAST, Advanced Manufacturing Partnership Steering Committee, Report to the President on Capturing Domestic Competitive Advantage in Advanced Manufacturing, July 2012, Appendix B, 47–50. Annexes to the report that contain detailed reports from each work group can be accessed through https://www .obamawhitehouse.archives.gov/administration/eop/ostp/pcast/docsreports.

35. PCAST, Advanced Manufacturing Partnership Steering Committee, Report to the President on Capturing Domestic Competitive Advantage, July 2012, Annex 6, Regional Meeting Summaries, https://obamawhitehouse.archives.gov/sites/default /files/microsites/ostp/amp_final_report_annex_6_amp_regional_meeting_summaries _july_update.pdf.

36. Eliza Eddison, Survey of Federal Manufacturing Efforts, MIT Washington Office, Washington, DC, September 2010, http://dc.mit.edu/resources/policy-resources; Aneesh Anand, Survey of Selected Federal Manufacturing Programs at NIST, DOD, DOE, and NSF, MIT Washington Office, Washington, DC, September 2014, http://dc.mit .edu/resources/policy-resources.

37. President's State of the Union Address, Full Text, *Wall Street Journal*, February 12, 2012, http://blogs.wsj.com/washwire/2013/02/12/full-text-obamas-state-of-the-union -address/.

38. White House, President Obama to Announce New Efforts to Support Manufacturing Innovation—Administration Proposed New National Network to Support Manufacturing, March 9, 2012, https://obamawhitehouse.archives.gov/the-press -office/2012/03/09/president-obama-announce-new-efforts-support-manufacturing -innovation-en; https://obamawhitehouse.archives.gov/photos-and-video/video/2012 /03/09/president-obama-speaks-manufacturing#transcript.

39. White House, Remarks by the President in the State of the Union Address, February 12, 2013, https://www.whitehouse.gov/the-press-office/2013/02/12/remarks -president-state-union-address.

40. Communication with Jason S. Miller, August 29, 2016.

41. PCAST, Advanced Manufacturing Partnership Steering Committee, Report to the President on Capturing Domestic Competitive Advantage, July 2012, 4.

42. Ibid., 1–2.

43. Ibid., 9.

44. Ibid., 12.

45. Ibid., 17.

46. AMP's focus was on production technologies, but it was not the first to pursue development of critical technology lists. In 1989, Senator Jeff Bingaman (D-N. Mex.) pushed the Defense Department and the White House Office of Science and Technology Policy to study and develop critical technologies needed across civilian and military sectors. This effort was also taken up by the Young Commission (see chapter 3), which surveyed nine industries on their critical technology needs. See Kent H. Hughes, *Building the Next American Century—The Past and Future of American Economic Competitiveness* (Washington, DC: Woodrow Wilson Center Press, 2005), 249, 255–257.

47. PCAST, Advanced Manufacturing Partnership Steering Committee, Report to the President for Capturing Domestic Competitive Advantage, July 2012, 21–24.

48. In the United States, both the Defense Department (DOD) and the National Aeronautics and Space Administration (NASA) have developed similar but somewhat different Technology Readiness Levels (TRLs); AMP applied the DOD terminology. See Department of Defense (DOD), Office of the Assistant Secretary for Research and Engineering, Technology Readiness Levels Guidance, updated May 13, 2011, http://www.acq.osd.mil/chieftechnologist/publications/docs/TRA2011.pdf.

49. PCAST, Advanced Manufacturing Partnership Steering Committee, Report to the President for Capturing Domestic Competitive Advantage, July 2012, 28–29.

50. The faculty commission and researchers are named at the front of the first volume: Berger and the MIT Task Force on Production in the Innovation Economy, *Making in America*, ii–iv. For disclosure, author Bonvillian was adviser to the study.

51. Ibid.

52. Richard M. Locke and Rachel L. Wellhausen, eds., *Production in the Innovation Economy* (Cambridge, MA: MIT Press, 2014).

53. These study areas are delineated in more detail on the MIT Production in the Innovation Economy (PIE) website, http://web.mit.edu/pie/research/index.html.

54. The major and Main Street firms are discussed in Berger and the MIT Task Force on Production in the Innovation Economy, *Making in America*, 25–64, 91–120.

55. Ibid., 65–90.

56. Ibid., 121–154.

57. Ibid., 155–178.

58. Ibid., 179–198.

59. Ibid., 6–7. See also statement on the PIE website, http://web.mit.edu/pie/research/index.html.

60. Berger and the MIT Task Force on Production in the Innovation Economy, *Making in America*, 7.

61. As listed in note 5 of this chapter, a number of articles and studies had considered aspects of innovation in developing manufacturing policies, although the MIT PIE study was the most far-reaching.

62. Berger and the MIT Task Force on Production in the Innovation Economy, *Making in America*, 17–20, 44–64.

63. Ibid., 20.

64. Jonas Nahm and Edward S. Steinfeld, The Role of Innovative Manufacturing in High-Tech Product Development: Evidence from China's Renewable Energy Sector, in Locke and Wellhausen, *Production in the Innovation Economy*, 139–174.

65. Berger and the MIT Task Force on Production in the Innovation Economy, *Making in America*, 91–102, 104–111.

66. Ibid., 111–114.

67. Elizabeth Reynolds, Hiram Semel, and Joyce Lawrence, Learning by Building: Complementary Assets and the Migration of Capabilities in U.S. Innovative Firms, in Locke and Wellhausen, *Production in the Innovation Economy*, 51–80.

68. Berger and the MIT Task Force on Production in the Innovation Economy, *Making in America*, 155–178. Sanjay Sarma of MIT was a major contributor on the "mass customization" model.

69. See, for example, Deloitte Ltd. and the Manufacturing Institute, Boiling Point? The Skills Gap in U.S. Manufacturing (2011), 6, www.themanufacturinginstitute.org /~/media/A07730B2A798437D98501E798C2E13AA.ashx, which found that 82% of manufacturing senior executives reported moderate to serious gaps in availability of qualified, skilled candidates; 74% of manufacturers reported that these shortages affected their ability to expand operations.

70. Andrew Weaver and Paul Osterman , Skills and Skills Gaps in Manufacturing, in Locke and Wellhausen, *Production in the Innovation Economy*, 17–50.

71. Andrew Weaver and Paul Osterman, The New Skill Production System, in Locke and Wellhausen, *Production in the Innovation Economy*, 76–77.

72. Berger and the MIT Task Force on Production in the Innovation Economy, *Making in America*, 21–23.

73. PCAST, Advanced Manufacturing Partnership 2.0 Steering Committee, Report to the President on Accelerating U.S. Advanced Manufacturing (Washington, DC: PCAST, October 2014), vii (list of AMP2.0 participants), https://obamawhitehouse .archives.gov/sites/default/files/microsites/ostp/PCAST/amp20_report_final.pdf.

74. Participants in AMP2.0 from Steering Committee firms and schools, as well as Obama administration participants, are listed in ibid., 52–55. For disclosure, author Bonvillian was a participant for MIT.

75. Ibid., 17.

76. Ibid., 66–70.

77. Ibid., 18.

78. Peter Dizikes, Reif Briefs Obama in White House—Advanced Manufacturing Partnership 2.0 Delivers Report on Developing Innovation Based Growth, MIT News

Office, October 28, 2014, http://news.mit.edu/2014/reif-briefs-obama-innovation-economy-1028.

79. White House, Office of the Press Secretary, Fact Sheet: President Obama Announces New Actions to Further Strengthen U.S. Manufacturing, Oct. 27, 2014, https://obamawhitehouse.archives.gov/the-press-office/2014/10/27/fact-sheet-president-obama-announces-new-actions-further-strengthen-us-m.

80. National Academies, Board on Science, Technology and Economic Policy, Innovation Policy Forum on Reinventing U.S. Advanced Manufacturing—A Review of the Advanced Manufacturing Partnership 2.0 Report, October 27, 2014, http://sites.nationalacademies.org/PGA/step/PGA_152473.

81. National Academy of Engineering (NAE), Making Value for America, report (Washington, DC: National Academies Press, 2016), http://www.nap.edu/catalog/19483/making-value-for-america-embracing-the-future-of-manufacturing-technology.

82. Ibid., vii.

83. Ibid., 1.

84. Ibid., 11.

85. Ibid., 20–45.

86. Ibid., 47–59.

87. Ibid., 40–45.

88. Ibid., 71–81, 104–107.

89. S.1468, 113th Cong., 2nd Sess. (2014), https://www.govtrack.us/congress/bills/113/s1468/text. It was reported as amended by the Senate Commerce Committee, chaired by Senator Jay Rockefeller (D-W.Va.), on August 26, 2014.

90. Report of the Committee on Science, Space and Technology, Report on H.R. 2996, Revitalize American Manufacturing and Innovation Act, H.R. Rep. No. 113-599, 113th Cong., 2nd Sess., September 15, 2014, Section IV (Hearing Summary).

91. H.R. 2996, Revitalize American Manufacturing and Innovation Act, 113th Cong., 2nd Sess., Congress.gov, bill actions, https://www.congress.gov/bill/113th-congress/house-bill/2996/actions.

92. Report of the Senate Committee on Commerce, Science and Transportation, on S.1468, Revitalize American Manufacturing and Innovation Act, S. Rep. No. 113-247, 113th Cong., 2nd Sess., August 26, 2014, Legislative History section, https://www.congress.gov/congressional-report/113th-congress/senate-report/247/1.

93. Report of the Committee on Science, Space and Technology, Report on H.R. 2996, Revitalize American Manufacturing and Innovation Act, H.R. Rep. No. 113-599, 113th Cong., 2nd Sess., September 15, 2014, Section IV (Hearing Summary).

94. William B. Bonvillian, Advanced Manufacturing Policies and Paradigms for Innovation, *Science* 342, no. 6163 (December 6, 2013): 1173–1175.

95. See, for example, on Germany, Forschungsunion and Acatech (National Academy of Science and Engineering), Securing the Future of German Manufacturing Industry, Recommendations for Implementing the Strategic Initiative Industrie 4.0, Final Report of the Industrie 4.0 Working Group, April 2013, http://docplayer.net /254711-Securing-the-future-of-german-manufacturing-industry-recommendations -for-implementing-the-strategic-initiative-industrie-4-0.html. On China, see Scott Kennedy, Made in China 2025, Center for Strategic and International Studies (CSIS), June 1, 2015 (summary of State Council's May 2015 manufacturing roadmap plan), https://www.csis.org/analysis/made-china-2025; China Unveils Internet Plus Action Plan to Fuel Growth, Xinhua, July 4, 2015 (announcement from the State Council to "integrate mobile Internet, cloud computing, big data and the Internet of Things with modern manufacturing"), http://english.cntv.cn/2015/05/22 /VIDE1432284846519817.shtml; China Establishes Fund to Invest in Advanced Manufacturing (State Council announces $3.05b fund), Xinhua, June 8, 2016, http://english.gov.cn/news/top_news/2016/06/08/content_281475367382490.htm; T. Whang, Y. Ahang, H. Yu, and F-Y. Wang, eds., *Advanced Manufacturing Technology in China: A Roadmap to 2050* (Chinese Academy of Sciences field-specific report) (Berlin: Springer, 2012). On Britain, see Manufacturing Technology Centre, Challenging the Boundaries of Manufacturing, http://www.the-mtc.org; Catapult, High Value Manufacturing Centres, https://hvm.catapult.org.uk/hvm-centres/. On Singapore, see Michael Tan and Jeffrey Chua, Industry 4.0 and Singapore Manufacturing, opinion, *Straits Times* (Singapore), February 10, 2016, http://www.straitstimes.com /opinion/industry-40-and-singapore-manufacturing; Economic Development Board of Singapore, Future of Manufacturing in Singapore (presentation, March 2015) (summarizing the Future of Manufacturing); $500m/5 year plan announced by the Deputy Prime Minister, Budget Speech in 2013, http://www.smartindustry.com /assets/Uploads/SI-PS-Singapore-Inofpack.pdf. On India, see Make in India Initiative (launched September 25, 2014, by Prime Minister Narenda Modi), http://www .makeinindia.com/home. On Japan, see Ministry of Economy, Trade and Industry (METI), Government of Japan, Growth Strategy 2016, Establishment of Public-Private Council for the 4th Industrial Revolution (components: regulatory reforms, individual healthcare services with personalized data and robotics, zero inventory supply chain, fintech open innovation system, smart factory, drone delivery, Internet of Things integration with accompanying cybersecurity, tripling of university R&D, and five strategic research centers), October 2016; Noriyuki Mita, Deputy Director General, Manufacturing Industries Bureau, METI, Responding to the Fourth Industrial Revolution (presentation, October 2016); Innovation 25 Council, Innovation 25—Creating the Future, Challenging Unlimited Possibilities, interim report, February 26, 2007, http://japan.kantei.go.jp/innovation/interimbody_e.html; Hideshi Semba, Science Counselor, Japan Mission to the European Union, Innovation Policy of Japan (presentation, June 15, 2012), http://www.j-bilat.eu/documents/seminar/as_2

/presentation_as2_hs.pdf. For a general discussion, see Shipp et al., *Emerging Global Trends in Advanced Manufacturing*.

6. The Advanced Manufacturing Innovation Institute Model

1. Michael Molnar (NIST), Steven Linder (DOD), and Mark Shuart (DOE), Building a New Partnership—The National Network for Manufacturing Innovation, presentation to the National Council for Advanced Manufacturing (NACFAM), April 29, 2016, 7.

2. Robert M. Solow, *Growth Theory, An Exposition*, 2nd ed. (New York: Oxford Univ. Press, 2000) (Nobel Prize Lecture, Dec. 8, 1987).

3. Paul Romer, "Endogenous Technological Change", *Journal of Political Economy*, 98(5) (1990), 72–102. http://www.nber.org/papers/w3210.pdf.

4. Richard Nelson, *National Systems of Innovation* (New York: Oxford University Press 1993), 3–21, 505–523. This "innovation organization" factor is elaborated on at length in William B. Bonvillian and Charles Weiss, *Technological Innovation in Legacy Sectors* (New York: Oxford University Press 2015), 25–27, 181–186, 190–192.

5. Vannevar Bush, *Science: The Endless Frontier* (Wash., D.C.: Government Printing Office 1945). http://www.nsf.gov/od/lpa/nsf50/vbush1945.htm.

6. Donald Stokes, *Pasteur's Quadrant, Basic Science and Technological Innovation* (Washington, DC: Brookings Institution Press, 1997).

7. Lewis Branscomb and Phillip Auerswald, *Between Invention and Innovation, An Analysis of Funding for Early-State Technology Development*. NIST GCR 02-841 (Washington, DC: NIST. November 2002), Part I: Early Stage Development. http://www.atp.nist.gov/eao/gcr02-841/contents.htm.

8. Vernon Ruttan, *Technology Growth and Development: An Induced Innovation Perspective* (New York: Oxford Univ. Press, 2001).

9. Bonvillian and Weiss, *Technological Innovation in Legacy Sectors*, 181–186.

10. William B. Bonvillian and Richard Van Atta, ARPA-E and DARPA, Applying the DARPA Model to Energy Innovation, *Journal of Technology Transfer* 36, no. 5, Oct. 2011, 469.

11. William B. Bonvillian, The New Model Innovation Agencies—An Overview, *Science and Public Policy*. Sept. 26, 2013, 1093.

12. Suzanne Berger and the MIT Task Force on Production and Innovation, *Making in America* (Cambridge, MA.: MIT Press, 2013).

13. Larry D. Browning and Judy C. Shetler, *Sematech: Saving the U.S. Semiconductor Industry* (College Station, TX: Texas A&M Press, 2000).

14. Bonvillian and Weiss, *Technological Innovation in Legacy Sectors*, 184–186.

15. James Womack, Daniel Jones and Daniel Roos, *The Machine that Changed the World.* (New York: Free Press, 1990).

16. Jonas Nahm and Edward Steinfeld, Scale-Up Nation: China's Specialization in Innovative Manufacturing." *World Development* 54 (2013): 288–300.

17. Bonvillian and Weiss, *Technological and Related Innovation*, 14–20, 55–66.

18. Philip Shapira and Jan Youtie, Presentation on the Next Production Revolution: Institutions for Technology Diffusion, Conference on Smart Industry: Enabling the Next Production Revolution, OECD and Sweden Ministry of Enterprise and Innovation, Stockholm, September 18, 2016.

19. David C. Mowery, The relationship between intrafirm and contractual forms of industrial research in American manufacturing, 1900–1940, *Explorations in Economic History,* 20, 1983, 351–374. The authors appreciate information from Ezequiel Zylberberg, post doctoral associate at MIT's Industrial Performance Center, on the literature cited here on innovation intermediaries.

20. Wesley M. Cohen and Daniel A. Levinthal, Absorptive Capacity: A New Perspective on Learning and Innovation, *Administrative Science Quarterly* 35, 1990, 128–152.

21. Robert W. Rycroft and Don E. Kash, Innovation Policies for Complex Technologies, *Issues in Science and Technology* 16, 1, Fall 1999, http://issues.org/16-1/rycroft/.

22. Jeremy Howells, Intermediation and the role of intermediaries in innovation, *Research Policy* 35, 2006, 715–728.

23. Christopher Freeman, Formal Scientific and Technical Institutions in the National System of Innovation, in B.-Å. Lundvall, ed., *National Systems of Innovation: Towards a Theory of Innovation and Interactive Learning* (London, New York: Pinter, 1992), 169–187.

24. Timothy J. Sturgeon, The New Digital Economy—Innovation, Economic Development and Measurement (United Nations Conference on Trade and Development (UNCTAD) ICT Analysis Section report March 25, 2017—in draft), 15–17.

25. The description of the challenge is from Paul Boris, The Industrial Internet of Things (IoT) at Work in Heavy Industry (General Electric Digital White Paper, General Electric Company, Fairfield, CT, September 22, 2016).

26. Discussion with Adele Ratcliff, Director, International Manufacturing and Innovation, Office of Manufacturing and Industrial Base Policy, Office of the Secretary of Defense, September 26, 2016.

27. Molnar et al., Building a New Partnership—The National Network for Manufacturing Innovation, 7. For a subsequent and more detailed summary of the role

of the institutes in the context of a new institute offering, see, Department of Defense (DOD) Mantech, Robots in Manufacturing Environments Manufacturing Innovation Institute, Proposers Day, slide presentation, August 15, 2016, https://s3 .amazonaws.com/sitesusa/wp-content/uploads/sites/802/2016/08/RIME_Proposers _Day_final.pdf.

28. The Defense Production Act, Pub. L. No. 81-774, 50 U.S.C. § 2061 et seq. (1950), was a Cold War and Korean War industrial mobilization tool.

29. Aside from Mantech, DARPA deputy director Ken Gabriel was involved in the AMP1.0 effort, and DARPA program manager Mick Maher led a sizable portfolio of DARPA advanced manufacturing R&D and advised on the AMP reports.

30. Discussion with Adele Ratcliff, DOD, September 26, 2016.

31. See the discussion of ARPA-E in William B. Bonvillian and Richard Van Atta, ARPA-E and DARPA: Applying the DARPA Model to Energy Innovation, *Journal of Technology Transfer* 36, no. 5 (October 2011).

32. Information in this section is drawn from the America Makes website, https:// www.americamakes.us/about/overview.

33. Descriptions of the institutes are drawn from their websites, and descriptions of the manufacturing technologies they aim to advance are drawn from National Science and Technology Council (NSTC), Subcommittee on Advanced Manufacturing, Advanced Manufacturing—A Snapshot of Priority Technology Areas across the Federal Government (Washington, DC: White House, Office of Science and Technology Policy, April 2016), 36–39, https://www.whitehouse.gov/sites/whitehouse.gov /files/images/Blog/NSTC%20SAM%20technology%20areas%20snapshot.pdf.

34. Details in Table 6.1 on the institutes are from the descriptions of each institute on their websites, available through, https://www.manufacturing.gov/nnmi -institutes/.

35. White House, Office of the Press Secretary, Fact Sheet: President Obama Announces Winner of New Smart Manufacturing Innovation Institute, June 20, 2016, 4, https:// www.whitehouse.gov/the-press-office/2016/06/20/fact-sheet-president-obama -announces-winner-new-smart-manufacturing.

36. Deloitte Ltd., Manufacturing USA: A Third-Party Evaluation of Program Design and Progress, report (Washington, DC: Deloitte, January 2017), 8–21, https:// www2.deloitte.com/content/dam/Deloitte/us/Documents/manufacturing/us-mfg -manufacturing-USA-program-and-process.pdf.

37. Ibid., 22–27.

38. Ibid., 28–35.

39. Ibid., 36–45.

40. This section draws on information prepared by NIST's Advanced Manufacturing National Program Office, slide presentation, July 2016; IACMI website, http://iacmi.org; and discussion with Craig Blue, CEO, and Robin Pate, workforce and communications director, IACMI, September 1, 2016. Bryan G. Dods succeeded Blue as IACMI CEO at the end of 2016 when the latter returned to Oak Ridge National Laboratory.

41. Oak Ridge National Laboratory, DOE, Manufacturing Demonstration Facility website, http://web.ornl.gov/sci/manufacturing/mdf/.

42. IACMI, Composites Workforce 2015, http://iacmi.org/wp-content/uploads/2016/04/IACMI_OnePager_FINAL_2015_UPDATE.pdf.

43. Indiana Economic Development Corporation, Indiana Adds Chief Innovation Officer to Economic Development Corporation, August 16, 2016, http://iacmi.org/2016/08/16/indiana-adds-chief-innovation-officer-economic-development-corporation/.

44. This section is based on discussions with Yoel Fink, CEO of AFFOA, on July 14, 2016; his slide presentation in a webinar for AFFOA participants on July 15, 2016; and the AFFOA website, join.affoa.org.

45. Points in this section are from a communication from Stephen Luckowski, U.S. Army, AFFOA federal program manager, October 25, 2016.

46. Stephen Luckowski, U.S. Army, AFFOA federal program manager, AFFOA 2017: First Projects, presentation to the American Fiber Manufacturers Association, Washington, DC, October 20, 2016, 30–34.

47. Ibid., 11–12; AFFOA website, Membership.

48. Communication from Luckowski, October 26, 2016.

49. Presentation by Luckowski, October 20, 2016, 8–10.

50. President's Council of Advisors on Science and Technology (PCAST), Advanced Manufacturing Partnership 2.0 Steering Committee, Report to the President on Accelerating U.S. Advanced Manufacturing (Advanced Manufacturing Partnership AMP2.0 Report) (Washington, DC: PCAST, October 2014), 22–25, 59–60, https://www.whitehouse.gov/sites/default/files/microsites/ostp/PCAST/amp20_report_final.pdf. Of course, these are not the only criteria that should be considered. For example, in comments to the authors on December 27, 2016, Adams Nager of ITIF suggested a fifth: "Filling a market gap: Does the MTA have a barrier that prevents adequate/socially optimal level of investment from private actors?"

51. Michael Molnar, NIST director of the Advanced Manufacturing National Program Office, presentation at MForesight National Summit 2016, Washington, DC, September 29, 2016.

52. See recommendations in Deloitte, Manufacturing USA, 58.

53. Ibid., 54.

54. PCAST, Accelerating U.S. Advanced Manufacturing, 4–5, 26–28, 64.

55. Ibid., 6, 30.

56. This work has not attempted to address the intellectual property issues faced by the institutes, because they are still a work in progress. Forming technology development collaborations between small and large firms as well as university researchers creates complex IP challenges. A work group of the Advanced Manufacturing Partnership focused on the IP framework for institutes, creating a series of guidelines. These included that institutes should not seek to hold IP themselves since that would be a disincentive for firms and researchers, that background IP should continue to be controlled by the IP holder, and that project agreements among groups of participants could set IP terms for the technology development project. See PCAST, Accelerating U.S. Advanced Manufacturing, Annex 30, Network for Manufacturing Innovation: Intellectual Property Management, https://www.whitehouse.gov /sites/default/files/microsites/ostp/PCAST/amp2.0_annex25-31_nnmi_analysis.pdf. Different institutes are forming somewhat different IP approaches based on their particular technology focus areas. As will be discussed, AFFOA has created a patent aggregator role for itself, particularly for university-held patents.

57. Deloitte, Manufacturing USA, 52–53.

58. Discussion with Prof. John Hart, MIT, April 19, 2017.

59. Discussion with Jason Miller, NEC, August 31, 2016.

60. President's Council of Advisors on Science and Technology (PCAST), Advanced Manufacturing Partnership Steering Committee, Report to the President on Capturing Domestic Competitive Advantage in Advanced Manufacturing (AMP1.0 Report) (Washington, DC: PCAST, July 2012), 21, https://www.whitehouse.gov/sites /default/files/microsites/ostp/pcast_amp_steering_committee_report_final_july_17 _2012.pdf.

61. Deloitte, Manufacturing USA, 55.

62. Ibid., 57.

63. The AMP study groups, however, did consult extensively with the National Governors Association in preparing their reports.

64. National Governors Association, Making Our Future—What States Are Doing to Encourage Growth of Manufacturing through Innovation, Entrepreneurship and Investment, an NGA Policy Academy Report, National Governors Association, Washington, DC, January 28, 2013, http://www.nga.org/cms/home/nga-center-for-best -practices/center-publications/page-ehsw-publications/col2-content/main-content -list/making-our-future.html.

65. National Governors Association, Seven States Selected to Develop Economic Strategies Focused on the Growth of Advanced Manufacturing Industries, press statement, October 6, 2011. (The states were Colorado, Connecticut, Illinois, Kansas, Massachusetts, New York, and Pennsylvania.)

66. See Economic Development Administration, Investing in Manufacturing Communities Partnership (IMCP), https://www.eda.gov/challenges/imcp/.

67. William B. Bonvillian, The Problem of Political Design in Federal Innovation Organization, in *The Science of Science Policy*, ed. Kaye Husbands Fealing, Julia Lane, John Marburger, and Stephanie Shipp (Stanford, CA: Stanford University Press, 2011), 302–326.

68. National Institute of Standards and Technology (NIST), Guidance on Institute Performance Metrics: National Network for Manufacturing Innovation, Advanced Manufacturing National Program Office, Gaithersburg, MD, August 2015, https://www.manufacturing.gov/files/2016/03/nnmi_draft_performance.pdf.

69. Deloitte, Manufacturing USA, 62–64.

70. Ibid., 48.

71. NSTC, Subcommittee on Advanced Manufacturing, Advanced Manufacturing—A Snapshot.

72. Government Accountability Office, Defense Additive Manufacturing—DOD Needs to Systematically Track Department-wide 3D Printing Efforts, GAO 16-56, Government Accountability Office, Washington, DC, October 2015.

73. Fraunhofer Gesellschaft, Fraunhofer Institutes and Research Establishments, http://www.fraunhofer.de/en/institutes-research-establishments/.

74. University College London, Evidence Submission to the House of Commons Committee on Science and Technology, December 2010, http://www.publications.parliament.uk/pa/cm201011/cmselect/cmsctech/619/619vw22.htm.

75. Work Foundation, Technology Innovation Centres, submission to the House of Commons, September 2010, 6, http://www.theworkfoundation.com/assets/docs/knowledgeeconomy%20newsletters/tics%20-%20applying%20the%20fraunhofer%20model%20to%20create%20an%20effective%20innovation%20ecosystem%20in%20the%20uk.pdf.

76. Herman Hauser for Lord Mandelson, Secretary of State, The Current and Future Roles of Technology and Innovation Centres in the UK, 13, https://interact.innovateuk.org/documents/1524978/2139688/The+Current+and+Future+Role+of+Technology+and+Innovation+Centres+in+the+UK/e1b5f4ae-fec8-495d-bbd5-28dacdfee186.

77. Statute of the Fraunhofer Gesellschaft, as revised in 2010, http://www.izm.fraunhofer.de/content/dam/izm/en/documents/Institut/Statute-of-the-Fraunhofer-Gesellschaft_tcm63-8090.pdf.

78. Ibid., Section 20, The Institutes.

79. Ibid., Section 21, Institute Management.

80. Ibid.

81. House of Commons, Committee on Science and Technology, Technology and Innovation Centres (2011), 23–30, http://www.publications.parliament.uk/pa/cm201011 /cmselect/cmsctech/619/619.pdf.

82. Ibid., Section 5, Operational Model, 33, http://www.publications.parliament.uk /pa/cm201011/cmselect/cmsctech/619/61908.htm.

83. For a general discussion, see John Goddard, Douglas Robertson, and Paul Vallance, Universities, Technology and Innovation Centres and Regional Development: The Case of the North-East of England, *Cambridge Journal of Economics* 36, no. 3 (2012): 609–627, http://cje.oxfordjournals.org/content/36/3/609.short. (Abstract.)

84. NSF's Engineering Center program is an exception. See NSF Engineering Research Centers (ERC) website, https://www.nsf.gov/funding/pgm_summ.jsp?pims_id=5502; and the ERC Association website, http://erc-assoc.org.

85. See, for example, Fraunhofer Center for Sustainable Energy Systems (CSE), http://www .cse.fraunhofer.org/about and http://www.cse.fraunhofer.org/about-fraunhofer-cse /labs-and-facilities.

86. MForesight (Alliance for Manufacturing Foresight) website, http://mforesight .org/about-us/#vision.

87. Data cited in a discussion by Charles Wessner, Georgetown University, MForesight National Summit 2016, Washington, DC, September 29, 2016.

88. Germany Trade and Invest, Industrie 4.0—Smart Manufacturing for the Future (Berlin: Germany Trade and Invest, July 2014), 20, http://www.gtai.de/GTAI/Content /EN/Invest/_SharedDocs/Downloads/GTAI/Brochures/Industries/industrie4.0-smart -manufacturing-for-the-future-en.pdf.

89. Manufacturing to Get Boost from 3D Printing, *Straits Times* (Singapore), March 17, 2016, http://www.straitstimes.com/business/manufacturing-to-get-boost-from-3d -printing.

90. National Academy of Sciences, Science, Technology, and Economic Policy (STEP) Board, *21st Century Manufacturing: The Role of the Manufacturing Extension Partnership* (Washington, DC: National Academies Press, 2013), Appendix A1, Canada's Industrial Research Assistance Program (IRAP), 196, 201.

91. Germany Trade and Invest, Industrie 4.0, 12.

92. Scott Kennedy, Made in China 2025, Center for Strategic and International Studies (CSIS), June 1, 2015 (summary of State Council's May 2015 manufacturing

roadmap plan), https://www.csis.org/analysis/made-china-2025; China Unveils Internet Plus Action Plan to Fuel Growth, Xinhua, July 4, 2015 (announcement from the State Council to "integrate mobile Internet, cloud computing, big data and the Internet of Things with modern manufacturing"), http://english.cntv.cn /2015/05/22/VIDE1432284846519817.shtml; People's Republic of China, The State Council, China Establishes Fund to Invest in Advanced Manufacturing (State Council announces $3.05b fund), Xinhua, June 8, 2016, http://english.gov.cn/news/top _news/2016/06/08/content_281475367382490.htm.

93. NSTC, Subcommittee on Advanced Manufacturing, Advanced Manufacturing—A Snapshot, Table 1, Selected Examples of Federal Investment in Advanced Materials Manufacturing, 8–9.

94. National Institute of Standards and Technology (NIST), Closing Tech Gaps Can Fortify Advanced Manufacturing (Gaithersburg, MD: National Institute for of Standards and Technology [NIST], November 17, 2016), https://www.nist.gov/news -events/news/2016/11/closing-tech-gaps-can-fortify-advanced-manufacturing-and -save-100-billion.

7. Start-up Scale-up: Addressing the Manufacturing Challenge for Start-ups

1. Jonathan Huebner, A Possible Declining Trend in Worldwide Innovation, *Journal of Technological Forecasting and Social Change* 72 (2005): 980–986, http://accelerating .org/articles/InnovationHuebnerTFSC2005.pdf.

2. Ibid., 981.

3. Ibid., 983, 985.

4. See, for example, John M. Smart, Measuring Innovation in an Accelerating World, *Technological Forecasting and Social Change* 72 (2005): 988–995, Acceleration Studies Forum, http://accelerating.org/articles/huebnerinnovation.html; Robert Adler, Entering a Dark Age of Innovation, *New Scientist*, July 2, 2005, https://www.newscientist .com/article/dn7616-entering-a-dark-age-of-innovation/. Compare Tyler Cowen, *The Great Stagnation* (New York: Dutton Penguin, 2011).

5. As discussed in chapters 4 and 9, and as noted later in this chapter, Gordon has argued that the IT innovation wave did not lead to the enduring productivity gains of prior innovation waves. See Robert Gordon, *The Rise and Fall of American Growth* (Princeton, NJ: Princeton University Press, 2015).

6. Peter Theil, What Happened to the Future, Founder's Fund, 2011, http:// foundersfund.com/the-future/; Pascal Goby, Facebook Investor Wants Flying Cars, Not 140 Characters, *Business Insider*, July 30, 2011, http://www.businessinsider.com /founders-fund-the-future-2011-7.

7. Lewis M. Branscomb and Philip E. Auerswald, Between Invention and Innovation, NIST Report GCR 02-841 (Gaithersburg, MD: National Institute of Standards and Technology, November 2002). See also Lewis M. Branscomb and Philip E. Auerswald, *Taking Technical Risks: How Innovators, Executives and Investors Manage High Tech Risks* (Cambridge, MA: MIT Press, 2001).

8. Branscomb and Auerswald preferred the term "Darwinian Sea" to "Valley of Death," arguing that the concept of a valley suggested a linear model of innovation, whereas innovation was instead an inherently more complex system. See Branscomb and Auerswald, Between Invention and Innovation, 35–37.

9. Ibid., 1.

10. Martin Weitzman, Recombinant Growth, *Quarterly Journal of Economics* 113, no. 2 (May 1998): 333.

11. Branscomb and Auerswald, Between Invention and Innovation, 4–5.

12. Robert E. Litan, Inventive Billion Dollar Firms: A Faster Way to Grow, SSRN Working Paper No. 1721608, *Social Science Research Network (SSRN)*, December 1, 2010, https://papers.ssrn.com/sol3/papers.cfm?abstract_id=1721608. The authors draw on, for ideas that appear in this chapter from this point forward, Peter S. Singer and William B. Bonvillian, "Innovation Orchards:" Helping Tech Start-Ups Scale, Washington, D.C.: Information Technology and Innovation Foundation (ITIF) March 2017, http://www2.itif.org/2017-innovation-orchards.pdf?_ga=1 .205014288.1283359406.1491740117.

13. Arnobio Morelix, E. J. Reedy, and Joshua Russell, 2016 Kauffman Index of Growth Entrepreneurship, National Trends (Kansas City, MO: Kauffman Foundation, May 2016), 14, http://www.kauffman.org/~/media/kauffman_org/microsites /kauffman_index/growth/kauffman_index_national_growth_entrepreneurship _2016_report.pdf.

14. Ian Hathaway and Robert Litan, Declining Business Dynamism in the United States: A Look at States and Metros, paper (Washington, DC: Brookings Institution Economic Studies, May 2014), 1, 2, http://www.brookings.edu/~/media/research/files /papers/2014/05/declining%20business%20dynamism%20litan/declining_business _dynamism_hathaway_litan.pdf.

15. Morelix, Reedy, and Russell, 2016 Kauffman Index of Growth Entrepreneurship, 14.

16. Ibid., 15, 17.

17. Ibid., 20.

18. Jorge Guzman and Scott Stern, The State of American Entrepreneurship: New Estimates of the Quantity and Quality of Entrepreneurship for 15 U.S. States,

1998–2014, NBER Working Paper 22095, National Bureau of Economic Research, Cambridge, MA, March 2016, http://jorgeg.scripts.mit.edu/homepage/wp-content /uploads/2016/03/Guzman-Stern-State-of-American-Entrepreneurship-FINAL .pdf.

19. Ibid., 6.

20. Ibid., 7–8.

21. Ibid., 32–33.

22. Catherine Fazio, Jorge Guzman, Fiona Murray, and Scott Stern, A New View of the Skew: A Quantitative Assessment of the Quality of American Entrepreneurship (paper, MIT Laboratory for Innovation Science and Policy, February 2016), 15, http:// innovation.mit.edu/assets/A-New-View_Final-Report_5.4.16.pdf.

23. Elizabeth Reynolds, Hiram Semel, and Joyce Lawrence, Learning by Building: Complementary Assets and Migration of Capabilities in U.S. Innovative Firms, in *Production in the Innovation Economy*, ed. Richard Locke and Rachel Wellhausen (Cambridge, MA: MIT Press, 2014), 81–108.

24. Gaddy, Benjamin, Varun Sivaram, Timothy Jones, and Libby Wayman. Venture Capital and Cleantech: The Wrong Model for Energy Innovation. *Social Science Research Network (SSRN)*, June 2, 2016. https://ssrn.com/abstract=2788919. See also Benajmin Gaddy, Varun Sivaram, and Francis O'Sullivan, Venture Capital and Cleantech, Working Paper, MIT Energy Initiative, July 2016, http://energy.mit.edu/wp -content/uploads/2016/07/MITEI-WP-2016-06.pdf.

25. Gaddy, Sivaram, and O'Sullivan, Venture Capital and Cleantech, July 2016, 1.

26. Ibid., 7.

27. Ibid., 5.

28. Benjamin E. Gaddy, Sivaram, Jones, and Wayman, Venture Capital and Cleantech, June 2, 2016, 20.

29. Price Waterhouse Coopers (PwC) with the National Venture Capital Association, Investment by Industry, PwC MoneyTree Report, Data, Q1 1995- Q2 2016.

30. Gaddy, Sivaram, and O'Sullivan, Venture Capital and Cleantech, July 2016, 10–12.

31. See PwC with the National Venture Capital Association, Investment by Industry. In the 2016 PwC MoneyTree Report Q4 2016 sectors were reclassified. While the same trends as before hold, the data (which is revised in every report) and sector definitions for older reports are no longer posted on the main PwC MoneyTree web page. The most recent report can be accessed at http://www.pwc.com/us/en/technology /moneytree.html.

32. National Venture Capital Association (NVCA), *Yearbook 2016* (Washington DC: NVCA, 2016), 63.

33. Ibid., 66.

34. David Braun, Mergers and Acquisitions: 2015 a Record Breaking Year, January 22, 2016, https://successfulacquisitions.net.

35. NVCA, *Yearbook 2016*, 69–70.

36. Jumpstart Our Business Startups (JOBS) Act, H.R. 3606, 112th Cong., 2nd Sess. (2012). See Securities and Exchange Commission, JOBS Act, https://www.sec.gov/spotlight/jobs-act.shtml. For a general discussion, see Chance Barnett, Crowdfunding Sites in 2014, *Forbes*, August 29, 2014; Stuart Dredge, Kickstarter's Biggest Hits—Why Crowdfunding Now Sets the Trends, *The Guardian*, April 17, 2014.

37. Ruth Simon, Few Businesses Take Advantage of Mini-IPOs, *Wall Street Journal*, July 6, 2016.

38. President's Council of Advisors on Science and Technology (PCAST), Advanced Manufacturing Partnership 2.0 Steering Committee, Report to the President on Accelerating U.S. Advanced Manufacturing (Advanced Manufacturing Partnership AMP2.0 Report) (Washington, DC: PCAST, October 2014), 38–43, 77–87, https://www.whitehouse.gov/sites/default/files/microsites/ostp/PCAST/amp20_report_final.pdf.

39. For a summary of potential federal financing mechanisms for start-ups or smaller firms for production scale-up, see Peter Singer, Manufacturing Scale-up: Summary of 14 Relevant Federal Financing Programs, report (Washington, DC: MIT Washington Office, May 27, 2014), http://dc.mit.edu/resources/policy-resources.

40. PCAST, Accelerating U.S. Advanced Manufacturing, 41–42.

41. Ibid., 42.

42. See discussion and sources cited in William B. Bonvillian and Charles Weiss, *Technological Innovation in Legacy Sectors* (New York: Oxford University Press, 2015), 44.

43. William B. Bonvillian, Donald Trump's Voters and the Decline of American Manufacturing, *Issues in Science and Technology* 32, no. 4 (Summer 2016): 37–38. For a general discussion, see Bonvillian and Weiss, *Technological Innovation in Legacy Sectors*, 37–54, 87–95, 215–239.

44. Bonvillian, Donald Trump's Voters and the Decline of American Manufacturing.

45. Lawrence Summers, Speech to IMF Economic Forum, November 8, 2013, https://www.youtube.com/watch?v=KYpVzBbQIX0.

46. World Bank, GDP Growth Per Capita (Annual Percentage)—United States, 1960–2015, http://data.worldbank.org/indicator/NY.GDP.MKTP.KD.ZG?locations=US.

47. McKinsey Global Institute, Poorer than Their Parents? A New Perspective on Income Inequality, July 2016, http://www.mckinsey.com/global-themes/employment-and-growth/poorer-than-their-parents-a-new-perspective-on-income-inequality.

48. Jason Furman, Chairman, Council of Economic Advisors, Trends in Labor Force Participation, presentation, National Press Club, August 6, 2015, https://obamawhitehouse.archives.gov/sites/default/files/docs/20150806_labor_force_participation_retirement_research_consortium.pdf.

49. Bonvillian and Weiss, *Technological Innovation in Legacy Sectors*, ix, 2–5, 7, 197, 253.

50. Erik Brynjolfsson and Andrew McAfee, *The Second Machine Age: Work, Progress, and Prosperity in a Time of Brilliant Technologies* (New York: Norton, 2014); Eric Brynjolfsson and Andrew McAfee, *Race against the Machine* (Lexington, MA: Digital Frontier, 2011). Compare David Autor, Why Are There Still So Many Jobs? The History and Future of Workplace Automation, *Journal of Economic Perspectives* 29, no. 3 (Summer 2015): 3–30.

51. Robert J. Gordon, Does the "New Economy" Measure Up to the Great Inventions of the Past? NBER Working Paper 7835, National Bureau of Economic Research, Cambridge, MA, August 2000, http://www.nber.org/papers/w7833, published in *Journal of Economic Perspectives* 14, no. 4 (Fall 2000): 49–74.

52. Bonvillian and Weiss, *Technological Innovation in Legacy Sectors*, 25, 184.

53. Ashlee Vance, *Elon Musk: Tesla, SpaceX and the Quest for a Fantastic Future* (New York: Ecco, HarperCollins, 2015).

54. This debate stems from Paul Romer, Endogenous Technological Change, *Journal of Political Economy* 98, no. 5 (1990), http://pages.stern.nyu.edu/~promer/Endogenous.pdf.

55. L. Rafael Reif, A Better Way to Deliver Innovation to the World, op-ed, *Washington Post*, May 28, 2015, https://www.washingtonpost.com/opinions/a-better-way-to-deliver-innovation-to-the-world/2015/05/22/35023680-fe28-11e4-8b6c-0dcce21e223d_story.html.

56. Cluster theory began with economist Alfred Marshall, who noted the importance of specialized industry sectors in particular regions, which he called "industrial districts." See Alfred Marshall, *Principles of Economics* (London: Macmillan, 1890). See, for example, Michael Porter, *Competitive Advantage of Nations* (New York: Free Press, 1990); Adrian T. H. Kuah, Cluster Theory and Practice: Advantages for the Small Business Locating in a Vibrant Cluster, *Journal of Research in Marketing and Entrepreneurship* 4, no. 3 (2002): 206–228 (sources on cluster theory).

57. The range of available programs is summarized in Joseff Kolman, Summary of Federal, State, University, and Private Programs for Supporting Emerging Technology,

MIT Washington Office, Washington, DC, July 10, 2015, http://dc.mit.edu/resources /policy-resources. See also William B. Bonvillian, The New Model Innovation Agencies: An Overview, *Science and Public Policy* 41, no. 4 (2014): 429–430 (programs from the 1980s to bridge the technology "Valley of Death").

58. This section draws on Nathalie Bockelt, Bridging the Innovation Gap in the U.S. Energy System (paper, MIT Washington Office, Washington, DC, February 2016), http://dc.mit.edu/resources-links.

59. Cyclotron Road website, http://www.cyclotronroad.org/home.

60. Cyclotron Road, in addition to getting support from Lawrence Berkeley Lab and DOE, has formed a 501c3 nonprofit called Activation Energy, which is mission aligned with CR but not associated with DOE. Through this entity, CR has received funds from the state of California's Clean Energy Commission (CEC) and corporate partners. See Johanna Wolfson, Director, Tech to Market (T2M), Department of Energy, Office of Energy Efficiency and Renewable Energy (EERE), communication, November 19, 2016.

61. Ibid.

62. Cyclotron Road, 2015 Report—A New Pathway for Hard Technology: Supporting Energy Innovators at Cyclotron Road, 2015, 10, http://static1.squarespace.com /static/543fdfece4b0faf7175a91ec/t/55efcf96e4b0fe570119a737/1441779606809 /Cyclotron_Road_A_New_Pathway_final.pdf.

63. Cyclotron Road, Building a Home for Hard Science Innovators—The Cyclotron Road Pilot, 2016 Annual Report, Berkeley CA.: Cyclotron Road March 2016, https://static1 .squarespace.com/static/543fdfece4b0faf7175a91ec/t/58cad7399de4bb7b62b0750f /1489688386385/2016-Cycloton-Road-Annual-Report-Online.pdf.

64. Argonne National Laboratory, Argonne Launches First Tech Incubator, May 20, 2016, http://www.anl.gov/articles/argonne-launches-first-tech-incubator. See also Chain Reaction Innovations website, http://chainreaction.anl.gov.

65. The Lab-Embedded Entrepreneurship program is a generalized model inspired by Cyclotron Road that has been developed at DOE's Advanced Manufacturing Office, along with EERE's Tech-to-Market office. This framework is being applied at two other labs—the Chain Reaction Innovations (CRI) program at Argonne National Lab and the Innovation Crossroads program at Oak Ridge National Lab (ORNL). Innovators selected to participate receive a fellowship, seed funding, and access and support at the lab. One aim of CRI is to make use of Argonne's expertise in battery storage capability, while Innovation Crossroads intends to leverage ORNL's strengths in additive manufacturing. Approximately $4 million will fund the first cohort of entrepreneurs at CRI through joint efforts between DOE and Argonne, and a similar figure will fund the first cohort for Innovation Crossroads

through joint funding from DOE and ORNL. See Wolfson, communication, November 19, 2016.

66. According to Johanna Wolfson, Fraunhofer's headquarters in Munich has recently adopted the TechBridge model at a corporate level and is working to grow it across the Fraunhofer Institutes in Germany. It is an interesting development—Fraunhofer came over to the United States, U.S. staff there created TechBridge to fill a U.S. need, and perhaps only in the United States could something like TechBridge have been developed. But then the TechBridge concept crossed back over the Atlantic; ironically, the model's success over time might be not in the United States but in Germany, depending on U.S. commitments to "hard"-technology start-ups. See Wolfson, communication, November 19, 2016.

67. TechBridge leverages the extensive resources of Fraunhofer CSE and the greater Fraunhofer network (including the Fraunhofer Energy Alliance of over 15 Fraunhofer Institutes) to perform industry-driven validation and demonstration projects that derisk disruptive technologies developed out of start-ups. While TechBridge did obtain some initial funding from venture capital firms, most venture capital investors proved very hesitant to fund the derisking of technologies until the model was proven. Specifically, TechBridge found that a rigid venture capital investing framework tended to create barriers to spending management funds on such derisking work. TechBridge, however, gained traction from an award from the Department of Energy in 2010, which provided $1 million in funding over three years. The investment helped TechBridge test out and refine its business concept and verify that the model could provide real value. See Wolfson, communication, November 19, 2016.

68. Ibid.

69. Fraunhofer Center for Sustainable Energy Systems, TechBridge website, http://www.cse.fraunhofer.org/techbridge/method.

70. Fraunhofer CSE Research Facilities website, http://www.cse.fraunhofer.org/about-fraunhofer-cse/labs-and-facilities.

71. Bockelt, Bridging the Innovation Gap, 16.

72. Johanna Wolfson, discussion with Nathalie Bockelt, MIT Washington Office, November 24, 2015.

73. Other models relevant to the "innovation orchard" concept include Case Western Reserve Sears [thinkbox], Invent NMU, and Otherlab, summarized in Benjamin J. Chazen, Venture Capital and Research Centers, MIT Washington Office, Washington, DC, August 2016, http://dc.mit.edu/resources/policy-resources. See also Dragon Innovation website, https://dragoninnovation.com (firm with facilities in Cambridge, MA, San Francisco, CA, and Shenzhen, China, which advises on and certifies

manufacturing design and production costs for new firms, and links start-ups with contract manufacturers for prototyping and initial production; originally organized to support crowdfunding but has broadened its mission).

74. Rafael Reif, Introducing The Engine, op-ed, *Boston Globe*, October 26, 2016. For disclosure, the authors of this book were involved for MIT in analyzing the "innovation orchard" models that contributed to The Engine.

75. Rob Matheson, The Engine closes its first fund for over $150 million, *MIT News*, April 6, 2017, http://news.mit.edu/2017/the-engine-closes-first-fund-150-million -0406.

76. Reif, Introducing The Engine.

77. This section draws on Katherine W. Nazemi, From Startup to Scale-Up: How Connecting Startups with Local Manufacturers Can Help Move New Technologies from Prototype to Production (paper, MIT Washington Office, Washington, DC, July 2016), http://dc.mit.edu/sites/default/files/doc/Connecting%20Startups%20to%20Small%20 Manufacturers%20Nazemi%20July%202016.docx.

78. Reynolds, Semel, and Lawrence, Learning by Building.

79. In part because of the successful work at Greentown Labs and MassMEP, DOE has focused on the manufacturing knowledge gap that prevents entrepreneurs from being ready to scale their hardware products. In September 2016, DOE announced that it would work with public and private sector partners to create a set of training materials to educate energy entrepreneurs on manufacturing fundamentals. This initiative, called Build4Scale, focuses on teaching entrepreneurs basics of manufacturing processes, core design-for-manufacturing principles, material selection trade-offs, and more. The intent is not to create manufacturing experts out of technical entrepreneurs but rather to provide a window into the manufacturing decision-making landscape so that entrepreneurs are better able to engage with experts and are better prepared for scale-up. Because this awareness can help avoid costly mistakes later, DOE believes that a small investment in training will yield greater economic return on its sizable research and development investments. See Wolfson, communication, November 19, 2016. See also Department of Energy (DOE), Office of Energy Efficiency and Renewable Energy, Build4Scale, http://energy.gov /eere/articles/build4scale-training-cleantech-entrepreneurs-manufacturing-success; Department of Energy (DOE), Office of Energy Efficiency and Renewable Energy website, http://energy.gov/eere/technology-to-market/build4scale-manufacturing -training-cleantech-entrepreneurs.

80. This section draws on Johanna Wolfson, Director of Tech-to-Market, DOE EERE, Emerging Models for a Better Innovation Pathway, DOE Office of Energy Efficiency and Renewable Energy, August 25, 2016 (presentation slides), and further discussions with Dr. Wolfson, August 25, 2016.

8. Workforce Education and Advanced Manufacturing

1. Statistics compiled in National Association of Manufacturers, Top 20 Facts about Manufacturing (2016), http://www.nam.org/Newsroom/Facts-About-Manufacturing/ (from Bureau of Economic Analysis, Census Bureau, Commerce Department, and Bureau of Labor Statistics data).

2. Stephen Gold, The Competitive Edge: Manufacturing's Multiplier Effect—It's Bigger than You Think, *Industry Week*, September 2, 2014, http://www.industryweek.com /global-economy/competitive-edge-manufacturings-multiplier-effect-its-bigger-you -think (citing ESA data). Compare, Robert Z. Lawrence, Does Manufacturing Have the Largest Employment Multiplier for the Domestic Economy? (blog) (Washington, D.C.: Peterson Institute of International Economics March 22, 2017, https://piie.com/blogs /realtime-economic-issues-watch/does-manufacturing-have-largest-employment -multiplier-domestic (argues multiplier effect includes foreign as well as domestic jobs).

3. The Manufacturing Institute and Deloitte, Overwhelming Support: U.S. Public Opinions on the Manufacturing Industry (report, 2014), 1, http://www2.deloitte.com /content/dam/Deloitte/us/Documents/manufacturing/us-mfg-public-perception -manufacturing-021315.PDF.

4. Craig Giffi, Ben Dollar, Jennifer McNelly, and Gardner Carrick, The Skills Gap in U.S. Manufacturing: 2015 and Beyond (Deloitte LLC, 2015).

5. Andrew Weaver and Paul Osterman, The New Skill Production System: Policy Challenges and Solutions in Manufacturing Labor Markets, in *Production in the Innovation Economy*, ed. Richard Locke and Rachel Wellhausen (Cambridge, MA: MIT Press, 2014), 17–50; Paul Osterman and Andrew Weaver, Skills and Skill Gaps in Manufacturing, in ibid., 51–80.

6. Jessica Nicholson and Regina Powers, The Pay Premium for Manufacturing Workers as Measured by Federal Statistics, ESA Issue Brief #05-15 (Washington, DC: U.S. Department of Commerce, Economics and Statistics Administration, October 2, 2015), http:// www.esa.doc.gov/sites/default/files/the-pay-premium-for-manufacturing-workers-as -measured-by-federal-statistics.pdf.

7. Susan Helper, Timothy Krueger, and Howard Wial, Why Does Manufacturing Matter? Which Manufacturing Matters? (paper, Metropolitan Policy Program, Brookings Institution, Washington, DC, February 2012), 4–5, https://www.brookings.edu /wp-content/uploads/2016/06/0222_manufacturing_helper_krueger_wial.pdf.

8. Susan Helper, How to Make American Manufacturing Great Again: Real Clear Policy, *The Mark-Up*, September 15, 2016.

9. Ken Jacobs, Zohar Perla, Ian Perry, and Dave Graham-Squire, *Producing Poverty: The Public Cost of Low Wage Production Jobs in Manufacturing* (Berkeley, CA: UC Berkeley Center for Labor Research and Education, May 2016), 3 (eight of the ten states with

the highest participation of production workers in public assistance programs are in the South).

10. Catherine Ruckelhaus and Sarah Leberstein, Manufacturing Low Pay (report National Employment Law Project [NELP], New York, November 2014), 6–7.

11. Nick Timiraos and Janet Adamy, U.S. Household Incomes Surged 5.2% in 2015, First Gain since 2007, *Wall Street Journal*, September 13, 2016, http://www.wsj.com /articles/u-s-household-incomes-surged-5-2-in-2015-ending-slide-1473776295 (based on Census Bureau data); Census Bureau, Income, Poverty and Health Insurance Coverage in the United States 2015, CB16-158, September 13, 2016, http:// www.census.gov/newsroom/press-releases/2016/cb16-158.html (2015 median U.S. household income increases 5.2%). See earlier discussion of this data in chapter 4, including another survey reporting a somewhat lower number. Concerning the slow wage recovery, see National Employment Law Project, The Low Wage Recovery, Data Brief, April 2014, http://www.nelp.org/content/uploads/2015/03/Low-Wage -Recovery-Industry-Employment-Wages-2014-Report.pdf.

12. Kevin Finneran, Middle Class Muddle, *Issues in Science and Technology* 33, no. 1 (Fall 2016): 40.

13. Osterman and Weaver, Skills and Skill Gaps in Manufacturing.

14. Bureau of Labor Statistics (BLS), Occupational Employment Statistics, 51-0000 Production Occupations, May 2015, http://www.bls.gov/oes/current/oes_stru.htm#51 -0000 (can compare wages for higher- and lower-skill manufacturing occupations).

15. See Bureau of Labor Statistics (BLS), Concepts and Methodology, http://www.bls .gov/cps/documentation.htm#concepts. For a more general discussion, see Elka Torpey, Got Skills, Think Manufacturing, *BLS Career Outlook*, June 2014, http://www.bls .gov/careeroutlook/2014/article/manufacturing.htm.

16. The difficulty of defining these categories is discussed in Jonathan Rothwell, Defining Skilled Technical Work, *Issues in Science and Technology* 33, no. 1 (Fall 2016): 47–51; Andrew Reamer, Better Jobs Information Benefits Everyone, *Issues in Science and Technology* 33, no. 1 (Fall 2016): 58–63.

17. Osterman and Weaver, Skills and Skill Gaps in Manufacturing, 17.

18. Ibid., 25, citing BLS Occupational Employment Statistics. For a more general discussion, see Patricia Panchak, Manufacturing's Wage and Job Security Problem, *Industry Week*, May 12, 2015, http://www.industryweek.com/compensation -strategies/manufacturings-wage-and-job-security-problem; Ruckelhaus and Leberstein, Manufacturing Low Pay, 5–8.

19. Madeline J. Goodman, Anita M. Sands, and Richard J. Coley, *America's Skills Challenge: Millennials and the Future* (Princeton, NJ: Educational Testing Service, 2015), https://www.ets.org/s/research/29836/.

20. Alicia Sasser Modestino, The Importance of Middle-Skill Jobs, *Issues in Science and Technology* 33, no. 1 (Fall 2016): 42.

21. Ibid.

22. Harry Holzer, Higher Education Workforce Policy: Creating More Skilled Workers (and Jobs for Them to Fill) (Washington, DC: Brookings Institution, 2014).

23. Achieve, The Future of the U.S. Workforce: Middle Skills and the Growing Importance of Postsecondary Education, September 2012, http://www.achieve.org/files /MiddleSkillsJobs.pdf; Harry J. Holzer and Robert I. Lerman, The Future of Middle-Skills Jobs (paper, Brookings Institution, Washington, DC, 2009), www.brookings.edu /~/media/Files/rc/papers/2009/02_middle_skill_jobs_holzer/02_middle_skill_jobs _holzer.pdf; Anthony P. Carnevale, N. Smith, and J. Strohl, Help Wanted: Projections of Jobs and Education Requirements through 2018 (Washington, DC: Georgetown University Center on Education and the Workforce, 2010), https://cew.georgetown .edu/wp-content/uploads/2014/12/fullreport.pdf.

24. Anthony P. Carnevale, Tamara Jayasundera, and Artem Gulish, America's Divided Recovery: College Haves and Have-Nots (Washington, DC: Georgetown University Center on Education and the Workforce, 2016), 2, https://cew.georgetown.edu/wp -content/uploads/Americas-Divided-Recovery-web.pdf.

25. Ibid., 3.

26. Maximiliano Dvorkin, Jobs Involving Routine Tasks Aren't Growing, Federal Reserve Bank of St. Louis, January 4, 2016, https://www.stlouisfed.org/on-the -economy/2016/january/jobs-involving-routine-tasks-arent-growing.

27. Carnevale, Jayasundera, and Gulish, America's Divided Recovery, 4.

28. Richard B. Freeman, *America Works: The Exceptional U.S. Labor Market* (New York: Russell Sage Foundation, 2007), 3.

29. Gary S. Becker, *Human Capital: A Theoretical and Empirical Analysis, with Special Reference to Education* (New York: National Bureau of Economic Research, 1975).

30. Pedro Nuno Teixeira, Gary Becker's Early Work on Human Capital, *IZA Journal of Labor Economics* 12, no. 3 (November 2014), section 4.2.

31. Suzanne Berger and the MIT Task Force on Production in the Innovation Economy, *Making in America* (Cambridge, MA: MIT Press, 2013), 18–20, 45–64, 115–120.

32. Robert Atkinson, Restoring Investment in America's Economy (report, Information Technology and Innovation Foundation [ITIF], Washington, DC, June 13, 2016), 8, http://www2.itif.org/2016-restoring-investment.pdf?_ga=1.113675271.1482316035 .1476207219.

33. German Federal Ministry for Economic Affairs and Energy, Make It in Germany: Introducing the German Mittelstand, http://www.make-it-in-germany.com/en/for

-qualified-professionals/working/mittelstand. This section draws on Dylan Binnie, Designed in California, Built in Oregon—Important Lessons for America to Learn from the German Workforce Education System (paper, Georgetown University, Washington, DC, May 10, 2016).

34. German Federal Ministry for Economic Affairs and Energy, The German Mittelstand: Facts and Figures about German SMEs, SME-shares in Germany in % (table), 2016, http://www.bmwi.de/English/Redaktion/Pdf/wirtschaftsmotor-mittelstand -zahlen-und-fakten-zu-den-deutschen-kmu,property=pdf,bereich=bmwi2012,sprache =en,rwb=true.pdf.

35. German Federal Ministry for Economic Affairs and Energy, The German Mittelstand.

36. Ibid.

37. The discussion here draws on Heike Solga, Paula Protsch, Christian Ebner, and Christian Brzinsky-Fay, The German Vocational Education and Training System: Its Institutional Configuration, Strengths, and Challenges, Discussion Paper SP I 2014-502 (WZB Berlin Social Science Center, 2014), https://bibliothek.wzb.eu/pdf/2014 /i14-502.pdf; David Soskice, Reconciling Markets and Institutions: The German Apprenticeship System, in *Training and the Private Sector*, ed. Lisa Lynch (NBER and University of Chicago Press, January 1994), 25–60, http://www.nber.org/chapters /c8776; Binnie, Designed in California, 6–9.

38. Soskice, Reconciling Markets and Institutions, 29–30.

39. Solga et al., The German Vocational Education and Training System, 13.

40. Fraunhofer Academy, Leitbild Der Fraunhofer Academy, 2016, http://www .academy.fraunhofer.de/de/ueber-uns/profil-selbstverstaendnis/leitbild.html.

41. President's Council of Advisors on Science and Technology (PCAST), Advanced Manufacturing Partnership 2.0 Steering Committee, Report to the President on Accelerating U.S. Advanced Manufacturing (Advanced Manufacturing Partnership AMP2.0 Report) (Washington, DC: PCAST, October 2014), 34.

42. Ibid., Appendix 2, 71–73.

43. Ibid., 35.

44. Automotive Manufacturing Technical Education Collaborative (AMTEC), http:// autoworkforce.org/about-amtec/.

45. White House, Ready to Work: Job-Driven Training and American Opportunity, July 2014, 13, https://www.whitehouse.gov/sites/default/files/docs/skills_report.pdf.

46. Discussion drawn from PCAST, Report to the President on Accelerating U.S. Advanced Manufacturing, 33–34.

47. Ibid., 34.

48. Ibid.

49. Florida Advanced Technology Education (FLATE) website, http://fl-ate.org /about-us/impact/. See also Infographic of Pathways (Which Are Not Linear), FLATE, http://fl-ate.org/wp-content/uploads/2014/12/10_2016-ET-Highlights.pdf.

50. Florida Department of Education, 2015–16 Frameworks, Manufacturing (pre-college through college framework for manufacturing education) website, http:// www.fldoe.org/academics/career-adult-edu/career-tech-edu/curriculum-frameworks /2015-16-frameworks/manufacturing.stml.

51. PCAST, Report to the President on Accelerating U.S. Advanced Manufacturing, 36.

52. Vannevar Bush, *Science, the Endless Frontier: A Report to the President on a Program for Postwar Scientific Research* (Washington, DC: U.S. Government Printing Office, July 1945; reissued by the National Science Foundation on NSF's tenth anniversary, July 1960), https://archive.org/stream/scienceendlessfr00unit/scienceendlessfr00unit_djvu.txt.

53. The Scientific and Advanced Technology Act of 1992, Pub. L. No. 102-476 (1992) (created the Advanced Technical Education program at NSF), summarized at https:// www.congress.gov/bill/102nd-congress/senate-bill/1146/all-info.

54. This summary draws from Maggie Lloyd, Review of the NSF's Advanced Tech-nological Education (ATE) Program: ATE's Role in Advanced Manufacturing Education and Training, report (Washington, DC: MIT Washington Office, February 2013), http://dc.mit.edu/sites/default/files/pdf/MIT%20Review%20of%20NSF%20ATE%20 Program.pdf.

55. Ibid., 5.

56. See Florida Advanced Technology Education (FLATE), Regional and Statewide Impacts, http://fl-ate.org/about-us/impact/; Florida Advanced Technology Education (FLATE), Regional and Statewide Impacts, http://fl-ate.org/about-us/impact/#sthash .N2cKo2c5.dpuf.

57. FLATE, Regional and Statewide Impacts; http://fl-ate.org/about-us/impact /#sthash.N2cKo2c5.dpuf.

58. Lloyd, Review of the NSF's Advanced Technological Education (ATE) Program, 6–12.

59. National Convergence Technology Center (NSF ATE-supported), Centers for Col-laborative Technical Assistance website, http://www.connectedtech.org/ccta.html.

60. Department of Labor (DOL), Employment and Training Administration, Work-force Investment Act—Adult and Dislocated Workers Program, https://www.doleta .gov/programs/general_info.cfm.

61. Workforce Investment Act of 1998, Public Law 105-220, 29 U.S.C. § 2810 et seq. (1998), summarized at https://en.wikipedia.org/wiki/Workforce_Investment_Act_of _1998.

62. The Workforce Innovation and Opportunity Act of 2014, Pub. L. No. 113-128 (2014), aimed to streamline the process of receiving services in core, intensive, and training areas into a more centralized process. See summary at https://en.wikipedia .org/wiki/Workforce_Innovation_and_Opportunity_Act.

63. See, for example, Workforce Investment Network, Tennessee Career Centers, http://www.workforceinvestmentnetwork.com/about-us/introduction.

64. Department of Labor (DOL), Employment and Training Administration, TAACCCT, https://www.doleta.gov/taaccct/. The Community-Based Job Training Grants program was designed to support workforce training for high-growth and emerging industries through community colleges, but the program ended after grants made in 2007. See Department of Labor (DOL), Employment and Training Administration, Business, Industry and Key Sector Initiatives, Community-Based Job Training Grants, https:// www.doleta.gov/business/Community-BasedJobTrainingGrants.cfm.

65. White House, Ready to Work.

66. This section is drawn from a discussion with Emily DeRocco, LIFT Education and Workforce Director, September 1, 2016; Lightweight Innovations for Tomorrow (LIFT), 2016 Education and Workforce Development programs, http://lift.technology /education-workforce-development/; Lightweight Innovations for Tomorrow (LIFT), Education and Workforce slide presentation, 2016; the summaries Lightweight Innovations for Tomorrow (LIFT), Workforce Profile 2016; Lightweight Innovations for Tomorrow (LIFT), 2016 Education and Workforce Roadmap and Master Plan; Lightweight Innovations for Tomorrow (LIFT), Investments as of May 2016; Lightweight Innovations for Tomorrow (LIFT), Workforce Metrics and Data; Lightweight Innovations for Tomorrow (LIFT), Talent Research; and from reports on its programs in Indiana, Ohio, Kentucky, Tennessee, and Michigan.

67. LIFT, 2016 Education and Workforce Development, 4–9.

68. Ibid., 17–45.

69. Ibid., 46.

70. Ibid., 3.

71. Government Accountability Office (GAO), Advanced Manufacturing: Commerce Could Strengthen Collaboration with Other Agencies on Innovation Institutes, GAO-17-320, Washington, DC April 6, 2017, http://www.gao.gov/products /GAO-17-320?source=ra (Department of Labor identified, in particular, as a nonparticipant).

72. Ibid., 12–14.

73. Communication from Thomas A. Kochan, September 7, 2016; also, Thomas A. Kochan, memo to author Bonvillian, Suggestions for Strengthening Workforce Components of NNMI Projects, Sept. 20, 2016.

74. William B. Bonvillian and Susan Singer, The Online Challenge to Higher Education, *Issues in Science and Technology* 29, no. 4 (Summer 2013), http://issues.org/29-4 /the-online-challenge-to-higher-education/.

75. Alliance for Manufacturing Foresight (MForesight), Manufacturing 101—An Education and Training Curriculum for Hardware Entrepreneurs, Report MF-RR-2016-0103, : Alliance for Manufacturing Foresight, Ann Arbor, MI, September 2016, http://mforesight.org/download-reports/.

76. National Defense Authorization Act for FY2017 (S.2943), 114th Cong., 2nd Sess., section 215, amending 10 U.S.C. § 2196. (Conference Report, Pub. L. No. 114-840 (2016); became law December 23, 2016. It created the "Manufacturing Engineering Education Grant Program.")

77. John Hart, Syllabus, Fundaments of Manufacturing Process, MITx and edX online education platforms, 2016, https://www.edx.org/course/fundamentals-manufacturing -processes-mitx-2-008x. See also MIT Innovation Initiative, Advancing Manufacturing Innovation on Campus and Online, *MIT News*, October 7, 2016, http://news.mit.edu /2016/advancing-manufacturing-innovation-campus-and-online-1007.

78. MIT, Supply Chain Management, Micromasters Credential website, http://scm .mit.edu/micromasters/faqs.

79. National Center for Supply Chain Technology Education (NSF/ATE supported) eTextbook website, http://www.supplychainteched.org/etextbook.html.

80. Department of Energy (DOE), Office of Energy Efficiency and Renewable Energy, Build4Scale, http://energy.gov/eere/articles/build4scale-training-cleantech -entrepreneurs-manufacturing-success; Department of Energy (DOE), Office of Energy Efficiency and Renewable Energy website, http://energy.gov/eere/technology -to-market/build4scale-manufacturing-training-cleantech-entrepreneurs.

9. Manufacturing and the Future of Work

1. Riots at Nottingham, *Times* (London, England), November 18, 1811, *The Times Digital Archive.*

2. Roger Luckhurst, Automation, in *The Oxford Handbooks Online* (Oxford: Oxford University Press, November 2014). http://www.oxfordhandbooks.com/view/10.1093 /oxfordhb/9780199838844.001.0001/oxfordhb-9780199838844-e-17.

3. John Beckett, Luddites, The Nottingham Heritage Gateway website, http://www .nottsheritagegateway.org.uk/people/luddites.htm.

4. Paul Lindholdt, Luddism and Its Discontents, *American Quarterly* 49, no. 4 (1997): 866.

5. Luckhurst, Automation.

6. Lindholdt, Luddism and Its Discontents, 868.

7. Joel Mokyr, Chris Vickers, and Nicolas L. Ziebarth, The History of Technological Anxiety and the Future of Economic Growth: Is This Time Different?, *Journal of Economic Perspectives* 29, no. 3 (2015): 34.

8. Susan Helper, Timothy Krueger, and Howard Wial, Why Does Manufacturing Matter? Which Manufacturing Matters? (paper, Brookings Institution, Washington, DC, February 22, 2016), 9–10.

9. Chester Levine, Laurie Salmon, and Daniel H. Weinberg, Revising the Standard Occupational Classification System, *Monthly Labor Review* (May 1999): 43–44.

10. Stanley Lebergott, Labor Force and Employment, 1800–1960, in *Output, Employment, and Productivity in the United States after 1800*, ed. Dorothy S. Brady (New York: National Bureau of Economic Research, 1966), 119.

11. Ibid., 36.

12. John Maynard Keynes, *Essays in Persuasion* (New York: Classic House Books, 2009), 197.

13. Lydia Saad, The 40-Hour Workweek Is Actually Longer—by Seven Hours, *Gallup*, August 29, 2014.

14. Erik Brynjolfsson and Andrew McAfee, *The Second Machine Age: Work, Progress, and Prosperity in a Time of Brilliant Technologies* (New York: Norton, 2014), 41.

15. Ibid., 42.

16. Ibid., 49.

17. Ibid., 62.

18. Martin Ford, *Rise of the Robots: Technology and the Threat of a Jobless Future* (New York: Basic Books, 2015), 77.

19. Sharon Pian Chan, Long Antitrust Saga Ends for Microsoft, *Seattle Times*, May 12, 2011.

20. Tyler Cowen, *Average Is Over: Powering America beyond the Age of the Great Stagnation* (New York: Plume, 2014), 69.

21. Ford, *Rise of the Robots*, 100–101.

22. Ibid., 113.

23. Atul Prakash, Rocky Markets Test the Rise of Amateur "Algo" Traders, Reuters, January 28, 2016.

24. Bureau of Labor Statistics (BLS), Employment, Hours, and Earnings, Current Employment Statistics, October 15, 2016. https://www.bls.gov/ces/.

25. Robin Wigglesworth, Banks Deflect Attempts to Bring Sunlight to Bond Dealing, *Financial Times*, October 10, 2016; Tracy Alloway and Michael MacKenzie, Bonds: Anatomy of a Market Meltdown, *Financial Times*, November 17, 2014.

26. Klint Finley, This News-Writing Bot Is Now Free for Everyone, *Wired*, October 20, 2015.

27. Ford, *Rise of the Robots*, 107.

28. Ben-Bright Benuwa, Yongzhao Zhan, Benjamin Ghansah, Dickson Keddy Wornyo, and Frank Banaseka Kataka, A Review of Deep Machine Learning, *International Journal of Engineering Research in Africa* 24 (2016): 132.

29. Brynjolfsson and McAfee, *The Second Machine Age*, 30–33.

30. Cowen, *Average Is Over*, 39–40.

31. Ibid., 244–245.

32. See Peter Temin, *The Vanishing Middle Class: Prejudice and Power in a Dual Economy* (Cambridge, MA: MIT Press, 2017).

33. Cowen, *Average Is Over*, 233.

34. A "Pigovian tax" is a fee imposed against private individuals or businesses for engaging in a specific activity. It is designed to discourage activities that create negative externalities (such as pollution) by bringing in line private and social costs. It was named after British economist Arthur C. Pigou, a leading early contributor to externality theory.

35. Brynjolfsson and McAfee, *The Second Machine Age*, 225–227, 237–238.

36. Cowen, *Average Is Over*, 77–80.

37. Ford, *Rise of the Robots*, 194–198.

38. Ibid., 257.

39. David H. Autor, Why Are There Still So Many Jobs? The History and Future of Workplace Automation, *Journal of Economic Perspectives* 29, no. 3 (Summer 2015): 5.

40. David Autor, presentation on the Future of Work, roundtable discussion, MIT, January 9, 2016.

41. Michael J. Handel, presentation on Skills, Job Creation and Labour Markets, Conference on Smart Industry: Enabling the Next Production Revolution, OECD and Sweden Ministry of Enterprise and Innovation, Stockholm, September 18, 2016.

42. David Mindell, *Our Robots, Our Selves: Robotics and the Myths of Autonomy* (New York: Penguin Random House, 2015).

43. J. C. R. Licklider, Man-Computer Symbiosis, *IRE Transactions on Human Factors in Electronics* 1 (March 1960): 4–11, http://groups.csail.mit.edu/medg/people/psz/Licklider.html.

44. Rethink Robotics, company website, http://www.rethinkrobotics.com.

45. Carl Benedikt Frey and Michael A. Osborne, The Future of Employment: How Susceptible Are Jobs to Computerization? Working Paper, Oxford Martin Programme on Technology and Employment, September 17, 2013, 44. http://www.oxfordmartin.ox.ac.uk/downloads/academic/future-of-employment.pdf.

46. Robert D. Atkinson, "It's Going to Kill Us!" and Other Myths about the Future of Artificial Intelligence, Information Technology and Innovation Foundation, Washington, DC, June 2016, 13–14.

47. Ibid., 14.

48. Tom Walker, Why Economists Dislike a Lump of Labor, *Review of Social Economy* 65, no. 3 (September 2007): 281–282.

49. Ibid., 285.

50. Melanie Arntz, Terry Gregory, and Ulrich Zierahn, Risk of Automation for Jobs in OECD Countries, a Comparative Analysis, OECD Social, Employment and Migration Working Paper 189, OECD, Paris, June 16, 2016.

51. David Autor and Michael Handel, Putting Tasks to the Test: Human Capital, Job Tasks, and Wages, *Journal of Labor Economics* 31, no. 2 (2013): S59–S96.

52. Organization for Economic Cooperation and Development (OECD), Automation and Independent Work in a Digital Economy, Policy Brief, OECD, Paris, May 2016, 2, http://www.oecd.org/employment/Policy%20brief%20-%20Automation%20and%20Independent%20Work%20in%20a%20Digital%20Economy.pdf.

53. Georg Duernecker, Technology Adoption, Turbulence, and the Dynamics of Unemployment (paper, University of Mannheim, 2009).

54. Constantine Alexandrakis, Sectoral Differences in the Use of Information Technology and Matching Efficiency in the U.S. Labour Market, *Applied Economics* 46, no. 29 (2014).

55. James Bessen, How Computer Automation Affects Occupations: Technology, Jobs, and Skills, *Vox, CEPR Economic Policy Portal*, September 22, 2016. http://voxeu.org/article/how-computer-automation-affects-occupations.

56. Georg Graetz and Guy Michaels, Robots at Work, Centre for Economic Performance Discussion Paper 1335, Centre for Economic Performance, London, England, March 2015, 4–5.

57. Daron Acemoglu and Pascual Restrepo, Robots and Jobs: Evidence from US Labor Markets, NBER Working Paper No. 23285, National Bureau of Economic Research,

March 2017, 2; Council of Economic Advisors to the President, Economic Report of the President Together with the Annual Report of the Council of Economic Advisors (Washington, DC: White House, February 2016), 234–235.

58. Acemoglu and Restrepo, Robots and Jobs, 1–5 and 36–37.

59. Ibid., 28.

60. Ibid., 36–37.

61. Michael A. Russo, Director of Government Relations, Regulatory Affairs & Strategic Initiatives—GlobalFoundries, GlobalFoundries Update, slide presentation, Nov. 27, 2013. See also, Charles W. Wessner and Thomas R. Howell, New York's Nanotechnology Initiative: Best Practices and Challenges (paper), March 12, 2017, 8 (jobs at the GlobalFoundries Malta, New York fab subsequently grew to 4000 direct and 20,000 indirect).

62. Hiawatha Bray, Teaching a driverless car to turn left, *The Boston Globe*, April 22, 2017, http://apps.bostonglobe.com/business/graphics/2017/04/driverless/series/teaching-a-driverless-car-to-turn-left/.

63. Nauna Hejlund, presentation on Skills, Job Creation and Labour Market, Conference on Smart Industry: Enabling the Next Production Revolution, OECD and Sweden Ministry of Enterprise and Innovation, Stockholm, September 18, 2016.

64. Population Council, Alvin Hansen on Economic Progress and Declining Population Growth, *Population and Development Review* 30, no. 2 (June 2004): 333.

65. Ibid., 338–339.

66. Ibid., 340.

67. Ibid., 341.

68. Benjamin Higgins, The Concept of Secular Stagnation, *American Economic Review* 40, no. 1 (March 1950): 160.

69. W. Robert Brazelton, Alvin Harvey Hansen: Economic Growth and a More Perfect Society: The Economist's Role in Defining the Stagnation Thesis and in Popularizing Keynesianism, *American Journal of Economics and Sociology* 48, no. 4 (October 1989): 437.

70. Anthony Scaperlanda, Hansen's Secular Stagnation Thesis Once Again, *Journal of Economic Issues* 11, no. 2 (June 1977): 225.

71. Morten Bech and Aytek Malkhozov, How Have Central Banks Implemented Negative Policy Rates? *BIS Quarterly Review*, March 2016.

72. Lawrence H. Summers, Demand Side Secular Stagnation, *American Economic Review: Papers and Proceedings* 105, no. 5 (2015): 61.

73. Ibid., 62.

74. Ibid., 63.

75. Ben S. Bernanke, Why Are Interest Rates So Low? Part 2: Secular Stagnation, Brookings Institution, March 30, 2015. Summers, Eggertsson, and Mehrotra released a paper that included an international dimension after Bernanke made this critique. In an open market, there must be similar conditions throughout the world. Bernanke proposes another explanation, deemed the global savings glut. Since the Fed's Paul Volcker raised interest rates to 15% in 1981, there has been a steady and continual decline in rates. The driver of this decrease is excessive savings in a number of emerging markets. Increasing capital outflows from these countries to the United States drive down the long-term interest rate. The dollar appreciates, and the U.S. saw current account balances grow. Unlike secular stagnation, monetary policy, mostly in developing countries, can correct the problem. This lack of balance is very evident in the current account number: in 2015, the United States had a deficit of $462 billion, while Germany had a surplus of $285 billion and China a surplus of $293 billion. Much of the appeal for this explanation likely lies in the fact that the burden of monetary and fiscal policy falls on developing countries. See Gauti B. Eggertsson, Neil R. Mehrotra, and Lawrence H. Summers, Secular Stagnation in the Open Economy, *American Economic Review: Papers and Proceedings* 106, no. 5 (2016); Ben S. Bernanke, Why Are Interest Rates So Low? Part 3: The Global Savings Glut, Brookings Institution, April 1, 2015; World Bank, Current Account Balance (BoP, current US$) http://data.worldbank.org/indicator/BN.CAB.XOKA.CD; Sean Miner, China's Current Account in 2015: A Growing Trade Surplus, Peterson Institute for International Economics, Washington, DC, February 8, 2016.

76. Robert J. Gordon, Secular Stagnation: A Supply-Side View, *American Economic Review: Papers and Proceedings* 105, no. 5 (2015): 55.

77. Ibid., 56.

78. Robert Gordon, *The Rise and Fall of American Growth* (Princeton, NJ: Princeton University Press, 2016), 607.

79. Roberto Cardarelli and Lusine Lusinyan, U.S. Total Factor Productivity Slowdown: Evidence from the U.S. States, IMF Working Paper, International Monetary Fund, Washington, DC, May 2015, 5.

80. Ricardo J. Caballero, Emmanuel Fari, and Pierre-Olivier Gourinchas,Safe Asset Scarcity and Aggregate Demand, January 26, 2016, 1, 10, later released as NBER Working Paper 22044, National Bureau of Economic Research, Cambridge, MA, February 2016. One piece of evidence supporting this theory is that between December 2009 and December 2015, the trade-weighted U.S. dollar index exchange value compared against major currencies appreciated from about 72 to 94. This was an increase of over 30%—with close to no change in interest rates. The yield on the ten-year Treasury note decreased from a range between 3.28% and 3.85% in December 2009 to between 2.13% and 2.33% in December 2015. See Federal Reserve System

Board of Governors , Trade Weighted U.S. Dollar Index: Major Currencies [DTWEXM]. https://fred.stlouisfed.org/series/DTWEXM. ; Department of the Treasury, Daily Treasury Yield Curve Rates. https://www.treasury.gov/resource-center/data-chart-center /interest-rates/Pages/TextView.aspx?data=yieldYear&year=2015.

81. Michael J. Fleming and Nicholas J. Klagge, The Federal Reserve's Foreign Exchange Swap Lines, *Federal Reserve Bank of New York Current Issues in Economics and Finance* 16, no. 4 (April 2010).

82. Chan Sewell, The 2010 Campaign: Democrats Are at Odds on Relevance of Keynes, *New York Times*, October 19, 2010.

83. Federal Reserve Bank of St. Louis and U.S. Office of Management and Budget, Federal Debt: Total Public Debt as Percent of Gross Domestic Product [GFDEGDQ188S]. https://fred.stlouisfed.org/series/GFDEGDQ188S.

84. See Mark Blyth, *Austerity: The History of a Dangerous Idea* (Oxford: Oxford University Press, 2013).

85. Carmen M. Reinhart and Kenneth S. Rogoff, *This Time Is Different: Eight Centuries of Financial Folly* (Princeton, NJ: Princeton University Press, 2009).

86. Christopher L. House, Christian Proebsting, and Linda Tesar, Austerity in the Aftermath of the Great Recession, NBER Draft, National Bureau of Economic Research, Cambridge, MA, November 24, 2015.

87. While Greece is a unique case because of its place in the Eurozone, it highlights the potentially devastating impact of austerity. In 2007, the GDP in Greece was around €63 billion (in chained 2010 euros), but by midway through 2016, it had fallen to €46 billion. About 27% of the country's GDP was lost, with poverty increasing from 2.2% to 15% between 2009 and 2015. The shortcomings of austerity are now more widely acknowledged, with the IMF, which had participated in the Greek bailout with its stringent conditions, changing tack in 2012. It is important to remember this episode in the wake of the crisis because in essence this delay likely contributed to the slow recovery.

88. Olivier Blanchard, Giovanni Dell'Ariccia, and Paolo Mauro, Rethinking Macroeconomic Policy, *Journal of Money, Credit and Banking* 42, no. 5 (September 2010): 205.

89. Olivier Blanchard and Daniel Leigh, Growth Forecast Errors and Fiscal Multipliers, IMF Working Paper, International Monetary Fund, Washington, DC, January 2013, 3.

90. Ibid., 19.

91. Alan J. Auerbach and Yuriy Gorodnichenko, Fiscal Multipliers in Recession and Expansion, in *Fiscal Policy after the Financial Crisis*, ed. Alberto Alesina and Francesco Giavazzi (Chicago: University of Chicago Press, 2013), 91–92.

92. American Society of Civil Engineers, 2013 Report Card for America's Infrastructure, http://www.infrastructurereportcard.org/.

93. Elena Holodny, The 11 Countries with the Best Infrastructure around the World, *Business Insider*, October 2, 2015.

94. Bureau of Labor Statistics (BLS), Table A-4. Employment Status of the Civilian Population 25 Years and Over by Educational Attainment, October 7, 2016. http://www.murraylax.org/eco120/fall2016/bls20161007_short.pdf.

95. Bureau of Labor Statistics (BLS), Table 3.3. Civilian Labor Force Participation Rate by Age, Gender, Race, and Ethnicity, 1994, 2004, 2014, and projected 2024 (in percent), December 8, 2015. https://www.bls.gov/emp/ep_table_301.htm.

96. Lawrence H. Summers, Building the Case for Greater Infrastructure Investment, *Financial Times*, September 11, 2016.

97. Congressional Budget Office (CBO), Public Spending on Transportation and Water Infrastructure, 1956 to 2014, March 2015, 10.

98. Ibid., 14.

99. Chris Mooney, The Gas Tax Has Been Fixed at 18 Cents for Two Decades. Now Would Be a Great Time to Raise It, *Washington Post*, December 3, 2014.

100. Governor of Connecticut's Transportation Finance Panel, Final Report, January 15, 2016, 7–8, http://portal.ct.gov/uploadedFiles/Departments_and_Agencies/Office_of_the_Governor/Learn_More/Working_Groups/2016.01.15%20TFP%20final%20report.pdf.

101. International Monetary Fund (IMF), World Economic Outlook 2014: Legacies, Clouds, Uncertainties (Washington, DC: International Monetary Fund, October 2014), 75.

102. Camilla Yanushevsky and Rafael Yanushevsky, Is Infrastructure Spending an Effective Fiscal Policy?, *Metroeconomica* 65, no. 1 (2014): 134–135.

103. Amitabh Chandra and Eric Thompson, Does Public Infrastructure Affect Economic Activity? Evidence from the Rural Interstate Highway System, *Regional Science and Urban Economics* 30 (2000): 459–460.

104. Barbara M. Fraumeni, The Contribution of Highways to GDP Growth, NBER Working Paper 14736, National Bureau of Economic Research, Cambridge, MA, February 2009; Gilles Duranton and Matthew A. Turner, Urban Growth and Transportation, *Review of Economic Studies* 1 (2012).

105. Daniel J. Wilson, Fiscal Spending Jobs Multipliers: Evidence from the 2009 American Recovery and Reinvestment Act, *American Economic Journal: Economic Policy* 4, no. 3 (2012): 258–259.

106. Ibid., 278.

107. Ibid., 258–259.

108. Robert D. Atkinson, *The Past and Future of America's Economy: Long Waves of Innovation That Power Cycles of Growth* (Cheltenham: Edward Elgar, 2004); Carlota Perez, *Technological Revolutions and Financial Capital: The Dynamics of Bubbles and Golden Ages* (Cheltenham: Edward Elgar, 2002).

109. Gordon, *The Rise and Fall of American Growth*, 170.

110. Ibid., 390–391.

111. Carl Kitchens and Price Fishback, Flip the Switch: The Impact of the Rural Electrification Administration 1935–1940, *Journal of Economic History* 75, no. 4 (December 2015).

112. World Bank, Age Dependency Ratio (% of Working-Age Population): United States. http://data.worldbank.org/indicator/SP.POP.DPND?locations=US.

113. Kerwin Kofi Charles, Erik Hurst, and Matthew J. Notowidigdo, The Masking of the Decline in Manufacturing Employment by the House Bubble, *Journal of Economic Perspectives* 30, no. 2 (Spring 2016): 181.

114. Peter L. Singer, Investing in "Innovation Infrastructure" to Restore U.S. Growth (Washington, DC: Information Technology and Innovation Foundation [ITIF], January 3, 2017), http://www2.itif.org/2017-innovation-infrastructure.pdf?_ga=1 .198109420.2108411368.1483563653.

115. Bureau of Economic Analysis (BEA), Real Value Added by Industry, April 21, 2016. https://fred.stlouisfed.org/release/tables?rid=331&eid=245.

116. This rise in real value added, according to the Bureau of Economic Analysis, was primarily driven by a 699% increase in the computer and electronic products sector. Only the petroleum and motor vehicles sectors increased by more than manufacturing as a whole, about 61% and 67%, respectively. Eight of the 19 sectors actually saw a decrease in value added, according to the government statistics. These very high increases in value added and output can distort analyses of the manufacturing industry as a whole. An ITIF study shows the distortion that measurement problems in computing and energy sector data introduce into manufacturing data. See Robert D. Atkinson, Luke A. Stewart, Scott M. Andes, and Stephen Ezell, Worse than the Great Depression: What the Experts Are Missing about American Manufacturing Decline (Washington, DC: Information Technology and Innovation Foundation [ITIF], March 19, 2012), http://www2.itif.org/2012-american-manufacturing-decline.pdf. Houseman, Bartik, and Sturgeon note that when the computer industry is dropped from measures, the data shows that an increase in demand for manufactured goods increases employment. See Susan N. Houseman, Timothy J. Bartik, and Timothy J.

Sturgeon, Measuring Manufacturing: How the Computer and Semiconductor Industries Affect the Numbers and Perceptions, Upjohn Institute Working Paper 14-209, Upjohn Institute, Kalamazoo, MI, January 2014, 4.

117. Perhaps the best articulation of this concern was in Charles L. Schultze, Industrial Policy: A Dissent, *Brookings Review* 2, no. 1 (Fall 1983): 3–12, http://www.brookings .edu/~/media/Files/rc/articles/1983/industrial_policy_schultze.pdf. For a conservative perspective on the industrial policy debates in the 1980s, see also Richard B. McKenzie, Industrial Policy, in *Concise Encyclopedia of Economics*, 2nd ed., 2007 (Library of Economics and Liberty), http://www.econlib.org/library/Enc1/IndustrialPolicy .html.

118. Helper, Krueger, and Wial, Why Does Manufacturing Matter? See also Stephen S. Cohen and John Zysman, *Manufacturing Matters: The Myth of a Post-industrial Economy* (New York: Basic Books, 1987).

10. Conclusion: Manufacturing Matters More Than Ever

1. Suzanne Berger and the MIT Task Force on Production and Innovation, *Making in America* (Cambridge, MA: MIT Press, 2013), 17–20, 44–64.

2. Discussed in Philip Shapira and Jan Youtie, Next Production Revolution: Institutions for Technology Diffusion, Conference on Smart Industry: Enabling the Next Production Revolution, OECD and Sweden Ministry of Enterprise and Innovation, Stockholm, September 18, 2016, 5.

3. Robert E. Scott, Manufacturing Job Loss: Trade Not Productivity Is the Culprit, report (Economic Policy Institute, August 11, 2015), http://www.epi.org/publication /manufacturing-job-loss-trade-not-productivity-is-the-culprit/ (citing BLS data).

4. David Autor, David Dorn, and Gordon H. Hanson, The China Shock: Learning from Labor Market Adjustment to Large Changes in Trade, NBER Working Paper 21906, National Bureau of Economic Research, Cambridge, MA, January 2016, http:// www.nber.org/papers/w21906. See also, Andrew Foote, Michel Grosz, and Ann Huff Stevens, Locate Your Nearest Exit: Mass Layoffs and Local Labor Market Response, NBER Working Paper No. 21618, National Bureau of Economic Research, Cambridge, MA, October 2015, http://www.nber.org/papers/w21618.

5. Danny Yagan, The Enduring Employment Impact of Your Great Recession Location (working paper, University of California—Berkeley, April 2016), https://sites .google.com/site/dannyyagan/greatdivergence.

6. Jon Coder and Gordon Green, Comparing Earnings of White Males by Education, for Selected Age Cohorts, High School vs College Graduates (Annapolis, MD: Sentier Research, October 2016), 1, charts 1 and 2 on 7, http://www.sentierresearch.com

/StatBriefs/Sentier_Income_Trends_WorkingClassWages_1996to2014_Brief_10_05 _16.pdf (based on Census Bureau data).

7. Melissa S. Kearney, Brad Hershbein, and Elisa Jacome, Profiles of Change: Employment, Earnings and Occupations from 1990–2013 (Washington, DC: Brookings Institution, 2015).

8. Stephen S. Cohen and John Zysman, *Manufacturing Matters: The Myth of a Post-industrial Economy* (New York: Basic Books, 1987).

References

Acemoglu, Daron, and David Autor. Skills, Tasks and Technologies: Implications for Employment and Earnings. In *Handbook of Labor Economics*, vol. 4b, edited by David Card and Orley Ashenfelter, 1043–1171. Amsterdam: Elsevier, 2011.

Acemoglu, Daron, and Veronica Guerrieri. Capital Deepening and Nonbalanced Economic Growth. *Journal of Political Economy* 116, no. 3 (2008): 467–498.

Acemoglu, Daron, and Pascual Restrepo. Robots and Jobs: Evidence from US Labor Markets, NBER Working Paper No. 23285, National Bureau of Economic Research, Cambridge, MA March 2017. http://www.nber.org/papers/w23285.

Achieve. The Future of the U.S. Workforce: Middle Skills and the Growing Importance of Postsecondary Education. September 2012. http://www.achieve.org/files/MiddleSkillsJobs.pdf.

Adler, Robert. Entering a Dark Age of Innovation. *New Scientist*, July 2, 2005. https://www.newscientist.com/article/dn7616-entering-a-dark-age-of-innovation/.

AFFOA website. join.affoa.org.

Aghion, Philippe, Ufuk Akcigit, and Peter Howitt. What Do We Learn from Schumpeterian Growth Theory? NBER Working Paper 18824, National Bureau of Economic Research, Cambridge, MA, February 2013. http://www.nber.org/papers/w18824.

Aghion, Philippe, and Rachel Griffith. *Competition and Growth: Reconciling Theory and Evidence*. Cambridge, MA: MIT Press, 2005.

Aguayo, Rafael. *Dr. Deming: The American Who Taught the Japanese about Quality*. New York: Simon and Schuster Fireside, 1991.

Alexandrakis, Constantine. Sectoral Differences in the Use of Information Technology and Matching Efficiency in the U.S. Labour Market. *Applied Economics* 46, no. 29 (2014): 3562–3571.

Alliance for Manufacturing Foresight (MForesight). Manufacturing 101—An Education and Training Curriculum for Hardware Entrepreneurs. Report MF-RR-2016-0103.

Ann Arbor, MI: Alliance for Manufacturing Foresight, September 2016. http:// mforesight.org/download-reports/.

Alloway, Tracy, and Michael MacKenzie. Bonds: Anatomy of a Market Meltdown. *Financial Times*, November 17, 2014.

Alvaredo, Facundo, Anthony B. Atkinson, Thomas Piketty, Emmanuel Saez, and Gabriel Zucman. The World Wealth and Income Database. http://www.wid.world/.

America Makes website. https://www.americamakes.us/about/overview.

American Society of Civil Engineers. 2013 Report Card for America's Infrastructure. http://www.infrastructurereportcard.org/.

Anand, Aneesh. Survey of Selected Federal Manufacturing Programs at NIST, DOD, DOE, and NSF. MIT Washington Office, Washington, DC, September 2014, http:// dc.mit.edu/resources/policy-resources.

Argonne National Laboratory. Argonne Launches First Tech Incubator. May 20, 2016. http://www.anl.gov/articles/argonne-launches-first-tech-incubator.

Arntz, Melanie, Terry Gregory, and Ulrich Zierahn. Risk of Automation for Jobs in OECD Countries: A Comparative Analysis. OECD Social, Employment and Migration Working Paper 189, OECD, Paris, June 16, 2016.

Arrow, Kenneth J. The Economic Implications of Learning by Doing. *Review of Economic Studies* 29, no. 3 (June 1962): 155–173.

Atkinson, Robert. Restoring Investment in America's Economy. Report. Washington, DC: Information Technology and Innovation Foundation (ITIF), June 13, 2016. http://www2.itif.org/2016-restoring-investment.pdf?_ga=1.113675271.1482316035 .1476207219.

Atkinson, Robert. *Think Like an Enterprise: Why Nations Need Comprehensive Productivity Strategies*. Washington, DC: Information Technology and Innovation Foundation (ITIF), May 2016. http://www2.itif.org/2016-think-like-an-enterprise.pdf?_ga=1 .141453106.1482316035.1476207219. (ebook).

Atkinson, Robert D. Enough Is Enough: Confronting Chinese Innovation Mercantilism. Report. Washington, DC: Information Technology and Innovation Foundation (ITIF), February 2012. http://www2.itif.org/2012-enough-enough-chinese -mercantilism.pdf.

Atkinson, Robert D. "It's Going to Kill Us!" and Other Myths about the Future of Artificial Intelligence. Washington, DC: Information Technology and Innovation Foundation (ITIF), June 2016.

Atkinson, Robert D. *The Past and Future of America's Economy—Long Waves of Innovation That Power Cycles of Growth*. Cheltenham: Edward Elgar, 2004.

Atkinson, Robert D., Luke A. Stewart, Scott M. Andes, and Stephen Ezell. Worse than the Great Depression: What the Experts Are Missing about American Manufacturing Decline. Washington, DC: Information Technology and Innovation Foundation (ITIF), March 19, 2012. http://www2.itif.org/2012-american-manufacturing-decline.pdf.

Auerbach, Alan J., and Yuriy Gorodnichenko. Fiscal Multipliers in Recession and Expansion. In *Fiscal Policy after the Financial Crisis*, edited by Alberto Alesina and Francesco Giavazzi, 63–98. Chicago: University of Chicago Press, 2013.

Automotive Manufacturing Technical Education Collaborative (AMTEC) website. http://autoworkforce.org/about-amtec/.

Autor, David. Presentation on the Future of Work. Roundtable discussion, MIT, January 9, 2016.

Autor, David. Why Are There Still So Many Jobs? The History and Future of Workplace Automation. *Journal of Economic Perspectives* 29, no. 3 (Summer 2015): 3–30.

Autor, David H., and David Dorn. The Growth of Low-Skill Service Jobs and the Polarization of the US Labor Market. *American Economic Review* 103, no. 5 (2013): 1553–1597.

Autor, David H., David Dorn, and Gordon H. Hanson. The China Shock: Learning from Labor Market Adjustment to Large Changes in Trade. NBER Working Paper 21906, National Bureau of Economic Research, Cambridge, MA, January 2016. http://www.nber.org/papers/w21906.

Autor, David, David Dorn, and Gordon Hanson. The China Syndrome: Local Labor Market Effects of Import Competition in the United States. MIT Economics paper, August 2011. http://economics.mit.edu/files/6613.

Autor, David, David Dorn, Gordon Hanson, and Kaveh Majlesi. Importing Political Polarization? The Electoral Consequences of Rising Trade Exposure. NBER Working Paper 22637, National Bureau of Economic Research, Cambridge, MA, September 2016. http://www.nber.org/papers/w22637.

Autor, David, David Dorn, Gordon H. Hanson, Gary Pisano and Pian Shu. Foreign Competition and Domestic Innovation: Evidence from U.S. Patents, NBER Working Paper 22879, National Bureau of Economic Research, Cambridge, MA, December 2016. http://www.nber.org/papers/w22879.

Autor, David, and Michael Handel. Putting Tasks to the Test: Human Capital, Job Tasks, and Wages. *Journal of Labor Economics* 31, no. 2 (2013): S59–S96.

Baicker, Katherine, and M. Marit Rehavi. Policy Watch: Trade Adjustment Assistance. *Journal of Economic Perspectives* 18, no. 2 (Spring 2004): 239–255.

Ballandonne, Matthieu. Creating Increasing Returns: The Genesis of Arrow's "Learning by Doing" Article. *History of Political Economy* 47, no. 3 (2015): 449–479.

Banister, Judith. China's Manufacturing Employment and Hourly Labor Compensation, 2002–2009. Bureau of Labor Statistics (BLS), June 7, 2003.

Barnett, Chance. Crowdfunding Sites in 2014. *Forbes*, August 29, 2014.

Baumol, William, and William Bowen. *Performing Arts, the Economic Dilemma: A Study of Problems Common to Theater, Opera, Music, and Dance.* New York: Twentieth Century Fund, 1966.

Bech, Morten, and Aytek Malkhozov. How Have Central Banks Implemented Negative Policy Rates? *BIS Quarterly Review*, March 2016.

Becker, Gary S. *Human Capital: A Theoretical and Empirical Analysis, with Special Reference to Education.* New York: National Bureau of Economic Research, 1975.

Beckett, John. Luddites. The Nottingham Heritage Gateway website. http://www.nottsheritagegateway.org.uk/people/luddites.htm.

Bennis, Warren, and Patricia Ward Biederman. *Organizing Genius.* New York: Basic Books, 1997.

Benuwa, Ben-Bright, Yongzhao Zhan, Benjamin Ghansah, Dickson Keddy Wornyo, and Frank Banaseka Kataka. A Review of Deep Machine Learning. *International Journal of Engineering Research in Africa* 24 (2016): 124–136.

Berger, Suzanne, and the MIT Industrial Performance Center. *How We Compete: What Companies around the World Are Doing to Make It in Today's Global Economy.* New York: Doubleday Currency, 2006.

Berger, Suzanne, and the MIT Task Force on Production and Innovation. *Making in America.* Cambridge, MA: MIT Press, 2013.

Berlin, Leslie. *The Man behind the Microchip: Robert Noyce and the Invention of Silicon Valley.* New York: Oxford University Press, 2005.

Bernanke, Ben S. Why Are Interest Rates So Low? Part 2: Secular Stagnation. Brookings Institution, Washington, DC, March 30, 2015.

Bernanke, Ben S. Why Are Interest Rates So Low? Part 3: The Global Savings Glut. Brookings Institution, Washington, DC, April 1, 2015.

Bernstein, Jared, Melissa Boteach, Rebecca Vallas, Olivia Golden, Kali Grant, Indivar Dutta-Gupta, Erica Williams, and Valerie Wilson. 10 Solutions to Fight Economic Inequality. Talkpoverty.org, June 10, 2015. https://talkpoverty.org/2015/06/10/solutions-economic-inequality/.

Bessen, James. How Computer Automation Affects Occupations: Technology, Jobs, and Skills. *Vox, CEPR Economic Policy Portal*, September 22, 2016. http://voxeu.org/article/how-computer-automation-affects-occupations.

Bhagwati, Jagdish. The Computer Chip vs. Potato Chip Debate. *Moscow Times*, September 2, 2010. https://themoscowtimes.com/articles/the-computer-chip-vs-potato-chip-debate-1075.

Bhagwati, Jagdish. The Manufacturing Fallacy. *Project Syndicate*, August 27, 2010.

Binnie, Dylan. Designed in California, Built in Oregon—Important Lessons for America to Learn from the German Workforce Education System. Paper, Georgetown University, Washington, DC, May 10, 2016.

Blanchard, Olivier, Giovanni Dell'Ariccia, and Paolo Mauro. Rethinking Macroeconomic Policy. *Journal of Money, Credit and Banking* 42 Supplement 1 (September 2010): 199–215.

Blanchard, Olivier, and Daniel Leigh. Growth Forecast Errors and Fiscal Multipliers. IMF Working Paper, International Monetary Fund, Washington, DC, January 2013.

Blyth, Mark. *Austerity: The History of a Dangerous Idea*. Oxford: Oxford University Press, 2013.

Bockelt, Nathalie. Bridging the Innovation Gap in the U.S. Energy System. Paper, MIT Washington Office, Washington, DC, February 2016. http://dc.mit.edu/resources-links.

Boeing. Everett Production Facility: Overview. http://www.boeing.com/company/about-bca/everett-production-facility.page.

Bonvillian, William B. Advanced Manufacturing: A New Policy Challenge. *Annals in Science and Technology* 1, no. 1 (2017): 1–131.

Bonvillian, William B. Advanced Manufacturing Policies and Paradigms for Innovation. *Science* 342, no. 6163 (December 6, 2013): 1173–1175.

Bonvillian, William B. The Connected Science Model for Innovation: The DARPA Model. In *21st Century Innovation Systems for the U.S. and Japan*, eds. Sadao Nagaoka, Masayuki Kondo, Kenneth Flamm, and Charles Wessner, 206–237. Washington, DC: National Academies Press, 2009.

Bonvillian, William B. Donald Trump's Voters and the Decline of American Manufacturing, *Issues in Science and Technology* 32, no. 4 (Summer 2016): 27–39. http://issues.org/32-4/donald-trumps-voters-and-the-decline-of-american-manufacturing/.

Bonvillian, William B. The New Model Innovation Agencies: An Overview. *Science and Public Policy* 41, no. 4 (2014): 425–437.

Bonvillian, William B. The Problem of Political Design in Federal Innovation Organization. In *The Science of Science Policy*, edited by Kaye Husbands Fealing, Julia Lane, John Marburger, and Stephanie Shipp, 302–326. Stanford, CA: Stanford University Press, 2011.

Bonvillian, William B. Reinventing American Manufacturing. *Innovations* 7, no. 3 (2012): 97–125.

Bonvillian, William B., and Susan Singer. The Online Challenge to Higher Education. *Issues in Science and Technology* 29, no. 4 (Summer 2013): 23–30. http://issues.org/29 -4/the-online-challenge-to-higher-education/.

Bonvillian, William B., and Richard Van Atta. ARPA-E and DARPA: Applying the DARPA Model to Energy Innovation. *Journal of Technology Transfer* 36, no. 5 (October 2011): 469–513.

Bonvillian, William B., and Charles Weiss. *Technological Innovation in Legacy Sectors.* New York: Oxford University Press, 2015.

Boris, Paul. The Industrial Internet of Things (IoT) at Work in Heavy Industry. General Electric Digital White Paper, General Electric Company, Fairfield, CT, September 22, 2016.

Branscomb, Lewis, and Philip E. Auerswald. *Taking Technical Risks: How Innovators, Executives and Investors Manage High Tech Risks.* Cambridge, MA: MIT Press, 2001.

Branscomb, Lewis M., and Philip E. Auerswald. Between Invention and Innovation. NIST Report GCR 02-841. Gaithersburg, MD: National Institute of Standards and Technology (NIST), November 2002.

Braun, David. Mergers and Acquisitions: 2015 a Record Breaking Year, January 22, 2016, https://successfulacquisitions.net.

Bray, Hiawatha. Teaching a driverless car to turn left. *The Boston Globe*, April 22, 2017. http://apps.bostonglobe.com/business/graphics/2017/04/driverless/series /teaching-a-driverless-car-to-turn-left/.

Brazelton, W. Robert. Alvin Harvey Hansen: Economic Growth and a More Perfect Society: The Economist's Role in Defining the Stagnation Thesis and in Popularizing Keynesianism. *American Journal of Economics and Sociology* 48, no. 4 (October 1989): 427–440.

Breznitz, Dan. Why Germany Dominates the U.S. in Innovation. *Harvard Business Review* , May 27, 2014. https://hbr.org/2014/05/why-germany-dominates-the-u-s-in -innovation/.

Breznitz, Dan, and Peter Cowhey. America's Two Systems of Innovation: Recommendations for Policy Changes to Support Innovation, Production and Job Creation. Report. San Diego, CA: Connect Innovation Institute, February 2012.

Breznitz, Daniel, and Michael Murphree. *Run of the Red Queen: Government, Innovation, Globalization and Economic Growth in China.* New Haven, CT: Yale University Press, 2011.

Browning, Larry D., and Judy C. Shetler. *Sematech: Saving the U.S. Semiconductor Industry.* College Station: Texas A&M Press, 2000.

Bryant, Randal E., Kwang-Ting Cheng, Andrew B. Kahng, Kurt Keutzer, Wojciech Maly, Richard Newton, Lawrence Pileggi, Jan M. Rabaey, and Alberto Sangiovanni-Vincentelli. Limitations and Challenges of Computer-Aided Design Technology for CMOS VLSI. *Proceedings of the IEEE* 89, no. 3 (March 2001): 341–365.

Brynjolfsson, Eric, and Andrew McAfee. *Race against the Machine.* Lexington, MA: Digital Frontier, 2011.

Brynjolfsson, Erik, and Andrew McAfee. *The Second Machine Age: Work, Progress, and Prosperity in a Time of Brilliant Technologies.* New York: Norton, 2014.

Bureau of Economic Analysis (BEA), Economic Industry Accounts, Percent Changes in Chain-Type Quantity for Value Added by Industry 2008–13, Table E.1, July 2014, (and prior year tables), https://www.bea.gov/scb/pdf/2014/07%20July/Dpages /0714dpg_e.pdf.

Bureau of Economic Analysis (BEA). Fixed Assets Accounts Tables, Investment in Private Fixed Assets by Industry, Table 3.7ESI, revised Sept. 7, 2016, https://www .bea.gov/iTable/iTable.cfm?ReqID=10&step=1#reqid=10&step=3&isuri=1&1003 =138&1004=2000&1005=2010&1006=a&1011=0&1010=x.

Bureau of Economic Analysis (BEA). Foreign Trade, Exports, Imports and Balance of Goods by Selected NAICS-Based Product Code, Exhibit 1 in FT-900 Supplement for 12/15, February 5, 2016. https://www.census.gov/foreign-trade/Press-Release/2015pr /12/ft900.pdf.

Bureau of Economic Analysis (BEA), Frequently Asked Questions, What Is Industry Value Added, March 2006, https://www.bea.gov/faq/index.cfm?.faq_id=184.

Bureau of Economic Analysis (BEA). Gross Private Domestic Investment [GPDI]. https://fred.stlouisfed.org/series/GPDI.

Bureau of Economic Analysis (BEA). Gross Private Saving [GPSAVE] https://fred .stlouisfed.org/series/GPSAVE.

Bureau of Economic Analysis (BEA). Personal Saving Rate [PSAVERT] https://fred .stlouisfed.org/series/PSAVERT.

Bureau of Economic Analysis (BEA). Real Personal Consumption Expenditures: Durable Goods [PCEDGC96]. FRED, Federal Reserve Bank of St. Louis. https://fred .stlouisfed.org/series/PCEDGC96.

Bureau of Economic Analysis (BEA). Real Personal Consumption Expenditures: Nondurable Goods [PCNDGC96]. FRED, Federal Reserve Bank of St. Louis. https://fred .stlouisfed.org/series/PCNDGC96.

Bureau of Economic Analysis (BEA). Real Value Added by Industry, April 21, 2016. https://fred.stlouisfed.org/release/tables?rid=331&eid=245.

Bureau of Economic Analysis (BEA). Shares of Gross Domestic Product: Gross Private Domestic Investment [A006RE1Q156NBEA]. https://fred.stlouisfed.org/series /A006RE1Q156NBEA.

Bureau of Economic Analysis (BEA). Shares of Gross Domestic Product: Personal Consumption Expenditures [DPCERE1A156NBEA]. https://fred.stlouisfed.org/series /DPCERE1A156NBEA.

Bureau of Economic Analysis (BEA). Trade in Goods with Advanced Technology Products, 2015, Exhibit 16. https://www.census.gov/foreign-trade/balance/c0007.html.

Bureau of Economic Analysis (BEA). U.S. International Trade in Goods and Services, Exhibit 1, February 5, 2016. https://www.census.gov/foreign-trade/Press-Release/2015pr /12/ft900.pdf.

Bureau of Economic Analysis (BEA). Value Added by Industry Group by Percentage of GDP (Table 5a) (Washington, DC: BEA 2013 data). https://www.bea.gov/iTable /iTable.cfm?ReqID=51&step=1#reqid=51&step=2&isuri=1.

Bureau of Economic Analysis (BEA). News Release BEA 17-02, Value Added by Industry Group as a Percentage of GDP (Table 5a), January 19, 2017 (2017 data). https:// www.bea.gov/newsreleases/industry/gdpindustry/2017/pdf/gdpind316.pdf.

Bureau of Economic Analysis (BEA). Value Added by Industry, Manufacturing Sector (2014 data). http://www.bea.gov/iTable/iTable.cfm?ReqID=51&step=1#reqid =51&step=51&isuri=1&5114=a&5102=1.

Bureau of Economic Analysis (BEA). Value Added by Private Industries: Manufacturing as a Percentage of GDP [VAPGDPMA]. FRED, Federal Reserve Bank of St. Louis. https://fred.stlouisfed.org/series/VAPGDPMA.

Bureau of Economic Analysis (BEA) and the Census Bureau. Trade Balance: Services, Balance of Payments Basis [BOPSTB]. FRED, Federal Reserve Bank of St. Louis. https://fred.stlouisfed.org/series/BOPSTB.

Bureau of Labor Statistics (BLS). All Employees: Manufacturing [MANEMP]. FRED, Federal Reserve Bank of St. Louis. https://fred.stlouisfed.org/series/MANEMP.

Bureau of Labor Statistics (BLS). All Employees: Total Nonfarm Payrolls [PAYEMS]. FRED, Federal Reserve Bank of St. Louis. https://fred.stlouisfed.org/series/PAYEMS.

Bureau of Labor Statistics (BLS). Civilian Unemployment Rate [UNRATE]. FRED, Federal Reserve Bank of St. Louis. https://fred.stlouisfed.org/series/UNRATE.

Bureau of Labor Statistics (BLS). Concepts and Methodology. http://www.bls.gov /cps/documentation.htm#concepts.

Bureau of Labor Statistics (BLS). Current Labor Statistics (CES) (Manufacturing Employment). https://www.bls.gov/ces/#tables.

Bureau of Labor Statistics (BLS). Databases, Tables & Calculators, Quarterly Census, Manufacturing Establishments 2001–2015. http://data.bls.gov/pdq/SurveyOutputServlet.

Bureau of Labor Statistics (BLS). *The Economics Daily*, December 8, 2009. http://www.bls.gov/opub/ted/2009/ted_20091208.htm.

Bureau of Labor Statistics (BLS). Employment, Hours, and Earnings, Current Employment Statistics, October 15, 2016. https://www.bls.gov/ces/.

Bureau of Labor Statistics (BLS). Industries at a Glance, Manufacturing, NACIS 31-33, Workforce Statistics, March 2016. http://www.bls.gov/iag/tgs/iag31-33.htm#workforce.

Bureau of Labor Statistics (BLS). Labor Force Statistics from the Current Population Survey, Unemployment Rate 2006–16, October 2016. http://data.bls.gov/timeseries/LNS14000000.

Bureau of Labor Statistics (BLS). Labor Productivity and Costs, Productivity Change in the Manufacturing Sector. http://www.bls.gov/lpc/prodybar.htm.

Bureau of Labor Statistics (BLS). Occupational Employment Statistics, 51-0000 Production Occupations, May 2015. http://www.bls.gov/oes/current/oes_stru.htm#51-0000.

Bureau of Labor Statistics (BLS). The Recession of 2007–2009. Spotlight on Statistics, Bureau of Labor Statistics (BLS), Washington, DC, February 2012. http://www.bls.gov/spotlight/2012/recession/pdf/recession_bls_spotlight.pdf.

Bureau of Labor Statistics (BLS). Table A-4. Employment Status of the Civilian Population 25 Years and Over by Educational Attainment, October 7, 2016. http://www.murraylax.org/eco120/fall2016/bls20161007_short.pdf.

Bureau of Labor Statistics (BLS). Table 3.3. Civilian Labor Force Participation Rate by Age, Gender, Race, and Ethnicity, 1994, 2004, 2014, and projected 2024 (in percent), December 8, 2015. https://www.bls.gov/emp/ep_table_301.htm.

Bush, Vannevar. *Science, the Endless Frontier: A Report to the President on a Program for Postwar Scientific Research*. Washington, DC: U.S. Government Printing Office, July 1945; reissued by the National Science Foundation on NSF's tenth anniversary, July 1960). https://archive.org/stream/scienceendlessfr00unit/scienceendlessfr00unit_djvu.txt.

Butler, Willem, and Ebrahim Rahbari. The "Strong Dollar" Policy of the U.S.: Alice in Wonderland Semantics vs. Economic Reality. *Vox, CEPR Economic Policy Portal*, July 28, 2011. http://voxeu.org/article/strong-dollar-policy-us.

Caballero, Ricardo J., Emmanuel Farhi, and Pierre-Olivier Gourinchas. Safe Asset Scarcity and Aggregate Demand, January 26, 2016, later released as NBER Working Paper 22044, National Bureau of Economic Research, Cambridge, MA, February 2016.

Cardarelli, Roberto, and Lusine Lusinyan. U.S. Total Factor Productivity Slowdown: Evidence from the U.S. States. IMF Working Paper, International Monetary Fund, Washington, DC, May 2015.

Carlaw, Kenneth I., and Richard G. Lipsey. Does History Matter? Empirical Analysis of Evolutionary versus Stationary Equilibrium Views of the Economy. *Journal of Evolutionary Economics* 22, no. 4 (2012): 735–766.

Carlino, Gerald, and William R. Kerr. Agglomeration and Innovation. NBER Working Paper 20367, National Bureau of Economic Research, Cambridge, MA, August 2014.

Carnevale, Anthony P., Tamara Jayasundera, and Artem Gulish. America's Divided Recovery: College Haves and Have-Nots. Washington, DC: Georgetown University Center on Education and the Workforce, 2016. https://cew.georgetown.edu/wp-content/uploads/Americas-Divided-Recovery-web.pdf.

Carnevale, Anthony P., N. Smith, and J. Strohl. Help Wanted: Projections of Jobs and Education Requirements through 2018. Washington, DC: Georgetown University Center on Education and the Workforce, 2010. https://cew.georgetown.edu/wp-content/uploads/2014/12/fullreport.pdf.

Catapult. High Value Manufacturing Centres. https://hvm.catapult.org.uk/hvm-centres/.

Census Bureau. 2014 Statistics of U.S. Businesses Annual Data Tables by Establishment, U.S., NAICS sectors, larger employment sizes up to 10,000+, September 29, 2016. https://www.census.gov/data/tables/2014/econ/susb/2014-susb-annual.html.

Census Bureau. Foreign Trade Statistics, Trade in Goods with Advanced Technology Products, 2015. https://www.census.gov/foreign-trade/balance/c0007.html#2015.

Census Bureau. Income, Poverty and Health Insurance Coverage in the United States 2015. CB16-158, September 13, 2016. http://www.census.gov/newsroom/press-releases/2016/cb16-158.html.

Census Bureau. New American Community Survey Statistics for Income, Poverty and Health Insurance. CB16-159, September 16, 2016. http://www.census.gov/newsroom/press-releases/2016/cb16-159.html.

Census Bureau. Real Median Family Income in the United States [MEFAINUSA672N]. FRED, Federal Reserve Bank of St. Louis. https://fred.stlouisfed.org/series/MEFAINUSA672N.

Census Bureau. U.S. Trade in Goods and Services—Balance of Payments (BOP) Basis, February 7, 2017. https://www.census.gov/foreign-trade/statistics/historical/gands.pdf.

Chain Reaction Innovations website. http://chainreaction.anl.gov.

Chan, Sharon Pian. Long Antitrust Saga Ends for Microsoft. *Seattle Times*, May 12, 2011.

Chandra, Amitabh, and Eric Thompson. Does Public Infrastructure Affect Economic Activity? Evidence from the Rural Interstate Highway System. *Regional Science and Urban Economics* 30, no. 4 (2000): 457–490.

Charles, Kerwin Kofi, Erik Hurst, and Matthew J. Notowidigdo. The Masking of the Decline in Manufacturing Employment by the House Bubble. *Journal of Economic Perspectives* 30, no. 2 (Spring 2016): 179–200.

Chazen, Benjamin J. Venture Capital and Research Centers, MIT Washington Office, Washington, DC, August 2016. http://dc.mit.edu/resources/policy-resources.

Chernow, Ron. *Titan*. New York: Vintage, 1997.

China Passes U.S. as Largest Manufacturer. *Wall Street Journal*, March 14, 2011. http://247wallst.com/2011/03/14/china-passes-the-us-as-largest-manufacturer/.

China Unveils Internet Plus Action Plan to Fuel Growth. Xinhua, July 4, 2015. http://english.cntv.cn/2015/05/22/VIDE1432284846519817.shtml.

Christensen, Clayton. *The Innovator's Dilemma*. Cambridge, MA: Harvard Business School Press, 1997.

Chu, Jessica. American Made? MIT Forum Examines the Role of Manufacturing in Rebuilding the Economy. MIT News Office, September 16, 2011. http://news.mit.edu/2011/manufacturing-event-pie-0916.

Coder, Jon, and Gordon Green. Comparing Earnings of White Males by Education, for Selected Age Cohorts, High School vs College Graduates. Annapolis, MD: Sentier Research, October 2016. http://www.sentierresearch.com/StatBriefs/Sentier_Income_Trends_WorkingClassWages_1996to2014_Brief_10_05_16.pdf.

Cohen, Stephen S., and John Zysman. *Manufacturing Matters: The Myth of a Post-industrial Economy*. New York: Basic Books, 1987.

Cohen, Wesley M. and Daniel A. Levinthal. Absorptive Capacity: A New Perspective on Learning and Innovation. *Administrative Science Quarterly* 35, 1990, 128–152.

Comin, D., and B. Hohij. Cross-Country Technological Adoption: Making the Theories Face the Facts. *Journal of Monetary Economics* 51 (2004): 39–83.

Congressional Budget Office (CBO). Public Spending on Transportation and Water Infrastructure, 1956 to 2014. Washington, DC: Congressional Budget Office, March 2015.

Council of Economic Advisors to the President, Economic Report of the President Together with the Annual Report of the Council of Economic Advisors. Washington, DC: White House, February 2016.

Cowen, Tyler. *Average Is Over: Powering America beyond the Age of the Great Stagnation*. New York: Plume, 2014.

Cowen, Tyler. *The Great Stagnation*. New York: Dutton Penguin, 2011.

Cross, Tim. After Moore's Law. *The Economist* (Technology Quarterly), March 12, 2016. http://www.economist.com/technology-quarterly/2016-03-12/after-moores-law.

Cummings, Jonathan, James Manyika, Lenny Mendonca, Ezra Greenberg, Steven Aronowitz, Rohit Chopra, Katy Elkin, Sreenivas Ramaswamy, Jimmy Soni, and Allison Watson. Growth and Competitiveness in the United States: The Role of Its Multinational Companies. McKinsey Global Institute, June 2010.

Cyclotron Road. 2016 Annual Report, Building a Home for Hard Science Innovators—The Cyclotron Road Pilot. March 2016. https://static1.squarespace.com /static/543fdfece4b0faf7175a91ec/t/58cad7399de4bb7b62b0750f/1489688386385 /2016-Cycloton-Road-Annual-Report-Online.pdf.

Cyclotron Road. 2015 Report—A New Pathway for Hard Technology: Support-ing Energy Innovators at Cyclotron Road, 2015. http://static1.squarespace.com /static/543fdfece4b0faf7175a91ec/t/55efcf96e4b0fe570119a737/1441779606809 /Cyclotron_Road_A_New_Pathway_final.pdf.

Cyclotron Road website. http://www.cyclotronroad.org/home.

Dahlman, Carl J. *The World under Pressure; How China and India Are Influencing the Global Economy and Environment*. Stanford, CA: Stanford University Press, 2012.

Davis, Donald R., and Prachi Mishra. Stolper-Samuelson Is Dead and Other Crimes of Both Theory and Data. In *Globalization and Poverty*, edited by Ann Harrison. Chi-cago: University of Chicago Press, 2007, 87–107.

Davis, Donald R., David E. Weinstein, Scott C. Bradford, and Kazushige Shimpo. Using International and Japanese Regional Data to Determine When the Factor Abundance Theory of Trade Works. *American Economic Review* 87, no. 3 (June 1997): 421–446.

Defense Advanced Research Projects Agency (DARPA). Adaptive Vehicle Make (AVM) website. http://www.darpa.mil/program/adaptive-vehicle-make.

Defense Production Act, Pub. L. No. 81-774, 50 U.S.C. § 2061 et seq. (1950).

Deloitte Ltd. Manufacturing USA: A Third-Party Evaluation of Program Design and Progress. Report. Washington, DC: Deloitte Ltd., January 2017. https://www2 .deloitte.com/content/dam/Deloitte/us/Documents/manufacturing/us-mfg -manufacturing-USA-program-and-process.pdf.

Deloitte Ltd. and the Manufacturing Institute. Boiling Point? The Skills Gap in U.S. Manufacturing (2011). www.themanufacturinginstitute.org/~/media/A07730B2A79 8437D98501E798C2E13AA.ashx.

Deloitte Ltd. and the Manufacturing Institute. The Skills Gap in U.S. Manufacturing: 2015 and Beyond (2015). http://www2.deloitte.com/us/en/pages/manufacturing /articles/boiling-point-the-skills-gap-in-us-manufacturing.html.

Department of Defense (DOD). DOD Announces Award of New Advanced Robotics Manufacturing (ARM) Innovation Hub in Pittsburgh, Pennsylvania. Release NR-009-17, January 13, 2016. https://www.defense.gov/News/News-Releases/News -Release-View/Article/1049127/dod-announces-award-of-new-advanced-robotics -manufacturing-arm-innovation-hub-i.

Department of Defense (DOD) Mantech, Robots in Manufacturing Environments Manufacturing Innovation Institute, Proposers Day, slide presentation, August 15, 2016, https://s3.amazonaws.com/sitesusa/wp-content/uploads/sites/802/2016/08 /RIME_Proposers_Day_final.pdf.

Department of Defense (DOD), Office of the Assistant Secretary for Research and Engineering. Technology Readiness Levels Guidance, updated May 13, 2011. http:// www.acq.osd.mil/chieftechnologist/publications/docs/TRA2011.pdf.

Department of Energy (DOE), Office of Energy Efficiency and Renewable Energy. Build-4Scale. http://energy.gov/eere/articles/build4scale-training-cleantech-entrepreneurs -manufacturing-success.

Department of Energy (DOE), Office of Energy Efficiency and Renewable Energy website. http://energy.gov/eere/technology-to-market/build4scale-manufacturing -training-cleantech-entrepreneurs.

Department of Labor (DOL), Employment and Training Administration. Business, Industry and Key Sector Initiatives, Community-Based Job Training Grants. https:// www.doleta.gov/business/Community-BasedJobTrainingGrants.cfm.

Department of Labor (DOL), Employment and Training Administration. TAACCCT. https://www.doleta.gov/taaccct/.

Department of Labor (DOL), Employment and Training Administration. Workforce Investment Act—Adult and Dislocated Workers Program. https://www.doleta.gov /programs/general_info.cfm.

Department of the Treasury, Daily Treasury Yield Curve Rates. https://www.treasury .gov/resource-center/data-chart-center/interest-rates/Pages/TextView.aspx?data =yieldYear&year=2015.

Dertouzos, Michael, Robert Solow, Richard Lester, and the MIT Commission on Industrial Production. *Made in America: Regaining the Productive Edge.* Cambridge, MA: MIT Press, 1989.

DG Trade Statistics. World Trade in Goods, Services, FDI, January 2016. http://trade .ec.europa.eu/doclib/docs/2013/may/tradoc_151348.pdf.

Dimitri, Carolyn, Anne Effland, and Neilson Conklin. The 20th Century Transformation of U.S. Agriculture and Farm Policy. Economic Information Bulletin No. 3, USDA Economic Research Service, June 2005.

Dizikes, Peter. A Manufacturing Renaissance for America? At an MIT Forum Experts Examine New Ways to Pursue a Good Old Idea: Making Things. MIT News Office, March 31, 2010. http://news.mit.edu/2010/future-manufacture-0331.

Dizikes, Peter. Reif Briefs Obama in White House—Advanced Manufacturing Partnership 2.0 Delivers Report on Developing Innovation Based Growth. MIT News Office, October 28, 2014. http://news.mit.edu/2014/reif-briefs-obama-innovation-economy -1028.

Dragon Innovation website. https://dragoninnovation.com.

Dredge, Stuart. Kickstarter's Biggest Hits—Why Crowdfunding Now Sets the Trends. *The Guardian*, April 17, 2014.

Driskell, James E., Paul H. Radtke, and Eduardo Salas. Virtual Teams: Effects of Technological Mediation on Team Performance, *Group Dynamics: Theory, Research and Practice* 7, no. 4 (December 2003): 297–323.

Duernecker, Georg. Technology Adoption, Turbulence, and the Dynamics of Unemployment. Paper, University of Mannheim, 2009.

Duranton, Gilles, and Matthew A. Turner. Urban Growth and Transportation. *Review of Economic Studies* 79, no. 4 (2012): 1407–1440.

Dvorkin, Maximiliano. Jobs Involving Routine Tasks Aren't Growing. Federal Reserve Bank of St. Louis, January 4, 2016. https://www.stlouisfed.org/on-the -economy/2016/january/jobs-involving-routine-tasks-arent-growing.

Economic Development Administration. Investing in Manufacturing Communities Partnership (IMCP). https://www.eda.gov/challenges/imcp/.

Economic Development Board of Singapore. Future of Manufacturing in Singapore. Presentation, March 2015. http://www.smartindustry.com/assets/Uploads/SI-PS -Singapore-Inofpack.pdf.

Eddison, Eliza. Survey of Federal Manufacturing Efforts. MIT Washington Office, Washington, DC, September 2010. http://dc.mit.edu/resources/policy-resources.

Eggertsson, Gauti B., Neil R. Mehrotra, and Lawrence H. Summers. Secular Stagnation in the Open Economy. *American Economic Review: Papers and Proceedings* 106, no. 5 (2016): 503–507.

Eli Whitney Museum and Workshop. Arms Production at the Whitney Armory, Mechanization in the Early Period, The Factory. https://www.eliwhitney.org/7/museum/eli -whitney/arms-production, and https://www.eliwhitney.org/7/museum/about-eli -whitney/factory.

ERC Association website. http://erc-assoc.org.

Ezell, Stephen. Our Manufacturers Need a U.S. Competitiveness Strategy, Not Special Treatment. The Innovation Files, Information Technology and Innovation Foundation

(ITIF), February 9, 2016. http://www.innovationfiles.org/our-manufacturers-need-a-u
-s-competitiveness-strategy-not-special-treatment/.

Fazio, Catherine, Jorge Guzman, Fiona Murray, and Scott Stern. A New View of the
Skew: A Quantitative Assessment of the Quality of American Entrepreneurship.
Paper, MIT Laboratory for Innovation Science and Policy, February 2016. http://
innovation.mit.edu/assets/A-New-View_Final-Report_5.4.16.pdf.

Federal Reserve Bank of St. Louis and U.S. Office of Management and Budget. Federal Debt: Total Public Debt as Percent of Gross Domestic Product [GFDEGDQ188S].
https://fred.stlouisfed.org/series/GFDEGDQ188S.

Federal Reserve Bank of St. Louis, Economic Research. Manufacturing as a Percentage of
GDP, Q3 2015, citing BEA data. https://research.stlouisfed.org/fred2/series/VAPGDPMA.

Federal Reserve Bank of St. Louis, Economic Research. Trade Weighted U.S. Dollar
Index: Major Currencies. https://research.stlouisfed.org/fred2/series/DTWEXM.

Federal Reserve Economic Data. Employment by Economic Activity for: Manufacturing: All Persons for the Republic of Korea, Persons, Monthly, Seasonally Adjusted;
Employment by Economic Activity: Manufacturing: All Persons for Japan, Persons,
Monthly, Not Seasonally Adjusted; All Employees: Manufacturing Vintage: 2016-08-
05, Thousands of Persons, Monthly, Seasonally Adjusted; All Employees: Manufacturing Vintage: 2016-09-02, Thousands of Persons, Monthly, Seasonally Adjusted;
Employment by Economic Activity: Manufacturing: All Persons for Germany, Persons, Quarterly, Not Seasonally Adjusted. https://fred.stlouisfed.org/.

Federal Reserve System Board of Governors. Trade Weighted U.S. Dollar Index:
Major Currencies [DTWEXM]. https://fred.stlouisfed.org/series/DTWEXM.

Fink, Yoel. Slide presentation in webinar for AFFOA participants on July 15, 2016.

Finley, Klint. This News-Writing Bot Is Now Free for Everyone. *Wired*, October 20,
2015.

Finneran, Kevin. Middle Class Muddle. *Issues in Science and Technology* 33, no.1 (Fall
2016): 39–40.

$500m/5 year plan announced by the Deputy Prime Minister, Budget Speech in
2013. http://www.smartindustry.com/assets/Uploads/SI-PS-Singapore-Inofpack.pdf.

Fleming, Michael J., and Nicholas J. Klagge. The Federal Reserve's Foreign Exchange
Swap Lines. *Federal Reserve Bank of New York Current Issues in Economics and Finance*
16, no. 4 (April 2010): 1–7.

Florida Advanced Technology Education (FLATE). Infographic of Pathways
Which Are Not Linear. http://fl-ate.org/wp-content/uploads/2014/12/10_2016-ET
-Highlights.pdf.

Florida Advanced Technology Education (FLATE). Regional and Statewide Impacts.
http://fl-ate.org/about-us/impact/.

Florida Department of Education. 2015–16 Frameworks, Manufacturing. http://www
.fldoe.org/academics/career-adult-edu/career-tech-edu/curriculum-frameworks/2015
-16-frameworks/manufacturing.stml.

Fong, Glenn R. ARPA Does Windows: The Defense Underpinning of the PC Revolution. *Business and Politics* 3, no. 3 (2001): 213–237.

Fong, Glenn R. Breaking New Ground or Breaking the Rules—Strategic Reorientation in US Industrial Policy. *International Security* 25, no. 2 (Fall 2000): 152–162.

Fong, Glenn R. Follower at the Frontier: International Competition and Japanese Industrial Policy. *International Studies Quarterly* 42, no. 2 (1998): 339–366.

Foote, Andrew, Michel Grosz, and Ann Huff Stevens. Locate Your Nearest Exit: Mass Layoffs and Local Labor Market Response. NBER Working Paper 21618, National Bureau of Economic Research, Cambridge, MA, October 2015. http://www.nber.org
/papers/w21618.

Ford, Martin. *Rise of the Robots: Technology and the Threat of a Jobless Future.* New York: Basic Books, 2015.

Forschungsunion and Acatech (National Academy of Science and Engineering). Securing the Future of German Manufacturing Industry, Recommendations for Implementing the Strategic Initiative Industrie 4.0. Final report of the Industrie 4.0 Working Group, April 2013. http://docplayer.net/254711-Securing-the-future-of
-german-manufacturing-industry-recommendations-for-implementing-the-strategic
-initiative-industrie-4-0.html.

Fraumeni, Barbara M. The Contribution of Highways to GDP Growth. NBER Working Paper 14736, National Bureau of Economic Research, Cambridge, MA, February 2009.

Fraunhofer Academy. Leitbild Der Fraunhofer Academy, 2016. http://www.academy
.fraunhofer.de/de/ueber-uns/profil-selbstverstaendnis/leitbild.html.

Fraunhofer Center for Sustainable Energy Systems (CSE) website. http://www.cse
.fraunhofer.org/about.

Fraunhofer Center for Sustainable Energy Systems (CSE) Research Facilities website. http://www.cse.fraunhofer.org/about-fraunhofer-cse/labs-and-facilities.

Fraunhofer Center for Sustainable Energy Systems (CSE) TechBridge website. http://
www.cse.fraunhofer.org/techbridge/method.

Fraunhofer Gesellschaft, Fraunhofer Institutes and Research Establishments website. http://www.fraunhofer.de/en/institutes-research-establishments/.

Fraunhofer Gesellschaft. Statute, as revised in 2010, Section 20, The Institutes; Section 21, Institute Management. http://www.izm.fraunhofer.de/content/dam/izm/en
/documents/Institut/Statute-of-the-Fraunhofer-Gesellschaft_tcm63-8090.pdf.

Freeman, Christopher. Formal Scientific and Technical Institutions in the National System of Innovation, in B.-Å. Lundvall, ed., *National Systems of Innovation: Towards a Theory of Innovation and Interactive Learning*. London, New York: Pinter, 1992, 169–187.

Freeman, Richard B. *America Works: The Exceptional U.S. Labor Market*. New York: Russell Sage Foundation, 2007.

Frey, Carl Benedikt, and Michael A. Osborne. The Future of Employment: How Susceptible Are Jobs to Computerization? Working Paper, Oxford Martin Programme on Technology and Employment, September 17, 2013. http://www.oxfordmartin.ox .ac.uk/downloads/academic/future-of-employment.pdf.

Fuchs, Erica, and Randolph Kirchain. Design for Location? The Impact of Manufacturing Offshore on Technology Competitiveness in the Optoelectronics Industry. *Management Science* 56, no. 12 (December 2010): 2323–2349.

Furman, Jason. Trends in Labor Force Participation. Presentation, National Press Club, August 6, 2015. https://www.whitehouse.gov/sites/default/files/docs/20150806 _labor_force_participation_retirement_research_consortium.pdf.

Gaddy, Benjamin, Varun Sivaram, Timothy Jones, and Libby Wayman. Venture Capital and Cleantech: The Wrong Model for Energy Innovation. *Social Science Research Network (SSRN)*, June 2, 2016. https://ssrn.com/abstract=2788919.

Gaddy, Benajmin, Varun Sivaram, and Francis O'Sullivan. Venture Capital and Cleantech. Working Paper, MIT Energy Initiative, July 2016. http://energy.mit.edu /wp-content/uploads/2016/07/MITEI-WP-2016-06.pdf.

German Federal Ministry for Economic Affairs and Energy. The German Mittelstand: Facts and Figures about German SMEs, SME-shares in Germany in % (table), 2016. http://www.bmwi.de/English/Redaktion/Pdf/wirtschaftsmotor-mittelstand-zahlen -und-fakten-zu-den-deutschen-kmu,property=pdf,bereich=bmwi2012,sprache =en,rwb=true.pdf.

German Federal Ministry for Economic Affairs and Energy. Make It in Germany: Introducing the German Mittelstand. http://www.make-it-in-germany.com/en/for -qualified-professionals/working/mittelstand.

Germany Trade and Invest. Industrie 4.0—Smart Manufacturing for the Future. Germany Trade and Invest, Berlin, July 2014. http://www.gtai.de/GTAI/Content/EN /Invest/_SharedDocs/Downloads/GTAI/Brochures/Industries/industrie4.0-smart -manufacturing-for-the-future-en.pdf.

Giffi, Craig, Ben Dollar, Jennifer McNelly, and Gardner Carrick. The Skills Gap in U.S. Manufacturing: 2015 and Beyond. Deloitte LLC, 2015.

Gini, Al. Work, Identity and Self: How We Are Formed by the Work We Do. *Journal of Business Ethics* 17 (1998): 707–714.

Glaeser, Edward L. Introduction. In *Agglomeration, Organization and Entrepreneurship, Agglomeration Economics*, edited by Edward L. Glaeser, 7. Chicago: University of Chicago Press, 2010, 1–14.

Global Macro Monitor. Chart, U.S. Employment in Manufacturing, using BLS data. https://www.creditwritedowns.com/2012/05/chart-of-the-day-us-manufacturing-unemployment-1960-2012.html.

Goby, Pascal. Facebook Investor Wants Flying Cars, Not 140 Characters. *Business Insider*, July 30, 2011. http://www.businessinsider.com/founders-fund-the-future-2011-7.

Goddard, John, Douglas Robertson, and Paul Vallance. Universities, Technology and Innovation Centres and Regional Development: The Case of the North-East of England. *Cambridge Journal of Economics* 36, no. 3 (2012): 609–627.

Gold, Stephen. The Competitive Edge: Manufacturing's Multiplier Effect—It's Bigger Than You Think. *Industry Week*, September 2, 2014. http://www.industryweek.com/global-economy/competitive-edge-manufacturings-multiplier-effect-its-bigger-you-think.

Goldin, Claudia, and Lawrence F. Katz. *The Race between Education and Technology*. Cambridge, MA: Harvard University Press, 2008.

Goldin, Claudia, and Lawrence F. Katz. The Race between Education and Technology: The Evolution of U.S. Educational Wage Differentials, 1890 to 2005. NBER Working Paper 12984, National Bureau of Economic Research, Cambridge, MA, March 2007.

Goodman, Madeline J., Anita M. Sands, and Richard J. Coley. *America's Skills Challenge: Millennials and the Future*. Princeton, NJ: Educational Testing Service, 2015. https://www.ets.org/s/research/29836/.

Gordon, Robert J. Does the "New Economy" Measure Up to the Great Inventions of the Past? NBER Working Paper 7835, National Bureau of Economic Research, Cambridge, MA, August 2000. http://www.nber.org/papers/w7833, published in *Journal of Economic Perspectives* 14, no. 4 (Fall 2000): 49–74.

Gordon, Robert J. *Productivity Growth, Inflation, and Unemployment: The Collected Essays of Robert J. Gordon*. Cambridge: Cambridge University Press, 2004.

Gordon, Robert. *The Rise and Fall of American Growth*. Princeton, NJ: Princeton University Press, 2016.

Gordon, Robert J. Secular Stagnation: A Supply-Side View. *American Economic Review: Papers and Proceedings* 105, no. 5 (2015): 54–59

Gordon, Robert J. U.S. Productivity Growth: The Slowdown Has Returned after a Temporary Revival. *International Productivity Monitor* 23 (Spring 2013): 13–19.

Government Accountability Office (GAO). Advanced Manufacturing: Commerce Could Strengthen Collaboration with Other Agencies on Innovation Institutes. GAO-17-320. Washington, DC: Government Accountability Office, April 6, 2017. http://www.gao.gov/products/GAO-17-320?source=ra.

Government Accountability Office (GAO). Defense Additive Manufacturing—DOD Needs to Systematically Track Department-wide 3D Printing Efforts. GAO 16-56. Washington, DC: Government Accountability Office, October 2015.

Governor of Connecticut's Transportation Finance Panel. Final Report, January 15, 2016. http://portal.ct.gov/uploadedFiles/Departments_and_Agencies/Office_of_the _Governor/Learn_More/Working_Groups/2016.01.15%20TFP%20final%20report.pdf.

Graetz, Georg, and Guy Michaels. Robots at Work. Centre for Economic Performance Discussion Paper 1335 Centre for Economic Performance, London, England, March 2015.

Grossman, Gene M., and Elhanan Helpman. Growth, Trade, and Inequality. Working Paper, Princeton University, Princeton, NJ, June 30, 2016. https://www.princeton .edu/~grossman/Growth_Trade_and_Inequality_063016.pdfgr.

Guzman, Jorge, and Scott Stern. The State of American Entrepreneurship: New Estimates of the Quantity and Quality of Entrepreneurship for 15 U.S. States, 1998–2014. NBER Working Paper 22095, National Bureau of Economic Research, Cambridge, MA, March 2016, http://jorgeg.scripts.mit.edu/homepage/wp-content/uploads/2016 /03/Guzman-Stern-State-of-American-Entrepreneurship-FINAL.pdf.

Hagemann, Harald. Solow's 1956 Contribution in the Context of the Harrod-Domar Model. Annual supplement, *History of Political Economy* 41 (2009): 67–87.

Handel, Michael J. Presentation on Skills, Job Creation and Labour Market, Conference on Smart Industry: Enabling the Next Production Revolution, OECD and Sweden Ministry of Enterprise and Innovation, Stockholm, September 18, 2016.

Hart, John. Syllabus, Fundaments of Manufacturing Process, MITx and edX online education platforms, 2016. https://www.edx.org/course/fundamentals-manufacturing -processes-mitx-2-008x.

Hartwig, Jochen. Has "Baumol's Disease" Really Been Cured? KOF Working Paper 155, Swiss Institute for Business Cycle Research, Zurich, Switzerland, November 2006.

Hatch, Nile W., and David C. Mowery. Process Innovation and Learning by Doing in Semiconductor Manufacturing. *Management Science* 44, no. 11, pt 1 of 2 (November 1998): 1461–1477.

Hathaway, Ian, and Robert Litan. Declining Business Dynamism in the United States: A Look at States and Metros. Paper, Brookings Institution Economic Studies, Washington, DC, May 2014. http://www.brookings.edu/~/media/research/files

/papers/2014/05/declining%20business%20dynamism%20litan/declining_business _dynamism_hathaway_litan.pdf.

Hauser, Herman, for Lord Mandelson, Secretary of State. The Current and Future Roles of Technology and Innovation Centres in the UK. https://interact.innovateuk .org/documents/1524978/2139688/The+Current+and+Future+Role+of+Technology+ and+Innovation+Centres+in+the+UK/e1b5f4ae-fec8-495d-bbd5-28dacdfee186.

Heilbroner, Robert. The Embarrassment of Economics. *Challenge*, November–December 1996, 47–49.

Hejlund, Nauna. Presentation on Skills, Job Creation and Labour Market, Conference on Smart Industry: Enabling the Next Production Revolution, OECD and Sweden Ministry of Enterprise and Innovation, Stockholm, September 18, 2016.

Helper, Susan. How to Make American Manufacturing Great Again. Real Clear Policy, September 15, 2016. http://www.realclearpolicy.com/blog/2016/09/15/how _to_make_american_manufacturing_great_again.html.

Helper, Susan, and Timothy Kruger. Supply Chains and Equitable Growth. Report. Washington Center for Equitable Growth, Washington, DC, September 2016. http://cdn.equitablegrowth.org/wp-content/uploads/2016/09/30134051/092816 -supply-chains.pdf.

Helper, Susan, Timothy Krueger, and Howard Wial. Why Does Manufacturing Matter? Which Manufacturing Matters? Paper, Metropolitan Policy Program, Brookings Institution, Washington, DC, February 22, 2016. https://www.brookings.edu/wp -content/uploads/2016/06/0222_manufacturing_helper_krueger_wial.pdf.

Helper, Susan, and Howard Wial. Strengthening American Manufacturing: A New Federal Approach. Paper, Metropolitan Policy Program, Brookings Institution, Washington, DC, September 2010.

Helpman, Elhanan. Increasing Returns, Imperfect Markets, and Trade Theory. In *Handbook of International Economics*, vol.1, edited by R. W. Jones and P. B. Kenen, 325–365. Amsterdam: Elsevier Science Publishers, 1984.

Helpman, Elhanan. *The Mystery of Economic Growth*. Cambridge, MA: Belknap, 2004.

Helpman, Elhanan. *Understanding Global Trade*. Cambridge, MA: Harvard University Press, 2011.

Hennigan, Michael. Germany's Record Trade Surplus in 2015. *finfacts*, February 10, 2016. http://www.finfacts.ie/Irish_finance_news/articleDetail.php?Germany-s -record-trade-surplus-in-2015-US-UK-France-in-deficit-520.

Herrendorf, Berhold, Richard Rogerson, and Akos Valentinyi. Growth and Structural Transformation. In *Handbook of Economic Growth*, vol. 2B, edited by Philippe Aghion and Steven N. Durlauf, 855–941. Amsterdam: Elsevier, 2014.

Higgins, Benjamin. The Concept of Secular Stagnation. *American Economic Review* 40, no. 1 (March 1950): 160–166.

High Performance Computing Act of 1991. Pub. L. No. 102-194, 105 Stat. 1594 (1991), 15 U.S.C. § 5501 (1991).

Hiltzik, Michael A. *Dealers of Lightning: Xerox PARC and the Dawn of the Computer Age*. New York: HarperCollins, 1999.

Hockfield to Co-chair U.S. Manufacturing Partnership. MIT News Office, June 24, 2011. http://news.mit.edu/2011/hockfield-obama-manufacturing-0624.

Holodny, Elena. The 11 Countries with the Best Infrastructure around the World. *Business Insider*, October 2, 2015.

Holzer, Harry J. Higher Education Workforce Policy: Creating More Skilled Workers (and Jobs for Them to Fill). Washington, DC: Brookings Institution, 2014.

Holzer, Harry J., and Robert I. Lerman. The Future of Middle-Skills Jobs. Paper, Brookings Institution, Washington, DC, 2009. www.brookings.edu/~/media/Files/rc /papers/2009/02_middle_skill_jobs_holzer/02_middle_skill_jobs_holzer.pdf.

House, Christopher L., Christian Proebsting, and Linda Tesar. Austerity in the Aftermath of the Great Recession. NBER Draft, National Bureau of Economic Research, Cambridge, MA, November 24, 2015.

Houseman, Susan N., Timothy J. Bartik, and Timothy J. Sturgeon. Measuring Manufacturing: How the Computer and Semiconductor Industries Affect the Numbers and Perceptions. Upjohn Institute Working Paper 14-209 Upjohn Institute, Kalamazoo, MI, January 2014.

Houseman, Susan, Christopher Kurz, Paul Lengermann, and Benjamin Mandel. Offshoring Bias in U.S. Manufacturing. *Journal of Economic Perspectives* 25, no. 2 (2011): 111–132. http://pubs.aeaweb.org/doi/pdfplus/10.1257/jep.25.2.111.

House of Commons (UK), Committee on Science and Technology. Technology and Innovation Centres, 2011. http://www.publications.parliament.uk/pa/cm201011 /cmselect/cmsctech/619/619.pdf.

Howells, Jeremy, Intermediation and the role of intermediaries in innovation. *Research Policy* 35, 2006, 715–728.

Huebner, Jonathan. A Possible Declining Trend in Worldwide Innovation. *Journal of Technological Forecasting and Social Change* 72 (2005): 980–986. http://accelerating .org/articles/InnovationHuebnerTFSC2005.pdf.

Hughes, Kent H. *Building the Next American Century—The Past and Future of American Economic Competitiveness*. Washington, DC: Woodrow Wilson Center Press, 2005.

IACMI. Composites Workforce 2015. http://iacmi.org/wp-content/uploads/2016/04/IACMI_OnePager_FINAL_2015_UPDATE.pdf.

IACMI website. http://iacmi.org.

Indiana Economic Development Corporation. Indiana Adds Chief Innovation Officer to Economic Development Corporation. August 16, 2016. http://iacmi.org/2016/08/16/indiana-adds-chief-innovation-officer-economic-development-corporation/.

Innovation 25 Council. Innovation 25—Creating the Future, Challenging Unlimited Possibilities. Interim Report, February 26, 2007. http://japan.kantei.go.jp/innovation/interimbody_e.html.

International Federation of Robotics and United Nations Economic Commission for Europe. World Robotics: 2015, 2014, 2013, 2010, 2009, 2005, 2004. https://ifr.org/worldrobotics/.

International Monetary Fund (IMF). World Economic Outlook 2014: Legacies, Clouds, Uncertainties. Washington, DC: International Monetary Fund, October 2014.

International Trade Administration (ITA). Trading Companies, One third of goods trade (by value) came from SMEs. http://www.trade.gov/mas/ian/build/groups/public/@tg_ian/documents/webcontent/tg_ian_005369.pdf.

International Trade Commission. Antidumping and Countervailing Duty Investigations, as of March 30, 2017. https://www.usitc.gov/trade_remedy/731_ad_701_cvd/investigations.htm.

Ishikawa, Kaoru. *What Is Total Quality Control? The Japanese Way*. Englewood Cliffs, NJ: Prentice–Hall, 1985.

Jacobs, Ken, Zohar Perla, Ian Perry, and Dave Graham-Squire. *Producing Poverty: The Public Cost of Low Wage Production Jobs in Manufacturing*. Berkeley, CA: UC Berkeley Center for Labor Research and Education, May 2016.

Jamshidi, Mo, ed. *System of Systems Engineering*. Hoboken, NJ: John Wiley and Sons, 2009.

Jensen, Bradford, Dennis Quinn, and Stephen Weymouth. Winners and Losers in International Trade: The Effects on U.S. Presidential Voting. Paper, Georgetown University, Washington, DC, June 10, 2016. http://cmepr.gmu.edu/wp-content/uploads/2016/10/jqw_trade_voting.pdf.

Johnson, R. Colin. Samsung Breaks Ground on $14 Billion Fab. *EE Times*, May 8, 2015.

Jones, Larry E., and Rodolfo E. Manuelli. Neoclassical Models of Endogenous Growth: The Effects of Fiscal Policy, Innovation and Fluctuations. In *Handbook of Economic Growth*, vol. 1A, edited by Philippe Aghion and Steven N. Durlauf, 13–65. Amsterdam: Elsevier, 2005.

Jorgenson, Dale. U.S. Economic Growth in the Information Age. *Issues in Science and Technology* 18, no. 1 (Fall 2001): 42–50. http://www.issues.org/18.1/jorgenson.html.

Jumpstart Our Business Startups (JOBS) Act, H.R. 3606, 112th Cong., 2nd Sess. (2012).

Kalil, Thomas, and Jason Miller. Advancing U.S. Leadership in High Performance Computing. White House Blog, July 29, 2015. https://obamawhitehouse.archives.gov/blog/2015/07/29/advancing-us-leadership-high-performance-computing.

Kearney, Melissa S., Brad Hershbein, and Elisa Jacome. Profiles of Change: Employment, Earnings and Occupations from 1990–2013. Washington, DC: Brookings Institution, 2015.

Kennedy, Scott. Made in China 2025. Center for Strategic and International Studies (CSIS), June 1, 2015. https://www.csis.org/analysis/made-china-2025.

Keynes, John Maynard. *Essays in Persuasion*. New York: Classic House Books, 2009.

Kharpal, Arjun. Apple plans two more R&D centers in China as its challenges in the country continue, CNBC, March 17, 2017. http://www.cnbc.com/2017/03/17/apple-china-two-more-research-centers-as-challenges-continue.html.

Kitchens, Carl, and Price Fishback. Flip the Switch: The Impact of the Rural Electrification Administration 1935–1940. *Journal of Economic History* 75, no. 4 (December 2015): 1161–1195.

Kolman, Joseff. Summary of Federal, State, University, and Private Programs for Supporting Emerging Technology. MIT Washington Office, Washington, DC, July 10, 2015. http://dc.mit.edu/resources/policy-resources.

KPMG. Innovated in China: New Frontier for Global R&D. *China 360*, August 2013.

Krafcik, John F. Triumph of the Lean Production System. *Sloan Management Review* 30, no. 1 (1998): 41–52.

Krugman, Paul. Border Tax Two-Step (Wonkish). *The New York Times,* January 27, 2017, https://krugman.blogs.nytimes.com/2017/01/27/border-tax-two-step-wonkish/?_r=0.

Krugman, Paul. Domestic Distortions and the Deindustrialization Hypothesis. NBER Working Paper 5472, National Bureau of Economic Research, Cambridge, MA, March 1996.

Krugman, Paul. How Did Economics Get It So Wrong? *New York Times*, September 2, 2009. http://www.nytimes.com/2009/09/06/magazine/06Economic-t.html.

Krugman, Paul. The Increasing Returns Revolution in Trade and Geography. Nobel Prize Lecture, December 8, 2008.

Kuah, Adrian T. H. Cluster Theory and Practice: Advantages for the Small Business Locating in a Vibrant Cluster. *Journal of Research in Marketing and Entrepreneurship* 4, no. 3 (2002): 206–228.

Langlois, R. N., and David C. Mowrey. The Federal Government's Role in the Development of the U.S. Software Industry. In *The International Computer Software Industry*, edited by David C. Mowrey, 71. New York: Oxford University Press, 1996.

Lardy, Nicholas R. Manufacturing Employment in China. *PIE Realtime Economic Issues Watch*, December 21, 2015.

Lawrence, Robert Z. Does Manufacturing Have the Largest Employment Multiplier for the Domestic Economy? (blog) Washington, D.C.: Peterson Institute of International Economics March 22, 2017. https://piie.com/blogs/realtime-economic-issues -watch/does-manufacturing-have-largest-employment-multiplier-domestic.

Lebergott, Stanley. Labor Force and Employment, 1800–1960. In *Output, Employment, and Productivity in the United States after 1800*, edited by Dorothy S. Brady, 117–204. New York: NBER, 1966.

Levine, Chester, Laurie Salmon, and Daniel H. Weinberg. Revising the Standard Occupational Classification System. *Monthly Labor Review* (May 1999): 36–45.

Licklider, J. C. R. Man-Computer Symbiosis, *IRE Transactions on Human Factors in Electronics* 1 (March 1960): 4–11. http://groups.csail.mit.edu/medg/people/psz/Licklider .html.

Lightweight Innovations for Tomorrow (LIFT). Education and Workforce Development programs. http://lift.technology/education-workforce-development/.

Lightweight Innovations for Tomorrow (LIFT). Education and Workforce slide presentation, 2016.

Lightweight Innovations for Tomorrow (LIFT). Investments as of May 2016.

Lightweight Innovations for Tomorrow (LIFT). Talent Research.

Lightweight Innovations for Tomorrow (LIFT). 2016 Education and Workforce Roadmap and Master Plan. https://lift.technology/wp-content/uploads/2014/07 /2016-LIFT-Education-and-Workforce-Roadmap.pdf.

Lightweight Innovations for Tomorrow (LIFT). Workforce Metrics and Data.

Lightweight Innovations for Tomorrow (LIFT). Workforce Profile 2016. https://lift .technology/wp-content/uploads/2014/07/LIFT_WorkforceEducation-Overview2016 .pdf.Lindholdt, Paul. Luddism and Its Discontents. *American Quarterly* 49, no. 4 (1997): 866–873.

Litan, Robert E. Inventive Billion Dollar Firms: A Faster Way to Grow. SSRN Working Paper 1721608, *Social Science Research Network (SSRN)*, December 1, 2010, https:// papers.ssrn.com/sol3/papers.cfm?abstract_id=1721608.

Liveris, Andrew. *Make It in America: The Case for Reinventing the Economy*. Hoboken, NJ: John Wiley and Sons, 2011.

Lloyd, Maggie. Review of the NSF's Advanced Technological Education (ATE) Program: ATE's Role in Advanced Manufacturing Education and Training. Report. Washington, DC: MIT Washington Office, February 2013. http://dc.mit.edu/sites /default/files/pdf/MIT%20Review%20of%20NSF%20ATE%20Program.pdf.

Locke, Richard M., and Rachel L. Wellhausen, eds. *Production in the Innovation Economy*. Cambridge, MA: MIT Press, 2014.

Lucas, Robert E., Jr. On the Mechanics of Economic Development. *Journal of Monetary Economics* 22 (1988): 3–42.

Luckhurst, Roger. Automation. In *The Oxford Handbooks Online*. Oxford: Oxford University Press, November 2014. http://www.oxfordhandbooks.com/view/10.1093 /oxfordhb/9780199838844.001.0001/oxfordhb-9780199838844-e-17.

Luckowski, Stephen. AFFOA 2017: First Projects. Presentation to the American Fiber Manufacturers Association, Washington, DC, October 20, 2016.

Lynn, Barry C. *End of the Line*. New York: Doubleday, 2005.

Maddison-Project website. http://www.ggdc.net/maddison/maddison-project/home .htm.

Majewska, Maria, and Urszula Szulczynska. Methods and Practices of Tacit Knowledge Sharing within an Enterprise: An Empirical Investigation. *Oeconomia Copernicana* 2 (2014): 35–48.

Make in India Initiative website. http://www.makeinindia.com/home.

Mandel, Michael. How Much of the Productivity Surge of 2007–2009 Was Real. *Mandel on Innovation and Growth* (blog), March 28, 2011. http://innovationandgrowth .wordpress.com/2011/03/28/how-much-of-the-productivity-surge-of-2007-2009-was -real/.

Mankiw, Greg. Is a VAT good for exports? *Greg Mankiw's Blog: Random Observations for Students of Economics,* May 18, 2010. http://gregmankiw.blogspot.com/2010/05/is -vat-good-for-exports.html.

Mankiw, Gregory. News Flash: Economists Agree. *Greg Mankiew's Blog,* February 14, 2009. http://gregmankiw.blogspot.com/2009/02/news-flash-economists-agree .html.

Mankiw, N. Gregory, David Romer, and David N. Weil. A Contribution to the Empirics of Economic Growth. *Quarterly Journal of Economics* 107, no. 2 (May 1992): 407–437.

Mann, Catherine L. Globalization of IT Services and White Collar Jobs. International Economics Policy Briefs PB03-11. Institute for International Economics, December 2003. http://www.iie.com/publications/pb/pb03-11.pdf .

Manufacturing Institute and Deloitte Ltd. Overwhelming Support: U.S. Public Opinions on the Manufacturing Industry. Report. 2014. http://www2.deloitte.com /content/dam/Deloitte/us/Documents/manufacturing/us-mfg-public-perception -manufacturing-021315.PDF.

Manufacturing Technology Centre. Challenging the Boundaries of Manufacturing. http://www.the-mtc.org.

Manufacturing to Get Boost from 3D Printing. *Straits Times* (Singapore), March 17, 2016. http://www.straitstimes.com/business/manufacturing-to-get-boost-from-3d -printing.

Markoff, John. Moore's Law Running Out of Room, Tech Looks for a Successor. *New York Times*, May 4, 2016.

Marshall, Alfred. *Principles of Economics*. London: Macmillan, 1890.

Matheson, Rob. The Engine closes its first fund for over $150 million. MIT News, April 6, 2017. http://news.mit.edu/2017/the-engine-closes-first-fund-150-million-0406.

McCallum, John. National Borders Matter: Canada-U.S. Regional Trade Patterns. *American Economic Review* 85, no. 3 (June 1995): 615–623.

McCausland, W. David, and Ioannis Theodossiou. Is Manufacturing Still the Engine of Growth? *Journal of Post Keynesian Economics* 35, no. 1 (Fall 2012): 79–92.

McKenzie, Richard B. Industrial Policy. In *Concise Encyclopedia of Economics*, 2nd ed., 2007. Library of Economics and Liberty. http://www.econlib.org/library/Enc1 /IndustrialPolicy.html.

McKie, Robin. James Watt and the Sabbath Stroll That Created the Industrial Revolution. *The Guardian*, May 29, 2015. http://www.theguardian.com/technology/2015 /may/29/james-watt-sabbath-day-fossil-fuel-revolution-condenser.

McKinsey Global Institute. Poorer than Their Parents? A New Perspective on Income Inequality. McKinsey Global Institute, July 2016. http://www.mckinsey.com/global -themes/employment-and-growth/poorer-than-their-parents-a-new-perspective-on -income-inequality.

Meckstroth, Dan. China Has a Dominant Share of World Manufacturing. Paper, Manufacturers Association for Productivity and Investment (MAPI) Foundation, Arlington, VA, January 2014. https://www.mapi.net/blog/2014/01/china-has-dominant-share -world-manufacturing.

Meckstroth, Dan. The Manufacturing Value Chain Is Bigger than You Think. Report. Washington, DC: Manufacturers Association for Productivity and Investment (MAPI) Foundation, Arlington, VA, February 16, 2016. https://www.mapi.net /forecasts-data/manufacturing-value-chain-much-bigger-you-think.

MForesight (Alliance for Manufacturing Foresight) website. http://mforesight.org /about-us/#vision.

Mindell, David. *Our Robots, Ourselves: Robotics and the Myths of Autonomy*. New York: Penguin Random House, 2015.

Miner, Sean. China's Current Account in 2015: A Growing Trade Surplus. Peterson Institute for International Economics, Washington, DC, February 8, 2016.

Ministry of Economy, Trade and Industry (METI), Government of Japan. Growth Strategy 2016, Establishment of Public-Private Council for the 4th Industrial Revolution, October 2016.

MIT Innovation Initiative. Advancing Manufacturing Innovation on Campus and Online. MIT News Office, October 7, 2016. http://news.mit.edu/2016/advancing -manufacturing-innovation-campus-and-online-1007.

MIT, Production in the Innovation Economy (PIE) website. http://web.mit.edu/pie /research/index.html.

MIT Roundtable on Developing National Innovation Policies, Summary, March 1, 2010. http://dc.mit.edu/sites/default/files/MIT%20Innovation%20Roundtable.pdf.

MIT Roundtable on The Future of Manufacturing Innovation—Advanced Technologies, Summary, March 29, 2010. http://dc.mit.edu/sites/default/files/Roundtable%20 The%20Future%20of%20Manufacturing%20Innovation.pdf.

MIT Supply Chain Management Micromasters Credential website. http://scm.mit .edu/micromasters/faqs.

MIT Washington Office, MIT Reports to the President, 2009–10, MIT Efforts on Policy Innovation Challenges, (Cambridge, MA: Massachusetts Institute of Technology 2010), 1-32-1-34, http://dc.mit.edu/sites/default/files/pdf/2010%20MIT%20 DC%20Annual%20Report.pdf.

Mita, Noriyuki. Manufacturing Industries Bureau, Ministry of Economy Trade and Industry (METI). Responding to the Fourth Industrial Revolution, presentation, October 2016.

Modestino, Alicia Sasser. The Importance of Middle-Skill Jobs. *Issues in Science and Technology* 33, no. 1 (Fall 2016): 41–46.

Mokyr, Joel, Chris Vickers, and Nicolas L. Ziebarth. The History of Technological Anxiety and the Future of Economic Growth: Is This Time Different? *Journal of Economic Perspectives* 29, no. 3 (2015): 31–50

Molnar, Michael. Presentation at MForesight National Summit 2016, Washington, DC, September 29, 2016.

Molnar, Michael (NIST), Steven Linder (DOD), and Mark Shuart (DOE). Building a New Partnership—The National Network for Manufacturing Innovation, presentation to the National Council for Advanced Manufacturing (NACFAM), April 29, 2016.

Mooney, Chris. The Gas Tax Has Been Fixed at 18 Cents for Two Decades. Now Would Be a Great Time to Raise It. *Washington Post*, December 3, 2014.

Morelix, Arnobio, E. J. Reedy, and Joshua Russell. 2016 Kauffman Index of Growth Entrepreneurship, National Trends. Kansas City, MO: Kauffman Foundation, May 2016. http://www.kauffman.org/~/media/kauffman_org/microsites/kauffman_index /growth/kauffman_index_national_growth_entrepreneurship_2016_report.pdf.

Morey, Mitchell. Preferences and the Home Bias in Trade. *Journal of Development Economics* 121 (2016): 24–37.

Morris, Charles R. *The Dawn of Innovation*. New York: Public Affairs, 2012.

Mowery, David C. The Relationship between Intrafirm and Contractual Forms of Industrial Research in American Manufacturing, 1900–1940. *Explorations in Economic History,* 20, 1983, 351–374

Mowrey, David C. The Computer Software Industry. In *Sources of Industrial Leadership: Studies of Seven Industries*, edited by D. C. Mowrey and R. R. Nelson, 145. Cambridge: Cambridge University Press, 1999.

Muro, Mark, Sid Kulkarni, Jacob Whiton, and David Hart. America's Advanced Industries: New Trends. Washington, DC: Brookings Institution, September 2016.

Nager, Adams. Calling Out Chinese Mercantilism. *International Economy* (Spring 2016): 62–64. http://www.international-economy.com/TIE_Sp16_Nager.pdf.

Nager, Adams B., and Robert D. Atkinson. The Myth of America's Manufacturing Renaissance: The Real State of U.S. Manufacturing. Washington, DC: Information Technology and Innovation Foundation (ITIF), January 2015. http://www2.itif.org /2015-myth-american-manufacturing-renaissance.pdf.

Nahm, Jonas, and Edward S. Steinfeld. The Role of Innovative Manufacturing in High-Tech Product Development: Evidence form China's Renewable Energy Sector. In *Production in the Innovation Economy*, edited by Richard M. Locke and Rachel L. Wellhausen, 139–174. Cambridge, MA: MIT Press, 2014.

Nahm, Jonas, and Edward Steinfeld. Scale-Up Nation: Chinese Specialization in Innovative Manufacturing. MIT working paper, March 12, 2012, later published in *World Development* 54 (2013): 288–300. http://dx.doi.org/10.1016/j.worlddev.2013.09.003.

National Academies, Board on Science, Technology and Economic Policy. Innovation Policy Forum on Reinventing U.S. Advanced Manufacturing—A Review of the Advanced Manufacturing Partnership 2.0 Report, October 27, 2014. http://sites .nationalacademies.org/PGA/step/PGA_152473.

National Academy of Engineering (NAE). Making Value for America. Report. Washington, DC: National Academies Press, 2016). http://www.nap.edu/catalog/19483/making-value-for-america-embracing-the-future-of-manufacturing-technology.

National Academy of Sciences, Science, Technology, and Economic Policy (STEP) Board. *21st Century Manufacturing: The Role of the Manufacturing Extension Partnership.* Washington, DC: National Academies Press, 2013.

National Association of Manufacturers. Top 20 Facts about Manufacturing (2016). http://www.nam.org/Newsroom/Facts-About-Manufacturing/.

National Center for Education Statistics, Fast Facts: Educational Attainment website. https://nces.ed.gov/fastfacts/display.asp?id=27.

National Center for Supply Chain Technology Education (NSF/ATE supported) eTextbook website. http://www.supplychainteched.org/etextbook.html.

National Convergence Technology Center (NSF/ATE supported) Centers for Collaborative Technical Assistance website. http://www.connectedtech.org/ccta.html.

National Defense Authorization Act for FY2017 (S.2943), 114th Cong., 2nd Sess., section 215, amending 10 U.S.C. § 2196 (Conference Report, Pub. L. No. 114-840 (2016)).

National Employment Law Project. The Low Wage Recovery. Data Brief, April 2014. http://www.nelp.org/content/uploads/2015/03/Low-Wage-Recovery-Industry-Employment-Wages-2014-Report.pdf.

National Governors Association. Making Our Future—What States Are Doing to Encourage Growth of Manufacturing through Innovation, Entrepreneurship and Investment, an NGA Policy Academy Report. National Governors Association, Washington, DC, January 28, 2013. http://www.nga.org/cms/home/nga-center-for-best-practices/center-publications/page-ehsw-publications/col2-content/main-content-list/making-our-future.html.

National Governors Association. Seven States Selected to Develop Economic Strategies Focused on the Growth of Advanced Manufacturing Industries. Press statement, October 6, 2011.

National Institute of Standards and Technology (NIST). Advanced Manufacturing National Program Office, slide presentation, July 2016.

National Institute of Standards and Technology (NIST). Closing Tech Gaps Can Fortify Advanced Manufacturing. Gaithersburg, MD: National Institute of Standards and Technology (NIST), November 17, 2016. https://www.nist.gov/news-events/news/2016/11/closing-tech-gaps-can-fortify-advanced-manufacturing-and-save-100-billion.

National Institute of Standards and Technology (NIST). Guidance on Institute Performance Metrics: National Network for Manufacturing Innovation. NIST Advanced

Manufacturing National Program Office, Gaithersburg, MD, August 2015. https://www.manufacturing.gov/files/2016/03/nnmi_draft_performance.pdf.

National Science and Technology Council (NSTC). Subcommittee on Advanced Manufacturing. Advanced Manufacturing—A Snapshot of Priority Technology Areas across the Federal Government. Washington, DC: White House, Office of Science and Technology Policy, April 2016. https://www.whitehouse.gov/sites/whitehouse.gov/files/images/Blog/NSTC%20SAM%20technology%20areas%20snapshot.pdf.

National Science Board (NSB). *Science and Engineering Indicators 2008*, Company and Other Nonfederal Funds for Industrial R&D Performance in the United States, by Industry and Company Size: 2001–05. Washington, DC: National Science Board, January 2008.

National Science Board (NSB). *Science and Engineering Indicators 2008*, R&D Performed Abroad by Majority-Owned Foreign Affiliates of U.S. Parent Companies, by Selected Industry of Affiliate and Host Region/Country/Economy: 2002–04. Washington, DC: National Science Board, January 2008.

National Science Board (NSB). *Science and Engineering Indicators 2012*, R&D Performed Abroad by Majority-Owned Foreign Affiliates of U.S. Parent Companies, by Selected Industry of Affiliate and Host Region/Country/Economy: 2012. Washington, DC: National Science Board, January 2012.

National Science Board (NSB). *Science and Engineering Indicators 2016*, Funds Spent for Business R&D Performed in the United States, by Size of Company: 2008–2013. Washington, DC: National Science Board, January 2016.

National Science Board (NSB). *Science and Engineering Indicators 2016*, Funds Spent for Business R&D Performed in the United States, by Source of Funds and Selected Industry: 2013. Washington, DC: National Science Board, January 2016.

National Science Board (NSB). *Science and Engineering Indicators 2016*, International Comparisons of Gross Domestic Expenditures on R&D and R&D Share of Gross Domestic Product, 2013 or Most Recent Year, Table 4.4. Washington, DC: National Science Board, January 2016.

National Science Board (NSB), *Science and Engineering Indicators 2016*, Table 4-7, Funds spent for business R&D performed in the U.S.: 2008–13. Washington, DC: National Science Board Jan. 2016.

National Science Board (NSB). *Science and Engineering Indicators 2016*, U.S. R&D Expenditures, by Performing Sector and Source of Funds: 2008–2013. Washington, DC: National Science Board, January 2016.

National Science Board (NSB), *Science and Technology Indicators 2016*, Chap. 4, R&D: National Trends and International Comparisons, Highlights. Washington, DC: National Science Board, January 2016.

National Science Foundation/National Science Board. *Science and Technology Indicators 2016*, Figure 4.3. http://www.nsf.gov/statistics/2016/nsb20161/#/downloads/chapter-4.

National Science and Technology Council (NSTC), Committee on STEM Education. Federal Science, Technology, Engineering, and Mathematics (STEM) Education: 5-Year Strategic Plan. Washington, DC: White House, Office of Science and Technology Policy, May 2013. https://www.whitehouse.gov/sites/default/files/microsites/ostp/stem_stratplan_2013.pdf.

National Science Foundation (NSF), Engineering Research Centers (ERC) website. https://www.nsf.gov/funding/pgm_summ.jsp?pims_id=5502.

National Science Foundation (NSF)/National Science Board (NSB). *Science and Technology Indicators 2016*, chap. 4. Washington, DC: National Science Foundation, January 2016. http://www.nsf.gov/statistics/2016/nsb20161/uploads/1/7/chapter-4.

National Venture Capital Association (NVCA). *Yearbook 2016*. NVCA, Washington, DC, 2016.

Nazemi, Katherine W. From Startup to Scale-Up: How Connecting Startups with Local Manufacturers Can Help Move New Technologies from Prototype to Production. Paper, MIT Washington Office, Washington, DC, July 2016. http://dc.mit.edu/sites/default/files/doc/Connecting%20Startups%20to%20Small%20Manufacturers%20Nazemi%20July%202016.docx.

Nelson, Richard R. *National Systems of Innovation*. New York: Oxford University Press, 1993.

Nelson, Richard R., and Sidney G. Winter. *An Evolutionary Theory of Economic Change*. Cambridge, MA: Harvard University Press, 1982.

Nicholson, Jessica R., and Ryan Noonan. What Is Made in America? U.S. Department of Commerce, Economics and Statistics Administration (ESA), Washington, DC, 2014. http://www.esa.doc.gov/sites/default/files/whatismadeinamerica_0.pdf.

Nicholson, Jessica, and Regina Powers. The Pay Premium for Manufacturing Workers as Measured by Federal Statistics. ESA Issue Brief 05-15. Washington, DC: U.S. Department of Commerce, Economics and Statistics Administration (ESA), October 2, 2015. http://www.esa.doc.gov/sites/default/files/the-pay-premium-for-manufacturing-workers-as-measured-by-federal-statistics.pdf.

Nordhaus, William D. Baumol's Diseases: A Macroeconomic Perspective. *B.E. Journal of Macroeconomics* 8, no. 1 (2009): Article 9, 1–37 .

Oak Ridge National Laboratory, DOE. Manufacturing Demonstration Facility website. http://web.ornl.gov/sci/manufacturing/mdf/.

Obama, Barack. Creating a National Strategic Computer Initiative. Executive Order, July 29, 2015. https://obamawhitehouse.archives.gov/the-press-office/2015/07/29 /executive-order-creating-national-strategic-computing-initiative.

Obama, Barack. The Way Ahead. *The Economist*, October 8, 2016.

Obama, Barack. 2004 Democratic National Convention Keynote Address. Speech, Democratic National Convention, Boston, July 27, 2004.

Office of the United States Trade Representative, Indonesia. https://ustr.gov/countries -regions/southeast-asia-pacific/indonesia.

Omnibus Foreign Trade and Competitiveness Act of 1988, Pub. L. No. 100-418, 19 U.S.C. § 2901 et seq. (1988).

Organization for Economic Cooperation and Development (OECD). Automation and Independent Work in a Digital Economy. Policy Brief, Organization for Economic Cooperation and Development, Paris, May 2016. http://www.oecd .org/employment/Policy%20brief%20-%20Automation%20and%20Independent%20Work%20in%20a%20Digital%20Economy.pdf.Organization for Economic Co-operation and Development (OECD). Revenue Statistics—OECD countries: Comparative tables, *OECD.Stat,* April 10, 2017. https://stats.oecd.org/Index.aspx ?DataSetCode=REV.

Panchak, Patricia. Manufacturing's Wage and Job Security Problem. *Industry Week*, May 12, 2015. http://www.industryweek.com/compensation-strategies/manufacturings -wage-and-job-security-problem.

Parente, Stephen. The Failure of Endogenous Growth. *Knowledge, Technology, and Policy* 13, no. 4 (Winter 2001): 49–58.

People's Republic of China, The State Council. China Establishes Fund to Invest in Advanced Manufacturing. Xinhua, June 8, 2016. http://english.gov.cn/news/top _news/2016/06/08/content_281475367382490.htm.

Perez, Carlota. *Technological Revolutions and Financial Capital: The Dynamics of Bubbles and Golden Ages*. Cheltenham: Edward Elgar, 2002.

Pisano, Gary, and Willy Shih. Restoring American Competitiveness. *Harvard Business Review*, 87, no. 7/8 (July–August 2009): 114–125. http://hbr.org/hbr-main/resources /pdfs/comm/fmglobal/restoring-american-competitiveness.pdf .

Pisano, Gary P., and Willy C. Shih. *Producing Prosperity*. Cambridge, MA: Harvard Business School Publishing, 2012.

Polanyi, Michael. *The Tacit Dimension*. Garden City, NY: Doubleday, 1966.

Population Council. Alvin Hansen on Economic Progress and Declining Population Growth. *Population and Development Review* 30, no. 2 (June 2004): 329–342.

Porter, Michael. *Competitive Advantage of Nations*. New York: Free Press, 1990.

Posey, Kirby G. Household Income 2015. American Community Survey Brief ACSBR/15-02. Washington, DC: Census Bureau, September 2016. https://www .census.gov/content/dam/Census/library/publications/2016/demo/acsbr15-02.pdf.

Prakash, Atul. Rocky Markets Test the Rise of Amateur "Algo" Traders. Reuters, January 28, 2016.

Preeg, Ernie. Farewell Report on U.S. Trade in Manufactures. Washington, DC: Manufacturers Association for Productivity and Investment (MAPI) Foundation, August 15, 2016. https://www.mapi.net/forecasts-data/my-farewell-report-us-trade -manufactures.

President's Council of Advisors on Science and Technology (PCAST). Report to the President on Ensuring American Leadership in Advanced Manufacturing. Washington, DC: PCAST, June 24, 2011. https://obamawhitehouse.archives.gov/sites/default /files/microsites/ostp/pcast-advanced-manufacturing-june2011.pdf.

President's Council of Advisors on Science and Technology (PCAST), Advanced Manufacturing Partnership Steering Committee. Report to the President on Capturing Domestic Competitive Advantage in Advanced Manufacturing. Washington, DC: PCAST, July 2012. https://obamawhitehouse.archives.gov/sites/default /files/microsites/ostp/pcast_amp_steering_committee_report_final_july_17_2012 .pdf.

President's Council of Advisors on Science and Technology (PCAST), Advanced Manufacturing Partnership 2.0 Steering Committee. Report to the President on Accelerating U.S. Advanced Manufacturing. Washington, DC: PCAST, October 2014. https://obamawhitehouse.archives.gov/sites/default/files/microsites/ostp/PCAST /amp20_report_final.pdf.

President's State of the Union Address, Full Text. *Wall Street Journal*, February 12, 2012. http://blogs.wsj.com/washwire/2013/02/12/full-text-obamas-state-of-the-union -address/.

Rassekh, Farhad, and Henry Thompson. Factor Price Equalization: Theory and Evidence. *Journal of Economic Integration* 8, no. 1 (Spring 1993): 1–32.

Reamer, Andrew. Better Jobs Information Benefits Everyone. *Issues in Science and Technology* 33, no.1 (Fall 2016): 58–63.

Reif, L. Rafael. A Better Way to Deliver Innovation to the World. Op-ed, *Washington Post*, May 28, 2015. https://www.washingtonpost.com/opinions/a-better -way-to-deliver-innovation-to-the-world/2015/05/22/35023680-fe28-11e4-8b6c -0dcce21e223d_story.html.

Reif, Rafael. Introducing The Engine. Op-ed, *Boston Globe*, October 26, 2016.

Reinhart, Carmen M., and Kenneth S. Rogoff. *This Time Is Different: Eight Centuries of Financial Folly*. Princeton, NJ: Princeton University Press, 2009.

Renwick, Trudi. How the Census Bureau Measures Income and Poverty. Census Bureau, September 8, 2016. http://blogs.census.gov/2016/09/08/how-the-census -bureau-measures-income-and-poverty-4/.

Rethink Robotics company website. http://www.rethinkrobotics.com.

Reynolds, Elizabeth, Hiram Semel, and Joyce Lawrence. Learning by Building: Complementary Assets and the Migration of Capabilities in U.S. Innovative Firms. In *Production in the Innovation Economy*, edited by Richard Locke and Rachel Wellhausen, 81–108. Cambridge, MA: MIT Press, 2014.

Reynolds, Kara M., and John S. Palatucci. Does Trade Adjustment Assistance Make a Difference? *Contemporary Economic Policy* 30, no. 1 (January 2012): 43–59.

Ricardo, David. *On the Principles of Political Economy and Taxation*, 1821. Library of Economics and Liberty. http://www.econlib.org/library/Ricardo/ricP2a.html.

Richardson, J. David. Trade Adjustment Assistance under the United States Trade Act of 1974: An Analytical Examination and Worker Survey. In *Import Competition and Response*, edited by Jagdish Bhagwati, 321–368. Chicago: University of Chicago Press, 1982.

Riley, Michael, and Ashlee Vance. It's Not Paranoia if They're Stealing Your Secrets. *Bloomberg Business Week*, March 19, 2012, 76–84.

Rodrik, Dani. *Economics Rules: The Rights and Wrongs of the Dismal Science*. New York: Norton, 2015.

Rogoff, Kenneth. Paul Samuelson's Contributions to International Economics. May 2005. http://scholar.harvard.edu/files/rogoff/files/samuelson.pdf.

Romer, Christina. Do Manufacturers Need Special Treatment? *New York Times*, February 4, 2012. http://www.nytimes.com/2012/02/05/business/do-manufacturers -need-special-treatment-economic-view.html?_r=0.

Romer, Paul. Endogenous Technological Change. *Journal of Political Economy* 98, no. 5 (1990): 71–102. http://pages.stern.nyu.edu/~promer/Endogenous.pdf.

Romer, Paul. The Trouble with Macroeconomics. *American Economist* (forthcoming; initially delivered as the Commons Memorial Lecture of the Omicron Delta Epsilon Society, January 5, 2016). https://paulromer.net/wp-content/uploads/2016/09/WP -Trouble.pdf.

Romer, Paul M. Increasing Returns and Long-Run Growth. *Journal of Political Economy* 94, no. 5 (1986): 1002–1037.

Rosen, William. *The Most Powerful Idea in the World*. New York: Random House, 2010.

Rosenberg, Nathan, ed. *The American System of Manufactures*. Edinburgh: University of Edinburgh, 1969.

Rosenthal, Stuart S., and William C. Strange. Small Establishments/Big Effects. In *Agglomeration, Organization and Entrepreneurship, Agglomeration Economics*, edited by Edward L. Glaeser, 277–302. Chicago: University of Chicago Press, 2007.

Rothwell, Jonathan. Defining Skilled Technical Work. *Issues in Science and Technology* 33, no. 1 (Fall 2016): 47–51.

Ruckelhaus, Catherine, and Sarah Leberstein. Manufacturing Low Pay. Report. New York: National Employment Law Project (NELP), November 2014.

Russo, Michael A., Director of Government Relations, Regulatory Affairs & Strategic Initiatives—GlobalFoundries, GlobalFoundries Update, slide presentation, Nov. 27, 2013.

Ruttan, Vernon. *Technology Growth and Development: An Induced Innovation Perspective*. New York: Oxford University Press, 2001.

Ruttan, Vernon W. *Is War Necessary for Economic Growth? Military Procurement and Technology Development*. New York: Oxford University Press, 2006.

Rycroft, Robert W. and Don E. Kash. Innovation Policies for Complex Technologies. *Issues in Science and Technology*, 16, no. 1 (Fall 1999). http://issues.org/16-1/rycroft.

Saad, Lydia. The 40-Hour Workweek Is Actually Longer—by Seven Hours. *Gallup*, August 29, 2014.

Samuelson, Paul A. Where Ricardo and Mill Rebut and Confirm Arguments of Mainstream Economists Supporting Globalization. *Journal of Economic Perspectives* 18, no. 3 (Summer 2004): 135–146. http://www.nd.edu/~druccio/Samuelson.pdf.

Sandmo, Agnar. *Economics Evolving: A History of Economic Thought*. Princeton, NJ: Princeton University Press, 2011.

Sawyer, L. A., and W. H. Mitchell. *The Liberty Ships: The History of the "Emergency" Type Cargo Ships Constructed in the United States during the Second World War*, 2nd ed. London: Lloyd's of London Press, 1985.

Scaperlanda, Anthony. Hansen's Secular Stagnation Thesis Once Again. *Journal of Economic Issues* 11, no. 2 (June 1977): 223–343.

Schlefer, Jonathan. *The Assumptions Economists Make*, Cambridge, MA: Belknap Harvard, 2012.

Schultze, Charles L. Industrial Policy: A Dissent. *Brookings Review* 2, no. 1 (Fall 1983). http://www.brookings.edu/~/media/Files/rc/articles/1983/industrial_policy_schultze.pdf.

Schumpeter, Joseph A. *Capitalism, Socialism, and Democracy.* New York: Harper Perennial Modern Thought, 2008. First published 1942.

Schwartz, Nelson D. Small Factories Emerge as a Weapon in the Fight against Poverty. *New York Times,* October 28, 2016.

Scientific and Advanced Technology Act of 1992, Pub. L. No. 102-476 (1992), summarized at https://www.congress.gov/bill/102nd-congress/senate-bill/1146/all-info.

Scott, Robert E. Manufacturing Job Loss: Trade Not Productivity Is the Culprit. Report. Economic Policy Institute, August 11, 2015. http://www.epi.org/publication/manufacturing-job-loss-trade-not-productivity-is-the-culprit/.

Securities and Exchange Commission. JOBS Act. https://www.sec.gov/spotlight/jobs-act.shtml.

Semba, Hideshi. Innovation Policy of Japan. Presentation, June 15, 2012. http://www.j-bilat.eu/documents/seminar/as_2/presentation_as2_hs.pdf.

Semiconductor Industry Association (SIA). *Factbook 2014.* Washington, DC: Semiconductor Industry Association, 2014.

Sewell, Chan. The 2010 Campaign: Democrats Are at Odds on Relevance of Keynes. *New York Times,* October 19, 2010.

Shapira, Philip, and Jan Youtie. Presentation on the Next Production Revolution: Institutions for Technology Diffusion, Conference on Smart Industry: Enabling the Next Production Revolution, OECD and Sweden Ministry of Enterprise and Innovation, Stockholm, September 18, 2016.

Shipp, Stephanie S., N. Gupta, B. Lal, J. Scott, C. Weber, M. Finin, M. Blake, S. Newsome, and S. Thomas. Emerging Global Trends in Advanced Manufacturing. Report P-4603. Arlington, VA: Institute for Defense Analysis, March 2012. https://www.wilsoncenter.org/sites/default/files/Emerging_Global_Trends_in_Advanced_Manufacturing.pdf.

Short, Doug. Household Incomes: The Decline of the Middle Class. *Advisor Perspectives,* September 16, 2016. https://www.advisorperspectives.com/dshort/updates/2016/09/19/household-incomes-the-decline-of-the-middle-class.

Simoes, Alexander. United States Data. The Observatory of Economic Complexity website. http://atlas.media.mit.edu/en/profile/country/usa/.

Simoes, Alexander. U.S.-Kenya Bilateral Trade. The Observatory of Economic Complexity website. http://atlas.media.mit.edu/en/profile/country/ken/.

Simoes, Alexander. What Does Germany Export to the United States? The Observatory of Economic Complexity website. http://atlas.media.mit.edu/en/visualize/tree_map/hs92/export/deu/usa/show/2014.

Simoes, Alexander. What Does the United States Export to Germany? The Observatory of Economic Complexity website. http://atlas.media.mit.edu/en/visualize/tree_map/hs92/export/usa/deu/show/2014/.

Simon, Ruth. Few Businesses Take Advantage of Mini-IPOs. *Wall Street Journal*, July 6, 2016.

Singer, Peter L. Federally Supported Innovations: 22 Examples of Major Technology Innovations That Stem from Federal Research Support. Washington, DC: Information Technology and Innovation Foundation (ITIF), February 2014. http://www2.itif.org/2014-federally-supported-innovations.pdf?_ga=1.194445550.2108411368.1483563653.

Singer, Peter L. Investing in "Innovation Infrastructure" to Restore U.S. Growth. Washington, DC: Information Technology and Innovation Foundation (ITIF), January 3, 2017. http://www2.itif.org/2017-innovation-infrastructure.pdf?_ga=1.198109420.2108411368.1483563653.

Singer, Peter L. Manufacturing Scale-up: Summary of 14 Relevant Federal Financing Programs. Report. Washington, DC: MIT Washington Office, May 27, 2014. http://dc.mit.edu/resources/policy-resources.

Singer, Peter L., and William B. Bonvillian. "Innovation Orchards:" Helping Tech Start-Ups Scale. Washington, D.C.: Information Technology and Innovation Foundation (ITIF) March 2017. http://www2.itif.org/2017-innovation-orchards.pdf?_ga=1.205014288.1283359406.1491740117.

Small Business Administration (SBA), Frequently Asked Questions About Small Business, Small Businesses Comprise What Share of the U.S. Economy (SBA Sept. 2012). https://www.sba.gov/sites/default/files/FAQ_Sept_2012.pdf.

Smart, John M. Measuring Innovation in an Accelerating World. *Technological Forecasting and Social Change* 72 (2005): 988–995. Acceleration Studies Forum. http://accelerating.org/articles/huebnerinnovation.html.

Smil, Vaclav. *Made in the USA: The Rise and Retreat of American Manufacturing*. Cambridge, MA: MIT Press, 2015.

Smith, Adam. *An Inquiry into the Nature and Causes of the Wealth of Nations*, edited by Edwin Cannan, 1904. Library of Economics and Liberty. http://www.econlib.org/library/Smith/smWN.html.

Smith, Douglas K., and Robert C. Alexander. *Fumbling the Future: How Xerox Invented, Then Ignored, the First Personal Computer*. New York: William Morrow, 1988.

Smith, Merritt Roe. Eli Whitney and the American System of Manufacturing. In *Technology in America: A History of Individuals and Ideas*, 2nd ed., edited by Carroll W. Pursell, Jr., 47–48. Cambridge, MA: MIT Press, 1990.

Smith, Merritt Roe. *Harpers Ferry Armory and the New Technology*. Ithaca, NY: Cornell University Press, 1977.

Smith, Merritt Roe. John H. Hall, Simeon North and the Milling Machine: The Nature of Innovation among Antebellum Arms Makers. *Technology and Culture* 14, no. 4 (October 1973): 573–591.

Smith, Merritt Roe. *Military Enterprise and Technology Change*. Cambridge, MA: MIT Press, 1985.

Solga, Heike, Paula Protsch, Christian Ebner, and Christian Brzinsky-Fay. The German Vocational Education and Training System: Its Institutional Configuration, Strengths, and Challenges. Discussion Paper SP I 2014-502, WZB Berlin Social Science Center, 2014. https://bibliothek.wzb.eu/pdf/2014/i14-502.pdf.

Solow, Robert M. A Contribution to the Theory of Economic Growth. *Quarterly Journal of Economics* 70, no. 1 (February 1956): 65–94.

Solow, Robert M. *Growth Theory: An Exposition*, 2nd ed. New York: Oxford University Press, 2000.

Solow, Robert M. Nobel Prize Lecture, December 8, 1987. http://nobelprize.org /nobel_prizes/economics/laureates/1987/solow-lecture.html.

Solow, Robert M. Technical Change and the Aggregate Production Function. *Review of Economics and Statistics* 39, no. 3 (August 1957): 312–320.

Song, Jae, David J. Price, Fatih Guvenen, Nicholas Bloom, and Till von Wachter. Firming Up Inequality. NBER Working Paper 21199, National Bureau of Economic Research, Cambridge, MA, May 2016.

Sonnenschein, Hugo. Do Walras' Identity and Continuity Characterize the Class of Community Excess Demand Functions? *Journal of Economic Theory* 6, no. 4 (1973): 345–354.

Soskice, David. Reconciling Markets and Institutions: The German Apprenticeship System. In *Training and the Private Sector*, edited by Lisa Lynch, 25–60. NBER and University of Chicago Press, January 1994. http://www.nber.org/chapters/c8776.

Spector, David. Is It Possible to Redistribute the Gains from Trade Using Income Taxation? *Journal of International Economics* 55, no. 2 (December 2001): 441–460.

Spence, A. Michael. The Impact of Globalization on Income and Employment: The Downside of Integrating Markets. *Foreign Affairs* 90, no. 4 (July–August 2011): 28–41. http://www.viet-studies.info/kinhte/MichaelSpence_Globalization_Unemployment .pdf.

Statistisches Bundesamt (Destatis), Foreign Trade, Ranking of Germany's trading partners in foreign trade—2016, Wiesbaden, April 12, 2016, https://www

.destatis.de/EN/FactsFigures/NationalEconomyEnvironment/ForeignTrade/Tables /OrderRankGermanyTradingPartners.pdf?__blob=publicationFile.

Steinfeld, Edward S. *Playing Our Game: Why China's Rise Doesn't Threaten the West.* Oxford: Oxford University Press, 2010.

Stettner, A., J. Yudken, and M. McCormack. Why Manufacturing Jobs Are Worth Saving. Century Foundation, June 2017.

Stewart, Luke A., and Robert D. Atkinson. Restoring America's Lagging Investment in Capital Goods. Washington, DC: Information Technology and Innovation Foundation (ITIF) (October 2013). http://www2.itif.org/2013-restoring-americas-lagging -investment.pdf.

Stokes, Donald. *Pasteur's Quadrant, Basic Science and Technological Innovation.* Washington, D.C.: Brookings Institution Press, 1997.

Stolper, Wolfgang, and Paul A. Samuelson. Protection and Real Wages. *Review of Economic Studies* 9 (1941): 58–73.

Sturgeon, Timothy J. The New Digital Economy—Innovation, Economic Development and Measurement. United Nations Conference on Trade and Development (UNCTAD) ICT Analysis Section report, March 25, 2017—in draft, 15–17.

Summers, Lawrence. Speech to IMF Economic Forum, November 8, 2013. https:// www.youtube.com/watch?v=KYpVzBbQIX0.

Summers, Lawrence H. Building the Case for Greater Infrastructure Investment. *Financial Times*, September 11, 2016.

Summers, Lawrence H. Demand Side Secular Stagnation. *American Economic Review: Papers and Proceedings* 105, no. 5 (2015): 60–65.

Tan, Michael, and Jeffrey Chua. Industry 4.0 and Singapore Manufacturing. Opinion, *Straits Times* (Singapore), February 10, 2016. http://www.straitstimes.com /opinion/industry-40-and-singapore-manufacturing.

Tassey, Gregory. Beyond the Business Cycle: The Need for a Technology-Based Growth Strategy. Paper, National Institute of Standards and Technology (NIST) Economic Analysis Office, Washington, DC, February 2012. http://www.nist.gov /director/planning/upload/beyond-business-cycle.pdf.

Tassey, Gregory. Rationales and Mechanisms for Revitalizing U.S. Manufacturing. *Journal of Technology Transfer* 35, no. 3 (June 2010): 283–333. http://www .scienceofsciencepolicy.net/sites/default/files/attachments/Tassey%20on%20 Manuf%20JTT%20June%202010.pdf.

Teixeira, Pedro Nuno. Gary Becker's Early Work on Human Capital. *IZA Journal of Labor Economics* 12, no. 3 (November 2014).

Temin, Peter, *The Vanishing Middle Class: Prejudice and Power in a Dual Economy.* Cambridge, MA: MIT Press, 2017.

Thaler, Richard H. *Misbehaving: The Making of Behavioral Economics.* New York: Norton, 2015.

Theil, Peter. What Happened to the Future? Founder's Fund, 2011. http://foundersfund.com/the-future/.

Thompson, Peter. How Much Did the Liberty Shipbuilders Learn? New Evidence for an Old Case Study. *Journal of Political Economy* 109, no. 1 (2001): 103–137.

Times. Riots at Nottingham, London, England. November 18, 1811, *The Times Digital Archive.*

Timiraos, Nick. Aid for Workers Untouched by Debate over Trade Deal. *Wall Street Journal,* May 10, 2015.

Timiraos, Nick, and Janet Adamy. U.S. Household Incomes Surged 5.2% in 2015, First Gain since 2007. *Wall Street Journal,* September 13, 2016. http://www.wsj.com/articles/u-s-household-incomes-surged-5-2-in-2015-ending-slide-1473776295.

Tocqueville, Alexis de. *Democracy in America,* translated by Gerald Bevan, introduction by Isaac Kramnick. London: Penguin, 2003. Originally published in 1835 and 1840.

Torpey, Elka. Got Skills, Think Manufacturing. *BLS Career Outlook,* June 2014. http://www.bls.gov/careeroutlook/2014/article/manufacturing.htm.

Trimble, William F. *William A. Moffett, Architect of Naval Aviation.* Annapolis, MD: U.S. Naval Institute Press/Bluejacket Books, 2007.

Triplett, Jack E., and Barry P. Bosworth. "Baumol's Disease" Has Been Cured: IT and Multifactor Productivity in U.S. Services Industries. Paper presented at 3rd ZEW Conference on the Economics of Information and Communications Technologies, July 4–5, 2003.

University College London. Evidence Submission to the House of Commons Committee on Science and Technology, December 2010. http://www.publications.parliament.uk/pa/cm201011/cmselect/cmsctech/619/619vw22.htm.

University of Pennsylvania. Openness at Constant Prices for United States [OPENRPUSA156NUPN]. FRED, Federal Reserve Bank of St. Louis. https://fred.stlouisfed.org/series/OPENRPUSA156NUPN.

U.S. Department of Agriculture (USDA). Food Availability (Per Capita) Data System. USDA Economic Research Service, August 2016. http://www.ers.usda.gov/data-products/food-availability-(per-capita)-data-system/summary-findings.aspx.

U.S. House of Representatives. Revitalize American Manufacturing and Innovation Act, H.R. 2996, 113th Cong., 2nd Sess. https://www.congress.gov/bill/113th-congress/house-bill/2996/actions.

U.S. House of Representatives, Committee on Science, Space and Technology. Report on H.R. 2996, Revitalize American Manufacturing and Innovation Act, H. Rep. No. 113-599, 113th Cong., 2nd Sess., September 15, 2014.

U.S. Senate. S.1468, 113th Cong., 2nd Sess., https://www.govtrack.us/congress/bills/113/s1468/text.

U.S. Senate, Senate Committee on Commerce, Science and Transportation. Report on S. 1468, Revitalize American Manufacturing and Innovation Act, S. Rep. No. 113-247, 113th Cong., 2nd Sess., August 26, 2014, Legislative History section. https://www.congress.gov/congressional-report/113th-congress/senate-report/247/1.

Vance, Ashlee. *Elon Musk: Tesla, SpaceX and the Quest for a Fantastic Future*. New York: Ecco, HarperCollins, 2015.

Walczak Jared, Location Matters: Effective Tax Rates on Manufacturers by State, Tax Foundation. Sept. 1, 2015. https://taxfoundation.org/location-matters-effective-tax-rates-manufacturers-state/.

Waldrop, M. Mitchell. *The Dream Machine*, Sloan Technology Series. New York: Viking, 2001.

Walker, Tom. Why Economists Dislike a Lump of Labor. *Review of Social Economy* 65, no. 3 (September 2007): 279–291.

Weaver, Andrew, and Paul Osterman. The New Skill Production System: Policy Challenges and Solutions in Manufacturing Labor Markets. In *Production in the Innovation Economy*, edited by Richard Locke and Rachel Wellhausen, 17–50. Cambridge, MA: MIT Press, 2014.

Weaver, Andrew, and Paul Osterman. Skills and Skill Gaps in Manufacturing. In *Production in the Innovation Economy*, edited by Richard Locke and Rachel Wellhausen, 51–80. Cambridge, MA: MIT Press, 2014.

Webb, Alex. Apple's Cook Announces New China R&D Center on Beijing Trip. *Bloomberg*, August 16, 2016.

Weiss, Charles, and William B. Bonvillian. *Structuring an Energy Technology Revolution*. Cambridge, MA: MIT Press, 2009.

Weitzman, Martin. Recombinant Growth. *Quarterly Journal of Economics* 113, no. 2 (May 1998): 331–360.

Wessner, Charles W. Presentation at MForesight National Summit 2016, Washington, DC, September 29, 2016.

Wessner, Charles W., and Thomas R. Howell. New York's Nanotechnology Initiative: Best Practices and Challenges (paper), March 12, 2017.

Whang, T., Y. Ahang, H. Yu, and F-Y. Wang, eds. *Advanced Manufacturing Technology in China: A Roadmap to 2050*. Berlin: Springer, 2012.

White House, Office of the Press Secretary. Fact Sheet: President Obama Announces Winner of New Smart Manufacturing Innovation Institute. June 20, 2016. https://www.obamawhitehouse.archives.gov/the-press-office/2016/06/20/fact -sheet-president-obama-announces-winner-new-smart-manufacturing.

White House, Office of the Press Secretary. Fact Sheet: President Obama Announces New Actions to Further Strengthen U.S. Manufacturing, Oct. 27, 2014, https:// obamawhitehouse.archives.gov/the-press-office/2014/10/27/fact-sheet-president -obama-announces-new-actions-further-strengthen-us-m.

White House, Office of the Press Secretary. President Obama Launches Advanced Manufacturing Partnership. Statement at Carnegie Mellon University, June 24, 2011. https://obamawhitehouse.archives.gov/the-press-office/2011/06/24/president -obama-launches-advanced-manufacturing-partnership.

White House, Office of the Press Secretary. Report to President Outlines Approaches to Spur Domestic Manufacturing Investment and Innovation. Press Release, July 12, 2012. https://obamawhitehouse.archives.gov/the-press-office/2012/07/17/report -president-outlines-approaches-spur-domestic-manufacturing-investm.

White House, Office of the Press Secretary. President Obama to Announce New Efforts to Support Manufacturing Innovation—Administration Proposed New National Network to Support Manufacturing, March 9, 2012. https://obamawhitehouse.archives .gov/the-press-office/2012/03/09/president-obama-announce-new-efforts-support -manufacturing-innovation-en; https://obamawhitehouse.archives.gov/photos-and -video/video/2012/03/09/president-obama-speaks-manufacturing#transcript.

White House. Office of the Press Secretary. Ready to Work: Job-Driven Training and American Opportunity, July 2014. https://www.whitehouse.gov/sites/default/files /docs/skills_report.pdf.

White House. Office of the Press Secretary. Remarks by the President in the State of the Union Address, February 12, 2013. https://obamawhitehouse.archives.gov/the -press-office/2013/02/12/remarks-president-state-union-address.

Whitney, Eli. The Manufacture of Firearms, 1812 memoir, Eli Whitney Collection, Yale University Archives. https://www.eliwhitney.org/7/museum/eli-whitney/arms -production.

Whitney, Eli. Letter to Treasury Secretary Oliver Wolcott, Jr., May 1, 1798, Eli Whitney Collection, Yale University Archives. https://www.eliwhitney.org/7/museum/eli -whitney/arms-production.

Whitney, Eli, III. Letter of March 20, 1890 from New Haven, CT, reprinted in Edward Craig Bates, The Story of the Cotton Gin, *New England Magazine*, May 1890, republished by Westborough, Massachusetts Historical Society, 1899. http://ebooks .library.cornell.edu/cgi/t/text/text-idx?c=newe;idno=newe0008-3.

Wigglesworth, Robin. Banks Deflect Attempts to Bring Sunlight to Bond Dealing. *Financial Times*, October 10, 2016.

Wilson, Daniel J. Fiscal Spending Jobs Multipliers: Evidence from the 2009 American Recovery and Reinvestment Act. *American Economic Journal: Economic Policy* 4, no. 3 (2012): 251–282.

Wolfson, Johanna. Emerging Models for a Better Innovation Pathway, DOE Office of Energy Efficiency and Renewable Energy, presentation slides, August 25, 2016.

Womack, James P., Daniel T. Jones, and Daniel Roos. *The Machine That Changed the World: The Story of Lean Production*. New York: Free Press, 1990.

Workforce Innovation and Opportunity Act of 2014, Pub. L. No. 113-128 (2014). Summarized at https://en.wikipedia.org/wiki/Workforce_Innovation_and_Opportunity_Act.

Workforce Investment Act of 1998, Pub. L. No. 105-220, 29 USC § 2810 et seq. (1998). Summarized at https://en.wikipedia.org/wiki/Workforce_Investment_Act_of_1998.

Workforce Investment Network. Tennessee Career Centers. http://www.workforce investmentnetwork.com/about-us/introduction.

Work Foundation. Technology Innovation Centres. Submission to the House of Commons, September 2010. http://www.theworkfoundation.com/assets/docs/knowledge economy%20newsletters/tics%20-%20applying%20the%20fraunhofer%20 model%20to%20create%20an%20effective%20innovation%20ecosystem%20in%20 the%20uk.pdf.

World Bank. Age Dependency Ratio (% of working-age population): United States. http://data.worldbank.org/indicator/SP.POP.DPND?locations=US.

World Bank. Current Account Balance (BoP, current US$). http://data.worldbank .org/indicator/BN.CAB.XOKA.CD.

World Bank. Data, Household Final Consumption Expenditure (% of GDP), table. http://data.worldbank.org/indicator/NE.CON.PETC.ZS.

World Bank. Foreign Direct Investment, Net Inflows (BoP, current US$). http://data .worldbank.org/indicator/BX.KLT.DINV.CD.WD.

World Bank. GDP Growth Per Capita (Annual Percentage)—United States, 1960–2015. http://data.worldbank.org/indicator/NY.GDP.MKTP.KD.ZG?locations=US.

World Bank. Historical GDP—GDP (current U.S.$) (United States and Japan totals for 1990 and 2005), http://data.worldbank.org/indicator/NY.GDP.MKTP.CD?locations =US; http://data.worldbank.org/indicator/NY.GDP.MKTP.CD?locations=JP.

Yagan, Danny. The Enduring Employment Impact of Your Great Recession Location. Working Paper, University of California—Berkeley, April 2016. https://sites .google.com/site/dannyyagan/greatdivergence.

Yanushevsky, Camilla, and Rafael Yanushevsky. Is Infrastructure Spending an Effective Fiscal Policy? *Metroeconomica* 65, no. 1 (2014): 123–135.

Zachary, G. Pascal. *The Endless Frontier: Vannevar Bush, Engineer of the American Century*. Cambridge, MA: MIT Press, 1999.

Zhang, Yiliu, Daniel Kuhner, Kathryn Hewitt, and Queenie Chan. Future of U.S. Manufacturing—A Literature Review, Parts I–III, MIT Washington Office, Washington, DC, August 2011, January 2012, July 2012. http://dc.mit.edu/resources/policy-resources.

Zimmerman, David. *Top Secret Exchange: The Tizard Mission and the Scientific War*. Montreal: McGill-Queen's University Press, 1996.

Index